THE
COMIC HISTORY
OF ROME

Gilbert Abbott À Beckett

Illustrated by
John Leech

Bolchazy-Carducci Publishers, Inc.
1996

Cover: Robert Emmet Meagher

The Comic History of Rome
Reprint of the Bradbury and Evans edition 1852 (London)

Printed in the United States of America
1996

BOLCHAZY-CARDUCCI PUBLISHERS, INC.
1000 Brown Street, Unit 101
Wauconda, IL 60084

ISBN 0-86516-333-2

Library of Congress Cataloging-in-Publication Data

À Beckett, Gilbert Abbott, 1811-1856.
    The comic history of Rome / Gilbert Abbott À Beckett : illustrated
by John Leech
       p.   cm.
    Originally published: London : Bradbury and Evans, 1852.
    ISBN 0-86516-333-2 (pbk. : alk. paper)
    1. Rome--History--Humor. 2. Wit and humor, Pictorial. I. Leech,
John, 1817-1864. II. Title.
DG210.A12 1996
937'.00207--dc20
                                              96-17098
                                                  CIP

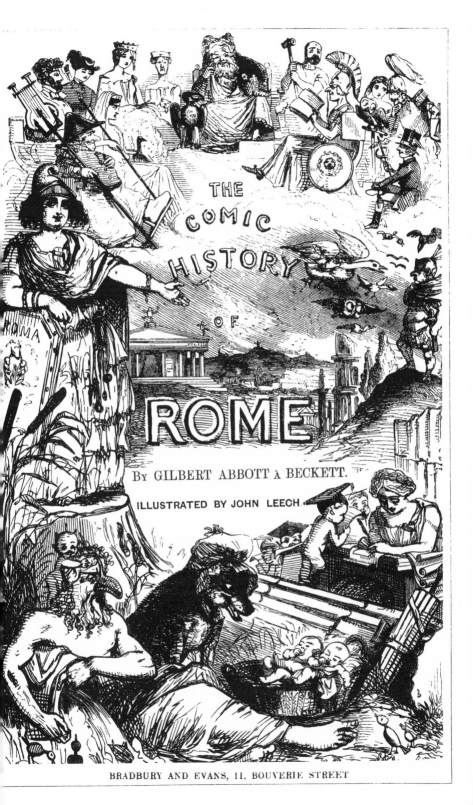

THE COMIC HISTORY OF ROME

BY GILBERT ABBOTT À BECKETT.

ILLUSTRATED BY JOHN LEECH.

BRADBURY AND EVANS, 11, BOUVERIE STREET

Romulus & Remus discovered by a gentle shepherd.

PREFACE.

Some explanation is perhaps due from a writer who adopts the title of Comic in relation to a subject which is ordinarily considered to be so essentially grave as that of History. Though the epithet may be thought by many inappropriate to the theme, this work has been prompted by a very serious desire to instruct those who, though willing to acquire information, seek in doing so as much amusement as possible.

It is true that professedly Comic literature has been the subject of a familiarity not unmixed with contempt on the part of a portion of the public, since that class of writing obtained the popularity which has especially attended it within the last few years; but as whatever disrepute it has fallen into is owing entirely to its abuse, there is no reason for abandoning an attempt to make a right use of it. The title of Comic has therefore been retained in reference to this work, though the author has felt that its purport is likely to be misconceived by many, and among them not a few whose judgment he would highly esteem, who would turn away from a Comic History solely on account of its name, and without giving themselves the trouble to look into it. Those persons are, however, grievously mistaken who have imagined that in this, and in similar books from the same pen, the object has been to treat History as a mere farce, or to laugh at Truth—the aim of the writer having invariably been to expose falsehood, and to bring into merited contempt all that has been injudiciously, ignorantly, or dishonestly held up to general admiration. His method of telling a story may be objected to; nevertheless, if he does his utmost to tell it truly, he ought not, perhaps, to be very severely criticised for adopting the style in which he feels himself most at home; and if his opinions are found to be, in the main, such as just and sensible persons can agree with, he only asks that his views and sentiments may be estimated by what they contain, and not by any peculiarity in his mode of expressing them.

The writer of this book is animated by an earnest wish to aid, as far as he is able, in the project of combining instruction with amusement; and he trusts he shall not be blamed for endeavouring to render such ability as he possesses available for as much as it is worth, in applying it to subjects of useful information.

Those who are not disposed to approve of his design, will perhaps give him credit for his motive; and he may with confidence assert, that, from the care and attention he has bestowed upon this work, it will be found to form (irrespective of its claims to amuse) by no means the least compendious and correct of the histories already in existence of Rome to the end of the Commonwealth. If he has failed in justifying the application of the title of Comic to his work, he has reason to believe it will be found accurate. Though the style professes to be light, he would submit that truth does not necessarily make more impression by being conveyed through a heavy medium; and although facts may be playfully told, it is hoped that narrative in sport may be found to constitute history in earnest.

CONTENTS.

ENGRAVINGS ON STEEL

———◆———

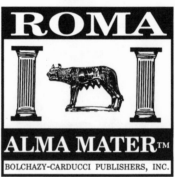

ENGRAVINGS ON WOOD.

COMIC HISTORY OF ROME.

CHAPTER THE FIRST.

FROM THE FOUNDATION OF ROME TO THE DEATH OF ROMULUS.

Æneas and Anchises.

HE origin of the Romans has long been lost in that impenetrable fog, the mist of ages ; which, it is to be feared, will never clear off, for it unfortunately seems to grow thicker the more boldly we try to grope about in it. In the midst of these fogs, some energetic individual will now and then appear with a pretty powerful link, but there are not enough of these links to form a connected chain of incidents.

One of the oldest and most popular traditions concerning the origin of the Romans, is that founded on the remarkable feat of filial pick-a-back alleged to have been performed by Æneas, who is frequently dragged in head and shoulders, with his venerable parent, to lead off the march of events, and, as it were, open the ball of history.

It is said that after * the siege of Troy, Æneas snatched up his Lares and Penates in one hand, and his father, Anchises, in the other;

---

* The Lares of the Romans are supposed to have been the Manes or shades of their ancestors, and consisted of little waxen figures—such as we should put under shades made of glass—which adorned the halls of houses. The Lares were sewn up in stout dog's-skin, durability being consulted more than elegance. The Penates were a superior order of deities, who were kept in the innermost parts of the establishment, and took their name from *penitus,* within, which caused the portion of the house they occupied to be afterwards called the *penetralia.*

when, flinging the former over the right shoulder, and the latter over the left, he ran down to the sea-shore, called "A boat a-hoy," and escaped from the jaws of destruction into the mouth of the Tiber There are many reasons for disbelieving this story, and it is quite enough to deprive it of weight to consider what must have been the weight of Anchises himself, and the large bundle of household images that Æneas is alleged to have been burdened with. Putting probability in one scale, and an elderly gentleman, with a lot of Lares and a parcel of Penates in the other, there can be no doubt which will preponderate. It happens, also, that Troy is usually said to have been destroyed 430 years before Rome was founded,* so that it would have been to this day as unfounded as the tale itself, if the city had had no other foundation than that which Æneas was supposed to have given it.

The Latin Bards have adorned this story in their own peculiar way, by adding that Æneas, on his arrival in the Tiber, resolved to sacrifice a milk white sow, in gratitude for his safety. The sow, who must have been an ancestor of the learned pig, got scent of her fate, and running two or three miles up the country, produced a sad litter of thirty little ones ; when Æneas, fancying he heard a voice telling him to build a town on the spot, determined, "please the pigs," to found a city there. The classical story-teller goes on to say, that Latinus, king of the Latins, happened to be at war with Turnus—or as we might call him Turner—King of the Rutuli, when the Trojans arrived, and the former, thinking it better worth his while to make friends than foes of the immigrants, gave them a tract of land, which rendered them extremely tractable. On the principle that one good turn deserves another, they turned round upon Turnus, and completely routed the Rutuli. Latinus, to show his gratitude, gave Lavinia—not the "lovely young" one, who Thomson tells us, "once had friends ; " but his own daughter of that name—in marriage to Æneas, who at the death of his father-in-law, ruled over the city, and called his colony Lavinium. Tradition tells us further that Æneas had a son, Ascanius, sometimes called Parvus Iulus, or little Juli, who subsequently left Lavinium, and built Alba Longa—a sort of classical long acre—in that desirable neighbourhood known as the Alban Mount, which, from its becoming subsequently the most fashionable part of the city, may deserve the name of the Roman Albany.

The descendants of Ascanius are said to have reigned 300 years, and an attempt has been made to fill up the gap of these three centuries with a quantity of dry rubbish of the antiquarian kind, which occupies space, without affording anything like a solid foundation for the structure to be built upon it. Of such a nature is the catalogue of matters alleged to have connected Æneas with the actual founders of Rome ; but though names and dates are given, there is little doubt that the value of names

---

* Troy destroyed, B. C. 1184.   Rome founded, B. C. 753.

is not even nominal, and that if we trust the dates, we shall rely on the falsest data.

The spirit of antiquarianism is as ancient as the subjects on which it employs its ingenuity, and the Romans began puzzling themselves at a very early period about their own origin. A long course of fabrication ended in rearing up a legendary fabric, which was acknowledged by all the Roman bards ; and however much they may have doubted the truth of the tale, they deserve some credit for the consistency with which they have adhered to it.

The legend states that one Procas, belonging to the family of the Silvii, or Silvers, had two sons,—the elder, to whom the kingdom was left, being called Numitor, and the younger going by the name of Amulius. Though Numitor was the bigger brother, he does not seem to have been, pugilistically speaking, the better man, for he was deprived of the kingdom by Amulius, who, to prevent the chances of the law of primogeniture again taking effect, by placing any of Numitor's descendants on the throne, caused Rhea Silvia, the only daughter of that individual to become a virgin in the Temple of Vesta. The Vestals were, in fact, the old original nuns, withdrawing themselves from the world, and entering into a solemn vow against marriage during thirty years ; after which period they were free to wed, though they were scarcely ever invited to avail themselves of their rather tardy privilege. The senior sister went by the highly respectable name of Virgo Maxima—or old maid in chief—and was doubtless something more than ordinary in her appearance, as well as in her position. The Vestals were required to be plain in their dress, and in order to extend this plainness as far as possible to their looks, their hair was cut very short, however much they may have been distressed at parting with their tresses. Their chief duty consisted in keeping up the fire on the altar of Vesta, and they were prohibited on pain of death from giving to any other flame the smallest encouragement. In the event of such an offence having been committed by an unfortunate Vestal, who found her position little better than being buried alive, she was made to undergo literally that awful penalty.

Though the duties of the Vestals were rigidly enforced, and the letting out of the sacred fire was, in some cases, punished by the extinction of the delinquent's vital spark, they enjoyed some peculiar advantages Though their acts were under strict control, they were, in one sense, allowed a will of their own ; for they were permitted, even when under age, to make their own testaments. They occupied re-served seats at public entertainments ; and if they happened to meet a criminal in custody, they had the privilege of releasing him from the hands of the police of the period. Notwithstanding these inducements, the office of Vestal was not in much request : and, in the event of a vacancy, it was awarded by lot to some young lady, whose dissatisfaction with her lot was usually very visible. Such is a brief outline of the duties and liabilities of the order into which Amulius forced his niece,

and it has been the subject of complaint in more recent times that
Rome still occasionally does as Rome used to do.   We will now return
to Rhea Silvia, who appears to have entered the service of the goddess
as a maid-of-all-work; for she was in the habit of going to draw water
from a well; and it was on one of these aquatic excursions she met
with a military man, passing himself off as Mars who paid his addresses
to her, and proved irresistible.

Rhea Silvia.

Rhea Silvia gave birth to twins; upon which her cruel uncle ordered
her to be put to death, and desired that her infant offspring should be
treated as a couple of unwelcome puppies, and got rid of by drowning in
the ordinary manner.

The children were placed in a cradle, or, as some say, a bowl, and turned adrift on the river; so that Amulius, if he had any misgiving as to the security of his crown, preferred to drown it in the bowl with his unhappy little relatives.

It happened that there had been such a run on the banks of the Tiber, that its coffers or coffer-dams had poured out their contents all over the adjacent plains, and caused a very extensive distribution of its currency. Among other valuable deposits, it chanced to lodge for security, in a branch connected with the bank, the children of Rhea Silvia, who, by the way, must have been very fortunate under the circumstances, in being able to keep a balance. The infants were not in a very enviable condition; for there was nobody to board and lodge them, though the Tiber was still at hand to wash and do for them. The high tide proved a tide of good fortune to the children, who were floated so far inland, that when the river receded, they were left high and dry at the foot of a fig * tree, with no one, apparently, to care a fig what became of them. Under these circumstances a she-wolf, who had gone down to the Tiber to drink, heard the whimpering of the babies among the trees, and, her attention being drawn off from the water in the river to the whine in the wood, she came forward in the most handsome manner in the capacity of a wet-nurse to give them suck and succour. How this wolf became possessed of so much of the milk of human kindness, does not appear, and it is not perhaps worth while to inquire.

The children, it is said, were awakened by receiving a gentle licking from the tongue of the animal standing *in loco parentis* over them. Finding the situation damp, the wolf removed the infants to her den, where they were visited by a philanthropic woodpecker; who, when they were hungry, would bring them some tempting grub, or worm, by which the woodpecker soon wormed itself into the children's confidence. Other members of the feathered tribe made themselves useful in this novel nursery, by keeping off the insects; and many a gnat found itself —or rather lost itself—unexpectedly in the throat of some remorseless swallow. However well-meaning the animal may have been, the children could not have profited greatly, if there had been no one ready to take them from the mouth; and happily Faustulus, the king's shepherd, who had watched them as they were being carried to the wolf's cave or loup-hole, provided them with another loophole to get out of it. Taking advantage of the wolf's temporary absence from home, the "gentle shepherd," resolving to rescue the children, by hook or by crook, removed the babes to his own hut, and handed them over to his wife Laurentia, as a sort of supplement to their previously rather extensive family.

Some historians, refusing to believe the story of the Wolf and the Woodpecker, have endeavoured to reconcile probability with tradition, by suggesting that the wife of Faustulus had got the name of the Wolf from the contrast she presented to her lamb-like husband, and that the supposed woodpecker was simply a hen-pecker, in the person of Laurentia.

---

* From this circumstance the fig was considered figurative of the foundation of the city, and held sacred in Rome for many centuries.

Romulus and Remus were the names of the two infants, who, as they grew up, began to take after their foster-mother the wolf, turning out exceedingly wild lads, with a lupine propensity for worrying the flocks, and going on altogether in a very brutal manner. Remus was taken up on a charge of sheep stealing, or something very like it, and brought before Numitor, his own grandfather, when a recognition took place in a manner not much in accordance with the ordinary rules of evidence. Romulus had also been apprised of his relationship by Faustulus, who must have made a pretty bold guess at a fact he could not have known ; and the two lads, being adopted by Numitor, were sent for their educato Gabii, where everything was taught that men of rank in those days were expected to learn, and whence the word Gaby is clearly derivable. Anxious to do something for the old gentleman, their grandfather, Romulus and Remus got up a demonstration in his favour, and they succeeded in restoring him to the throne of Alba Longa, a long row of white houses, which was less of a territory than a Terrace, and it is a strange coincidence that Terracina, or little Terrace, formed one end of it. Amulius was killed, and leaving Numitor sole master of White's Row, Romulus and Remus resolved on a building speculation a great deal higher up—that is to say on the spot where they had passed the days of their infancy. Before the new city was commenced, a dispute

Romulus consulting the Augury.

arose, first, about what it should be called, and secondly, as to who should govern it. Romulus and Remus, being twins, could not bring the law of primogeniture to bear upon their little differences, and it was therefore agreed to refer the matter to augury, which should decide who was to be inaugurated as the ruler of the new colony. Romulus mounted the Palatine Mount, and Remus took his station on the Aventine, when both began to keep a very sharp look out for something ominous. Remus was the first to remark something odd in the shape of six vultures flying from north to south, but Romulus no sooner heard the news than he declared he had· seen twelve, and the question arose whether, figuratively speaking, the one bird in hand seen by Remus should outweigh the two in the bush that subsequently appeared to Romulus. The augur, when appealed to, gave, as usual, a very ambiguous answer. It amounted, in effect, to the observation that there were six of one and a dozen of the other; so that the soothsayer, instead of having said anything to soothe, was far more likely to irritate. Both parties claimed the victory; Remus contending for the precedence usually granted to the early bird, and Romulus maintaining that he had been specially favoured, by having been permitted to see so many birds of a feather flock together. Romulus accordingly commenced drawing his plans in the Etruscan fashion, by causing a boundary line to be marked out with a plough, to which were yoked a heifer and a bull, a ceremony from which, perhaps, the English term bulwarks, and the French word boulevards or bulvards, may or may not be derivable. The line thus traced was called the Pomœrium, and where an entrance was to be made, it was customary to carry the plough across the space—a

little engineering difficulty that gave the name of Porta to a gate, from the verb *portare*, to carry. Remus looked on at the proceedings in a half-quizzing, half-quarrelsome spirit, until the wall rose a little above the ground, when he amused himself by leaping derisively over it. " Thus," said he, " will the enemy leap over those barriers." " And thus," rejoined the superintendent or clerk of the works— one Celer, who acted in this instance with thoughtless celerity —" thus shall die whoever may

Remus jumping over the Walls.

leap over my barriers." * With these words he gave Remus a mortal

---

* The Pomœrium was not the actual wall, but a boundary line, held very sacred by the Romans. It consisted of nothing but the clod turned inwards by the furrow, and, it is probable, that the offensive act of Remus was not his leaping over the wall, but his hopping over the clod, which would, naturally, excite indignation against him as an unmannerly clod-hopper.

blow, and the legend goes on to state, that Romulus was immediately
seized with remorse, and subsequent visits from his brother's ghost
rendered Romulus himself little better than the ghost of what he used
to be. Remus showed as much spirit after his decease as during his
lifetime ; and took the form of the deadly nightshade, springing up at
the bed-side, to poison the existence of his brother.

Awful appearance of the Shade of Remus to Romulus

Tradition tells us that Romulus came at length to terms with
the ghost, who agreed to discontinue his visits, in consideration of
the establishment of the festival of the Lemuria—called, originally,
Remuria—in honour of his memory. The rites were celebrated bare-
footed—an appropriate penalty for one who had stepped into a brother's
shoes; the hands were thrice washed—a process much needed, as
a sort of expiation for dirty work ;—and black beans were thrown
four times behind the back, with the superstitious belief that the
growing up of the beans would prevent the stalking abroad of evil
spirits. The unfortunate twin was buried on Mount Aventine, and

Romulus ordered a double set of sceptres, crowns, and royal badges, in order that he might set up one set by the side of his own, in honour of his late relative. These duplicates of mere senseless symbols served only to commemorate the double part which Romulus had acted ; for a vacant throne and a headless crown were but empty tributes to a murdered brother's memory.

The city having been built, was found considerably too large for the people there were to live in it ; and as a place cannot, like a garment, be made to fit by taking it in, there was no alternative but to fill the city with any stuff that might serve for stuffing. Romulus, therefore, threw open his gates to any one who chose to walk in, which caused an influx of those who, from having no character at all, usually go under the denomination of all sorts of characters. Society became terribly mixed, and, in fact, the place was a kind of Van Demon's Land, crammed with criminals, replete with runaway slaves, and forming—in a word—a regular refuge for the morally destitute. It says something for the females of the period, that women were very scarce at Rome, and it is surprising that some learned philologist has never yet made the remark, that the fact of the word Ro-man being familiar to us all, while there is no such term as Ro-woman, may be taken as a collateral proof of the scarcity of the gentler sex in the city founded by Romulus.

The ladies of the neighbourhood were indisposed to listen to the addresses of the male population of Rome, which was quite bad enough to suggest the possibility of the Latin word *male-factor* having supplied the distinctive epithet " male " to the ruder sex in general. In vain were proposals of marriage made to the maidens of the adjoining states, who one and all declared they would not change their state by becoming the wives of Romans. Irritated by these refusals, Romulus determined to prove himself more than a match for these women, every one of whom thought herself too good a match for any of his people. He announced his intention to give a party or pic-nic for the celebration of the Consualia, which were games in honour of Consus, the god of Counsel,—a sort of lawyer's frolic, in which a mole was sacrificed, probably because working in the dark was always the characteristic of the legal fraternity. Invitations to these games were issued in due form to the Latins and Sabines, with their wives and daughters, many of whom flocked to the spot, under the influence of female curiosity.

The weather being propitious, all the Sabine beauty and fashion were attracted to the place, and the games, consisting of horse-racing, gave to the scene all the animation of a cup day at Ascot. Suddenly, at a pre-concerted signal, there was a general elopement of the Roman youth with the Sabine ladies, who were, in the most ungallant manner, abandoned to their fate by the Sabine gentlemen. It is true that the latter were taken by surprise, but they certainly made the very best of their way home before they thought of avenging the wrong and insult that had been committed. Had they been all married ladies who were carried off, the cynic might have suggested that the Sabine husbands would not

The Romans walking off with the Sabine Women.

have objected to a cheap mode of divorce, but—to make use of an **Irishism**—there was only one single woman who happened to be a wife in the whole of the "goodly company." The small Latin states, Antennæ, Crustumerium, and Cœnina, were very angry at the supineness of the Sabines, whose King—one Tatius—seemed disposed to take the thing rather too tacitly. The three states above mentioned commenced an action on their own account, and Acron, the King of Cœnina, fell in battle by the hand of Romulus, who, stripping off the apparel of the foe, caused it to be carried to Rome and hung upon an oak, where the arms and armour of Acron, glittering among the acorns, were dedicated, as *Spolia opima*, to Jupiter Feretrius. *

Though Tatius had been the last, he was not destined to be the least of those taking part in the Sabine war; and he determined to rely less on strategy than stratagem. The water in those days was not so well laid on as in later times; when the lofty aqueducts, still running in ruins about the neighbourhood of Rome, were carried to an elevation fitted for the very highest service that could be desired. Rome, instead of being well supplied, was supplied by wells; and ladies of rank were accustomed to draw the water required for domestic purposes. It chanced, one afternoon, that Tarpeia, the daughter of Tarpeius, the commander of the Roman city, on the Capitoline Hill, was proceeding on an errand of the sort, when she met with Tatius, who, addressing her in the language of a friend, requested " a drink " of her pitcher. Tarpeia, dazzled by the splendour of his gold bracelets and glittering armour, could not resist the request of such a highly polished gentleman. Tatius had purposely electrotyped himself for the interview, and, seeing the effect he had produced, he intimated that he had several friends, who were covered with metal quite as attractive as that he wore, and that, if Tarpeia would only open the gate of the citadel to himself and party, she should have more gold than she could carry. The bargain was faithfully kept on both sides; for Tarpeia opened the gate to Tatius and the Sabines, who, on their part performed their contract to the letter, for, as they entered, they threw at her not only their bracelets but their breast-plates, completely crushing her with the weight of the gold she had coveted; and making her think, no doubt, that " never was poor woman so unmercifully put upon." So thorough an illustration of an *embarras des richesses* is not often met with in history.

Being now possessed of the Capitoline, the Sabines were in an improved position; and the Romans, having tried in vain to recover the citadel, saw that they must either give in or give battle. Determining on the latter course, Romulus selected the valley between the Palatine and the Capitoline, where a general engagement began ; but the Romans seemed to have special engagements elsewhere, for they were all running away, when their leader, with great tact, vowed a Temple to Jupiter Stator—the flight-stayer. This gave to the action a decided re-action ; for the Romans, being rallied upon their cowardice,

---

* The word Feretrius will strike the merest tyro as being derived from *fero*, to strike, and meaning to designate Jupiter in his character of Striker, or Smiter.

by their chief, began, in their turn, to rally. The contest grew fierce on both sides, when suddenly the Sabine ladies, who were the primary cause of the quarrel, threw themselves into the midst; and, though female interference has rarely the effect of making peace, the women were, on this occasion, the cause of a cessation of hostility. It was agreed that the two nations should be henceforth united under the name of Romans and Quirites, each having a distinct king, a distinction which, had it continued, must in time have led to a difference. In a few years, however, Tatius was slain at a sacrifice which he had attended without the remotest idea of being made a victim himself; and Romulus, finding nothing said about a successor, thought it politic to hush the matter up without even avenging his late colleague. Romulus is said to have reigned for seven-and-thirty years; but when we enquire into the exact time and manner of his death we learn nothing, beyond the fact that nobody knows what became of him. According to the statement of one set of authorities, he was attending a review in the Palus Capræ—a marsh near the Tiber—when a total eclipse of the sun took place, and on the return of light, Romulus was nowhere visible. If this was really the case, it is probable that he got into a perilous swamp, where he felt a rapid sinking; and all his attendants being in the dark as to his situation were unable to extricate him from the marsh in which, according to some authorities, he went down to posterity.

It must, however, be confessed, that when we look for the cause of the death of Romulus in this fatal swamp, we have but very poor ground to go upon. It is, nevertheless, some consolation to us for the mystery that overhangs the place and manner of his decease, that his existence is, after all, quite apocryphal; and we are not expected to go into an elaborate inquiry when, where, and how he died, until the fact of his having ever lived at all has been satisfactorily settled.

Before we have quite done with Romulus, it will be proper to state how he is said to have divided the people under his sovereignty. He is alleged to have separated them into three tribes—the Latin word *tribus* will here suggest itself to the acute student—namely the Ramnes, called after the Romans; the Tities, after Titus Tatius; and the Luceres, who derived their appellation either from one Lucumo, an Etruscan ally of Romulus, or Lucerus a king of Ardea; or *lucus* a grove, because there was no grove, and hence we get *lucerus a non luco*, on the same principle as *lucus a non lucendo:* or lastly, according to Niebuhr's opinion, from a place called Lucer or Lucerum, which the Luceres might have inhabited.

Each tribe was divided into ten *curiæ*,* every one of which had a chapel for the performance of sacred rites, and was presided over by a *curio;* and the reader must have little curiosity, indeed, if he does not ask whether our modern word curate may not be referred to this remote

---

* The best derivation of the word *curia* is *quiris*, which, on inquiry, is found to correspond with *curis*.

origin. The *curiæ* were subdivided into gentes, or clans, and each gens consisted of several families, called gentiles; so that a man of family and a member of the gentes, became somewhat synonymous. In time, however, the gentiles got very much mixed by unsuitable marriages; and hence there arose among those who could claim to belong to a gens, a distinction similar to that between the *gentes*, or *gents*, of our own day, and the *gentiles*, or *gentlemen*. Romulus is said to have selected his body-guard from the three tribes, taking one hundred from each, and as Celer, the Etruscan, was their captain, the guards got the name of Celeres—the fast men of the period.

In addition to the tribes, there existed in those early times a separate body, consisting of slaves, and a somewhat higher class, called by the name of clients.* The latter belonged to the common people, each of whom was permitted to choose from among the patricians a *patronus*, or patron, who could claim the life and fortune of his client in exchange for the cheaper commodities of protection and patronage. The patron gave his countenance and advice when asked, the client giving his labour and his money when wanted—an arrangement which proves that clients, from the remotest times to the present hour, were liable to pecuniary mulcts, even to the extent of the entire sacrifice of the whole of their subsistence, for the benefit of those who had the privilege of advising them.

The Senate—a term derived from the Latin word *Senes*, old men—formed the chief council of the state, and its first institution is usually referred to the reign of Romulus. Three members were nominated by each tribe, and three by each of the thirty *curiæ*, making ninety-nine in all, to which Romulus himself is said to have added one, for the purpose of making up round numbers, and at the same time nominating a sort of president over the assembly, who also had to take care of the city, in the absence of the sovereign. There is a difference of opinion as to whether one hundred new members were added to the Senate at the time of the union with the Sabines, for Dionysius says there were; but Livy says there were not; and we are disposed to attach credit to the former, for he was an extremely particular man, while Livy was frequently oblivious of caution in giving credence and currency to mere tradition.

Before closing this portion of the narrative of the History of Rome, it is necessary to warn the reader against believing too much of it. The current legends are, indeed, *Legenda*, or things to be read, because every body is in the habit of repeating them; but the student must guard himself against placing credence in the old remark, that " what everybody says must be true," for here is a direct instance of what everybody says being decidedly otherwise. The life and reign of Romulus, are to be taken not simply *cum grano salis*—with a grain of salt—but with an entire cellar of that condiment, which is so useful in correcting the evil consequences of swallowing too much of anything.

---

* The word " client " is probably derived from *cluere*, to hear or obey—at all events cluere is the best clue we can give to the origin of the word in question.

CHAPTER THE SECOND.

oMULUS having been swamped in the marsh of
Capra, or having disappeared down one of
those drains, which have carried away into the
great sea of conjecture so many of the facts of
former ages, the senate put off from week to
week, and from this day se'nnight to that day
se'nnight the choice of a successor. The
honourable members agreed to try their hands
at Government by turns, and they took the
sceptre for five days each by a constant rotation, which any wheel, and more particularly
a commonwheal, was sure to suffer from. The
people growing tired of this unprofitable game
of fives, which threw everything into a state
of sixes and sevens, clamoured so loudly to be
reduced under one head, that permission was
given them to elect a sovereign. Their choice
fell upon Numa Pompilius, because he was
born on the day of the foundation of the city ;
so that he may be said to have succeeded by
birth to the berth of chief magistrate. Numa
Pompilius was a Sabine, who we are told had
been instructed by Pythagoras, and we should
be happy to believe what we are told, if we did
not happen to know that the sage belonged to
quite a different time, having lived two hundred
years later than the alleged existence of the pupil.

Before entering on his duties, the newly chosen king consulted the
augurs, with one of whom he walked up to the Temple on the Saturnian
Hill, where Numa, seated on a stone, looked to the south as far as he
could see, in order to ascertain whether there was any impediment to
his views and prospects. In the earliest periods of the history of Rome
no office was undertaken without a consultation of the augurs, or
auspices ; and the continued use of these words affords proof of the
ancient custom to which they relate ; though inauguration now takes
place under auspices of a very different character. The recognised
signs of those times were only two, consisting of the lightning, by
means of which the truth was supposed to flash across the augur's

mind ; and, secondly, the birds, who, by being consulted for something
singular in their singing, or eccentric in their flying, might, had they
known it, have fairly plumed themselves on the honours done to them.
A crow on the left betokened that things were looking black, but the
same bird on the right imparted to everything a brighter colour ; and as
these birds are in the habit of wandering right and left, the augurs could
always declare there was something to be said on both sides.

Numa Pompilius was, according to all accounts, a just ruler, and he
began his career in a ruler-like manner by drawing several straight
lines about Rome, to mark its boundaries. He placed these under a
deity, termed Terminus, and he erected twelve stones within a stone's
throw of each other, at regular intervals along the frontier. These
were visited once a year by twelve officers, called Fratres Arvales,
appointed for the purpose, and the custom originated, no doubt, the
parochial practice of perambulating parishes with wands and staves,
placed in the hands of beadles, who not unfrequently add the luxury
of beating the boys to the ceremony of beating the boundaries.

Numa, though he had come to the throne, was fond of the retired
walks of life, and frequently took a solitary stroll in the suburbs.
During one of his rambles chance brought him to a grotto, and he was
induced to remember the grotto by the surpassing loveliness of its fair

Numa Pompilius remembering the Grotto.

inhabitant. Her name was Egeria, her profession that of a fortune-
teller, which gave her such an influence over the superstitious mind of
Numa, that she ruled him with her divining rod as completely as if it
had been a rod of iron. He professed to act under the advice of this
nymph, to whom tradition—an inveterate match-maker—has married
him, and he instituted the Flamines, an order of priests, to give weight
to the falsehoods or " flams " he thought fit to promulgate. The
privileges of the Flamines were not altogether of the most comfortable

kind, and consisted chiefly in the right of wearing the Apex—a cap made of olive wood—and the Laena, a sort of Roman wrap-rascal, shaggy on both sides, and worn above the toga, as an overcoat. The Flamen was prohibited from appearing in public without his Apex, which could not be kept on the head without strings; but such was the stringency of the regulations, that one Sulpicius* was deprived of his priesthood, in consequence of his official hat, which was as light as a modern zephyr, having been blown off his head in the midst of a sacrifice.

Numa added, also, a sort of *ballet* company to the mythological arrangements of his day, by establishing twelve *Salii*, or dancing priests, whose duty it was to execute a grand *pas de douze* on certain occasions through the principal public thorough fares. The Salii, though a highly respectable, were not a very venerable order, for no one could remain in it whose father and mother were not both alive, the existence of the parents of the dancing priests being, no doubt, required as a guarantee that their dancing days were not yet over.

Several temples are dated from this reign, including that of Janus, the double-faced deity, who presided over peace and war—a most appropriate office to one capable of looking two ways at once, for there are always two sides to every quarrel. This temple must have been perfectly useless during the life of its founder, for it was never to be opened in the time of peace, and Numa preserved for Rome forty-three years of undisturbed tranquillity. He was emphatically the friend of order, and its usual consequences, prosperity to trade, with soundness of credit, and he encouraged commerce by giving a patron-saint or Lar to every industrial occupation. He marked also the value of good faith by building a temple to Bona Fides, and it may be presumed that the creditor, who, putting up with the loss of his little bill, sacrificed a bad debt in this Temple, was still in hope that he should eventually find his account in it.

If it cannot be said that Numa never lost a day, it must be admitted that he made the most of his time ; for he added two whole months to the year of Romulus. January and February were the names given to the time thus gained ; but as the year did not then correspond with the course of the sun, it was usual to introduce, every other year, a supplementary month, so that if one year was too short, the next, by being too long, made it as broad as it was long in the aggregate.

Numa Pompilius lived to be eighty-two ; when he had the beatitude of dying as peacefully as he had lived ; and so gently had Nature dealt with him, that she had suffered him to run up more than four scores, before her debt was satisfied. Certain stories are told of the funeral ceremonies that followed Numa's death ; and it is said that the Senators acted as porters to his bier, in token of their appreciation of the imperial measures which Numa had himself carried. It has been stated, also, that he caused to be placed, within his tomb, a copy, on papyrus, or

* Val. Maximus, i. 1. § 4.

palm leaves,* of his own works, in twenty-four books; and it is certainly a happy idea to bury an author with his writings, when, if they have been provocative of sleep in others, he may eventually reap the benefit of their somniferous properties.

On the death of Numa, the country having been taught, by past experience, the danger of allowing the crown to go from head to head, without the slightest regard to a fit, determined that the interregnum should be short, and the election of a new king was at once proceeded with. The choice fell upon Tullus Hostilius, who was of a decidedly warlike turn, and was ever on the look-out for a pretext to commence hostilities. The Albans, our old friends of Alba Longa, or White's Row, were the nearest, and consequently the most conveniently situated, for the indulgence of his pugnacious propensities; and tradition relates that on one occasion some Alban peasants, having been attacked and stripped by the Romans, the former, who had lost even their clothes, sought redress at the hands of their rulers. In the course of ah attempt to settle the dispute between Alba and Rome, each place sent ambassadors, who crossed each other on the road, as if the two states were determined to be in every way at cross purposes. The Alban envoys were beguiled of all ideas of business by invitations to banquets and feasts, so that whenever they attempted to ask for explanations, their mouths were stopped with a dinner or a supper, given in honour of their visit. The Roman messengers were prohibited, on the contrary, from accepting invitations, or giving up to parties what was meant for Romankind; and had received peremptory instructions to demand an immediate settlement of their long-standing account from the Albans. The parties could not understand each other, or, rather, they understood each other too well; for war was the object of both, though neither of them liked the responsibility of beginning it. The Albans, however, prepared to march on Rome, and encamped themselves within the confines of a ditch, into which ditch their King, Cluilius, tumbled, one night, very mysteriously, and died, which caused them to dignify the ditch with the name of *fossa Cluilia.*

Death of Cluilius.

The Albans appointed one Mettius Fuffetius, a fussy and nervous personage, as Dictator, in the place of the late King; and Fuffetius

---

* There exist, in the British Museum, books older than the time of Numa, written by the Egyptians, on these palm leaves, which show, in one sense, the palmy state of literature at that early period.

requested an interview with Tullus, who agreed to the proposition, with a determination, before meeting the Dictator, not to be dictated to. Mettius represented the inconvenience of wasting whole rivers of blood, when a few pints might answer all the purpose; and it was finally agreed to settle the matter by a grand combat of six, sustained on either side by three champions, chosen from each army. The Alban and the Roman forces were graced, respectively, with a trio of brothers, whose strength and activity rendered them worthy to be ranked with the small family parties who attach the epithet of Herculean, Acrobatic, Indian rubber, or Incredible, to the fraternal character in which they come forward to astonish and amuse the enlightened age we live in.

These six young men were known as the Horatii and Curiatii,—the former being on the Roman, the latter on the Alban side; and to them it was agreed, by mutual consent, to trust the fate of the battle. The story-tellers have done their utmost to render everything Roman as romantic as possible; and the legend of the Horatii and Curiatii has been heightened by making one of the latter batch of brothers the accepted lover of the sister of the Horatii.

All the arrangements for the sanguinary *sestetto* having been completed, the six champions came forward, looking fresh and confident, not one of them displaying nervousness by a shaking of the hand, though they shook each other's hands very heartily. Having taken their positions, the men presented a picture which we regret has not been preserved for us by some sporting annalist of the period. Imagination, who is "our own reporter" on this occasion, and, perhaps, as accurate a reporter as many who profess to chronicle passing events, must fill up the outlines of the sketch that has been handed down to us.

The contest commenced with a great deal of that harmless, but violent exercise, which goes on between Shakspeare's celebrated pair of Macs—the well known 'Beth and 'Duff—when the former requests the latter to " lay on " to him, and there ensues a clashing of their swords, as vigorous as the clashing of their claims to the crown of Scotland At length one of the Curiatii, feeling that they had all met for the despatch of business, despatched one of the Horatii, upon which the combatants, being set going, they continued to go one by one with great rapidity. A few seconds had scarcely elapsed when a second of the Horatii fell, and the survivor of the trio, thinking that he must eventually become number three if he did not speedily take care of number one, resolved to stop short this run of ill-luck against his race, by attempting a run of good luck for his life; or, in other words, having a race for it. The excellence of his wind saved him from drawing his last breath, for the Curiatii, starting off in pursuit, soon proved unequal in their speed, and one shot far in advance of the other two, who, though stout of heart, were somewhat too stout of body to be as forward as their nimbler brother in giving chase to their antagonist. The survivor of the Horatii perceiving this, turned suddenly round upon the nearest of his foes, and having at once disposed of him, waited patiently for the

other two, who were coming at unequal speed, puffing and panting after
him. A single blow did for the second of the Curiatii, who was already

Combat between the Horatii and Curiatii.

blown by the effort of running, and it was unnecessary to do more with
the third, who came up completely out of breath, than to render him
incapable of taking in a further supply of that vitally important article.
The last of the Horatii had consequently become the conqueror, and
though when he began to run his life seemed to hang on a thread,
which an unlucky stitch in his side would have finished off, his flight
was the cause of his coming off in the end with flying colours. After
the first of the Curiatii fell, fatness proved fatal to the other two, for
Horatius, by dealing with them *en gros*, as well as *en detail*, settled all
accounts with both of them.

Seeing the result of the contest, Fuffetius, on the part of the Albans,
gave out that they gave in, and the Romans returned home with
Horatius at their head, carrying—in a huge bundle—the spoils of the

Curiatii.   At the entrance of the city he met his sister, who, perceiving among the spoils, a garment of her late lover, embroidered with a piece of work from her own hands, commenced another piece of work of a most frantic and desperate character.   Maddened at the sight of the yarn she had spun for the lost object of her affections, she began spinning another yarn that threatened to be interminable, if her brother had not soon cut the thread of it.   She called him by all kinds of names but his own, and was, in fact, as noisy and abusive as a conventional " female in distress," or, as that alarming and dangerous nuisance, " an injured woman."   Horatius, who had found the blades of three assailants less cutting than a sister's tongue, interrupted her as she ran through her wrongs, by running her through with his sword, accompanying the act with the exclamation, " Thus perish all the enemies of Rome."   Notwithstanding the excitement and *éclat* attending the triumphant entry of Horatius into Rome, the proper officer of the period, whoever he may have been, was evidently not only on duty, but prepared to do it, for the victorious fratricide, or sororicide, was at once hurried off to the nearest Roman station.   Having been taken before the king, his majesty saw great difficulties in the case, and was puzzled how to dispose of it.   Taking out the scales of justice, he threw the heavy crime of Horatius into one ; but the services performed for his country, when cast into the other scale, seemed to balance the matter pretty evenly.   Tullus, therefore, referred the case to another tribunal, which sentenced the culprit to be hanged, but he was allowed to have so capitally acquitted himself in the fight, that he was acquitted of the capital punishment.   This was commuted for the penalty of passing under the yoke, which consisted of the ceremony of walking under a pike raised upright on two others, and at these three pikes the only toll placed upon his crime was levied.

The fallen warriors were honoured with tombs in the form of sugar-loaves, by which the unsatisfactory sweets of posthumous renown were symbolised.   Fuffetius, who though not wounded in his person, was fearfully wounded in his pride by the result of the conflict, felt so jealous of Tullus, that the former, though afraid to burst into open revolt, determined on the really more revolting plan of treachery.   The rival soldiers had now to combine their forces against the Veientines and the Fidenates, and, having set out together, they soon found the foe drawn up in battle array, when Tullus with his Romans faced the Veientines, and Mettius with his Albans formed a *vis à vis* to the Fidenates.   When the conflict commenced, the Alban wing showed the white feather, and Fuffetius gradually withdrew his forces to an adjacent hill, which he lowered himself by ascending for the purpose of watching the turn of events, so that he might declare himself on the side of victory.   Tullus saw the unmanly manœuvre, but winked at it, and rushed like winking upon the Fidenates, who ran so fast that their discretion completely out-ran their valour.   The Roman leader then turned his eyes, arms, and legs towards the Veientines, who fled towards the Tiber, into which they desperately dived, but many of them, for divers reasons, never got out again. The perfidious Albans, headed by Mettius Fuffetius, now came down into the plain, and putting on a plain, straightforward manner, he congratulated Tullus on the victory. Pretending not to have noticed their treachery, he invited them all to a sacrifice on the following day, and having particularly requested them to come early, they were on the ground by sunrise, but were completely in the dark as to the intentions of T. Hostilius. The Romans at a given signal closed in upon the Albans, who were informed that their city should be razed, or rather, lowered to the ground, and, that their chief, who had pulled a different way from his new ally, should be fastened to horses who should be driven in opposite directions. This cruel sentence, upon which we have scarcely patience to bestow a sentence of our own, was barbarously carried into execution. Alba fell to the ground; which is all we have been able to pick up relating to the subject of this portion of our history.

The remainder of the reign of Hostilius was occupied with military successes; but he neglected the worship of the gods, who it is said evinced their anger by a tremendous shower of stones on the Alban Mount, in order to soften his flinty heart, by making him feel the weight of their displeasure. From the extreme of indifference he went to the opposite extreme of superstition, and called upon Jupiter to send him a sign—which was, in fact, a sign of the King's head being in a lamentable condition. The unhappy sovereign, imitating his predecessor Numa, attempted some experiments in the hope of drawing down some lightning, but it was not likely that one who had conducted himself so badly could be a better conductor of the electric fluid, and the result was, that though he learned the art of attracting the spark, it flashed upon him with such force that he instantly expired.

Such is the tradition with reference to the death of Tullus; but it is hard to say whether the accounts handed down to us have been over-charged, or whether the clouds were in that condition. Some speculators insinuate that the royal experimentalist owed his sad fate to some mis-management of his electrical jar while attempting to produce an unnatural jarring of the elements. The good actions of Tullus were so few, that his fame will not afford the omission of one, and being desirous to put the best construction we can upon his works, we give him credit for the construction of the Curia Hostilia, whose site still meets the eye near the northern angle of the Palatine. Ambassadors are spoken of as existing in the reign of Tullus Hostilius, but whether they owe their origin to Numa, who went before, or to Ancus Martius, who came after him, is so much a matter of doubt, that some historians, in trying to meet the claims of both half-way, stop short of giving the merit to either. Tullus may, at all events, have the credit of employing, if he did not institute, the art of diplomacy in Rome; for he appointed ambassadors, as we have already seen, to negotiate with the Albans. These envoys were called Feciales, the chief of whom wore on his head a fillet of white wool, with a quantity of green herbs, formed into a turban, which must have had somewhat the appearance of a fillet of veal, with the ingredients for stuffing. His duty was to proceed to the offending country, and proclaim his wrongs upon the border, though there might be no one there to listen, and having crossed the boundary—if his indignation happened to know any bounds—he was to astonish the first native he met by a catalogue of grievances. On reaching a city, the ambassador went over the old story to the soldier at the gate, just as though, at Storey's gate, an irritated foreigner should pour out his country's real or imaginary wrongs to the sentinel on duty. To this recital the soldier would, of course, be as deaf as his post, and the Fecialis would then proceed to lay his complaint before the magistrates. In the event of his obtaining no redress, he returned home for a spear, and killing a pig with one end, he poked the fire with the other. The instrument being thus charred in the handle and blood-stained at the point, became an appropriate emblem of hostility, and the Fecialis declared war by stirring it up with the long pole, which he threw across the enemy's boundary.

After the death of Tullus Hostilius, the people lost no time in choosing Ancus Martius, a grandson of Numa, for their sovereign. The new king copied his grandfather, which he had a perfect right to do, but he imposed on the Pontifex Maximus the very severe task of copying on white tables the somewhat ponderous works of Pompilius, which were posted up for the perusal of the populace.

Though partial on the whole to peace, Ancus was not afraid of war, and, when his kingdom was threatened, he was quite ready to fight for it. He subdued the Latins, and having first settled them in the field, allowed them to settle themselves in the city. He enlarged Rome, but abridged the distance between different parts by throwing the first bridge across the Tiber, and his name has come down to posterity in the ditch of the Quirites which he caused to be dug for the defence of the city, against those who were unlikely to go through thick and thin for the purpose of invading it. He also built a prison in the heart of the city, and what might be truly termed a heart of stone, for the prison was formed of a quarry, and is still in existence as a monument of the hard lot of its inmates. Ancus Martius further signalised his reign by founding the city of Ostia at the Tiber's mouth, and thus gave its waters the benefit of that port which so much increased their value. On the spot may still be seen some ruins supposed to belong to a temple dedicated to the winds, among whom the greater part of the temple has long since been promiscuously scattered. Salt-works were also established in its neighbourhood, but the *sal* was of that volatile kind that none now remains from which buyers could fill their cellars. Ancus Martius reigned for a period of twenty-four years, and either in tranquillity or war—whether engaged in the works of peace, or embroiled in a piece of work—he proved himself thoroughly worthy of his predecessors, and, in fact, he left far behind him many who had gone before him in the task of government.

CHAPTER THE THIRD.

FROM THE ACCESSION OF TARQUINIUS PRISCUS TO THE DEATH OF
SERVIUS TULLIUS.

IT is the opinion of the best authorities that the Muse of History has employed her skipping-rope in passing, or rather skipping, from the grave of Ancus Martius to the throne of Tarquinius Priscus ; for there is a very visible gap yawning between the two ; and as we have no wish to set the reader yawning in sympathy with the gap, we at once drag him away from it.

Plunging into the times of Tarquinius Priscus, we describe him as the son of a Corinthian merchant, who, being compelled to quit his country for political reasons, had withdrawn all his Corinthian capital, and settled at Tarquinii, an Etruscan city. Having fallen in love with a lady of the place, or, more poetically speaking, deposited his affections in an Etruscan vase, he became a husband to her, and the father of two children, named respectively Lucumo and Aruns. Poor Aruns had a very brief run, and soon met his death ; but we cannot say how or where, for we have no report of the meeting. Lucumo married Tanaquil, an Etruscan lady, of great beauty and ambition, who professed to dive into futurity ; and, guided by this diving belle, he threw himself into the stream of events, in the hope of being carried onwards by the tide of fortune. She persuaded him that Tarquinii was a poor place, where nothing was to be done ; that his foreign extraction prevented him from being properly drawn out ; and that Rome alone could afford him a field wide enough for his vast abilities. Driven by his wife, he jumped up into his chariot, which was an open one, and was just entering Rome, when his cap was suddenly removed from his head by a strange bird, which some allege was an eagle ; though, had they said it was a lark, we should have believed them far more readily. Lucumo followed his hat as well as he could with his eyes ; but his wife was so completely carried away with it, that she declared the circumstance told

her he would gain a crown, though it really proved how nearly he had
lost one; for until the bird replaced his hat upon his head, there was
only a bare possibility of his getting it back again.

The wealth of his wife enabled Lucumo to live in the first style of
fashion; and having been admitted to the rights of citizenship, he
changed his name to Lucius Tarquinius: for the sake, perhaps, of
the sound, in the absence of any sounder reason.   He was introduced
at Court, where he won the favour of Ancus, who was so much taken
by his dashing exterior, that he gave him a commission in the army, as
Tribunus Celerum, a sort of Captain of the Guards, who, from the
title of Celeres, appear to have been, as we have before observed, the
fast men, as opposed to the " slow coaches " of the period.

Celeres.

The Captain made himself so generally useful to Ancus, that when
the latter died, his two sons were left to the guardianship of the
former, who, on the day fixed for the election of a new king, sent his
wards to the chase, that they might be pursuing other game, instead of
looking after the Crown, which Tarquinius had set his own eye upon.
In the absence of the youths, Tarquinius, who had got the name of
Priscus, or the old hand, which he seems to have well deserved, proposed himself as a candidate; and, in a capital electioneering speech,
put forth his own merits with such success, that he was voted on to the
throne without opposition.

The commencement of his reign was not very peaceful, for he was
attacked by the Latins; but he gave them a very severe Latin lesson,
and, crushing them under his feet, sent them back to that part of Italy
forming the lower part of the boot, with the loss of considerable booty.
He, nevertheless, found time for all manner of games; and he instituted
the Ludi Magni, which were great sport, in a space he marked out as
the Circus Maximus.

The position of the Circus was between the Palatine and Aventine

Hills, there being a slope on either side, so that the people followed the
inclination of nature as well as their own in selecting the spot for
spectacular purposes. In the earliest times a Circus was formed of
materials brought by the spectators themselves, who raised temporary
scaffolds, from which an unfortunate drop, causing fearful execution among
the crowd, would frequently happen. Tarquinius Priscus, desirous of giving
more permanent accommodation to the Roman sight seers, built a Circus
capable of containing 150,000 persons, and, from its vast superiority in
size over other similar buildings, it obtained the distinction of Maximus.
The sports of the Circus were extremely attractive to the Romans, who
looked to the *libelli*, containing the lists of the horses, and names and
colours of the drivers, with all the eagerness of a "gentleman sports-
man" seeking information from Dorling's correct card at Epsom. In
the early days of Rome the amusements of the Circus were limited to
the comparatively harmless contests of equestrian speed ; and it was not
until the city had reached a high state of refinement—cruelty having
become refined like everything else—that animals were killed by
thousands, and human beings by hundreds at a time, to glut the
sanguinary appetites of the prince and the people. The ancient Circus
was circular at one end only, and the line of seats was broken by a sort
of outwork, supposed to have comprised the box and retiring-room of the
sovereign ; while, at the opposite side, was another deviation from the
line of seats, to form a place for the *editor spectaculorum*—a box for
the manager. Though Tarquinius is said to have founded the Circus
Maximus in commemoration of his victory over the Latins, they were
not the only foes whom he might have boasted of vanquishing.

Having fought and conquered the Sabines, he took from them
Collatræ, as a collateral security for their good behaviour; and coming
home with a great deal of money, he built the Temple of Jupiter on the
capitol.

Tarquinius, being desirous of increasing the army, was opposed by a
celebrated augur of the day, one Attus Navius, whose reputation seems
to have been well deserved, if the annexed anecdote is to be believed ;
for it indicates that he could see further into a whetstone than any one
who has either gone before or followed him. Navius declared that augury
must determine whether the plan of Tarquinius could be carried out,
which caused the latter to ask, sneeringly, whether he knew what he
was thinking about. The question was ambiguous, but Navius boldly
replied he did, and added, that what Tarquinius proposed to do was
perfectly possible. "Is it indeed," said the King, "I was thinking
of cutting through this whetstone with this razor." "It will be a close
shave," was the reply of the augur, "but it can be done, so cut away ;"
and the bluntness of the observation was only equalled by the sharpness of the blade, which cut the article in two as easily as if it had been
a pound of butter, instead of a stone of granite. This reproof was
literally more cutting than any other that could have been possibly
conveyed to the king, who ever afterwards paid the utmost respect to

the augurs, of whom he was accustomed thenceforth to say, that the affair of the whetstone proved them to be much sharper blades than he had been willing to take them for.

Having been at war with the Tuscans, whom he vanquished, he was admitted into the ranks of the Kings of Etruria; a position which led him to indulge in the most extravagant desires. He must needs have a crown of gold, which often tears or encumbers the brow it adorns; a throne of ivory, on whose too highly polished surface the foot is apt to slip; and a sceptre, having on its top an eagle, which frequently gives wings to the power it is intended to typify. His robe was of purple, with so costly an edging, that the border exceeded all reasonable limits, and furnished an instance of extravagance carried to the extreme, while the rate at which he went on may be judged from the fact of his always driving four in hand in his chariot. He did not, however, wholly neglect the useful in his taste for the ornamental; and though his extravagance must have been a drain upon the public pocket, he devoted himself to the more honourable drainage of the lower portions of the city. He set an example to all future commissioners of sewers, by his great work of the *Cloaca Maxima*, some portion of which still exists, and which contains, in its spacious vault, a far more honourable monument than the most magnificent tomb that could have been raised to his memory.

Tarquinius had reigned about thirty-eight years, when the sons of Ancus Martius, who had been from the first brooding over their own ejection from the throne, carried their brooding so far as to hatch a conspiracy, which, though regarded by the best authorities as a mare's nest, forms one of those " lays " of ancient Rome which tradition gives as part of her history. The youths, expecting that Tarquinius would secure the succession to a favourite, named Servius Tullius, made an arrangement with a couple of shepherds, who, pretending to have a quarrel, went with hatchets in their hands to the king, and requested him to settle their little difference. Tarquinius seems to have been in a most accommodating humour, for he is said to have stepped to the door of the palace, to arbitrate between these most un-gentle shepherds, who, pretending that they only came with their hatchets to axe his advice, began to axe him about the head; and while he was endeavouring to act as an arbitrator, they, acting as still greater traitors, cruelly made away with him. The lictors who stood by must have had their faces and their fasces turned the wrong way, for they administered a beating to the shepherds when too late, after the regal crown was already cracked beyond the possibility of repair, and the king was almost knocked to pieces before he had time to collect himself.

Tarquinius was a practical reformer, and rested his fame on the most durable foundations, among which the still-existing remains of the Cloaca Maxima, or largest common sewer, have already been noticed. Those who are over nice might feel repugnant to come down to posterity by such a channel; but that country is fortunate indeed in which genius seeks "the bubble reputation" at the mouth of the sewer, instead of in the mouth of the cannon.

It must be recorded, to the honour of Tarquinius, that he organised the plebeians, and elevated some of them to the rank of patricians, thus giving vigour to the aristocratic body, which runs the risk of becoming corrupt, and losing its vitality, unless a supply of plebeian life-blood is from time to time poured into it.

This measure would have been followed by other wholesome reforms, but for the short-sighted and selfish policy of the patricians themselves, who could not perceive the fact, full of apparent paradoxes, that if anything is to remain, it must not stand still; that no station can be stationary with safety to itself; and that nothing possessed of vitality can grow old without something new being continually added.

The sixth king of Rome was Servius Tullius, who is said to have been the son of a female in the establishment of Tanaquil. His mother's name was Ocrisia; but there is something vague about the paternity of the boy, which has been assigned sometimes to the Lar, or household god of the establishment, and sometimes to Vulcan. Whoever may have been the father, it was soon intimated that the child was to occupy a high position; and on one occasion, when sleeping in his cradle, his head was seen to be on fire; but no one was allowed to blow out the poor boy's brains, or otherwise extinguish the flame, which was rapidly consuming the hair on the head of the future heir to the monarchy. The nurses and attendants were ordered to sit down and see the fire burn out of its own accord, which, the tradition says, it did, though common sense says it couldn't; for the unfortunate infant must have died of consumption had he been suffered to blaze away in the cool manner spoken of. Though of common origin, at least on his mother's side, young Servius Tullius was supposed to have been completely purified by the fire, which warmed the hearts of all who came near him; and not only did the queen adopt him as her own son, but the partial baking had produced such an effect upon his very ordinary clay, that he was treated like a brick required for the foundations of the royal house into which Tarquinius cemented him, by giving him, as a wife, one of the daughters of the royal family.

Tanaquil having kept secret her husband's death, Servius Tullius continued for some time to carry on the business of government, just as if nothing had happened. When it was at length felt that the young favourite of fortune had got the reins fairly in his hands, the murder came out, and the barbarous assassination of Tarquinius was published to the multitude. Servius was the first instance of a king who mounted the throne without the aid of the customary pair of steps, consisting of an election by the Senate, and a confirmation by the Curiæ.

It might have been expected that Servius, when elevated above his own humble stock, might have held his head so high and become so stiff-necked as to prevent him from noticing the rank from which he had sprung; but, on the contrary, he exalted himself by endeavouring

to raise others. His reign was not a continued round of fights, for
he preferred the trowel to the sword, and, instead of cutting his name
with the latter weapon, he wisely chose to build up his reputation
with the former instrument. His first care was to complete the city,
to which he added three hills, feeling, perhaps, that his fame would
become as ancient as the hills themselves; and with a happy perception
that if "walls have ears" they are just as likely to have tongues, he
surrounded Rome with a wall, which might speak to future ages of his
spirit and enterprise. He was a friend to insolvent debtors, to whom
he gave the benefit of an act of unexampled liberality. Desiring them
to make out schedules of their liabilities, he paid off the creditors in a
double sense, for they were extremely reluctant to receive the cash, the
payment of which cashiered their claim on the person and possessions
of their debtors. He abolished imprisonment for debt, giving power
to creditors over the goods and not the persons—or, as an ingenious
scholar has phrased it, the *bona* and not the bones—of their debtors.

Debtor and Creditor.—Seizure of Goods for a Debt.

Servius found that while he was raising up buildings he was knocking down a great deal of money ; but being nevertheless anxious to erect a temple to Diana on the Aventine Hill he persuaded the Latins, who had made the place a sort of *quartier Latin*, to subscribe to it. The Latins, the Romans, and the Sabines, were every year to celebrate a sort of union sacrifice on this spot, where the cutting up and cooking of oxen formed what may be termed a joint festival. It happened that a Sabine agriculturist had reared a prize heifer, which caused quite an effervescence among his neighbours, and taking the bull quietly by the horns, he asked the augur what it would be meet for him to do with it. The soothsayer looked at the bull, who turned his brilliant bull's eye upon the astonished sage, with a sort of supercilious stare that almost amounted to a glaring oversight. The augur, not liking the look of the animal, and anxious, no doubt, to put an end to the interview, declared that whoever sacrificed the beast to Diana, off-hand, would benefit his race, and cause his nation to rule over the other confederates. The animal was led away with a shambling gait to the sacred shambles, where the Roman priest was waiting to set his hand to any Bull that might be presented to him. Seeing the Sabine preparing to act as slaughterman, the pontiff became tiffy, and suggested, that if the other was going to do the job, he might as well do it with clean hands, upon which the Sabine rushed to the river to take a finger bath While the owner was occupied about his hands the Roman priest took advantage of the pause to slaughter the animal, and, on his return, the Sabine found that he had unintentionally washed his hands of the business altogether The oracle was thus fulfilled in favour of the Romans, who trumpeted the fact through the bull's horns, which were hung up in front of the temple in memory of this successful piece of priest-craft.

The growing popularity of Servius with the plebs made the patricians anxious to get rid of him, for they had not the sense to feel that if they aspired to be the pillars of the state, a close union with the class beneath, or, as they would have contemptuously termed it, the base, was indispensable. It happened that Servius, in the hope of propitiating the two sons of Tarquinius, had given them his two daughters as their wives, though it was a grievous mistake to suppose that family marriages are usually productive of family union. Jealousy and quarrelling ensued, which ended in the elder, Tullia, persuading her sister's husband Lucius Tarquinius to murder his own brother and his own wife, in order that he might make a match with the lump of female brimstone that had inflamed his brutal passions. Not satisfied with the double murder, which would have qualified her new husband to be struck in the hardest wax and to occupy chambers among the worst of horrors, Tullia was always whispering into his ear that she wished her father farther, and by this demoniac spell she worked on the weak and wicked mind of Lucius Tarquinius. It having been reported that Servius Tullus intended to crown his own reign by uncrowning himself, and exchanging, as it were, the royal stock for consuls, the patricians thought it would be a good opportunity to speculate for a fall, by attempting the king's overthrow. Tullia and her husband were asked to join in this conspiracy, when it was found that the wretched and corrupt pair would be quite ripe for any enormity. It was arranged, therefore, that Lucius Tarquinius, at a meeting of the Senate, should go down to the House with all the insignia of royalty, and, having seated himself upon the throne, the trumpeters in attendance were, by one vigorous blow, to proclaim him as the sovereign. When Servius heard the news he proceeded to the Assembly, where all things—including the trumpets—seemed to be flourishing in favour of the traitor. As the sound of the instruments fell upon the old king's ears, he seemed to tremble for a moment before the rude blast which threatened the blasting of all his benevolent views, but calling out from the doorway in which he stood, he rebuked the insolence and treachery of his son-in-law. A disgraceful scene ensued, in which other blows than those of the trumpeters were exchanged, and Servius, who had in vain desired the traitor to "come off the throne," was executing a threat to "pull him off" as well as the old man's strength, or rather, his feebleness, would allow him. The senators were watching the scene with the vulgar interest attaching to a prize fight, and were no doubt backing up the combatants with the ordinary expressions of encouragement, which we can only interpret by our own familiar phrases of, "Go it," "Now then young 'un," "Bravo old 'un," and "Give it him." Getting rather too near the edge of the throne, but holding each other firmly in their respective grasps, the two combatants rolled together down the steps of the throne—an incident not to be met with in the rolls of any other Parliament. Getting immediately on to their legs they again resumed their hostile footing, when Tarquinius being younger and fresher than his antagonist, seized up the old man, now as feeble as an infant in arms, and carried his brutality to such a pitch as to pitch him down the steps of the Senate House. Servius tried in vain to pick up his courage, and being picked up himself, he was on his road home when he was overtaken and murdered in a street, which got the name of *Vicus Sceleratus*, or Rascally Row, from the disgraceful row that occurred in it. Tullia was driving down to the House to hear the news when her coachman pulled up at the horrid sight of the king lying in the street, but the female fury only ordered the man to "drive on," and it is said that she enforced her directions by flinging a footstool at his head, though, on subjecting the story to the usual tests, we find the footstool without a leg to stand upon. Servius Tullus had reigned forty-four years, and his memory was cherished for centuries after his death, his birthday being celebrated on the Nones of every month, because he was known to have been born on some nones, but which particular nones were unknown to any one. We have already noticed the wall of Servius, but we must not forget the Agger, or mound, connected with it, the value of which was equal to that of the wall itself, and, indeed, those who give the preference to the Agger over the wall do not much ex-aggerate. There remains to this day a great portion of the mound, which was sixty feet high and fifty broad, skirted with flag stones towards the outer side, and the Romans no doubt would derive more security from laying down their flags on the outer wall than from hanging out their banners.

The greatest work, however, of the reign of Servius was the reform of the Constitution, which he constructed with a view to the reconciling of the wide differences between the patricians and the plebeians, so as to form one powerful body by making somebodies of those who had hitherto been treated as nobodies His first care was to divide the plebeians into thirty tribes—a name derived from the word *tribus,* or three, and applied to the three plebeian tribes—the derivation being so simple that were we to ask any schoolboy if he understood it, his answer would be, that " he might be whipped " and he would assuredly deserve to be whipped " if he didn 't." These thirty tribes were placed under an officer called a *tribunus,* whose duty it was to keep a list of the members and collect the *tributum*—a word, to which in the reader's ready mind, the word tribute will at once be attributed. Besides the orders of patricians and plebeians, whose position was determined by descent alone, Servius thought there were many who might be connected together by a tie proper to them all, namely, that of property. He accordingly established a census to be held every five years, in which the name of every one who had come to man's estate was put down, together with the amount of his other estate, if he was lucky enough to have any. The whole number was divided into two heads, one of which was foot, or *pedites,* and the other horse, or *equites,* among whom an equitable share of rights and duties had to be distributed. The *pedites,* or infantry, were not all on the same footing, but were subdivided into six classes, according to the amount of their possessions, which determined their position in the army; but even the sixth class, or those who had no other possession than their self-possession, were not excluded from the service. Each class was divided into seniors and juniors, the former being men between forty-five and sixty ; the latter, including all below forty-five and above seventeen, at which early age, though frequently not bearded themselves, they were expected to go forth and beard the enemy. In addition to the two assemblies of the curiæ (the *comitia curiata*) and the tribes (the *comitia tributa*), there was instituted by Servius a great national assembly called the *comitia centuriata,* and consisting of the whole of the centuries. Of these centuries there were altogether one hundred and ninety-three ; but, instead of every individual member being allowed a separate vote, the suffrage was distributed amongst classes according to their wealth or the number of asses they possessed, a principle which the opponent of a mere property qualification will regard as somewhat asinine. By this arrangement the poor were practically excluded from voting at all, unless the rich were disagreed among themselves, when the merely industrious classes, such as the *Fabri*—the very extensive family of the Smiths and the

Carpenters—the *Cornicines*—the respectable race of Hornblowers—and others of similar degree sometimes had sufficient weight to turn the balance.

Though the equestrian centuries comprised the richest class, they seem to have been in one respect little better than beggars on horseback, for each eques received from the treasury a sum for the purchase of his horse and an annual grant for its maintenance. The amount was levied upon orphans and widows, who were, it is true, exempt from other imposts, though their contributing from their slender means to keep a horse on its legs caused many to complain that the law rode rough-shod over them. The Assembly of the Centuries was a grand step towards self-government, and, though many may think that wealth had an actual preponderance, it was always possible for a member of a lower class to get into a higher, and thus an inducement to self-advancement was secured, which is, certainly, not one of the least useful ends of government. There were numerous instances of energetic Romans rising from century to century with a rapidity showing that they were greatly in advance of the age, or, at all events, of the century in which they were originally placed by their lot, or rather by their little.

Servius introduced into Rome the Etruscan As, of the value of which we can give no nearer notion than by stating the fact that a Roman sheep was worth about ten Etruscan asses. To the poorer classes these coins could have been of little service, and by way of small change they were permitted to use shells, from which we no doubt get the phrase of "shelling out," a quaint expression sometimes used to describe the process of paying. In some parts of the world shells are still current as cash, and even among ourselves fish are employed at cards as the representatives of money. Though in ordinary use for the smaller purposes of commerce, shells were not receivable as taxes, for when the Government required the sinews of war it would not have been satisfied with mussels or any other similar substitute.

The Roman As was of bronze and stamped on one side with a portrait of Janus, whose two heads we never thought much better than one, though they appeared appropriately on a coin as a sign, perhaps, that people are often made doublefaced by money. On the other side was the prow of a ship, which might be emblematical of the fact that money is necessary to keep one above water.

In the time of Servius all were expected to arm themselves according to their means, and the richest were thoroughly clad in bronze for the protection of their persons, while the poorer, who could not afford anything of the kind, were obliged to trust for their self-defence to their own natural metal. The patricians carried a clypeus, or shield, of such dimensions as to cover frequently the whole body, and by hiding himself behind it the wearer often escaped a hiding from the enemy. The material of which the clypeus was composed was wood covered with a bull's skin that had been so thoroughly tanned as to afford safety against the severest leathering.

Tarquinius Superbus makes himself King.

CHAPTER THE FOURTH.

FROM THE ACCESSION OF TARQUINIUS SUPERBUS TO THE BANISHMENT
OF THE ROYAL FAMILY, AND THE ABOLITION OF THE KINGLY DIGNITY.

TARQUINIUS had ascended the throne more by the force of his fists, than by the strength of his arms; for he had aimed a blow, not only at the crown, but at the face of the unhappy sovereign who had preceded him. Carrying his hostility beyond the grave, Tarquinius refused to bury his animosity, or to grant his victim a funeral. The upstart nature of the new king gained for him the nickname of Superbus, or the proud, though he had as little to be proud of as some of the most contemptible characters in history. He, however, asserted himself with so much audacity, that the people were completely overawed by his pretensions, and many made away with themselves, to insure their lives, by a sort of Irish policy, against Tarquin's violence. He took away the privileges of the plebeians, and sent many to the scaffold, by employing them as common bricklayers; but there were several who preferred laying violent hands on themselves, to laying a single brick of the magnificent buildings which he planned, in the hope, perhaps, that the splendour of the constructions of his reign would induce posterity to place the best construction on his character.

He coolly assumed the whole administration of the law, and added the office of executioner to that of judge, while he combined with both the character of a criminal, by seizing the property of all those whom he punished, and thus adding robbery to violence. To prevent the possibility of a majority against him in the Senate, he cut off several of the heads of that body; and though he never condescended to

D

submit to the Assembly a single question, he treated the unhappy
members as if they had much to answer for.

Finding the continued ill-treatment of his own people getting rather
monotonous, he sought the pleasures of variety by harassing the
Volscians, whom he robbed of a sufficient sum to enable him to commence a temple to Jupiter.   Bricks and mortar soon ran up above
the estimated cost; and Tarquin had scarcely built the lower floor,
when he came to the old story of shortness of funds, which he supplied
by making the people pay as well as work, and taxing at once their time
and their pockets.   This temple was on the Capitoline Hill; and it is said
that in digging the foundations the workmen hit upon a freshly-bleeding
human head, which, of course, must be regarded as an idle tale; nor
would it be right for history to hold an elaborate inquest on this head,
since it would be impossible to find a verdict without having first found
the body.   The augur, who, according to the legend, was present on
the occasion, is reported to have made a *post-mortem* examination of the
head, which he identified as that of one Tolus; but who Tolus was, or
whether he ever was at all, we are told nothing on any competent
authority.   The augur, whose duty it was to be ready to interpret
anything that turned up, no sooner saw the head, than putting upon it
the best face he could, he declared it to be a sign that Rome was destined to be the head of the world—an obvious piece of fulsome adulation, worthy of being offered to the flattest of flats, by one disposed to
flatter.   The temple itself was a great fact, notwithstanding the numerous fictions that are told concerning it; and there is little doubt that
though, as some say, Tarquinius Priscus (the old one) may have begun
it, Tarquinius Superbus put to it the finishing touch, and surmounted it
with a chariot and four in baked clay, which, had it been preserved to
this day, would have been one of the most interesting of Potter's
Antiquities.

A curious anecdote, connected with the bookselling business of the
period, has been handed down to us; and it is sufficiently interesting
to be handed on to the readers of this work, who are at liberty either to
take it up, or to set it down at its real value.   It is said that Tarquin
was waited upon by a female, who brought with her nine books, and,
expressing herself willing to do business, asked three hundred pieces of
gold for the entire set of volumes.   The King pooh-poohed the proposition, on the ground of the exorbitant price, and desired her to be off with
the books, when she solemnly advised him not to off with the bargain.
Finding him obstinate, the woman, who was, it seems, a sibyl, and eked
out her bookseller's profits by the business of a prophetess, threw into
the flames three of the volumes, which, assuming, for a few minutes,
the aspect of illuminated copies, soon left no traces—not even a spark—
of any genius by which they might have been inspired.   The sibyl,
soon after, paid a second visit to Tarquin, bringing with her the six
remaining volumes; and having asked in vain the same sum for the
imperfect copy as she had done for the whole work, she went through a

sort of second edition of Burns, by throwing three more of her books
into the fire.   To the surprise of Tarquin, she appeared a third
time with her stock of books, now reduced to three; and upon the
King's observing to her " What do you want for these ? " she replied
that three hundred pieces of gold was her price; that she made no
abatement; that if the books were not instantly bought, they would
speedily be converted into light literature, and being condensed
into one thick volume of smoke, would, of course, take their final
leaves of the royal residence.   The King, astonished at the woman's
pertinacity, resolved at last to send for a valuer, to look at the books,

Tarquinius Superbus has the Sibylline Books valued.

who declared them to be well worth the money.   They contained a
variety of remedies for diseases, directions for preparing sacrifices, and

other interesting matter, with a collection of the oracles of Cumæ, by way of appendix, so that the volumes formed a sort of encyclopædia, embracing the advantages of a Cookery Book, a Buchan's Domestic Medicine, and a Complete Fortune-teller.   Tarquin* became the purchaser of these three very odd volumes, which seem to have been estimated less according to their intrinsic value, than the price they had brought; and they were carefully put away in the Temple library.

It was the desire of the Government to prevent the people from knowing what these books might contain, and the office of librarian was entrusted to two individuals of illustrious birth, under the idea—not very flattering to aristocracy—that patricians would be found the best promoters of ignorance.   One of these officers, having acted so inconsistently with his rank, as to have imparted some information to a fellow-citizen, was dismissed from his place and thrown into the sea in a bag; so that he may be said, by the heartless punster, to have got the sack in a double meaning.

While building operations were going on at home, destruction was being dealt out abroad; and the Gabii being about twelve miles from Rome, were the objects of the King's hostility.   Having sent one of his captains against them, who was repulsed by a major force, Tarquinius resolved on trying treachery.   He accordingly despatched his son, Sextus, to complain of ill-treatment at his father's hands, and to implore the pity of the Gabii, who were gabies enough not only to believe the story, but even to appoint Sextus their general.   He was ultimately chosen their governor; and finding the Gabii completely in his hands, he sent to his own governor—Tarquinius—to know what to do with them.   The King was in the garden when the messenger arrived; and whenever the latter asked a question, the former made no reply, but kept knocking off the heads of the tallest poppies with his walking-stick.   The messenger ventured to intimate, once or twice, that he was waiting for an answer; but the heads of the poppies flying off in all directions, he began to tremble for his own, and he flew off himself, to prevent accidents.   On his return, he mentioned the circumstances to Sextus, who regarded the poppies as emblems of the Gabii; and, indeed, the latter seemed so thoroughly asleep, that the comparison was no less just than odious.

Sextus, taking the paternal hint, knocked off several of the heads of the people; and keeping up the allegory to the fullest extent, cut off the flower of the Gabii.   Many of their fairest blossoms perished by a too early blow; and being thus deprived of what might fairly be termed its primest pick, the soil was soon planted with the victorious standards of Tarquinius.   He, however, instead of introducing any apple of discord, judiciously grafted the Gabian on the Roman stock; and thus cultivated the only really valuable fruits of victory.

---

* Some say that Tarquinius Priscus bought the books ; but it is of little consequence who was the real buyer, as the whole story is very probably "a sell" on the part of the narrators, as well as of the sibyl.

Tarquin was a great deal troubled by the signs of the times; or, rather, he was made so uncomfortable by an evil conscience, that if a snake appeared in his path, it seemed to hang over him like a horrible

The Evil Conscience of Tarquin.

load; and if he went to sleep, there was a mare's-nest always at hand, to trouble him with a night-mare. He dreamed that some eagles had built in his gardens, and that in their temporary absence from the nest, some vultures had breakfasted on the new-laid eggs, and, armed with their beaks, taken possession of the deserted small tenement. Unable to drive the vultures out of his head, he was anxious to ascertain the meaning of the omen, for he had become so superstitious, that if he saw a sparrow dart from a branch, he regarded it as an emblem that he was himself about to hop the twig in some unexpected manner. Doubting the efficiency of his own augurs, on whom he was beginning to throw some of the discredit to which prophets in their own country are liable, Tarquin resolved on seeking the aid of foreign talent; and as the omens were worse than Greek to him, he sent to the oracles at Delphi, thinking if the matter was Greek to them they would be able to interpret it. His messengers to the fortune-tellers were his two sons, Aruns and Titus, together with his nephew, one Lucius Junius Brutus, who, though an extremely sensible young man, was in the habit of playing the fool, in order to avert the suspicions of his uncle. Though Brutus assumed the look of an idiot, and generally had his eye on vacancy, it was only to conceal the fact that a vacancy on the throne was what he really had his eye upon. Valuable gifts were taken to the oracle, which was slow to speak in the absence of presents. When Brutus put a *bâton* into the hand of the Priestess, she knew, by the weight, that the *bâton* was a hollow pretext for the conveyance of a bribe, which she looked for, found, and pocketed. On the strength of a large lump of gold, thus cunningly conveyed to the Priestess, Brutus ventured to ask who would be the next King of Rome, to which she replied by a recommendation that all the applicants should go home to their mothers, for that " he who kissed his mother first should be the one to govern." Titus and Aruns made at once for their mamma, and eager to kiss her, ran as fast as they could to catch the first bus, but Brutus, whom they had perhaps tripped up, to prevent his getting a fair start, saluted his mother earth with a smack of the lip in return for the blow on the face that his fall had occasioned him.

When the ambassadors returned to Rome they found Tarquin as nervous as ever ; and there is little doubt, that if tea had been known in those days, the King would have sat for ever over his cups, endea-vouring to read the grounds for his fears in the grounds of the beverage. The treasury having been exhausted by his building speculations, the people were growing more dissatisfied every day ; and, in order to turn their discontent away from home, he engaged them in a quarrel with Ardea, a city situated on a lofty rock, against which the Romans threw themselves with a sort of dashing energy. The attempt to take the place by a common assault and battery was vain, for the rock stood firm ; and it was probable, that if the Romans remained at the gates, and continued knocking over and over again, they would ultimately be com-pelled to knock under. They therefore resolved on hemming the Ardeans in, as there was no chance of whipping them out, and military works were run in a continuous thread round the borders of the city.

The Romans, acting as a sort of army of occupation, had, of course, scarcely any occupation at all ; and there being nothing that soldiers find it so difficult to kill as their time, the officers were in the habit of going halves in suppers at each other's quarters. At one of these entertainments the King's sons, and their cousin, one Tarquinius, sur-named Collatinus, from the town of Collatia, were discussing the merits of their respective wives, and each of the officers, with an uxuriousness among the military that the commonest civility would have restrained, was praising his own wife at the expense of all others.

It was at length agreed that the husbands should proceed forthwith to Rome, and that having paid an unexpected visit to all the ladies, the palm should be awarded to her who should be employed in the most praise-worthy way, when thus unceremoniously popped in upon. They first visited the wife of Sextus, who had got a large evening party and ball at home, and who was much confused by this unexpected revelation of her midnight revels. Dancing was at its height; and as a great writer has said of dancing among the Romans, " *Nemo fere saltat sobrius, isin forte insaniat,*"*—any one who dances must be either very drunk, or stark mad,—we may guess the state of the company that Sextus found at his residence. In one corner the game of *Par et Impar*—" odd or even "—might perhaps have been played ; for nothing can be more purely classical than the origin of some of those sports which form

---

* Cicero. It is true this was said at a much later time than that of which we are now writing ; but dancing, except in connection with certain ceremonies, was considered degrading by the Romans from the earliest period.

almost the only pretexts for the employment of our modern street-
keepers.   A portion of the guests might have been amusing themselves
with the *Tali,* or "knuckle-bones," others might have been employed
at *Jactus bolus*—"pitch and toss;" while here and there among the
revellers might have been heard the familiar cry of *Aut caput aut navem*
—the "heads or tails" of antiquity.

Mrs. Sextus consoles herself with a Little Party.

Their next call was at the house of Collatinus, whose wife, Lucretia,
was also engaged with a ball, but it was of cotton, and instead of
devoting herself to the whirl of the dance, she was spinning with
her maids, by way of spinning out the long, dreary hours of her
husband's absence.   Sextus at once admitted that Collatinus had
indeed got a treasure of a wife, and the officers returned to the camp ;
but a few evenings afterwards, availing himself of the introduction of

her husband, Sextus paid the lady a second visit. Being a kinsman, he was asked to make himself at home, but his manner became so strange, that Lucretia could not make him out; and as he did not seem disposed to go home till morning, she retired to her chamber, with the impression, no doubt, that being left alone in the sitting-room he would take the hint, order his horse, and proceed to his lodgings. Lucretia was, however, disturbed in the middle of the night by Sextus, who was standing over her with a drawn sword, and who was guilty of such brutal insolence, that she sent a messenger, the first thing in the morning, to fetch her husband from Ardea, and her father from Rome, who speedily arrived with his friend, P. Valerius, a highly respectable man, who afterwards got the name of Publicola. Collatinus brought with him L. J. Brutus, and Lucretia having rapidly run through the story of her wrongs, she still more rapidly run through herself before any one had time to arrest the deadly weapon. Revenge against Tarquin and his whole race was instantly sworn, in a sort of quartette, by the four friends, and L. J. Brutus, snatching up the dagger, made a great point of it in a speech he addressed to the people in the market place. Indignation was now thoroughly roused against the Tarquin family, and Brutus, proceeding to Rome, called a public meeting in the Forum. He opened the business of the day by stating what had been done, and having made his deposition he proposed the deposition of the king; when it was moved, by way of amendment, and carried unanimously, that the resolution should be extended by the addition of the words, " and the banishment of his wife and family." A volunteer corps was at once formed to set out for Ardea, where the king was supposed to be ; but on hearing of the insurrection, he had at once decamped from the camp, and proceeded to Rome, where he found the gates closed, and feeling himself shut out from the throne, he took refuge with his two sons, Titus and Aruns, at Caere, in Etruria. There history loses sight of the old king, but Sextus has been traced to Gabii, a principality of which he thought he was the head; but the people soon undeceived him, by showing him they would have no head at all, for they cut him off one day in a tumult.

Tullia had fled, and it is not known whither ; but mercy to the' fallen king would lead us to hope that the queen had gone in a different direction from that which he had taken. The Ardeans agreed to a truce for fifteen years—a somewhat lengthy letter of license—during which all hostile proceedings were to be stayed, and the people decreed the total abolition of the kingly dignity. The royal stock was converted, as it were, into consuls, and L. Junius Brutus, with L. Tarquinius Collatinus, were elected for one year, to fill the latter character.

Before closing an account of what is usually termed the kingly period of the history of Rome, it is due to truth to state, that though some of the alleged kings were good and others were bad, they must all be considered as very doubtful characters. The fact of their existence depends on no better authority than certain annals, compiled more than a century and a half after the materials for compiling them had been destroyed; and we are thus driven to rely upon the statements of certain story-tellers, belonging, we fear, to a class, whose memories, according to the proverb, ought to be excellent. In pretending to recollect what they never knew, they have sometimes forgotten themselves, and in building up their stories, they have shown how mere fabrication may raise an ostensibly solid fabric.

Of the seven kings, who are said to have ruled in Rome during a period of nearly two hundred and fifty years, three or four were murdered; another subsided in a bog, and another ran for his life, which he saved by his speed, though he was the last of the race of royalty. It is difficult to spread these seven sovereigns over a space of two centuries and a half, and we feel that we might as well attempt to cover an acre of bread with a thin slice of ham, or turn the river Thames into negus by throwing a few glasses of sherry into it. Of the earliest Roman annals, some were burnt, leaving nothing to the student but the tinder, from which it is, in these days, hardly possible to obtain much light, but the greater portion of the early history of Rome has come down to us by tradition, that extraordinary carrier, who is continually adding to the bulk, but diminishing the weight of the matters consigned to it for delivery.

Of the condition of the people at this early period little or nothing can be known, and to amuse ourselves with idle guesses, would be scarcely better than to turn into a game of blindman's buff the important business of history. We can however state, with confidence, that the earliest Romans had no regular coinage, but were in the habit of answering with brass, in the rudest shape, the demands of their creditors. Servius Tullius is reputed to have been the first who converted the brass into coin, and marked it with the figure of a horse or some other animal,* as an emblem, perhaps, of the fact, that money runs away very rapidly.

Among the early Romans, the most honourable occupations were agriculture and war; the latter enabling the citizens to make a conquest of the soil with the sword, and the former teaching them to subdue it to their purposes by the implements of husbandry. Trade and commerce were held in contempt, and left to the plebeians; the patrician considering himself suitably employed only when he was thrashing his corn, or performing the same operation on his enemies.

During the early existence of the city the native artists were few, and the great works of architecture undertaken by the later kings were embellished by foreign talent from Etruria. The writing-master had made so little progress in ancient Rome, that it is doubtful whether many of the patricians could write their own names; and even some of the most distinguished characters of the day were men of mark, not only by their position, but by their signatures.

---

* Hence, from the word *pecus*, cattle, was derived *pecunia*, signifying money, and giving rise to our own word "pecuniary."

It is not very gratifying to the friends of education to find that though ignorance was almost universal among the early Romans, there was a wholesome tone of morality among the people, which led them, not only to condemn in their traditions the cruelty and laxity of principle prevailing in the family of their last king, but to pay due reverence to the domestic virtues of Lucretia. The legend of the latter being found spinning with her maids, while the princesses of the house of Tarquin were reeling in the dance, during the absence of their respective husbands, is sufficient to show the estimation in which decency and sobriety were held, as well as the odium that attached to riotous revelry. The patrician youth of infant and unlettered Rome would have been ashamed of those nocturnal gambols which have prevailed among portions of the juvenile aristocracy and gentry in more civilised countries, and in a more enlightened age, when door-knockers, and bell-handles, have been carried off as the *spolia opima* of some disorderly triumph.

CHAPTER THE FIFTH.

FROM THE BANISHMENT OF TARQUINIUS SUPERBUS TO THE BATTLE OF
LAKE REGILLUS.

RUTUS, who had gained his eminence by swearing that there should be no monarch or single ruler in Rome, found himself in sole possession of the supreme authority. His position presents nothing very remarkable to the modern observer, who is accustomed to see those who have denounced a system yesterday participating in the profits of the same system to-day, and declaring their own arguments to be thoroughly out of place, as applied to themselves when in office. Brutus, however, could not consistently exercise a power he had sworn to overthrow; and to carry out his anti-monarchical principles, he had either to go out himself, or to ask for a colleague. On the same principle that prefers the half quartern to utter loaflessness, Brutus proposed a partnership in the government; and Collatinus was taken into the firm, which proved to have no firmness at all, for it was dissolved very speedily. The difficulty of agreement between two of the same trade was severely felt by the two popular reformers, who were dividing the substance without the name of that power they had vowed to destroy; it was soon evident that if they had thought it too much for one, they considered it not enough for two; and they were accordingly always quarrelling. To prevent collision, they tried the experiment of taking the supreme authority by turns, each assuming the fasces for a month at a time; but this alternate chopping of the regal sticks, or fasces, which were the emblems of power, led to nothing satisfactory.

A question at length arose, upon which the duality of the ruling mind was so distinctly marked, that the two consuls, whose very name is derived from *con*, with, and *salio*, to leap, were trying to leap in two opposite ways; and an end of their own power was the only conclusion to which they were likely to jump together. Tarquin had retired to Caere, waiting the chances of a restoration of his line; but his line had fallen into such contempt, that he was fishing in vain for his recal, though he nevertheless sent ambassadors to demand the restoration of himself, or at all events of his private property.

The senate decreed that though Tarquin could not have the fasces, he was at liberty to make a bundle of all the other sticks that might belong to him. On this question Brutus and Collatinus were violently opposed, and both becoming hot, their excessive warmth led to a mutual coolness that ended in an open hostility, which shut out every hope of compromise. Collatinus gave in by going out, and was succeeded by P. Valerius, one of the party of four who had roused the popular spirit over the bier of Lucretia.

Tarquin's ambassadors, instead of being satisfied with the permission to remove his goods, had other objects in the back-ground; for they had a plan for his restoration in the rear, while they let nothing appear in the van, but the late king's furniture. The plot was being discussed after dinner, by a party of the conspirators, when one of the waiters, who had concealed himself behind the door, overheard the scheme, and ran to Valerius with the exclusive intelligence. The traitors were secured, and when they were brought up before the consuls, Brutus recognising among the offenders his two sons, subjected both them and himself to a very severe trial. Asking them what they had to say to the charge, and getting " nothing " in reply, he looked in the faces of his sons, and declaring that he must class all malefactors under one general head, which must be cut off, he called upon the lictors to do their duty. In leaving the other prisoners to be tried by Valerius, Brutus whispered to his colleague, " Now try them, and acquit them, if you can;" but he could only execute the law, and the law could only execute the criminals. The ambassadors were allowed to remain at large, though their plotting proved that they had been at something very little; and the government withdrew the permission that had been granted for the removal of Tarquin's goods, which were divided by means of a scramble among the populace.

Thus Tarquin, who had broken the twenty valuable tables of Servius, was doomed to have the tables turned upon him by the destruction of his own, while every leaf of the former was restored under the Consular government. The landed estates of the Tarquins were distributed among the plebeians, so that the banished family had no chance of recovering their lost ground, which was afterwards known as the Field of Mars, or Campus Martius. The corn on the confiscated property was ripe; but the people felt a conscientious objection to consuming the produce which no labour of their own had reared; and they did not allow the tyrant's grain to outweigh their honest scruple. Throwing all idea of profit overboard, they cast the corn into the Tiber, which, it is said, was so shallow, that the sheaves stuck in the mud, and formed the small island known as the Insula Tiberina. That a piece of land, however small, should be formed by a crop of corn, however plentiful, is difficult to believe: but the story of the wheat can only find reception from the very longest ears; for common sense will admit that in the effort to give credit to the tale, it must go thoroughly against the grain on a proper sifting of all the evidence.

Tarquin relinquishing his hopes of a restoration by stratagem, resolved on resorting to strategy, and brought into the field a large army, of which the Veii formed a considerable part, and his son Aruns headed the Etruscan cavalry. The Roman consuls commanded their own forces; Valerius being at the head of the foot, and Brutus mounted on a clever cob, with a strong sword, that might be called a useful hack, taking the lead of the equestrians. When Aruns entered the field, he recognised Brutus in Tarquin's cloak, and the young man felt the blood mantling with indignation into his cheek at the first sight of the mantle. He instantly made for Brutus, who with equal eagerness made for Aruns, and so violent was the collision, that the breath was knocked at one blow out of both their bodies.

Aruns and Brutus.

The hostile leaders having fallen to the ground, the battle shared their fate, and both armies withdrew to their camps; but neither would allow the other the credit of a victory. The legend goes on to state that the god Silvanus—an alarmist among the classical deities, and synonymous with Pan—was heard shouting in the night that the Etruscans having lost one man more than the Romans, the latter had gained the battle. This announcement of the result of the contest, though only by a majority of one, so alarmed the Etruscans, who were always panic struck at the voice of Pan, that they took to flight, leaving the enemy to carry everything before them, including all the property that the fugitives had left behind them. The remains of Brutus were brought to the Forum, where they lay in state; but the state in which they lay was truly deplorable; for the deceased consul had been so knocked about, that had he been alive, he would scarcely have known himself, even by the aid of reflection. His colleague, Valerius, delivered an oration over his departed virtues, making a catalogue of the whole, and fixing the highest price to every one of them.

The question of " Shall Brutus have a statue?" was soon answered in the affirmative, and he was placed among the kings, though he had destroyed the monarchy. Where failure constitutes the traitor, success makes the patriot: and upon the merest accident may depend the question whether the originator of a design against a bad government shall go to the block of the sculptor, or to that of the executioner.

P. Valerius was in no hurry to ask the people for a colleague, and he for some time did the whole of the business of the chief magistracy himself; so that had it not been for the mere name of the office, Rome might just as well have remained a monarchy. This fact seems to have flashed at last on the public mind; and when it was found that P. Valerius was building himself a stone residence, in a strong position, a rumour was spread abroad that he was aiming at the foundation of his own house, or family, in the kingly power. On hearing the report he immediately stopped the works of his intended residence, and having called a meeting of the curiæ, he appeared before them with his fasces reversed; a sign that the bundles of rods were not intended to be used on the backs of the people alone, but that they were held, as it were, in trust, and in pickle for the punishment of delinquency in general. This treatment of the fasces so fascinated the people, that they acquitted P. Valerius of every charge, and acknowledging their suspicions of a plot to be groundless, they gave him a plot of ground to build his house upon. Pleased with the taste of popularity, he continued to court it with so much success, that he gained the name of Publicola, or one who honours the public; and he certainly introduced many very wholesome legal reforms, by dabbling in law, in a spirit truly lau-dable. He gave an appeal from the magistrate to the people, in cases where the punishment awarded had been a fine, a whipping, or a hanging; and in the last instance the provision was extremely salutary, for the suspending of a sentence might often avoid the necessity for suspending an alleged criminal. This right of appeal was, however, limited to within a mile from the city; an arrangement that would have justified the formation of a league to abolish the mile, as an unnecessary distinction, of which we can only expose the absurdity, by suggesting the possibility of an offence committed at Knightsbridge being punishable at Newgate with immediate death; while the culprit of Holborn Hill, though nearer the place of execution, would be further from the scaffold.

Having passed several salutary acts, and secured, as it were, the cream of popularity to himself, he proposed the election of a colleague who might share the skim with him. The new consul was Spurius Lucretius; but poor Spurius enjoyed none of the genuine sweets of power. He was so far advanced in years, at the period of his advancement to office, that he had already one foot in the grave, and the other foot went in after it immediately on his taking his new position. M. Horatius Pulvillius was chosen in the poor old man's stead, and an incident speedily happened which caused a difference, leading to something more than personal indifference between the two consuls. The temple of Jupiter, on the Capitoline, so called from the incident already related, of the Caput Toli, or head of Tolus, had not yet been dedicated; and it having been arranged that the thing was to be done, the next question that arose was, " Who is to do it? " Both consuls were anxious for the job; and it was at length arranged that lots should be drawn, in order to settle the undecided point, which had led to such a decided coolness between P. Valerius and his colleague. Horatius was the happy man whom fortune favoured by her choice ; and he was in the act of performing the ceremony, when, without any ceremony at all, a messenger rushed in, exclaiming that the son of the consul had suddenly expired. Believing the alarm to be false, Horatius hinted at his suspicion of its being one of the blackest of jobs, by suggesting that those who brought the news should go and attend the funeral. " As for me," he exclaimed, " I have other engagements just now ;" and, continuing the work of dedication, he proceeded to mark the commencement of a new era, by driving a huge nail into the wall of the temple. Such was the mode by which chronology was taught to the early Romans, who had their dates literally hammered into them ; and, as long as the consul hit the right nail upon the head, or went upon the proper tack, mistake was almost impossible.

The first specimen of diplomacy to be met with in the records of Rome must be referred to the first year of the Republic, when a treaty was concluded with Carthage, and engraved on brazen tables. The material was appropriate to the purpose it served; and the language was so obscure, that a modern treaty could scarcely have surpassed it in ambiguity. Some parts of it were unintelligible to the most learned of the Romans themselves ; and, had any difference arisen as to the interpretation of the treaty, the tables must have been left to brazen it out ; for no one could have explained their meaning. Though the document may have mystified many things, it made one thing clear, for it proved history to have been wrong in stating that Horatius succeeded Brutus, for they are described as both being consuls together at the date of the treaty. In following the ordinary version or perversion of the facts or fictions connected with the rise of Rome, we take history as we find it; and though much of it is known to be false, we, by continually making the admission, prevent the bane from remaining very long without the antidote.

P. Valerius was still consul, with P. Lucretius for a colleague, when the old King Tarquin happened to be on a visit, at Clusium, in Etruria, with the local Lar, Porsenna.* After supper, Tarquin often grew garrulous about his alleged wrongs, and worked on the sympathies of his host, who declared the Romans should receive, through the medium

---

* Niebuhr spells the word with a double n, in the penultimate syllable ; but Macaulay, who quotes four verses from different writers in favour of his orthography, writes the word Porsena, with the penultimate short.

of Porsenna, a tremendous physicking. The Lar accordingly set forth
at the head of his army, and its approach being announced, the people
in the suburbs of Rome were frightened out of their wits, and into the
city. Throughout the whole of his journey, Porsenna administered a
strong dose to all that opposed his way; and he scoured the country by
the most drastic system of pillage. On arriving at Rome, he at once
forced the Janiculum, the garrison rushing with their leader at their
head, and the foe almost at their heels, into the city. Nothing was now
between the Romans and their assailants but the wooden bridge, or
Pons Sublicius; and when the people asked for consolation from their
consul, he had none to offer them. Looking at the water, he saw there
was no time for reflection; and he ordered the bridge to be cut down,
when Horatius Cocles, the gatekeeper, volunteered to offer a check to
the enemy. " I want but two," cried Horatius, " two only are wanted,
to join with me in throwing for that great stake, the safety of Rome;"
and there immediately presented themselves, as ready to " stand the
hazard of the die," if die they must, the youthful Spurius Lartius of the
Neminian race, and Herminius, belonging to the Tities. The three
heroes took their station at the foot of the bridge, resolved that no one
should pass without paying a poll-tax, in the shape of a blow on the
head, which the valiant trio stood prepared to administer. A shout of
derisive laughter was the only salute they received from the Etruscan
army; but the laughter was soon transferred to the other side of the
Etruscan mouth, and subsided altogether when no less than half-a-dozen
tongues were found to have licked the dust, instead of the enemy.
Porsenna's army had advanced to the sound of trumpets, which seemed
no longer in a flourishing condition, but were as incapable of dealing
out a blow as the soldiers themselves. A few of the troops in the rear
shouted " Forward ! " to those in the van ; but there was such a determined cry of " Keep back ! " among the foremost men, that all were
under the influence of a general gib, and every rank gave evidence of
rank cowardice.

While the Etruscans were shaking in their shoes on one side of the
river, the Romans were shivering their own timbers, and knocking
down beams and rafters on the other. They had razed the bridge to
the ground, or rather lowered it to the water, when they called to their
gallant defenders to come back, while there was still a plank left—a
single deal to enable them to cut over to their partners.

Lartius and Herminius, seeing the game was nearly over, thought the
only card they had to play was to discard their companion, and save
themselves by a trick, which, however, would leave all the honours to
Horatius. The two former darted across just before the remainder of
the bridge fell, splashing into the water below, and rendering the tide
untidy with the broken fragments.

Horatius was now alone in his glory, with the foe before him, and
the flood behind ; his only alternative being between a fatally hot reception by the one, and an uncomfortably cold reception by the other.

Disdaining to beg for mercy from Porsenna, he prayed for pity from the
Tiber, and making a bold plunge, he threw himself on the kind indulgence of the river. Being fastened up in armour, his case was a par-

Horatius Cocles Defending the Bridge.

ticularly hard one, and being encumbered as he was with his arms, to
use his legs was scarcely possible. He nevertheless got on swimmingly,
for his heart never sank, and at length, feeling his foot touch the
bottom, he knew that his hopes were not groundless.

By courage and strength Horatius prevailed over every obstacle, and
Cocles owed to the cockles of his heart, as well as to the muscles of his
body, the happy results of his hazardous experiment. To recompense
him for his risk by water, the grateful nation gave him a large portion
of land, and erected his statue in the Comitium, a portion of the Forum
from which orators were in the habit of holding forth, and where the

E

figure of Horatius was placed to speak for itself to the populace. Though the enemy was kept out of the city, the Romans were kept in, while provisions were growing shorter and shorter every day—a sort of growth that led of course to a constant diminution. Such was the gratitude of the citizens to Horatius, that they subscribed to give him always as much as he could eat; and although the fact involves a pun we abominate, we are obliged to state the truth, that, in order to give him his desert, many went without their dinners.

The Romans had declared they would hold out to the last, and though they were left with scarcely any food, though they might have at once procured it, had they consented to eat their own words, they declined to satisfy their hunger by such a humiliating process. All hope of saving the city being apparently lost, the senate entered into an agreement with one Caius Mucius, who could talk a little Tuscan, and who undertook to go across the water for the purpose of killing Porsenna. Mucius disguised himself in an Etrurian helmet —a sort of Tuscan bonnet—and with a sword concealed under the folds of his ample Roman wrap-rascal, he arrived at Porsenna's camp, just as the salaries were being paid to the soldiers. While the troops were intent on drawing their pay, Mucius slily drew his sword, and seeing an individual rather handsomely dressed, rushed upon him to administer to him, with the weapon, a most unhandsome dressing.

The individual thus assailed was rapidly despatched, but it turned out that the victim, instead of being the king, was an unfortunate scribe, or writer, who could have been by no means prepared for this unusual fate of genius. Had the critics unmercifully cut him up, the scribe would have felt that his death was, to a certain extent, in the way of business; but to be murdered by mistake for a king, was a result that any member of the republic of letters might fairly have objected to. It may appear at first sight startling that a literary man should have been well-dressed, and in the company of a king, but it must be remembered that the scribe was not necessarily a man of remarkable ability. His art was that of a mere copyist, which, even in these days, frequently gains a reputation for the imitator, who is often confounded with, instead of being confounded by the man of original genius. The scribes of antiquity, like many modern writers, did no more than set down the thoughts of others, and, as their style was extremely hard, consisting of a piece of iron, with which they wrote upon wax, their works were not likely to make a very deep or lasting impression.

Our pity for the unfortunate literary character is considerably lessened by the fact, that being in the camp he had no doubt been dining with the guards; and we know he was wearing a showy dress—two circumstances indicating an affectation of the manners of the fast man, which are always unbecoming to the man of letters.

Mucius was about to retire after the execution of the deed, but he was seized by the attendants, and then seized by remorse when he was informed that he had despatched a harmless literary man instead of Porsenna. Being taken to the king, Mucius found him sitting before the fire of a large altar.   The Etruscan chief, on hearing the charge, pointed out the penalty that had been incurred, when the prisoner, thrusting his right hand into the fire, allowed it to remain, with extraordinary coolness, or, rather, with most intense heat, until it was consumed as far as the wrist ;

Mucius Scævola before Porsenna.

and he concluded the act of self incendiarism, by declaring there were three hundred others who were just as ready as himself to take up arms and burn off a hand, in defiance of their oppressor.   Porsenna, who had watched the painful process with extreme interest, was so delighted at the fortitude displayed, that he jumped from his seat, and mentally remarking that " the fellow was a wonderfully cool hand at an operation of the kind," ordered some guards to conduct him in safety to Rome ; at the same time advising Mucius to conduct himself more wisely for the future.

Mucius returned to Rome, where he obtained the name of Scævola (from *Scævus*) in consequence of his being left-handed, or it might have been because of his having evinced such an utter want of dexterity in the business he had undertaken.

Porsenna, having heard that there were three hundred Romans ready to take his life, felt uneasy at such fearful odds as three hundred to one against him; nor could he enjoy a moment's peace with himself until a peace with Rome was concluded. He sent ambassadors to negotiate a treaty, which was soon arranged; the only difficulty arising on the subject of the proposed restoration of Tarquin, which his subjects would not listen to; and, though he and Porsenna had hitherto rowed in the same boat, the latter found it absolutely necessary to throw the former overboard. Rome was compelled to return the territory taken from the Veii, and Porsenna claimed several hostages, among whom were sundry young ladies of the principal Roman families. One of these was named Clælia, who, with other maidens, having resolved on

Clælia and her Companions escaping from the Etruscan Camp.

a bold plunge for their liberty, jumped into the Tiber's bed, and swam like a party of ducks to the other side of the river. Clælia ran home in her dripping clothes, but, instead of a warm reception, she was met with a wet blanket, for her father fearing that her having absconded would be visited upon Rome, sent her back like a runaway school-girl to the camp of Porsenna. That individual behaved with his usual magnanimity, for he not only pardoned Clælia and her companions, but sent them home to their parents, who, perhaps, knew better than Porsenna how to manage them.

The Etruscan monarch seems to have been one of those who could do nothing by halves, but having once granted quarter to the foe, he was not satisfied until he had surrendered the whole of what he had taken from the vanquished. He gave them unprovisionally all the provisions remaining in his camp, and, in fact, he left behind him so many goods and chattels, that at public auctions it was customary for many years afterwards to advertise the effects as " the property of King Porsenna." Returning to Clusium, he is believed to have shut himself up at home, and never stirred out again, for we meet with him no more in any of the highways or byways of history.

The Romans having recovered from the blow, or series of blows, they had received from Porsenna, were prepared to turn their anger on the subject nearest at hand, and the Sabines were conveniently situated to receive a great deal of it. Irritated by the enemy, the Sabines lost their temper towards each other, and several of them, among whom were Atta Clausus, or Appius Claudius and family, went over to Rome. The renegades were received by their new allies with honour; for apostacy, which should carry with it disgrace, was even in those days treated too often as a virtue. The Claudii were made patricians of Rome, which seems to have always courted converts by offering the highest price to those who were ready to part with their old opinions and principles. Valerius Publicola—or as some call him, Popli-cola, one who honoured the people—died soon after the last-mentioned event, and received the compliment of a magnificent funeral. The procession commenced with a band of pipers, every one of whom the public paid, and the crown was carried in state; but on such an occasion as this, the empty crown could be suggestive of nothing but its own hollowness.

The armour belonging to the deceased was buried with him, as if in mockery of its uselessness against the attacks of the grim enemy; and the face was painted, as is still the custom in Italy, where the attempt to disguise the complexion to which we must come at last, only gives to the reality a hideousness neither necessary nor natural. After the funeral of a great or a much lamented man, it was usual to hang branches of cypress on his house, and his gates were decorated with pine by those who were left pining after him.

It was about this period that the great battle of Lake Regillus is supposed to have been fought, when the Latins, who had been trying to translate into Latin everything belonging to Rome, were at length taught that the Roman character was strong enough to maintain its own individuality.

In times of extreme peril, it has always been found that two heads, instead of being better than one, are likely to neutralise each other, and to reduce the supreme power under one head is the best mode of making it effectual. The Romans, when seriously threatened by the Latins, proceeded at once to the appointment of a dictator, from whose decrees there should be no appeal; so that whatever he said should be no sooner said than done—a principle of action which contributes materially to the success of every great enterprise. P. Lartius was the first dictator; but we can find no traces of his dictation, and he seems to have been speedily superseded by Aulus Postumius, whose sword is said to have been known " to bite," * — a propensity which must have rendered his blade rather liable to snap, unless its temper was excellent. The appointment of dictator was only for six months ; so that the people were soon absolved from the absolute power under which they placed themselves. The best piece of patronage at the disposal of the dictator, was the place of Master of the Horse, which Aulus conferred on Æbutius ; the latter acting completely under the guidance of the former, who never parted with the reins while deputing the mastership of the horse to another. Aulus and Æbutius set forward towards the Lake Regillus, on the margin of which they waited till it was pitch dark before they pitched their tent, with the intention of preparing for a pitched battle.

The Latins were led by Mamilius, and the foe being face to face, engaged themselves hand to hand with the most desperate energy. According to the legend, Æbutius and Mamilius, meeting in the thick of the fight, came individually to blows, which resulted in the unhorsing of the Master of the Horse, who was almost bored to death with the points of the swords of the enemy. At one time the battle seemed so much in favour of the Latins, that Aulus entreated the Romans not to resign themselves to the ravens, to be crowed over in a double sense, by the birds of prey and the enemy. So mutual was the slaughter, and so equal the bravery on both sides, that it would have been difficult to decide the battle ; and the legend, in its equal apportionment of valour to each party, would have come to no practical result, had not supernatural agency stepped in opportunely to give to one side the victory. Two gigantic youths were seen fighting on the Roman side, and though nobody knew their names, their address was the admiration of every one. Their valour was shown at the expense of the unfortunate Latins, who, unable to sustain the heavy charge that was now made upon them, made no further attempt to meet any engagement, but resorted to flight, as the only act that seemed to offer benefit.

The warriors wore nothing on their heads, and many surmises arose as to who they could be ; but nobody suspected the truth,—that the heroes, without helmets or hats, were Castor, who never was unaccompanied by his friend Pollux, and Pollux, who never went anywhere without his Castor. The same noble youths were the first to announce in Rome the news of the victory, acting as " their own reporters " of their own exploits. Having delivered their message, they disappeared as mysteriously as they came ; for the legend loses sight of them in a horse-trough near the temple of Vesta. Hither they repaired to water their steeds, and to refresh themselves at an adjacent well ; and those who feel the insatiable thirst of curiosity, are referred to the bottom of

---

* " Camerium knows how deeply
  The sword of Aulus bites,
  And all our city calls him
  The man of seventy fights."

MACAULAY's *Lay of the Battle of the Lake Regillus.*

this well for the truth, if a deeper inquiry into the legend is desired. For many ages a superstitious reverence was shown for the margin of the Lake Regillus, where a mark, said to be the impression of a celestial horse's hoof, remained, to make a lasting impression on the softness of credulity.

We have hitherto been swimming, as well as we can, in the sea of conjecture, catching eagerly at the lightest cork or bladder, in the shape of fact, to keep us afloat in the stream of events flowing from legendary sources.

The continuation of the journey will be chiefly on the *terra firma* of fact; and, instead of being, now and then, so thoroughly at sea as to find ourselves wandering into the wildest latitudes, with no other pilot than tradition, we shall henceforth, in our progress, have good and substantial grounds to go upon. Hitherto we have had credulity pulling at the oars, the idle and uncertain breezes of rumour filling our sails, and our rudder in the hands of various authorities distinguished for nothing but their disagreement with each other, and who would, in fact, be without distinction of any kind if they were without a difference.

We are now about to pursue our journey by a more certain road, to carry on our history, as it were, by the rail; and, though the line may be a peculiar one of our own, the train of facts will be regular, coming, we trust into no violent collision with others pursuing the same path, and arriving, in due time, at the appointed terminus.

CHAPTER THE SIXTH.

FROM THE BATTLE OF THE LAKE REGILLUS TO THE CLOSE OF THE WAR WITH THE VOLSCIANS.

HE resources of Rome had hitherto been derived from the plunder taken in war, but the field of battle is always far less fertile than the field of industry. In the former case, the crop once gathered is rendered for ever unproductive, and to beat the same enemy twice over, is like the useless operation of thrashing straw; for if, in either case, the first thrashing has been complete, there is nothing to be got by a second. The plebeians had been so long withdrawn from the cultivation of the land, that they found it extremely awkward to cultivate a second time an acquaintance once dropped; and the earth having been hitherto regarded as *infra dig.*, was not likely to yield much to those who had despised until they wanted it. The plebeians could only reap what they had sown, and as they had sown nothing of any value, they had fallen into a state of extreme seediness. Begging and borrowing were the only alternatives of those who could no longer steal, and the patrician body became a sort of loan society to the plebeians, who pledged themselves not only morally, but physically, for the return of the money that had been advanced to them. The law of debtor and creditor was extremely stringent in ancient Rome; and indeed its stringency amounted almost to a rope round the debtor's neck; for if he could not pay within a certain time, he was tied down as the slave of his creditor. In this position the assailant was called an *addictus*, for he was regularly sold, without even the equity of redemption being allowed to him. If the borrower had only pledged himself without an actual sale, he was simply a *nexus*, with the power of paying off his debt by either money or work; but if he could do neither, he became an *addictus** forthwith, when he was thrown into chains, and

---

* This law is said to have been altered by Servius Tullius ; but if legislation on the subject was at one time loose, it became very binding afterwards, and was extremely strict at the date above alluded to.

wore nothing but the stripes, which were the ordinary livery of that disgraceful state of servitude.

Appius Claudius had been chosen Consul, with P. Servilius as a colleague, in the year of the City 258, when a miserable old insolvent, with his hair like a mat, giving evidence of the severe rubs that had fallen on his head, rushed into the forum. His face had the paleness of ashes, and many tried to sift his countenance, in which the marks of his having been ground down to the dust were plainly visible. His back bore traces of recent scores, every one of which he declared should be accounted as a score to be paid off upon his oppressors. His farm had been burned down, and its contents burned up; his cattle had been driven he knew not where, while he himself had been driven to distraction. The tax-gatherer had, nevertheless, been as punctual as ever in his calls, and having soundly rated the ruined agriculturist for not being ready with his rates, the latter had been compelled to run into debt; for the Romans had not made insurance against fire any feature of their policy. Having been unable to pay his debts, the impoverished farmer became the slave of his creditor; and the shoulders of the former bore unmistakeable marks of the latter having got the whip-hand of him. The excitement in the forum was intense; for all were seized with indignation, who might possibly be seized for debt; and every one who owed anything to anybody began to feel that he owed a great deal more to common humanity. A popular outbreak seemed to be close at hand, and the two Consuls consulted together on the crisis. Appius Claudius gave it as his opinion, that as the people were put up, the best way was to put them down; but his colleague, Servilius, was an advocate for a milder regimen. At this juncture, news arrived of the Volscian army having set out for Rome; and the plebeians being called upon to enlist, declared that they would not enlist themselves at the bidding of those who would do nothing to enlist their sympathies. In this difficult dilemma, P. Servilius promised that if they would come out and fight, they should be released from prison during the war; and guaranteed that if they would present a bold front to the enemy's sword, their backs should be safe from the scourge of domestic tyranny. There was an immediate rush of insolvents into the ranks, which were soon filled almost to overflowing; for as a great majority of the population happened to be hopelessly in debt, a summons to the field was the only sort of summons their appearance to which might have been reasonably relied upon.

They fought with the energy of desperation, for each rank had sworn an oath, and there was an affidavit, therefore, on every file, to do execution on the Volscians. Never were bankrupts more determined to avoid a surrender than the band of defaulters who went forth to meet the foe with a confidence, which would, probably, have disappeared had they recognised at the meeting a single one of their creditors. The success of the Romans was complete, and those who had fought upon the understanding that every blow they struck was to wipe out a debt, returned home in the expectation that every old liability had been rubbed off, and that they would be free to rub on as they best could for the future.   They were, however, doomed to bitter disappointment, for Appius Claudius declared that no faith ought to be kept with those who had kept no faith with their creditors ; and all the debtors who were not prepared to pay upon the nail had the screw cruelly applied to them. The debtors were sent back to their prisons, and many an unfortunate insolvent, as he thought of the imposition that had been practised upon him, could only cast his eyes upon the walls of his dungeon, and murmur at the dreadful cell of which he had become the victim.   The bolts and bars of oppression would have brought liberty to a dead lock, had it not been for the people outside the gaols, who threatened to rise for the purpose of falling upon the tyrants.   At this critical period Rome was menaced by the Sabines, when the plebeians were called upon to enlist ; but they declared they would be recruits of the very rawest description if they allowed themselves to be again done as they had been already.   Public meetings were held on the Esquiline and Aventine hills, where liberal sentiments, which have now become as old as the hills themselves, fell upon the popular ear with all the charm and force of novelty.   The patricians were divided as to the best means of dealing with the difficulty their own misconduct had created, and it was obvious that the fatal error having been committed of refusing to accede to a just demand, the scarcely less dangerous mistake of yielding to violence and clamour was the only course that could now be followed.   The patricians would have stood by their order ; but the difficulty was to know how public order, as well as their own órder, could be preserved ; and it was at length agreed that a dictator should be appointed.   The choice fell upon M. Valerius, a moderate man, whom the plebeians could trust, for he came of a good stock, his father being no other than that great gun of the popular party, the famous Publicola.   A large army was soon ready to take the field, or to take anything else that came in the ordinary course of battle.   Valerius marched against the Sabines, who fled, or, more literally speaking, decamped ; for they left behind them their camp, which was taken by the enemy.

On his return to Rome in triumph, the dictator asked for an inquiry into the people's wrongs, with a view to giving them their rights ; but the patrician party in the senate refusing him his committee, Valerius sent in his resignation, which was accepted by the senate.   He apologised to the plebeians for not having been able to carry his measures of reform ; and the patricians, pleased by his moderation in resigning his seat, gave him a curule chair—a sort of portable stall, or reserved seat, which, at the Circensian games he was privileged to occupy.

The Curule Chair, or Sella Curulis, invites us to pause for a moment, and hold a short sitting upon it, for the purpose of inquiring into its origin.   Comfort seems to have been supplied most charily in the construction of this official chair ; but there was a fine touch of morality in giving uneasiness to the seat of unlimited power.   The legs of the Sella Curulis folded like those of a camp-stool; a device which may have been emblematical of the fact, that the dictatorial office was liable to a speedy shutting up, for the appointment was never more than of six months' duration. The material of which the chair was formed was the smoothest and most highly-polished ivory; so that the fatal facility of a fall must have been frequently suggested to the occupant of the seat by its exceedingly slippery surface.*

The Consuls, fearing an outbreak if the army was disbanded, ordered the soldiers to remain on duty in the capacity of special constables over each other—the staff being held responsible for the conduct of the main body. To be continued thus as a standing army, was more than the troops felt disposed to stand; and, determining to take high ground, they withdrew to the top of the Mons Sacer or Sacred Mount, in the neighbourhood of Crustumenium. Electing L. Sicinius as their leader, they accommodated themselves as well as they could, until matters should be accommodated with the senate.

The patricians began to be greatly alarmed at the secession of the plebeians; for though the former had been accustomed to trample the latter under foot, all the foundations of society seemed to be withdrawn in the absence of that part which, though it may be called the base, is essential to the existence of the capital. Rome, in fact, was beginning to find out that an aristocracy cut off from all connection with the people at large, is little better than a flower separated from the tree, and doomed to fall speedily into bad odour. The patrician order happily recognised the important truth, that the most delicate tendrils owe all their vitality to the sap, carried up to the top of the tree from those portions that are in the closest connection with the soil; and steps were therefore taken to prevent the final severing of the sturdy trunk from the higher branches. An embassy, consisting of ten patricians, was sent to negotiate; but as the patricians were no orators, and their stupidity spoke for itself, Menenius Agrippa, who had once been a plebeian, was sent as their head, which of course included their mouth-piece.

Menenius, using his authority as spokesman for the common weal, cited the fable of the Belly and the Members, to the bellicose *plebs*, who seemed struck by his relation of it to them, and its own relation to their existing position. He told them that, once upon a time, all the members of the human body resolved on aiming a blow at the stomach, which was accused of leading a life of idleness. The hands struck with no particular aim; the legs, moved to rebellion, refused to stir; the eye shut down its lid; the mouth went into open hostility, and the nose joining in the general blow, there seemed every prospect that the proud stomach would be glad to eat humble pie in the absence of all other provisions. It was, however, soon found that, in nourishing their

* The Curule Chair is said to have been imported, with other articles of state furniture, from Etruria. In some cases, the feet were formed of ivory in the shape of elephant's tusks; but there are other proofs of their Tuscan origin.

animosity, the members were keeping all nourishment from themselves, and that they and their revenge were about equally wasted.

The plebeians, understanding the moral of the story, were disposed to treat, on the understanding that they should henceforth be better treated. An agreement was entered into, by which the sponge was to be applied to all old debts ; and all who had lost their liberty by being the slaves of bad circumstances were restored to freedom. The new compact provided also for the institution of two officers, named Tribunes, who were invested with authority over the concerns of the plebeians ; and it was certainly one of the best investments ever made for the profit of the Roman people. The person of the Tribune was so sacred, that a common assault upon this officer, when in the execution of his duty, rendered the assailant liable not merely to be taken up, but to be knocked down and killed in the streets by any one having a mania for manslaughter.

The Tribune was allowed such an unlimited liberty of speech, that it was punishable to interrupt him ; and in default of bail, it was death to cough him down while addressing the people. Even to yawn during one of his discourses, was to open an abyss into which the yawner might be plunged before he was aware of it ; and the involuntary action of his distended jaws would often render them the jaws of his own destruction.

The house of the Tribune was open day and night ; so that it was as easy to find one of these officers as it is in these days to find a policeman, and sometimes rather easier. The Tribunes had power to bring parties before them, or, in other words, to issue summonses, as well as to enforce fines, which, if not paid, involved the forfeiture of property, or, in simpler terms, were recoverable by distress warrant upon the defaulter's goods and chattels. One of the greatest privileges of the Tribunes was the right of exercising a veto on any decree of the senate. Though they had no seats in the assembly, they were permitted to look in at the door ; and if any act was passing that they disapproved, they had the privilege of exercising, by a shout of " No," a sort of negative authority. This power of prevention left fewer evils to be cured ; and the plebeians, having at last obtained an organ of their own, may be said to have found the key to their liberties.

The Tribunes seem to have had power to add to their number, for they selected three colleagues, soon after they themselves had been chosen ; and, from this time forth, a struggle ensued between plebeian energy, seeking its fair share of right, and patrician tenacity, holding on with obstinate determination to exclusive advantages.

Contemporaneously with the institution of the Tribunes, some new officers were appointed, under the name of Ædiles, who were something like our Commissioners of Woods and Forests, of Sewers, and of Paving combined ; for they had the care of public buildings, roads, and drains, as well as of baths and washhouses. They sometimes decided small disputes, and acted as Inspectors of Markets, examining weights, settling quarrels, and holding the scales of justice as well as of merchandise. They kept an eye to unwholesome provisions, and a nose to stale fish; their ears took cognisance of bad language; in their hands they carried a staff; and they were, in fact, a curious compound of the beadle, the commissioner, the policeman, and the magistrate.

While the plebeians had been sulking on the Mons Sacer, a treaty between the Latins and the Romans had been brought about by Spurius Cassius, a Consul, who, though his name sounds like counterfeit coin, seems to have possessed a good deal of the true metal. By the treaty, both nations were to be almost entirely equal in every respect; and, even with regard to booty, they were to be on the same footing.

By another clause in the act, those insolvent debtors who had been converted into "alarming sacrifices!" and were reduced to slavery, because their creditors "must have cash," or its equivalent, were restored to freedom. The ceremony of manumission was curious, and comprised so many indignities done to the slave, that, although free, he could not have been very easy under the process. He was first taken before the Consul by his master, who gave him a blow on the cheek, which was rather a back-handed mode of making an independent man of him. The Consul then laid his wand about the insolvent's back, at the same time declaring him perfectly free, and telling him to go about his business—if he happened to have any. The beating having been gone through, there was still more lathering to be endured; for the head of the freedman was closely shaved, as a precaution, perhaps, against his going mad on the attainment of his liberty. His release from his chains was not complete until he had been deprived of his locks; and to crown all, he was invested with that emblem of butchery in a political, as well as a social point of view, the red cap of liberty.

During the internal quarrels of Rome, agriculture had been so thoroughly neglected, that the harvest had completely fallen to the ground, or, rather, had never come out of it. The husbandman had husbanded nothing, either for himself or others; and as nothing had been sown but civil dissension, there was nothing to reap but the fruit of it. The Romans, who, until lately, had been thirsting for power, were now hungry for food; and, to prevent the people from dying at home, envoys were sent to scour the surrounding countries,—a process which involved many a brush with the inhabitants. It is stated, by some historians, that, during the famine, an order was forwarded to Gelo, of Syracuse, for corn, which that individual was quite ready to supply, but for which he was so thoroughly unbusiness-like as to refuse the money. The incident, though utterly without commercial interest, would have been pleasing in a different point of view, were it not for the stern realities of chronology, which prove that Gelo could not have acted as a gratuitous corn-dealer at the time specified, for he was not alive at the period.

While Rome was suffering from want of corn, it was wasting the very flower of its population in a war with the Volscians. Among the most distinguished warriors on the side of the Romans was Caius Marcius, a young patrician, who led all his own clients into an action in which the defendants—the unfortunate Volscians—were subjected to enormous damages. He subsequently proceeded against Corioli, which made an obstinate defence; but was ultimately beaten, and compelled to pay the whole of the costs of the conflict. From this affair he took the name of Coriolanus, by which he is better known than by his original appellation of C. Marcius, for mankind will too often award the largest measure of fame to the most extensive perpetrator of mischief; and he who would carve himself a name, may carve it much more deeply and durably with the sword than with any other instrument.

When the corn arrived from Sicily, the popular party proposed a gratuitous distribution of the boon; but the patricians, headed by Coriolanus, who was a tyrant in grain, recommended that the plebeians should pay for what they required. Complaint is never so open-mouthed as when it has nothing to eat; and the people became desperate when they found Coriolanus advising, without a scruple, that not a grain should be given, nor an ear lent to their sufferings. He proposed the abolition of the Tribunes as the condition of food being supplied to the people; but they, becoming every day more crusty from the want of bread, insisted on his being tried for treason. Coriolanus saw the people waxing resolute to seal his doom, and he accordingly made his escape, so that when the time came for him to be tried, he was found wanting. Judgment went against him by default; his name was struck out of the list of patricians—a sort of peerage of the period. He was sentenced, moreover, to *aquæ et ignis interdictio*—prohibition from fire and water; a punishment which, looking at the fiery nature of all spirituous liquors, may be fancifully supposed to have involved especially a stoppage of grog, as it certainly prevented everybody from entertaining him. This sentence amounted, in fact, to banishment; and, indeed, it was designed to do so; for the interdiction of fire and water left the culprit nothing on earth but air, which of course it was quite impossible to live upon.

Stung with what he called the ingratitude of his countrymen, though they had really not much to thank him for, Coriolanus, in a spirit not very magnanimous, proceeded to offer his services to the enemy. Taking leave of his wife Volumnia, a voluminous woman, who had had greatness thrust upon her by nature to an awkward extent, he departed for the country of the Volscians, and arrived at Antium about supper time. His name was taken up at once to Attius Tullius, who, though sitting at his meal with the usual accompaniment of *manus unctæ*, or greasy hands, determined not to allow the illustrious stranger to slip through his fingers. Coriolanus was hospitably entertained, and induced to take the command of the Volscian army against the Roman colonists. He drove them from place to place until he had got them up against the Cluilian ditch, and into it many were thrown; a sad proof of his animosity

having been carried to a pitch that must always leave a black stain on
his memory.   Here also he pitched his tent within almost a stone's
throw of Rome ; and as the plebeians were unwilling to fight, ambassadors
were sent to entreat Coriolanus to lay down his sword ; but, contemptuously folding his arms, he returned no answer.   The priests next
tried their powers of persuasion, but though they did all they could
to convert Coriolanus to the cause of Rome, it was not until female
influence was brought into requisition, that the attempt proved successful.   His mother Veturia, accompanied by his considerably better
half, Volumnia, and a party of Roman ladies made up for the occasion,

Coriolanus parting from his Wife and Family.

visited him at his camp, when the clamour of the strong-minded, the
sighs and sobs of the weaker, the sneers of some, the tears of others,
and the importunity of all, proved irresistible.   He had been resolute

for some time; but when his wife, with a heavy heart added to her natural weight, fell upon his neck, he seemed to be sinking under that which he could no longer stand up against.

His mother, Veturia, following up the advantage that had been gained, tried the power of the female tongue, to which time seems to go on adding all the force of which it deprives the rest of the body. The old lady raved and shouted with a degree of anile energy that struck Coriolanus with dismay; and when she threw herself on the ground, declaring he should walk over her body if he attempted to march upon Rome, he felt that he could not take another step without trampling on the tenderest relations of humanity. With Volumnia hanging to his neck, and Veturia clinging to his heels,—with a wife pouring the loudest lamentations into his ear,—with a mother cursing everything in general, but his own birthday in particular,—with a bevy of Roman ladies shrieking and sobbing in the background,—Coriolanus could no longer resist, but ordered his camp to be broken up, and led his legions back again. Tradition differs as to the date of the death of Coriolanus, who, according to some accounts, sunk under the attack made upon him by the weaker sex; while others assert that he lived to a good old age, which is likely to have been the case, if the scene we have described was not immediately the death of him—for the constitution that could have survived so severe a trial must have been of a strength truly wonderful.

Coriolanus has been held up as a model of disinterestedness, but we cannot help setting him down as a selfish upstart, who turned traitor to his country, because it did not form the highest estimate of his personal merits. His deserts are overbalanced by the fact of his being a deserter; and it was, assuredly, the reverse of magnanimity to evince his spite against the nation to which he belonged, merely because his own value had not been put upon his own services. Such is our view of Coriolanus without the masquerade dress in which he has been often made to appear; for truth compels us to take off the gilt in which he has hitherto shone, and to substitute the guilt that really belongs to him.

The Temple of Fortuna Muliebris was raised, in compliment to the women who, by their hysterical, and now historical efforts, were said to have saved Rome; and indeed, considering the frequency with which female influence operates the other way, the fact of its having been exercised for the prevention of mischief, deserves the commemoration of a monument.

CHAPTER THE SEVENTH.

FROM THE CLOSE OF THE WAR WITH THE VOLSCIANS TO THE PASSING
OF THE BILL OF TERENTILLUS.

FTER the war with the Volscians was at an end, the Romans are said to have entered into a treaty with their former foe, the object of which was a sort of partnership in plunder; it being agreed that the new allies should take the field together, and divide the produce. Ill-gotten gain is never a source of real profit; and the land stolen in war became a ground of contention among the Romans. The patricians had hitherto grasped the whole of the conquered soil, though they could not do so with clean hands; and Spurius Cassius proposed that the plebeians should have a share of it. The suggestion, though violently resisted, became the law of the land; but the land was not appropriated in conformity with the law until a much later period. Spurius Cassius did not long survive, when the year of his Consulship had expired; for the patricians caused him to be impeached, and his head was struck off upon a block, though, from the services he had performed, it deserved rather to have been struck off upon a medal.

The patricians tried to divert the attention of the plebeians from domestic affairs by leading them constantly into battle; but the latter, though compelled to march into the field, would take no steps to secure a victory. Like horses brought to the water but refusing to drink, the soldiers, though conducted to the field, evinced no thirst for blood; but firmly declining to aim a single blow, they presented a striking picture of passive disobedience. In vain did the officers suggest, that for those ambitious of a soldier's grave, there was at length an eligible opening; they would gain no laurels, but allowed themselves to be kept at bay; they laughed outright at their commanders, and, instead of

F

straining every nerve for success, they kept their risible muscles only in full exercise.

There existed at this time a gens in Rome which had managed to obtain such a share of power for itself, that it was generally recognised as the governing family. The gens alluded to was that of the Fabii, whose union formed their chief strength; for no member of the family, though he might be unmindful of his antecedents, was ever known to forget his relatives. The Fabii derived their name from Faba, a bean, because their ancestors had cultivated that kind of pulse; but in later times the gens became remarkable for feeling the popular pulse, and making a cat's-paw of the patricians. By an arrangement with the order to which they belonged, the Fabii were ensured one of the consulships, on condition of their influencing their clients to elect a patrician to the other; and thus both the people and the senate were played off against each other for the special advantage of the "family." Fortunately for society, there is in all corruption a rottenness which is always bringing it towards its conclusion while it seems to be gaining its end; and the usual difficulty of getting unprincipled men to hang long together by a rope of sand, was illustrated in the case of the patricians and the Fabii. The quarrels among themselves helped to render them contemptible to the plebeians, and the troops had become so accustomed to treat their leaders with disrespect, that many an intended fight ended without a sword being taken from its sheath, and nothing was drawn but the battle.

One of the Consuls had, for several years, been chosen from the family of the Fabii; when its members growing tired, at last, of their patrician stock being a laughing-stock to the army, determined to make themselves popular. Marcus Fabius won the hearts of the soldiers, by dressing their wounds, and promising to redress their grievances. Kæso Fabius, his successor, recommended the distribution of the land among the plebeians, by whose sweat it had been gained; but he had not been always equally anxious to acknowledge the claims of popular perspiration; for he had been one of those who condemned Spurius Cassius for having made a similar proposition.

Tradition states that the Fabii afterwards emigrated in a body, upwards of three hundred strong, taking with them four thousand clients; but whether the clients went at their own solicitation, or whether the Fabii were the solicitors, we are not in a position to determine. It is said that the whole party of four thousand three hundred went into action together, and paid with their lives the costs of the sad affair; but the critical authorities doubt the whole story; and it is satisfactory to our best feelings to know that we, on this point, know nothing.*

The Etrurians soon after wasted the country near Rome, and wasted their own time into the bargain, for they were at last glad to treat,

---

* Among the other difficulties of this story is the comparatively trifling one, that the Fabian race did not become extinct; but tradition hops over this dilemma, by leaving one of the family behind to serve as a father to future Fabii.

though not until they had retreated. A peace was concluded ; and the parties held their peace for forty years,—or, at all events, if they ever had words, they did not come to blows during that lengthened period.

As some of the events recorded in this chapter arose out of the Roman law of debtor and creditor, it may be just as well to include in this account a few items of a commercial character. When a man ran into debt, he was almost sure to be brought to a stand-still, for compound interest continued to accrue so rapidly that there was no chance of compounding with those to whom he owed money. Thirty days after a debt being demanded, the defaulter was handed over to his creditor, and bound with a cord, by way of accord and satisfaction ; but, at the end of sixty days, a crier, whose office was enough to make him shed tears, advertised the insolvent for sale as a slave in the market-place. It is not surprising that the plebeians should rise against their being put up to this degrading auction, more particularly when the masters to whom they were knocked down were in the habit of beating and cruelly ill-treating them. The patricians laid violent hands, not only upon the plebeians, but upon all the property of the State, assuming to the utmost all its rights, and repudiating all its duties. They took as a matter of right all the offices of state ; and so complete was the seizure made by the patricians of every thing in the shape of a Government situation, that the name of the order which absorbed to itself all the good things is to be traced in the modern word "patronage." The whole of the profits of war went into the pockets of the upper class ; and though the plebeians drew the sword, the patricians drew whatever money was to be obtained from the enemy.

The patricians, however, were not allowed to exercise their tyranny always without resistance ; for, if their conduct was revolting to human nature, it was to be expected that human nature would revolt against them when opportunity offered. An instance occurred during the Consulship of Appius Claudius, who had been elected by the senate, and who, wishing to levy troops, caused the names of all the men between eighteen and forty-five to be called over in a list, which furnished the materials for enlistment. Amongst the names was that of Publilius Volero, who had formerly held a commission as a centurion, or captain ; and, being now selected to serve as a common soldier, declared indignantly that rather than go as a private into the ranks, he would continue in a private station. Publilius, in fact, kicked violently against the orders of the Consul, and being a man of very powerful stamp, it was felt that when Publilius kicked in earnest, there was something on foot that it was not easy to contend against. Appius intimating that the Consuls must be obeyed, desired one of the lictors to do his duty ; when Volero, being a strong and robust man, received the lictor with open arms, and lifting him from the ground, gave him a setting down that shook the nerves of the astonished officer. Having thrown the lictor on the ground, where the unhappy functionary took

his own measure, instead of carrying out those of his superiors, Volero
threw himself on the public, upon whom he made a very strong
impression.

A Lictor is sent to arrest Publilius Volero.

Publilius from this moment had considerable weight with the plebeians, who made him one of their Tribunes ; and he at once proposed
a large measure of reform in the mode of electing those officers. He
suggested an extension of the suffrage, by giving it to the tribes instead
of the centuries ; and public meetings were got up in support of the
project.   These meetings were attended by the patricians, and disturbances ensued, owing to the attempts of one party to put the other
party down ; for public discussion in all ages seems to have been
conducted on the principle that it is to be all on one side, and that any
opinion opposed to that of the majority is not to be listened to.   When
the strength of lungs happens to be with the party having the strength
of argument, there is not much harm done ; but as the patricians and
plebeians mustered in nearly equal numbers at the meetings alluded to,
personal altercations frequently took place ; and the Tribunes as well as
the Consuls sent their respective officers to arrest each other.
    At length Lætorius, who had been elected as the colleague of Publi-
lius Volero, marched into the Forum with an armed force, determined

that he would that morning carry the day; and as he drew his sword, he declared he would go through with it. The patricians, losing their own resolution, offered to agree to any that he might propose; but, refusing to trust them, he took possession of the Capitol, as a guarantee for the fulfilment of their promise. The *Lex Publilia* was accordingly passed, to the great annoyance of Appius, who always treated the plebeians as if different sorts of clay, as well as different moulds, were employed by Nature in her great man—ufacture. When his year of office was over, he was impeached by the Tribunes; but on the day when the trial ought to have come on, the worldly trials of Appius were all past, for he died the night before the cause stood for hearing. Posterity has agreed on the verdict which the judges were not required to pronounce; and it has even been said that he fell by his own hand, in consequence of his sense of guilt preventing him from knowing how to acquit himself.

To add to its troubles, Rome was visited by a double plague, in the shape of an external foe and an internal pestilence. The enemy having approached the gates of the city, the country people had taken refuge inside the walls, bringing with them their cattle in such numbers that the place was literally littered with pigs, while the oxen and sheep were packed in pens to an extent of which our own pen can furnish but a faint outline. The summer was at the height of its heat, and the sufferings of the poor dumb animals, as they lost their fat, and met their fate, were enough to melt not only a heart of stone, but many a stone of suet. The foe, fearing from the pestilence a plaguy deal of trouble, broke up their camp; and Rome was allowed to enjoy an interval of peace, though disease did more havoc than might have been expected at the hands of an enemy.

We now come to the legend of Cincinnatus; and though it is no better than a legend, which, as the smallest student will be aware, is so called from *legendum*, a thing to be read, we must proceed upon the assumption that, as it is a thing to be read, it is *à fortiori* a thing to be written. Lucius Quinctius, surnamed Cincinnatus from his curly locks—for nature had dressed his hair to a turn—was of a high patrician family. He passed his life as a country gentleman occupying his own estate, and occupying himself in looking after it. His land, it must be admitted, was better cultivated than his manners, which were haughty and imperious. His virtues were all of the domestic kind; he was equally attached to his wife and his farm, and he was an excellent husband, as well as a good husbandman.

It happened that Rome was in such a perilous state as to need a strong hand, when Cincinnatus, being famed for the use of the spade, was invited to leave his *otium cum dig.*—as everybody knows already, and somebody may have said before—that he might assume the office of dictator. When the messengers arrived from the senate, Cincinnatus was at work in the fields, perhaps sowing up some old tares, or examining the state of his pulse—a favourite crop in those days—or cutting out the sickliest of his corn with the sickle. The soil being loamy, and Cincinnatus being in the thick of his work, he was not very presentable ; but hastily throwing his toga round him, he made the best appearance he could before the messengers of the senate. They at once hailed him as dictator, and carried him to Rome, where he called out every man

Cincinnatus chosen Dictator.

capable of bearing arms ; and every man thus called out, accepted the patriotic challenge. Every soldier was to carry with him food for five days, and twelve stakes cut into lengths to form a barricade; so that, as the stakes weighed several pounds, and the eatables were solid, the burden of each man, together with his accoutrements—which included a cask on the head from which the perspiration poured—must have been inconveniently ponderous. Notwithstanding their heavy load, the legend, which is less weighty than their equipments, goes on to state that the soldiers started at sunset, with Cincinnatus at their head, and reached the camp, a distance of two-and-twenty miles, at a quick march, or rather at a fast trot, by midnight. Though the story runs thus, we are compelled to doubt the running of the troops, who, with their legs encumbered by their arms and other equipments, must have found speed impossible. On arriving at Mount Algidus, where the enemy was encamped, Cincinnatus made his soldiers surround the place, and by aiming at all in the ring, they were sure to hit somebody. Finding themselves in the midst of a circle by no means social, the Æquians sued for mercy ; but Cincinnatus threw Gracchus Clœlius and his lieutenants into chains, which was equivalent to making them enter into bonds for their future good behaviour. Clœlius continued in his command after having been thus formally tied down, and Cincinnatus returned to Rome in triumph. Having held the dictatorship only sixteen days, he laid it quietly down, and returning to his farming operations, after having submitted the enemy to the yoke, he fitted it once more to the necks of his oxen.

While engaged in fighting with an external enemy, a nation often forgets the foes she has within; and it is the cruel policy of despotism to waste the popular energy on quarrels with strangers, in order to divert the attention of the public from domestic grievances. The war being ended, the people began to look at home, and they soon perceived that, while the sword of aggression had been in constant use, the sword of justice had been rusting in the scabbard, or had been only drawn forth to inflict, occasionally, a wound on public liberty. A movement arose in favour of law reform, and C. Terentillus Arsa brought in a bill for getting the patricians and plebeians to a better understanding, by putting them on nearly the same footing. The measure led to considerable agitation; for, though the tribunes passed it, the senate could not get over it at all; and, the latter having thrown it out, the former brought in a bill, containing a great deal more than the original demand, in the year following. In political, as well as pecuniary affairs, a just claim carries interest, which accumulates as long as the claim remains unsatisfied; and every day, while it augments the debt due, increases the difficulty of meeting it.

The proposition of Terentillus was much discussed in large assemblies, the harmony of which was disturbed by some of the young patricians; for, even in the early days of which we write, the noble art of laughing down, or crowing over a discomfited orator, was understood by some of the juvenile scions of aristocracy. It happened that Cincinnatus had four sons, who were exceedingly fine young men, with very coarse manners. One of them, named Kæso, was continually getting into street rows, or disturbing public meetings; and frequently went so far as to interfere with Virginius, a tribune, in the execution of his duty. The officer was for a long time patient; but, at length, was goaded to take the matter, as well as the offender, up; and Kæso was charged with a series of assaults, of a more or less aggravated and aggravating character. While these accusations were hanging over him, an old case of manslaughter came to light; the victim having been an aged invalid, whom Kæso, in a disreputable night brawl, had cruelly maltreated. He was already under heavy sureties when this fresh charge was brought up, and, to avoid meeting it, this proud patrician ran away from his bail, leaving their recognizances to be forfeited.

Reports were soon afterwards spread, that the man who had left the city as a contemptible runaway, was about to return to it in the more formidable character of a robber and a murderer. One night when the people had gone to bed, many of them heard in their sleep the trampling of horses, which seemed to come like a tremendous nightmare over the city. Presently a shout arose, which beat upon the drum of every ear like a call to battle. The Consuls sprang out of bed, and throwing about them the first substitute for a toga that the bedclothes presented, they made at once for the walls of the city. The plebeians, when called upon, refused to serve; and the Consuls, feeling how weak they were in going to the wall alone, made the usual promises, which the people, as usual, were induced to discount, at a great personal sacrifice. Proceeding to the Capitol, they found it in the possession of a large band of exiles and runaway slaves, who would have been glad to run away a second time, had escape been possible. Many fell, and were felled to the earth, on both sides, while P. Valerius after putting several to the sword, had the sword put to him in a most uncomfortable manner.

The exiles took nothing by their expedition as far as the attack was concerned; but many of them owed something to the expedition with which they fled from the contest. After this battle, all traces of Kæso Quinctius are lost; but whether he fell in the fray, or whether the thread of his existence was frayed out in some other way, is a mystery we have no means of unravelling.

Appius Claudius was now called upon, as the surviving partner of P. Valerius, to redeem the pledge given by the latter; but Appius, with a chicanery worthy of Chancery in its best, or rather in its worst days, pleaded the death of his colleague as a bar to the suit, declaring that both consuls must be joined in it, though he knew all the while that a bill of revivor for the purpose of including the deceased consul was quite impossible. During these unhappy differences between the two orders, many of the leading plebeians were murdered at the instigation of the patricians, who, however, were rapidly cutting their own throats; for violence, while it thinned the body, added to the stoutness of heart of the popular party. The tribunes were increased in number from five to ten; and, somewhat later, a still higher point was gained for the plebeians by limiting to a couple of sheep and thirty beeves the fines to which they were liable. These exactions were, however, enforced with such rigour that the tenderest lamb was allowed no quarter if a fine had been incurred, and the smallest stake in the country—if the stake happened to be beef—was seized without remorse if the owner had become subject to a penalty.

It was many years before the Bill of Terentillus—which has been specially noted—was at length taken up, when the patricians graciously consented to a change in the laws, and offered the benefit of their services into the bargain, by taking upon themselves to determine the sort of change that was required. Hitting, by anticipation, on the modern expedient for delaying useful measures, the patricians appointed a select committee to inquire into law reform, and, by way of rendering the chances of legislation still more remote, they ordered the members to proceed to Athens, where, under the enervating influence of Attic associations, they were likely to go to sleep over the subject of their labours. The special commissioners became, no doubt, so thoroughly Greek in all their ideas, that, even the preparation of their report was deferred until the Greek Kalends.

CHAPTER THE EIGHTH.

FROM THE ESTABLISHMENT OF THE DECEMVIRATE TO THE TAKING
OF VEII.

Roman Bull and Priest of the period.

THE Romans, being at peace abroad, began to think of improving the means of quarrelling among themselves at home, and a desire for law reform became general. Three senators had been sent to Athens to collect information, but what they picked up in Greece was so thoroughly Greek to them, that they were obliged to get it translated into Latin by one Hermodorus, an Ephesian refugee, before they could understand a word of it.* As one job naturally leads to another, it was arranged that three commissioners having been employed in cramming, the process of digesting should be entrusted to ten more, who were called the Decemviri. These were appointed from the patricians, after a struggle on the part of the plebeians to get five selected from their own order; but, with a laudable regard to public order, they withdrew their opposition. The especial object for which the Decemviri had been appointed was to frame a new code of laws, but it seems to have been always understood that the practical purpose of a commission is to delay an object, quite as much as to further it. Lest the Decemviri should proceed too rapidly with the work they had been specially chosen to do, arrangements were made for distracting their attention from it by throwing on them the whole business of Government. Had they been

* It has been often a subject of regret that the particulars of this expedition have not been handed down to us, and that the three Roman excursionists did not put their heads together to form a log during their voyage. It is, however, seldom that the marine expeditions of the sages are fully detailed, for nothing can be scantier than the account of the journey of the three wise men of Gotham who went to sea in a bowl ; and there is reason to believe that many a chapter has been lost to the philosophical transactions of the world, by the chapter of nautical accidents.

modern commissioners of inquiry, they would have needed no excuse for delay ; but, with a stubborn resolution to get through their task, they surmounted, or avoided, the obstacles they might have been excused for stumbling at. Instead of making their administrative duties an interruption to their legislative labours, and urging the necessity for attending to both as a plea for the performance of neither, the commissioners took the sovereignty in rotation for five days at a time, and as ten rulers acting all at once would have kept nothing straight, this arrangement for obtaining the strength of unity was altogether a judicious one. At the expiration of their year of office the Decemviri had completed a system of laws, which was engraved on ten tables ;— a proof of the industry of the Government of the day, for in these times it would be hopeless to expect ten tables from those who might be, at the same time, forming a cabinet.

Though the Decemviri had done enough to win the public favour, they had left enough undone to afford a pretext for the prolongation of their powers. It was suggested that though the ten tables were very good as far as they went, there was room for two more; and to give an opportunity for this small sum in addition being completed, the continuance of the decemviral form of government was agreed upon. As the time for the election approached, the most disgraceful election intrigues were practised, and in order to disqualify Appius Claudius— one of the former Decemviri—the patricians put him in the chair, or elected him president, on the day of the nomination of the candidates. Appius had for some time been acting the character of the " people's friend," and he had shown himself a consummate actor, for, being a tyrant by nature, he must have been wholly indebted to art for appearing otherwise. Having been called upon to preside, he opened the business of the day by proposing nine names of little note—including five plebeians—and then, with an air of frankness, he suggested himself as a fit and proper person to complete the number. The people— surprised and amused at the coolness of the proposition—proceeded to elect the very candid candidate, who, being joined with a number of nonentities, formed the unit to the ten of which the rest composed the cipher. Soon after their election, the new Decemviri proceeded to complete the twelve tables—and as they formed the origin of the Civil Law, embodying principles which the best jurists have been unable to improve —we will spread these tables before the student, and ask him to sit down with us for a few moments over them.

We cannot promise him any other than a dry repast, with little or nothing to whet his curiosity ; and unless his appetite for information is extremely vigorous, there will be little to suit his taste on those plates of bronze or ivory—the material is immaterial, and has been variously described—on which the provisions we are about to serve up were originally carved.

The first table coincided in some respects with our County Courts Act, and furnished a cheap mode of bringing a defendant into court by a simple summons, though if he refused to walk, a mule, an appropriate type of obstinacy, was to be provided for him.

By the second table, it was justifiable to kill a thief in the night; but a person robbed in the day was to have the thief as his slave; a privilege equal to that of being allowed to take into your service, as your page, the urchin who has just picked your pocket. Such an exploit would no doubt indicate a smart lad, and, in order to make him literally smart, the Roman law, in the spirit of our Juvenile Offenders Act, ordered the knave a whipping.

The third table was in some respects an interest table; for it prohibited the taking of more than 12 per cent. on a loan; but if a debtor did not pay within thirty days, he might be bound with chains; an arrangement by which his exertions to get out of difficulty must have been grievously fettered. Having been made to enter into these unprofitable bonds for sixty days, the debtor, if his creditors were more than one, might have been divided between them; but human nature must have found it difficult, under such circumstances, to declare a dividend.

The fourth table seems hardly to have a sound leg to stand upon; for it gave a father the right of life and death over all his children, together with the privilege of selling them. To prevent a parent from pursuing a disgraceful traffic in a series of alarming sacrifices of his family stock, he was not permitted to sell the same child more than three times over, when the infant was permitted to go into the market on his own account, free of all filial duty.

The fifth table related to the estates of deceased persons; and if a freedman died without a will or a direct heir, the law provided for the distribution of his goods without providing for his family. Fallacious hopes among poor relations were checked by handing over to the patron all that remained; and thus the client may be said to have been subject to costs, even after the debt of nature had been satisfied.

In the sixth table, there is nothing worthy of remark; but the seventh guards against damage done by quadrupeds, and not only meets the old familiar case of the donkey among the chickens, but declares that any one wilfully treading on a neighbour's corn shall pay a suitable penalty.

Agriculture was protected by making it a capital offence to blast by incantation another's wheat; so that had the farmers of the day moaned over each other's ruined prospects as they have done in more recent times, performing a sort of incantation by singing the same old song of despair, they might have been liable to lose their heads in the literal as well as in the intellectual sense of which the phrase is susceptible. By the same table, a man breaking another's limb was exposed to retaliation; and a simple fracture was compensated by a simple fracture, though the parties were allowed to compound if they preferred doing so.

The eighth table was equivalent to a Building Act; and by providing a space of two feet and a half between house and house, it prevented collisions among neighbours; while the fruit dropping from one person's tree into another's garden, fell by law into the hands of the latter.

The purity of justice was provided for by the ninth table, which ordered the execution of a judge who accepted a bribe in the execution of his office. It inflicted the same penalty on a corrupt arbitrator, or —that greater traitor still—the wretch who should deliver up a Roman citizen to the enemy.

The tenth table might teach a lesson to our own enlightened age, in which it is too generally the custom to waste in hollow and costly ceremonies over the dead, much that might be made serviceable to the living. More than twenty centuries have passed since the Roman lawmakers seeing how mourners might be caught by the undertakers in the traps and trappings of woe, limited to a certain sum the costs of a funeral. The outlay upon the "infernal deities," to whom sacrifices were made in those days, and to whom, therefore, we may compare the black job-masters of our own time, was also reduced to the very lowest figure. In measures of health the Romans were equally in advance of us; for we still accumulate our dead in the grave-yards of our towns, though by the laws of the twelve tables, burials within the city were prohibited.

The eleventh and twelfth tables have come down to us in such mere fragments, that it is difficult to make up an entire leaf from both of them put together. To the eleventh, is attributed the aristocratic provision against marriages between the patricians and the plebeians; but as the law could not always prevent a flame, it was at last found expedient to allow a match which was permitted five years later by the Lex Canuleia.*

Such is a brief account of the Laws of the Twelve Tables; which although cut up by the shears of time into very little bits, say much, in broken sentences, to the honour of their authors. Even as late as the days of Cicero, it was a part of a boy's education to learn these laws as a *carmen necessarium*—or necessary verse—though they were not necessarily in verse at all; for the better opinion is, that they were all in prose, and that they were, in fact, as free from rhyme as they were full of reason.

The Decemvirs had now completed their allotted task; but, though elected for a limited time, they seemed determined to remain in their offices after their office hours were fairly over. During the first Decemvirate the members had taken the Government alternately for twenty-four hours at a time, on the principle of every lucky dog having his day; but now the whole ten assumed, at once, the insignia of royalty. Unable to resist the fascination of the fasces, the Decemvirs were each of them preceded, when they walked abroad, by a bundle of those imposing sticks; the sight of which, at last, aroused public attention to the number of rods that might be in pickle for the backs of the people.

---

* "Law of the Twelve Tables," B.C. 450.   "Lex Canuleia," B.C. 445.

Murmurs at home were echoed by rumours of war abroad; the Æquians and Sabines had renewed their hostility; and the Decemvirs, who could not levy troops or money, summoned the country gentlemen from their seats out of town to their seats in the senate. Many honourable members protested strongly against the Government, but agreed to the necessary supplies; from which it seems that the practice of speaking one way and voting another is a very ancient one. The Decemvirs stuck to their places with an adhesiveness that might suggest a comparison with Roman cement, but for the fact that the adhesiveness is not uncommon in modern times, though the secret of the Roman cement has perished. Armies were despatched to meet the foe, the people having met the expenses, and Appius remained at home with one of his colleagues. The Roman forces abroad had to contend with internal as well as external enemies; for a venerable, but too garrulous soldier, one Dentatus, called also Siccius, was constantly declaring himself heartily sick of the tyranny of the Decemvirs. He had even talked of another secession of the plebs; and, to prevent him from taking himself off, a plan was formed to cut him off by a summary process. He received orders from his superior officer to go up the country, with a few others, and select a spot where a tent might be pitched, in the event of a pitched battle. His companions were assassins in disguise, who, on arriving at a lonely spot, threw off their masks, and appeared in their true features. They immediately fell upon the astonished Dentatus; who must have seen through his assailants before he died, for many were found perforated with the sword of the veteran.

While the rest of the Decemvirs were disgusting the people by their tyranny, Appius was proceeding to render himself one of those objects of contempt at which not only the Roman nose, but the nose of all humanity, was destined to turn up, and at which scorn was to point her imperishable finger-post.

A centurion, named Virginius, had an only daughter, named Virginia, whom her father, with a want of caution pardonable, perhaps, in a widower, permitted to go backwards and forwards alone through the public streets to a private day-school.* The young lady, in all the playful innocence of sixteen, was in the habit of dancing and singing along the thoroughfare, when the smallness of her feet, and the beauty of her voice, struck the eye and ear of Appius. According to some authorities, Virginia was attended by a nurse-maid; but it is scarcely necessary to remark, that the same fatal fascination, which in military neighbourhoods attracts female attention from children that ought to be, to men that are, in arms, was no less powerful in the Via Sacra than in Rotten Row,— by the banks of the Tiber, than on the shores of the Serpentine. One morning, as Virginia was passing through the market-place, on her way

* It seems, however, to have been the custom of the period for plebeians to send their daughters from six to sixteen to a scholastic establishment from about nine to-five; and it is ten to one that Virginia was a pupil at one of these cheap nursery grounds, in which young ideas were planted out for the purpose of shooting.

to the seminary, with her tablets and school-bag—or more familiarly speaking, her slate and satchel—on her arm, a minion, under the dominion of Appius, seized an opportunity for seizing the maiden by the wrist. The nurse was either absent, or more probably talking to one

Virginia carried off by a Minion in the pay of Appius.

of the officers on duty round the corner; for the fasces were as irresistible to the female servants of the day, as the honied words and oilskin capes of a similar class of officials at a much later period. Virginia screamed for assistance, and they only who have heard the cry of a female in distress, can imagine the shrillness of the shriek that rang through the market. Marcus—for such was the minion's name—was instantly surrounded by a circle of respectable tradesmen, who knew and desired to rescue Virginia. The smith, though he had other irons in the fire, left his bellows to deal Marcus a blow; the butcher, with uplifted cleaver, was preparing a most extensive chop; and the money-changer was just on the point of paying off the ruffian in a new kind of coin, when he declared Virginia to be his slave, and announced himself as the client of the dreaded Appius. At this formidable name, the smith's work seemed to be done, the butcher became a senseless block, and there was a sudden change in the note of the money-changer.

The officer on duty, who had arrested the attention of the nurse, being at length called away by some trifling charge, had left her at leisure to look after the more precious charge with which she had been entrusted. As those usually talk the loudest who do the least, the remonstrances of the female attendant were, no doubt, vehement in proportion to her neglect; and, indeed, the confusion created by the shrieks of the nurse was rather calculated to draw off the attention of the crowd from Virginia herself, who was carried away by Marcus, with an intimation that he should at once take the case before a magistrate. Among the other consequences of the neglect of the maid, was an attachment that had sprung up between the day-school miss and a young gentleman, named Icilius. This impetuous youth, having heard of what had happened, proceeded to the court at which the case was about to come on, and which was presided over by the tyrant Appius. Icilius prayed for an adjournment, on the ground of the absence of the young lady's father; and it was found impossible to resist the application of such an earnest solicitor. This point having been conceded, the friends of Virginia applied for her admission to bail; and there was such a general tender of securities among the throng, that Appius felt he could not calculate on his own security if he refused the request that had been made to him. The next morning the matter again came on, in the shape of a remanded case; and Virginius, who had been on duty with his regiment the day before, was now present at the hearing.

Had there been in those days the same love of the horrible that has prevailed in our own times, the startling incident of a girl killed by her own father, would have probably come down to us, through the medium of the fullest reports, amplified by "other accounts," and a long succession of "latest particulars." We must, however, on the present occasion, be satisfied with the merest summary; for the Romans, in the time of Appius, were equally destitute of relish for the details of the spilling of blood, and of "family Sunday newspapers," whose respectable proprietors are always ready to avail themselves of a sanguinary affair, with an eagerness that seems to show that they look upon blood as essential to the vitality of a journal, and involving the true theory of the circulation. It remains only to be told, that Virginius, after taking leave of his daughter, and finding her escape from the power of Appius impossible, stabbed her with a knife, snatched up from a butcher's stall, and, brandishing the weapon in the air, threatened perdition to the tyrant. Appius, at the sight of the blood-stained steel, felt his heart fluttering, as if affected by magnetic influence; and losing, for the time, his own head, he offered ten thousand pounds of copper for that of Virginius.*

It is the common characteristic of a moving spectacle to strike every one motionless; and the guards of Appius, when ordered to seize Virginius, found themselves fixed to the spot by so many stirring incidents. In vain did Appius call upon his clients and his lictors to do their duty. Among all his numerous attendants there was not a sole but shook in its shoe, while the tyrant trembled from head to foot with bootless anger. Urged at length by the commands of Appius, the officers attempted to clear the spot, when a severe scuffle ensued, and the authorities were assailed with all sorts of missiles. The market-place supplied abundance of ammunition. Ducks and geese flew in all directions. Some of the lictors found calves' heads suddenly lighting on their shoulders. Others, who were treated, or rather maltreated, with oysters, suffered severely from an incessant discharge of shells, and many received the entire contents of a Roman feast, *ab ovo usque ad malum*,—from the assault and battery of the egg, to the *malum in se* of a well-aimed apple. The stalls of the dealers in vegetables were speedily cleared of their contents; and a trembling lictor, smothered—like a rabbit—in onions, might be seen, trying to creep away unperceived, while others, who were receiving their desert in the form of fresh fruit, fled, under a smart shower of grape, from the fury of the populace. At length, the stock of the market being exhausted, the assailants had recourse to stones; and Appius, feeling that he was within a stone's throw of his life, entreated the lictors to remove him from the scene of danger. Four of the stoutest of his attendants, hoisting his curule chair on to their shoulders, made the best of their way home, where Appius at length arrived, with the apple of his eye damaged by a blow from a pear, his mouth choked with indignation and mud, his lips blue with rage and grape juice, his robe caked with confectionary, and his head, which had been made spongy with the loaves thrown at it, affected with a sort of drunken roll.† Such is the melancholy portrait which historical truth compels us to draw of the unhappy Appius, for whom, however, no pity can be felt, even though his case and his countenance presented many very sad features. The assault in

---

*   " Then up sprung Appius Claudius, ' Stop him—alive or dead,
            Ten thousand pounds of copper to the man who brings his head.' "—
                                        Macaulay's Lays of Ancient Rome.

† This description is not exaggerated, at least, if the authority of Macaulay is to be relied upon; and for the incidents of this remote period we are perhaps justified in trusting quite as much to the lay of the poet, as to any other source. The following lines refer to the state of Appius, when taken home, after the death of Virginia :—

        " One stone hit Appius in the mouth, and one beneath the ear,
        And ere he reached Mount Palatine he swooned with pain and fear.
        His cursed head, that he was wont to hold so high with pride,
        Now like a drunken man's, hung down, and swayed from side to side.
        And when his stout retainers had brought him to his door,
        His face and neck were all one cake of filth and clotted gore."

Appius Claudius punished by the People.

the market-place must have rendered it difficult for an artist of the day to have taken his likeness, after the carrots, whirling about his head, had settled in his hair, the rich oils having given to his Roman nose a touch of grease, and the eggs thrown by the populace, who continued to egg each other on, having lengthened his round cheeks into an oval countenance.

Having gained his palace, the wretched tyrant ran up stairs, in the hope that he might save himself by such a flight; but he was overtaken, and thrown into gaol, where he, who had hitherto been permitted to do precisely as he pleased, was allowed just rope enough to hang himself; a process, it is believed, he performed, though the subject is so knotty, that we are not prepared to disentangle it.

Virginius had returned to the camp, where the soldiers, having heard of the fall of the decemvir, proceeded to hit him, as usual, when down, renouncing the authority of Appius and his colleagues. The valour of the insurgents was, however, of a negative kind ; for in times of danger they seemed to think absence of body better than presence of mind, and their policy was to secede from the city. They withdrew to the Sacred Mount, where ambassadors from the Senate were sent after them, to see if matters might not be arranged ; when the popular chiefs, with a sort of one-sided liberality, in which some friends of freedom are too apt to indulge, asked an amnesty for themselves, and the immediate putting to death of the whole of the late government. The ambassadors, not liking a precedent, which might be applied to succeeding administrations, of which themselves might form a part, suggested the propriety of trying the decemvirs first, and executing them, if necessary, afterwards. It was some time before the friends of freedom and justice could bring themselves to consent to the trial preceding the punishment; but upon being assured that the decemvirs would have little chance of escape, it was at length agreed to allow them the preliminary forms of a trial.

The plebeians having got the upper hand, became almost as intolerant as the tyrants they had displaced,—a common error, unfortunately, among the professing lovers of liberty. They demanded that the Tribunes should be restored, which was well enough; that the Tribunate should be perpetual,—which was an insolent and overbearing interference with the will of any succeeding generation; and, by way of climax, they required that any one suggesting the abolition of their favourite office should be burnt as a traitor. They were no doubt fully justified in having a will of their own, but they had no authority to entail that will upon a subsequent age ; and least of all had they the right to make bonfires of those who were of a different way of thinking. It is true that, at such a moment, few are willing to put their lives literally at stake, by uttering their opinions ; but these arbitrary pranks, so frequently committed in the name of freedom, account sufficiently for the frequent use of the words " more free than welcome." The truth is, that when Liberty becomes a notorious public character, she seems to disappear from private life ; and, indeed, how is she to be found at home, if she is occupied out of doors, knocking off the hats of those who will not give her a cheer, or breaking the windows of those who will not illuminate in her honour?

The plebeians having gained the permission of the Senate to hang and burn to their hearts' content all who might give way to difference of opinion, under the weak-minded impression that it would never alter friendship, proceeded to the election of Tribunes in place of the Decemvirs, who were thrown into prison. This is said to have been the first instance of the incarceration of any one belonging to the patrician order; and the sensation in the upper circles was immense when they heard that a few exclusives of their own set were in actual custody. Some aristocratic families went into mourning on the melancholy occasion, and offered any fine, as a matter of course, for the release of their kindred.

Appius Claudius and Spurius Appius — probably an illegitimate member of the family—were thrown into the same cell, where, it is said, they made away with themselves or each other; but whether there is any truth in this story of the cell, or whether it is merely a cellular tissue of falsehood, it is difficult to decide, after so long an interval. The eight remaining Decemviri went into exile, or, in other words, were transported for life; while Marcus Claudius, who had claimed Virginia, repaired to Tibur, now Tivoli, and may be said to have taken his conscience out to wash in the famous baths of the neighbourhood. Other authorities say that he fled to avoid the ironing for life with which he had been threatened, or that he feared the mangling to which he might be exposed at home, at the hands of the infuriated populace.

Consuls had already been elected, in the persons of L. Valerius and M. Horatius; but ten Tribunes were now chosen, among whom, of course, were the leaders in the revolution; for it is a popular notion, that those who have overthrown one government, must necessarily be the fittest persons to construct another. It is, however, much easier to knock down than to build up; and those who have shown themselves extremely clever at bowling out, are often bowled out rapidly in turn, when they get their innings.

It is a characteristic of nations, as well as of individuals, that those who have no affairs of their own immediately on hand, are apt to concern themselves with the affairs of their neighbours. The Romans having arranged matters among themselves, began to look abroad, and having rid themselves of domestic foes, they sent their Consuls, L. Valerius and M. Horatius, to deal with foreign enemies. Valerius seized upon the camp of the Æqui, just as they were canvassing their prospects under their tents; and Horatius, after routing the Sabines, made them free of the city; thus converting into respectable tradesmen those who had been hitherto extremely troublesome customers.

When the Consuls returned to Rome, they expected the Senate would pay them the usual compliment of a triumph; and instead of entering the city at once, they put up at the temple of Bellona, outside the walls, waiting for orders. The patricians, who were jealous of the

generals, thought to deprive them of the customary honours, by a low
trick; but the tribes dealing more fairly with the warriors, or, to use a
familiar expression, lending them a hand, decreed the triumph which
the Senate had denied to them.   Thus did the patricians lose a privilege
they had abused; and the two Consuls drove four-in-hand into the city
in spite of them.

In the foreground of the Tableau may be observed a Patrician looking very black at the
Triumph of the General.

In modern times, the nearest approach we have to a triumph is the
entrance into a country town of a company of equestrians, or a travelling
menagerie.   The arrangements were in many respects suitable to a
fair, and it would seem to have been the opinion of the Romans that
none but the brave deserved the fair, for it was only the most eminent
warriors who were awarded the honours of a triumph.   There was,
however, something very undignified in the practice of hanging about
the outskirts of the town until regularly called in, which was the usual
course adopted by those who anticipated the glory of a summons from
the senate.   It sometimes happened that the summons never arrived,
and the General, who had hoped to make his entry in a chariot and
four, was at last compelled to sneak, unattended, into the city.   Such
might have been the lot of L. Valerius and M. Horatius, had it not
been for their popularity, aided, probably, by the senseless love of show,
which often causes the hero to be degraded into the mountebank.   As
triumphs, like Lord Mayors' shows, were nearly all the same, the following account will comprehend, or lead the reader to comprehend, the
general features of these military pageants.
     The procession opened with a band of trumpeters, and as much
breath as possible was blown out of the whole body.   Next came
some men with boards, inscribed with numerous achievements, and
forming, in fact, the posting bills, or puffing placards, of the principal

character.   These were followed by a variety of objects, taken from the
enemy, and may be compared to the properties used in the show, the
next feature of which was a file of flute-players, who walked in a sort of
fluted column.   Next in order came the white bulls, or oxen devoted
for sacrifice, accompanied by the slaughtering priests, or holy butchers;
and immediately afterwards a remarkable beast, odd fish, or strange

In all probability something of this sort.

bird, that had been snared, hooked, or caged, in the conquered country.
These were followed by the arms of the foe, with as many captives as
possible, in chains, and the larger the string of fettered victims, so
much the greater was the amount of "linked sweetness, long drawn out"
before the eye of the conqueror.   After these were carried the gifts the
General had received from allied or friendly powers, consisting usually
of crowns made of grass, every blade of which was a tribute to the
sword of the victor.   Next came a file of lictors, and then the General
himself, in a chariot and four, with a slave on the footboard behind,
whispering in his ear, to remind him of his being still "a man and a
brother."

The Consuls having gained a civil as well as a military triumph, by
their defeat of the patricians, would have been re-elected by acclamation
for another year; but they had the good sense to retire upon the popularity they had gained, without waiting to become bankrupt of that very
fleeting commodity.   The patricians, getting tired of an exclusiveness
which seemed likely to exclude them from real power, condescended to
vie with the plebeians as candidates for the office of Tribune.   They
judiciously came to the conclusion that it was better to cast their pride
under foot, than to stand too much upon their dignity; and the result
was, that, by the election of two of their order, they obtained a voice in
the new government.

Popular measures were now the order of the day; and C. Canuleius,
one of the tribunes, brought in a bill to legalise the connubium
between the Patres and the Plebs, so that the fathers of the senate

might marry the daughters of the people. This proposition for an enlargement of the connubial noose gave rise to several very knotty points, and to much opposition on the part of the patricians. The greater number of them believed themselves to be the essence of all that was rare and refined, until the more sensible portion of them perceived that the essence was growing rarer every day, and that unless it formed a combination with something more solid, it would all very soon evaporate. The law was accordingly allowed to pass; and by the timely application of some common clay, the roots of aristocracy were saved from the decay that had threatened them. Many of the patricians, who had long been wedded to old prejudices, found it far more agreeable to be married to young plebeians; and matrimony was contracted, or, rather, greatly extended, among the different classes of society.

The Reform party had now become strong enough to propose that one of the consuls should always be a plebeian; and though the Senate tried very hard to maintain the principle, that those only are fit for a snug place who have been qualified by a good birth, the tide of opinion had set in so strongly the other way, that it was hopeless, with the thickest sculls, to pull against the current.

Tribuni militum, with the power of consuls, were instituted; but the patricians managed, by a trick, to reduce these consuls into a sort of stock for their own use, by selecting from their own body two officers named Censors, who were to be employed in taking the census, an extremely important part of the consular authority. The mere enumeration of the people was not of itself a high privilege, and required no acquaintance with the law, or of any of the twelve tables, excepting, perhaps, the simple tables of arithmetic. Besides the privilege of looking after the numbers of the people, the office gave especial opportunities of looking after number one; for the administration of the finances of the state was committed to the Censor;* and it has too often happened that a collector of duties has considered that there was a duty owing to himself, out of those received on behalf of the Government. They were also Commissioners of the Property Tax, with full inquisitorial powers; but, most odious part of all, they had authority to ascertain the dates of the birth of females, as well as males, and could mercilessly surcharge a lady for her age, as well as her husband for his income. They were also controllers of virtue and morality, their duty being to maintain the *mos majorum*, or manners of the old school; for it seems to have been always the custom of mankind to lament the past as "the good old times," no matter how bad the old times may have been, and how infinitely inferior to the present.

The Censors, however, derived their chief influence from their power of determining the rank of every citizen; for, from the very earliest times,

* At a later period, the Censors had the entire control over the public expenditure, even to the feeding of the sacred geese; and there is no doubt that even the geese were made to yield a considerable nest egg to a dishonest functionary.

the multitude were in the habit of pursuing, through thick and thin, that perilous Will o' the Wisp—a wisp that reduces many a man of substance to a man of straw—a position in society. This the Censors could award; and people were ready to pay any price for that most costly of all stamps—though perhaps, after all, the most difficult to purchase—the stamp of fashion. From the early days of Rome to the present hour, we meet with frequent counterfeits of the stamp in question, the forgery of which has spoiled, and continues to spoil, a quantity of calves' skin, and asses' skin, that might otherwise be found of service, at least to its owners.

Rome had begun to enjoy a short repose, like an infant in its cradle, when it was unexpectedly made to rock to its very foundations, by a shortness of provisions; for the absence of anything to eat is sure to afford food to the disaffected. Grumbling is the peculiar attribute of an empty stomach; and flatulence, caused by hunger, is an ill wind, that blows good to nobody. During the scarcity, a wealthy citizen, one Spurius Maelius, anxious to give his fellow-citizens a genuine meal, purchased corn at his own expense, and sold it for a mere song—taking the produce, perhaps, in promissory notes—to his poorer countrymen. This liberality rendered Maelius extremely popular with all but the patricians, who declared that they saw through his design in selling cheap corn; that as old birds they were not to be caught with chaff: and that his real aim was the kingly dignity. Under the pretext of preventing him from accomplishing this object, the patricians appointed a Dictator; and poor old Cincinnatus, bowed down with age and agriculture, which had been his natural bent, was dragged from the tail of the plough to the head of the state, though his own state was that of extreme bodily decrepitude. His Master of the Horse, who really held the reins, was Servilius Ahala, by whom Maelius was summoned before the Dictator, to answer any charge that might be brought against him. If the mode of making the accusation was strange, the method of answering it was equally irregular; for Maelius, instead of meeting it with dignity, ran away from it, with a butcher's knife, which he snatched from a stall in the market-place. Flourishing the formidable weapon, he cut in among the crowd, and was immediately followed by Servilius Ahala, with a party of young patrician blades, who, in a manner that would have pierced a heart of stone, plunged their swords into their victim's bosom.

Ahala was charged with the murder, but he was enabled to avoid the consequences, as men of consequence in those days could do, by a voluntary exile. Though domestic cookery had received a check from the dearth at home, there was no scarcity of foreign broils, and the Romans created Mam. Æmilius dictator, to encounter the Fidenates and Veientines. Three ambassadors were sent to Fidenae, but the diplomatic service could not have been so desirable in those days as in our own, for the three ambassadors were slain, and perhaps the financial reformers would say that it was very proper to cut down such a piece of gross extravagance. The order emanated from Lar Tolumnius of Veii; and while it said little for his heart, it cost him his head, which was cut off by Cornelius Cossus—the master of the horse to Æmilius.

The Veientines continuing troublesome, Furius Camillus was appointed dictator, when, with an engineering talent rare in those days, he commenced a mine, and overcoming all minor, as well as major, or general difficulties, he forced a way into the city. The King of Veii was offering a sacrifice in the Temple of Juno, just as the Romans had completed their tunnel, and as the soldiers burst like a crop of early champions through the earth, he saw his fate written in bold Roman characters. Everything was given to the conquerors, and it is said that the statue of Juno, followed of its own accord ; but the probability is, the statue remained *in statu quo*, for miraculous instances of going over to Rome were not in those days numerous.

Rome was once more at peace, when the citizens, with peculiar ingratitude, having no other foes, began to quarrel with Camillus himself, to whom they owed their tranquillity. They accused him of having unduly trafficked in shares, by appropriating more than his due portion of the booty. His unpopularity had not, however, come down upon him until it was found that he had, in a fit of piety, dedicated a tenth of the spoils of Veii to the Delphic God—a circumstance he had forgotten to mention, until he had disposed of the whole of his own share of the prize, and it became necessary for the other participators in the plunder to redeem his promise at their own cost, and, with their own ready money, to save his credit. His name fell at once from the highest premium of praise to the lowest discount of disparagement, and he incurred the especial detestation of those whom he had served ; for kindnesses are often written in marble in the hearts of those who remember them only to repay them with ingratitude. Not liking to lie under the imputation of dishonesty, and being unable to get over it, he chose a middle course, and passed a sort of sentence of transportation upon himself by going into voluntary exile. He, however, with a littleness of mind that was not uncommon among the early Romans, vented his spite as he left the city gate, expressing a wish that Rome might rue his absence ; but Rome consoled herself for the loss she might sustain in him by confiscating the whole of his property.

Among the incidents of the life of Camillus, a story is told of an event that happened, when, after having subdued the Veientines, he drove the Faliscans out their city of Falerii. There existed within the walls a fashionable boys' school, to which the patricians sent their sons, who were frequently taken out walking in the suburbs. One morning the pupils, who were two and two, found themselves growing very tired one by one, for their promenade had been prolonged unusually by the pedagogue. The wretch and his ushers had, in fact, ushered the unsuspecting infants into the camp of Camillus, with an intimation that the parents of the boys were immensely opulent, that the schooling was regularly paid, and there could be no doubt that a

rich ransom could be procured for such a choice assemblage of fathers'
prides and mothers' darlings. Camillus nobly answered, that he did
not make war on young ideas not yet taught to shoot, and he concluded
by giving the schoolmaster a lesson ; for, causing him to be stripped, and
putting a scourge into the hands of the boys, the young whipper-
snappers snapped many a whip on the back of their master.

School-boys flogging the Schoolmaster.

CHAPTER THE NINTH.

FROM THE TAKING OF ROME BY THE GAULS, TO ITS SUBSEQUENT
PRESERVATION BY MANLIUS.

A Gaul.

As a prophet is sure to come right in the end, if he will go on prophesying a thing until it really happens; so the soothsayers, who had been constantly predicting the taking of Rome, seemed likely, at last, to have their forebodings verified.

The Gauls were destined to be the invaders, and tradition tells us that they were attracted to cross the Alps by the reputation of the Italian grapes, which induced them to expect a superior glass of wine on the other side of the mountains. The Gauls were remarkable for the hugeness of their bodies, which presented a series of gigantic pictures in their iron frames; and their faces being covered with long shaggy hair, they seemed ready, by their ferocious aspect, to beard an enemy. These people were the ancient inhabitants of modern France, and it is a curious fact, that the occupants of the country have, up to the present time, cultivated that hairiness of visage, in which they may be said to have literally aped their ancestors. Tradition—that wholesale carrier, who delivers so many parcels at the historian's door, some of which are scarcely worth the carriage—has handed to us a small packet, with reference to the Gauls and their origin, the contents of which we proceed to examine. On taking it up, we find that it possesses very little weight; but we, nevertheless, proceed to the operation of unpacking. Beginning as we would with a basket, we find ourselves hampered to a considerable extent, for on opening the lid, and using the eye of discernment, we turn over the contents with eagerness, and after all catch at little better than straw, in our attempts to take hold of something tangible. Turning over the flimsy mass, we arrive at very little of a solid description, though, on getting to the bottom of it, we establish the fact that the Gauls, under Brennus, their chief, marched upon Clusium, one of the states of Etruria. People in difficulties are apt to grow exceedingly amiable towards those who are in a position to help them ; the man of money becomes the very " dear Sir " of one who needs a loan, and the Clusians appealed to their " friends," the Romans, of whom they knew nothing, for their kind assistance.

The Roman Senate, adopting the quarrel of the Clusians, sent three ambassadors, the sons of M. Fabius Ambustus, to the Gauls, desiring them to withdraw ; but the Gauls sent back a very galling answer. They declared their own country was little, and their necessities were large ; that they had not land enough to supply them with bread ; and, though they wished not to tread on a neighbour's corn, they could not help feeling where the shoe was pinching. They added, that, as to Clusium, they did not want it all, but would willingly share it with its owners ; a proposition similar to that of a pickpocket, who, while robbing you of your handkerchief, politely offers you the joint use of it.

This arrangement not having been acceded to, the Clusians and the Gauls came into collision ; when the Roman ambassadors, who only went to have a few words, so far forgot their diplomatic character as to come to blows ; and, though it is not unusual for peace-makers to cause more mischief than they prevent, it was rather too much to find the pacificators, who had gone forth to knock discord on the head, engaged in fracturing the skulls of those whom they went to propitiate. One of the Fabii not only killed a Gallic chief, but, having made away with the individual, was making off with his arms and accoutrements ; when a cry of " shame ! " arose from the Gauls, who did not approve of an arrangement by which the envoy was killing several of them, while a delicate regard to the law of nations prevented them from killing the envoy. It is difficult for men to stand upon a point of etiquette when threatened with the point of the sword ; but the Gauls, with extreme moderation, resolved on sending envoys to complain of the envoys ; and thus, as it were, fight the ambassadors with their own weapons. The Roman Senate felt the justice of the complaint ; but, seeing that public feeling ran the other way, the Senators were base enough to do an injustice rather than make an honourable stand against the wilfulness of the people.

The Fabii, whom the Senate had been too cowardly to punish, the million thought proper to reward by appointing them Consular Tribunes for the year ensuing ; and when the news reached the Gauls, it excited in them a very natural bitterness. After their first burst of rage, they began to collect themselves ; and finding, when collected, they could muster 30,000 strong, they were joined by upwards of 40,000 Senones, in alliance with whom they reached Allia, a little stream flowing towards the Tiber. Here they were met by the Romans, who threw up entrenchments to prevent the enemy from entrenching upon their domain ; but being comparatively few in numbers, they endeavoured to spread themselves out as far apart as possible.

As a kettle of water thrown upon a spoonful of tea, with the intention of making it go further, produces a weakening effect; so did the expansion of the Roman line dilute its strength to such a degree, that the right wing became panic-stricken, and the left catching the infection, both wings began to fly together. Several of the Romans plunged into the Tiber, to save their lives, and the dux or general set the ignominious example. Some lost all self-possession, and fell helplessly into the possession of the enemy; while others finding their heads beginning to swim violently on shore, could not obtain the chance of safety by swimming across the river.

A few only of the soldiers got home in safety, soaked to the skin; and though there may be something ignoble in the picture of a party of Roman warriors dripping in their wet clothes, we are compelled to follow the dry threads of history. Those who escaped by means of the friendly tide, took the sad tidings to Rome, which would now have fallen an easy prey to the Gauls, had they not remained on the field of battle, uttering horrid yells, shaking their yellow locks, and intoxicating themselves with something more potent than the stream cup of success which they had quaffed so easily. When the bad news reached Rome, the citizens began to fly apace, and some were startled by their own shadows, as if, like guilty creatures, they were unable to bear their own reflections. Many of the patricians ran for safety into the Arx, or topmost part of the city, which was carrying cowardice to the utmost height; and some who tried to save their goods as well as their lives, packed their property in casks with the hope of preserving it.

On the arrival of the Gauls, they found the walls and the inhabitants completely unmanned, and though nearly every one who remained was somebody beside himself, the population had, owing to the foolish panic, been most sensibly diminished. Among those who remained were eighty old patricians, who had filled in their turns, the chief offices of state, and who, having sworn to die, took the oaths and their seats in the Forum. They wore their official robes, occupied their ivory chairs, and being carefully got up with venerable white beards, they had all the imposing effect of a *tableau vivant* upon the Gauls who entered the Forum. One of the barbarians, attracted by the singularity of the scene, stroked the beard of the aged Papirius to ascertain if he was real, when the aged P. having returned the salutation by a smart stroke with his sceptre, the inquisitive Gaul found his head and the charm broken together. Though the patricians had, at first, worn the appearance of mere wax-work, they now began to wax warm, which led to their speedy dissolution; for the Gauls, falling violently upon them, converted the whole scene into a chamber of horrors. The eighty senators were slain, to the immense satisfaction of the Romans themselves, who felt a conviction that after this alarming sacrifice they were sure of a triumph. They seemed to look upon the venerable victims as so much old stock that must be cleared off, and the previously depressed citizens began to rally with all the renewed vigour of a bankrupt who has just undergone the operation of an extensive failure. The Gauls invested the Capitol, but its defenders feeling that no one had a right to invest that Capitol but themselves, did their utmost to keep it standing in their own names; and, not even for the sake of ensuring their own lives, would they agree to an unconditional surrender. The barbarians, finding nothing better to do, commenced firing the city in several parts, pulling down the walls and throwing them into the Tiber; a species of sacking that must have been very injurious to the bed of the river.

The occupants of the Capitol continued to hold out, or rather, to keep in, and it being desirable to communicate with them, a bold youth, named Pontius Cominius, attempted the hazardous enterprise. Having encased himself in a suit of cork, he crossed the Tiber, and clambering on his hands, he performed the wonderful feat of reaching the Capitol. He returned in the same manner; and, on the following day the Gauls observing the track, thought to be all fours with him, by stealing up on the points of their fingers and the tips of their toes, to the point he had arrived at. With a cat-like caution, which eluded even the vigilance of the dogs, and while the sentinels were off their guard, a party of the Gauls crept up one by one to the top of the rock, which was the summit of their wishes. Just as they had effected their object, a wakeful goose,* with a head not unworthy of the sage, commenced a vehement cackle, and the solo of one old bird was soon followed by a full chorus from a score of others. Marcus Manlius, who resided near the poultry, was so alarmed at the sound that he instantly jumped out of his skin—for, in those days, a sheep's skin was the usual bedding—and ran to the spot, where he caught hold of the first Gaul he came to, and, giving him a smart push, the whole pack behind fell like so many cards to the bottom.

Manlius was rewarded with the scarcest luxury the city contained, in the shape of plenty to eat, and it cannot be said that we have greatly improved upon the early Romans in matters of the same kind, for a dinner is still a common mode of acknowledging the services of a public man, and literally feeding his vanity.

The Gauls continued to invest Rome, and heard with savage delight of the diminishing supplies, or rather, to use an Irishism, the increasing scarcity. News at last came that the garrison had been for some time living upon soles, and it is an admitted fact that they had consumed all but a few remaining pairs belonging to the shoes of their generals. Driven at length to desperation, they baked as hard as they could the flour they still had on hand, and making it up into quarterns, or four pounders, threw it at the enemy. The Gauls looked up with astonishment, when another volley of crust satisfied them that bread was coming " down again;" and not wishing to get their heads broken with the staff of life, which they fancied must be very plentiful in Rome, they offered

---

* These geese were sacred to Juno, who was the goddess of marriage; but we cannot say whether the goose became identified with her on that account.

terms of ransom. The price fixed upon was one thousand pounds of
gold, in the weighing of which the Gauls are said to have used false

The Citadel saved by the cackling of the Geese.

weights, but it is difficult to say what weight ought to be given to the
accusation. The story goes on to say that the Gallic king, on being
remonstrated with for his dishonesty, cut dissension short with his
sword, and throwing it into the scale with a cry of *Væ victis*, turned
the balance still more in his own favour.

In the meantime the Romans at Veii had called Camillus from exile,
and chosen him Dictator ; for it was the opinion of the day that good
use could always be made of a man after thoroughly ill-using him.
Camillus arrived at Rome just as the gold was being weighed, when he

declared that he would deliver his country, but would not allow the delivery of the treasure. He added, that the metal with which all claims upon Rome should be met was steel; that he cared not who might draw upon him, for he was ready, at sight, with prompt acceptance. While the discussion was proceeding, a Roman legion arrived; and the Gauls were driven out of the city, having lost not only their self-possession, but possession of the gold that had been assigned to them. On the road to Gabii a battle ensued, in which every Gaul, it it is said, was slain, not one being left alive to tell the tale; and as there are two sides of a story, as well as of a fight, it is impossible, in the absence of the other party, to say which side was victorious.

When the Romans returned to their city, they found it little better than a dust-heap, or a plot of ground on which a shooting party had met for the purpose of shooting dry rubbish. The people were called upon to rebuild their houses; but even in those days the principle of the proverb, that fools build houses for wise men to live in, appears to have been recognised. There was a general disinclination to dabble in mortar; and there seemed to be a conspiracy not to enter upon a plot for building purposes.

Rome seemed very unlikely to be built in that day; and it might never have been restored, had not an accident—on which they put an ominous construction—caused the citizens to proceed to the re-construction of their city. While Camillus was "on his legs" in the senate, a centurion, passing the House of Assembly with a flag in his hand, was heard to say, "Let us plant our banner here, for this is the place for us to stop at." The senators, rushing forth, declared their acceptance of the omen, though there was nothing ominous in the fact; and the people, carried away, or rather attracted to the spot, by the same stupidly superstitious feeling, declared that on that place they would rebuild the city. There is no doubt that the anxiety of the senators for the restoration of Rome was owing to the fact of their own property lying near at hand; and they were desirous, therefore, of improving the neighbourhood. There was very little patriotism, and a large amount of self-interest, in a suggestion that materially enhanced their own estates; and it was extremely easy to find an omen that would put twenty or thirty per cent. upon the value of their property. In pursuance of the "omen," they liberally gave bricks that did not belong to them, and followed up their munificence by allowing stone to be cut from the public quarries, in order that the works might be hastened; while, as a further act of generosity, it was permitted to the citizens to pull to pieces their houses at Veii, for the purpose of embellishing Rome and its vicinity. Speed being the order of the day, every other kind of order was neglected. All idea of a general plan fell to the ground, in consequence of every one having a ground plan of his own. The houses, instead of wearing the aspect of uniformity, showed a variety of faces, and told each a different story; while the streets were so constructed, with reference to the sewers, that the latter were as useless as if they had been devised by a modern commission.

Rome was still exposed to aggression on various sides from numerous foes; but Camillus, in his capacity of Dictator, first vanquished them, and then, admitting them to the franchise, received them in the light of friends, as if, like old carpets, a thorough beating brought them out in new colours. Whatever may be the fortune of war, it is its misfortune invariably to entail a heavy debt; and it is a truth of universal application, that a country, like an individual, no sooner gets into hot water, than liquidation becomes extremely difficult. Such was the case with Rome, where taxation became so high, that the poor were compelled to borrow of the rich, who, with the usual short-sightedness of avarice, added an exorbitant claim for interest to the principal debt, and thus, by insisting on both, got in most cases neither.

Manlius, whose quick apprehension of a goose's cackle had rendered him the deliverer of his country, was exceedingly hurt at the neglect with which he had been treated, though he had little cause of complaint; for his merit, after all, consisted chiefly in the fact of his living within hearing of the fowl-house. He was, however, jealous of the honours conferred on others; for he expected, no doubt, that the whole of the plumage of the sacred geese would have been feathers in his cap in the eyes of his countrymen. Seeking, therefore, another mode of gaining popularity, he cast his eye upon some unfortunate birds of a different description—the unhappy plebeians, who were being plucked like so many pigeons in the hands of their patrician creditors. He went about with purses in his hand, like the philanthropist of the old school of comedy, releasing prisoners for debt; and declaring his determination to extend his bounty to all who needed it. This advertisement of his intention brought crowds of applicants to his house; for there was always " a case of real distress " at hand, for the indulgence of one whose greatest luxury was the liquidation of other people's liabilities. The popularity of Manlius excited the jealousy of the patricians, who, not appreciating his magnanimity, thought him little better than a goose that was always laying golden eggs, and he retaliated upon them by declaring he had rather be a fool than a knave; that the money he disposed of was his own, but that they had grown rich upon gold embezzled from the price of the city's ransom. Their only answer to the charge was to get him thrown into prison for making it. The plebeians, finding their friend and banker in gaol, with nobody to pay their debts, were dissolved in tears—the only solvency of which they were capable. Some went into mourning, while those who could not afford it put on black looks, and threatened to release him from custody.

The Senate, unable to maintain any charge, and tired, perhaps, of the expense of keeping him in prison, sent him forth to maintain himself at his own charge; but his means having been greatly reduced, he found a corresponding reduction in his popularity. While his resources flowed in a golden stream, he was a rich pump that any one was ready to make a handle of; but no sooner did the supply fall off, and the pump cease to act, than he was left destitute of the commonest succour. He was eventually brought to trial; and being called upon for his defence, he produced four hundred insolvents whose debts he had paid—and who passed through the Court of Justice—as witnesses to his liberality. He then showed his wounds, which were not the sore places of which the patricians complained; and he ultimately pointed to the Capitol, in the preservation of which he had acquitted himself so well, that on the recollection of it, his acquittal was pronounced by the citizens. His persecutors, however, obtained a new trial, upon which he was condemned to death; and a slave having been sent with the despatch containing the news, proceeded to the despatch of Manlius himself in a treacherous manner. Proposing a walk along the cliff, under the pretence of friendship, the slave gradually got Manlius near the edge, until the latter suddenly found himself driven to the last extremity. Upon this he received a push which sent him down the Tarpeian Rock; and the man who pretended to have come as a friend, had been base enough to throw him over. The sudden idea of the traitor was afterwards carried into frequent execution; for the practice he had commenced, was subsequently applied to the execution of criminals.

After the death of Manlius, his house was levelled with the ground, and he himself experienced the fate of most men when thoroughly down, for he was repudiated even by his own family. The gens, or gents, of the Manlii, with a contemptible want of manliness, resolved that none of the members should ever bear the name of Marcus, which they avoided as a mark of disgrace, though at one time it had been a title of honour.

Rome seemed now to be declining, and going down all its seven hills at once; pestilence killed some, and gave the vapours to others, and the sewers no longer fulfilled their office, but overflowing, in consequence of the irregular rebuilding of the city, they threw a damp upon the inhabitants. The free population was growing daily less, while the number of patricians continued the same, and there seemed reason to fear that Rome would soon become one of those most inconvenient of oligarchies, in which there are many to govern and comparatively few to be governed. The " eternal city " was in danger of being prematurely cut off by an early decline, for its constitution was not yet matured; and though it had once been saved by mere quackery,* it was now to be preserved by a bolder and wiser regimen.

* See *ante*, the anecdote of the Sacred Geese.

CHAPTER THE TENTH.

FROM THE TRIBUNESHIP OF C. LICINIUS TO THE DEFEAT OF THE
GAULS BY VALERIUS.

Roman Soldier.

OME was now overwhelmed with debt, and fresh taxes were imposed to rebuild the wall of stone; but it would have been as easy to have got blood out of the stones themselves, as money from the pockets of the people. The more they went on not paying, the more were they called upon to pay; and ruin appeared inevitable, until it occurred to the great financial reformers of the day that there can be no permanent balance to the credit of a state without a due adjustment of the balance of power. Happily for the interests of humanity, there is scarcely ever a crisis requiring a hero, but there is a hero for the crisis,—no situation demanding a man, without a man for the situation; and though there may be on hand a formidable list of those who perpetually " Want places," we have the consolation of feeling that when there is a vacant place to be filled up, there is no lack of the material required to fill it.

The man for the situation in which Rome then happened to be, was a certain C. Licinius, who had married the younger daughter of the patrician, M. Fabius. The lady was considered to have wed below her station, and the Roman noses of her relatives were converted into snubs, by the habit of turning up for the purpose of snubbing her. Being on a visit with her sister, who was the wife of Servius Sulpicius, the Consular Tribune, she was one day alarmed by such a knocking at the door as she had never yet heard, and on inquiring the cause, she found that the lictors of old, like the modern footmen, were in the habit of estimating, by the number of raps he was worth, the dignity of their master. The elder Fabia, perceiving her sister's surprise, took the opportunity of administering a rap on the knuckles, through the medium of the knocker, and observed, that if the latter had not married a low plebeian, she would have been accustomed to hearing her own husband knock as loud, instead of being obliged to knock under.

The vanity of Fabia had received a blow which had deprived her of

H

sense; and the effect of the knocking at the door had been so stunning, that she could scarcely call her head her own. She was resolved that her husband should make as much noise in the world as her brother-in-law,—that he should gain an important post, and win the privilege of knocking as violently as he chose at his own threshold.

Miss Fabia, the Younger, astonished at the Patrician's double-knock.

Those who would supply a higher motive to the ambition of C. Licinius, have asserted that his wife must have been accustomed to the loud knockings at the house of her father, who had once been consul; but whether the young lady heard them, unless she remained at home to answer the door, may be an open question. Whatever may have been the spur used to stir up ambition in his breast, we, at all events, know the fact, that C. Licinius was elected a tribune of the people, in conjunction with his friend Lucius Sextius; so that even if the former were roused by the knocker, it is not likely that ambition was hammered into the latter by the same ignoble instrument.

Having obtained their places, they began to bid very high for popularity; but, like many other bold bidders in the same market, it was by no means at their own expense that they proposed to make their purchases. They introduced three new laws: the first, touching other people's money; the second, touching other people's land; and, in reference to both these matters, touching and taking were nearly synonymous.

The first of these laws related to the debts of the plebs, and fur nished an easy mode of payment, by providing that all the money paid as interest should be considered as principal. By this arrangement, if Spurius owed his tailor one hundred asses, and paid him five per cent., by way of interest, the tailor would, in thirty years, not only have had his debt cancelled, without receiving his money, but he would have to refund no less than fifty asses to Spurius.

This law was sure to obtain for its framers a certain kind of popularity; for as those who do not meet their engagements are always a numerous class, it is a safe clap-trap to legislate in favour of the insolvent classes of the community. C. Licinius became at once the idol of all those who were continually running into debt one day, and out of the way the next, and whose valour far outstripped the discretion of those who had trusted them.

The second law related to land, enacting that no one should occupy more than five hundred jugera, or acres, and that if he had a surplus, he should be deprived of it, for the benefit of those who wished to settle their own liabilities with other people's property. From this arrangement there was no appeal, for the land was taken away; and if the owner wished to complain, he had no ground for it.

The third law provided for the restoration of the Consuls, and stipulated that one should always be a plebeian; but the patricians, who wanted everything their own way, just as the plebeians wanted everything theirs, succeeded in putting a veto upon the propositions.

In the meantime, the people, placed between two parties—one of which was seeking popularity at any price, while the other was endeavouring to preserve its exclusive interests at any cost—were for eight years deprived of all benefit from either side; and though the public would have accepted a compromise, Licinius, who knew that when the point was settled his popularity would be on the wane, declared that they should either have all or nothing. This policy, which is the same as that of prohibiting a starving man from accepting a moderate meal, unless he is invited to a banquet, was well adapted to the purposes of those whose happiness depends upon the dissatisfaction of all around, and to whom the success of all their avowed designs is the consummation of failure.

As long as the bills continued to be thrown out year after year, C. Licinius and Sextius were pretty sure of their annual election to the tribuneship. At about the end of the fifth year, the opposition began to wane, and it became exceedingly likely that the three bills would pass, when Licinius kept the popularity market brisk, by proposing a fourth measure, which was sure to be strenuously objected to. This was a proposal to put on eight new hands to the keeping of the Sibylline books, by increasing from two to ten the number of the librarians. As the books were but three, there would, of course, be no less than three book-keepers and a fraction to each volume,—an arrangement as objectionable as pluralism, though in an opposite direction; for it is scarcely worse to give ten offices to one man, than to put ten men into one office. Excuses were, however, found for the suggestion, on the ground that as five of the book-keepers were to be plebeians, the skill they would acquire in the interpretation of auguries would qualify a larger number for the consulship; the patricians having maintained that at least a smattering of the fortune-telling art was required for the due execution of the office.

Rome was now suffering from domestic wounds, when, fortunately, a little counter-irritation was got up, by an attack of the Veliternians on Tusculum. There is no better cure for a family quarrel, than the sudden incursion of a neighbour; and when relatives are breaking each other's heads at Number One, a stone thrown from the garden of Number Two will frequently, by the establishment of a single new wound, be the cause of healing half-a-dozen. The threatened aggression from without had caused the ten Tribunes to agree to the measures of their colleagues, Licinius and Sextius; but the patricians still held out, and appointed the veteran Furius Camillus to the dictatorship. The tribes were in the act of voting, when Furius ordered them away, with violent menaces; but the fury of Furius was impotent from age, and the Tribunes coolly threatened him with a fine of five hundred thousand asses. They had come to the correct conclusion that he could not get together so many asses without selling himself up; he thought it better to abdicate, and P. Manlius was chosen to stop the fermentation that the sour old man had created.

The bills were now all passed; and L. Sextius had been appointed plebeian consul, when the patricians, refusing to sanction what they could not prevent, declined to ratify the election. As the avalanche does not wait for the consent of the object it is about to sweep away, so the will of the public overcame the feeble opposition of the patricians. The latter, however, succeeded in taking a large portion of power from the consuls, and giving it to a new magistrate, called a Prætor, who was invested with authority that some historians have described as almost preternatural. He was chosen from the patricians, and was, in fact, a sort of third consul, whose duty it was *Jus in urbe dicere*,* to lay down the law—a privilege that, if improperly exercised, might include the prostration of justice—in the city. The patricians thus kept to themselves the power of interpreting the law; and as ambiguity seems inherent in the very nature of law, almost any latitude was left to those who were at liberty to declare its meaning. The power of the patricians was further augmented by the appointment of two curule or aristocratic Ædiles, in addition to the two chosen from the plebeians; and though their duties related chiefly to the mending of the roads, they had opportunities of paving the way for many encroachments on the part of their own order.

The struggle between the patrician and the plebeian parties was severe, and each endeavoured to represent itself as the only real friend

---

* Livy, vi., 42.

of the people.   Among other acts, in the interest of the masses, was a measure introduced by C. Poetelius, consisting of a *lex de ambitû*, an election law, relating to the getting round, or circumventing, of the electors by the candidates.   It will astonish those acquainted with election practices to be told, that the word " candidate " is derived from *candidus*, in allusion to the white robe usually worn as an emblem of purity by the seeker of popular suffrages.   The white robe, however, was notoriously, in many cases, a white lie, and the law *de ambitû* was passed to prohibit canvassing on market-days, when many more things were purchased than the articles ostensibly sold ; and the butcher has been known to include in the price of a calf's head, the value he placed upon his own judgment.

The cause of reform made slow but inevitable progress, though it was occasionally discredited by some of those incidents which still cause us to look well to our pockets in the presence of the professional lover of liberty.   C. Licinius, the framer of the law against occupying more than a certain quantity of the public land, was, it is said, the first to pay the fine, for holding a double allowance, comprising five hundred jugera in his own name, and five hundred in that of his son ; a piece of duplicity which was detected and duly punished. Other instances of private peculation were discovered among those most clamorous for the public good ; and it became necessary in those days, as in our own, to look among the loudest talkers for the smallest doers, and the greatest doos of the community.

The law of debt had been rendered somewhat less severe ; but the impossibility of permanently helping those who could not help themselves was strikingly exemplified.   The rate of interest had been reduced ; and advances were to be made by the State to those who could give security ; but those who could give none were to have no assistance whatever.   To those who could pay no interest at all, it mattered little whether the interest was moderate or high ; and an extension of time for discharging a debt, in the case of a man who could pay nothing, was only like lengthening the rope with which he was to hang himself.

In the year of the City 390, a plague broke out in Rome, and the calamity, which swallowed up thousands, being ascribed to the gods, repasts were prepared for them, under the title of *lectisternia*, in order to draw off their appetites from the people.   The richest luxuries were laid out upon tables, to which the gods were invited ; but these tables caused no diminution in the tables of mortality.   As the guests did not accept in person the invitations addressed to them, they were represented by images ; but this imaginary attendance at a real feast fed nothing but the superstition of the people.   A statue of Jupiter was laid, at full length, upon a couch of ivory, covered with the softest cushions ; but it was found impossible to produce the sort of impression that was so earnestly desired.   Chairs were also set round for the goddesses, but none came forward to take the chair at this unfortunate

banquet.   An effort was then made to divert the attention of the gods,
by getting up stage plays, or histriones : * but the gods did not patronise
the drama in those days, more than in our own ; and whether the
Olympian dinner-hour interfered, or whether no interest was felt in an
entertainment translated from Etruria, as the English drama is from
France, the result was the same in both cases, for the plays, during
their short-lived career, were dead failures.   To add to the misery
of the whole affair, while the stage performances were unattended,
there was an inconvenient "succession of overflows" of the Tiber's
banks, which damped the spirits and deluged the houses of the
inhabitants.

Seizing hold of every piece of superstition, instead of taking the
pestilence fairly in hand, the Romans, hearing that a plague had once
been stopped by knocking a nail into the wall of a temple, resolved on
going on that absurd tack ; and, for this purpose, a hammer was put
by the ninny-hammers into the hands of Manlius.   As the pestilence
had by this time begun to wear itself out, the people were foolish
enough to suppose that the plague had been driven in with the nail ;
and Manlius having fulfilled the task, which any carpenter might have
performed, resigned the dictatorship.

It is always the fate of a real or supposed benefactor of the public to
have plenty of private foes ; and, indeed, an elevated position is usually
an inviting mark for the arrows of malevolence.   Manlius became a
target forthwith ; and, had the very bull's eye been aimed at, the apple
of his eye could not have been more effectually hit, than by a wound
sought to be inflicted on him, through his son Titus.   The youth had,
it seems, an unfortunate hesitation in his speech, which irritated his
hasty parent ; and as the boy could scarcely stammer out a word, a few
words with his father became a very frequent consequence.   As he
laboured so much in his speech, the unhappy lad was sent to labour
with his hands among the slaves ; and Pomponius, the plebeian
tribune, having a spite against the father, began to regard the son with
the most enlarged benevolence.

Pomponius, by way of prosecuting his vindictive plans, resolved on
prosecuting Manlius, for cruelty to his son ; but the boy, in a powerful
fit of filial piety, though he had a considerable hesitation in his own
delivery, had no hesitation whatever about the delivery of his father
from the hands of his enemies.   Proceeding to the house of Pomponius,
under the cloak of friendship, and with a dagger under his cloak, he
desired to speak with the Tribune, who was still in bed, and not being
up to the designs of Titus, ordered his admission to the chamber.
The young man had been received in a spirit of friendly confidence by

---

* The word "Histriones" is said to be derived from the Etruscan *hister*, a dancer.
The earliest performers introduced into Rome were dancers—in fact, a ballet company—
from Etruria.   Those sensitive admirers of the purely classical in the entertainments of
the stage, who clamour against opera and ballet, will, perhaps, be surprised to learn that
the most truly classical performances are those which they most energetically protest
against.

Pomponius, who only discovered that young Manlius was at daggers-drawn, when he was seen to brandish a glittering weapon.   He demanded an unconditional withdrawal of the charge against his father; when the terrified Tribune, finding it impossible to bolster up his

Titus threatening Pomponius.

courage, muttered a promise to stay all proceedings; and Titus, who had formerly irritated his father by stammering, was received with open arms, for having spoken out so boldly in his favour.

No sooner were the divisions of the people healed, than the city itself began to be torn to pieces in a most extraordinary manner. Rome was convulsed to its centre: the earth began to quake, and the citizens to tremble.   A tremendous chasm appeared at length in the Forum; and as the abyss yawned more and more, it was thought unsafe for the people to go to sleep over it.   Some thought it was a freak of Nature, who, as if in enjoyment of the cruel sport she occasioned, had gone into convulsions, and split her sides.   Others formed different conjectures; but the chasm still remained,—a formidable open question. Some of the people tried to fill it up with dry rubbish, but they only filled up their own time, without producing the least effect upon the cavity.   In vain did the largest contractors undertake the job, for it was impossible to contract the aperture, that, instead of being small by degrees and beautifully less, grew every day large by fits and starts, and horribly greater.

At length the augurs were consulted, who, taking a view of the hole, announced their conviction that the perforation of the earth would continue, and that, in fact, it would become in time a frightful bore, if the most precious thing in Rome were not speedily thrown into it. Upon this, a young guardsman, named Marcus Curtius, fancying there could be nothing more precious than his precious self, arrayed himself in a full suit of armour, and went forth, fully determined to show his metal. Notice was given that at an appointed time a rapid act of horsemanship would be performed by M. Curtius; and as there is always great attraction in a feat which puts life in jeopardy, the attendance, at a performance where death for the man and the courser was a matter of course, was what we should call numerous and respectable. All the rank and fashion of Rome occupied the front seats, at a spectacle throwing every thing else into the shade, and the performer himself into the very centre of the earth, which was to prove to him a centre of so much gravity. Having cantered once or twice round the ring, he prepared for the bold plunge; but his horse having looked before he leaped, began to plunge in a different direction. Taking another circuit, M. Curtius, spurred on by ambition, put his spurs into the animal's side, and the poor brute was hurried into the abyss, though, had there been any way of backing out, he would have eagerly jumped at it. The equestrian performance was no sooner over, than the theatre of the exploit was immediately closed, and a lake arose on the spot, as if to mark the scene as one that might command a continued overflow. The place got the name of the Lacus Curtius, in honour of the hero, if such he may be called; and his fate certainly involved the sacrifice of one of the most precious articles in Rome, for it would have been impossible to find in the whole city such a precious simpleton.

Rome continued at war with the Gauls, who made frequent inroads; and on one occasion, during the dictatorship of T. Quinctius Pennus, came within a short distance from the city. The two armies were divided by the Anio, when the Gauls, who had a giant in their van, sent him on to the bridge, with an offer to fight any one of the enemy. The Gaul being at least twenty stone, was far above the ordinary pitch; but Titus Manlius, a tight-built light-weight—the plebeian pet, who had already proved himself too much for the Tribune, Pomponius—came forward to accept the polite offer of the giant. The fight was one of extreme interest, and both parties came up to the encounter with surly confidence. The plebeian pet wore a suit of plain bronze; but the giant was painted in various colours, presenting a formidable picture. The giant aimed the first blow with his right, but the young one having got away cleverly, commenced jobbing his opponent with such effect, that the latter, finding it a bad job, fell heavily. The giant was unable to continue the contest, and young Manlius, taking the collar, or torques, from his victim's neck, got the title of Torquatus, which, from its connection with his neckcloth, descended to his domestic ties, and became a stock name in his family.

The gallant Curtius leaping into the gulf.

The Gauls retreated for a while, but having subsequently joined the Volscii, they got into the Pontine Marshes, and resolved to go through thick and thin for the purpose of attacking the Romans. Again a giant appeared in the Gallic ranks, where, it would seem, a giant was

Terrific Combat between Titus Manlius and a Gaul of gigantic stature.

always to be found,—an appendage indicating less of the brave than of the fair in the composition of the Gallic army. Again a young Roman was ready to meet an opponent twice his size; and Marcus Valerius declared that if the giant meant fighting, he, Marcus Valerius, was to be heard of at a place agreed upon. The terms were concluded, and the giant came up, with the appearance of contemplating mischief, when a crow, settling on the Gaul's helmet, by way of crest, soon enabled the Roman to crow over his crest-fallen antagonist. The bird, flapping his wings whenever the giant attempted to hit out, put so many feathers in his face as to render his position ticklish; and as he could not see with a bundle of crow-quills in his eye, his look-out became rather desperate. Valerius, in the mean time, laid about him with such vigour and effect, that the giant, who was doubly blinded with rage and feathers, knew not where to have him. The contest soon terminated in favour of the Roman youth, who took the name of Corvus, or the Crow, from the cause already mentioned. The Gauls were vanquished, and Valerius was awarded no less than ten prize oxen; so that he obtained in solid beef, rather than in empty praise, an acknowledgment of his services. At his triumph, 4000 Volscians were drawn up on each side of him in chains; but there is something in the idea of his passing through this Fetter Lane which is repugnant to our more civilised notions of true glory.

CHAPTER THE ELEVENTH.

FROM THE FIRST WAR AGAINST THE SAMNITES TO THE PASSING OF
THE LAWS OF PUBLILIUS.

THE Romans were now about to encounter a truly formidable foe, in the
Samnites,—a warlike people, who had
been extending their territory, by going
to great lengths. and allowing themselves extraordinary latitude. Coming
down upon Campania, they overlooked
Capua, or rather they did not overlook
it; for, having an eye to its wealth,
they resolved to do their utmost to
become possessed of it. Under these
circumstances, the Campanians, being
unable to find the means of a successful campaign, applied to Rome for
assistance.

Two consular armies were equipped; one under M. Valerius Corvus,
or the Crow, who was really ravenous for glory, and the other under
A. Cornelius Cossus; this A. Cossus being in fact THE Cossus already
spoken of.*

Corvus was an enormous favourite with the soldiers; less, however,
on the strength of his moral qualities, than on the strength of his arms
and legs; for he was an athlete of remarkable power. He could leap
so high as to be able to jump over the heads of others of his own standing; and the rapidity of his promotion is therefore not astonishing. He
was no less light with his tongue than with his legs; for he could run
on almost as pleasantly with the former as he could with the latter.
He was, in fact, an agreeable rattle, who could make and take a joke
with equal ease,—a quality common in more modern times; for those
who profess to make jokes of their own are very much in the habit of
taking those of other people. He loved a glass of wine, and could
drink it without professing his connoisseurship, after the manner of those
learned wine-bibbers of the present day who are addicted to talking so
much unmeaning buzz on the subject of bees-wing. His relish for the
grape allured him to Mount Gaurus, then clad with vines, where he
could take his observations among the raisins, and make in his mind's
eye a sort of *catalogue raisonnée* of the enemy.

On this spot a battle ensued, which was fought with such fierceness on

* *Vide* page 87.

the side of the Romans, that the Samnites afterwards declared they had seen fire in their opponents' eyes; but the Samnites must have been light-headed themselves, so have made so absurd a statement. Valerius having been thus far successful, advanced into the Apennines, where, what are called the mountain fastnesses, are rendered dangerous by those occasional loosenesses of the earth that give rise to, or cause the fall of, an avalanche. Though nothing of this sort fell upon him, he was expecting the descent of the foe, which suddenly appeared on the topmost heights, and came down with such a run, that the escape of the Romans seemed impossible. In this difficult dilemma, a subordinate officer proved to be the safeguard of the whole Roman army; and as the noble lion, when netted to the profit of a bold hunter, was delivered by a mouse, so was the noble-hearted Valerius indebted to P. Decius Mus for the safety of himself and his followers. P. Decius laid, in fact, a snare for the Samnites, who were caught in this trap of Mus, or military mouse-trap. He climbed, with a little band, a height so narrow, that large numbers could not reach it to dislodge him, though it was necessary to keep an eye upon him; and, while the Mus attracted the cat-like vigilance of the whole Samnite army, Valerius and his followers were allowed to steal away unperceived to their own quarters.

When the enemy, tired with watching, had fallen asleep, Mus crept out, as quietly as his name would imply, and reached his camp in safety. He received immediately from the Consul an ox, with gilded horns, through which he might trumpet his fame; and the soldiers presented him with a *corona obsidionalis*—a crown made of blades of grass—in commemoration of their having been gallantly rescued from the blades of the enemy. The materials for a crown of this description were plucked on the spot, in memory of the pluck shown on the spot by the gallant recipient. Such a crown conveyed a finer lesson of morality than anything that the cold brilliance of gold or jewels could suggest; for the wreath of grass, converted, by the very sunshine in which it basked, into the dry and lifeless hayband, told, in a few hours, the perishable nature of glory.

Aided by the manœuvre of the Mus, the success of Valerius was complete: the Samnites fled in such consternation that they left behind them 40,000 shields and 170 standards; so that the Romans must have found the way literally paved with the flags of the vanquished. A triumph was decreed to both the Consuls, and foreign nations sent to congratulate the Romans on their success; the Carthaginians forwarding a crown of gold, twenty-five pounds in weight, the mere cartage of which from Carthage must have been costly and difficult. Compliments poured in upon the conquerors from every side; for good fortune increases the number of addresses to a state, just as the success of an individual causes a sensible, or rather a senseless, addition to the contents of his card-basket. Rome was inundated with calls upon her—many of which were for assistance from feeble countries, whose weak states seemed to be threatened with speedy dissolution.

It was about this time (B. C. 342) that the garrison at Capua broke out into revolt, arising, it is said, from the fact that Capua was extremely rich, and the soldiers very poor; that the latter were hopeless debtors, and forgot what they owed their country in the vast sums they owed to their creditors. The story goes on to say, that a corps of heavy insolvents first originated the idea of sacking the city and bagging its wealth, by placing it among their own baggage. The Consul, C. Martius Rutilius, was sent to take the command, and he attempted the soothing system; but the soldiers were goaded with the fetters of debt, and refused to be smoothed over, or to submit to remain under irons. Being in want of a leader, they seized on T. Quinctius, an aged veteran, whose head was so completely bowed down, that he could not do otherwise than bow when asked if he would lead them as their general. The nod of palsy was interpreted into the nod of assent, and T. Quinctius was selected to oppose Corvus, or the Crow, though the only chance for the veteran was, that in the capacity of a scare-crow he might succeed in

A Scare-crow.

frightening his antagonist. The armies at length met, when the insurgents, led by a shivering veteran, began to follow their leader, and to shake with fear, which induced Valerius to offer them terms, and the quaking Quinctius was the first to recommend his troops to accept an amnesty. Thus ended an insurrection, of which the motive appears vague, and the management thoroughly contemptible. The best opinion of its origin seems to be, that the army abounded in debtors, who were afraid to go home, and who preferred the chances of a mutiny to the certainty of having to meet their creditors. The only concession they asked was the cancelling of all their debts ; a proposition that savours rather of the swindler than the patriot. It is, however, an almost universal fact, that the insolvent classes of a community are to be found in opposition to the constituted authorities ; and, indeed, the strength or weakness of such an opposition is no bad test, after all, of the merits of an administration ; for if the majority of the people are well-to-do, the inference must be favourable to the government.

Peace was concluded with the Samnites, but Rome was now on the brink of a war with the Latins, who sent ambassadors, proposing that the two people should henceforth be considered as one, in order to establish their unity. The Senate was to be half Latin and half Roman ; but the latter declared they would not recognise this sort of half and half in any of their measures. The Consul, T. Manlius, when he heard the terms, went off into a series of clap-traps, in which he knew he was perfectly safe ; for the contingency in which he might have been called upon to keep his word, was not at all likely to happen. He exclaimed, that if the Senate should be half Latin, he would enter the assembly with his drawn sword, and cause vacancies in half the seats of the house by slaying all the Latin occupants. This species of paulo-post-future patriotism is equally common and convenient, for it pledges the professor to do nothing until after the doing of something else, which, in all probability, may never happen. T. Manlius was not put to the test, though he certainly proved himself, in some respects, ready for the Latins, had they come on in earnest ; for poor Annius, their spokesman, having tumbled down stairs from top to bottom, the consul brutally chuckled over the weak legs of the unhappy legate. " Ha ! ha ! " roared Manlius, with savage mirth, " thus will I prostrate all the Latins ; " and he proceeded to kick at the ambassador, who, being a man of several stone, was completely stunned by his too facile descent from the upper landing to the basement of the Temple of Jupiter.

The two Consuls went forth to fight, and both commenced their campaign by going to sleep, which led naturally to the inquiry, what they could both have been dreaming about. So thoroughly sympathetic were they in their drowsiness, that they had dreamed precisely the same dream, in which each had seen a ghost, who had addressed both in the same spirit. The spectre, who was decidedly on the shady side of existence, professed through his lantern jaws to throw a light upon Rome's future destiny. He told the Consuls that the general on one side was doomed ; but, as this was merely dealing with generalities, he went on to add, that the whole army on one side was to be buried in the earth ; a suggestion neither side would be very anxious to fall in with. The spectre, who was rather more communicative than spectres usually are, and who was not so monosyllabic as a fair average ghost, proceeded to further explanations, in the course of which he remarked, that " the general who first devoted himself to the infernal gods, would, by that act of devotion, consign the whole of the opposing army to " a most unpleasant neighbourhood. Both agreed that the one whose army was the first to back out, should be the first to rush into danger. The hostile armies accordingly began to recede as far as they could, and the only contest was to ascertain who could be the cleverest and quickest in walking in one direction, whilst looking in another. It was an understood thing that nobody was to fight unless first attacked, and the general aim was to avoid aiming at anything. Foraging parties went out daily to try and provoke each other to an onslaught, and the prevailing sentiment on both sides was a hope, that " somebody would only just do so and so." Titus Manlius, the son of Torquatus, approached the Latin camp, when Metius, of Tusculum, attempted by all sorts of provoking signals to induce the raw youth to commence a combat; but the

Metius aggravating Titus Manlius.

boy for some time combated nothing but his own inclination, which would have set him on to an onset. At length he became so irritated that he could restrain himself no longer, but hurling his javelin with all his might, it stuck in the mane of the horse of Metius. The poor brute, looking for sympathy to his master, fell back upon him for protection; but this act of affectionate confidence was fatal to Metius, who, being brought to the ground, was saddled with the whole weight of the unfortunate quadruped. Titus, taking advantage of the position of Metius, stabbed him with his sword, and the latter, feeling himself pierced, could only set up a piercing cry, by way of retaliation upon his antagonist. Having stripped off the armour of his victim, young Titus bore it in triumph to his father, Torquatus Manlius, who proceeded to imitate Brutus; but, like most imitations, the appearance of T. Manlius in the part of the "heavy father" was by no means successful.

Collecting the troops by the sound of trumpet, so that the audience might be sufficiently large, he threw himself into an imposing attitude; but the imposition was seen through, and the reception he met with was far from flattering. He next called forward his son, and denouncing him as an officer who had disobeyed his governor in a double sense— his father and his consul—the lictors were ordered to proceed, by the execution of the son, to the execution of their duty. Manlius, having witnessed the ceremony, buried his face in his toga, expecting at least three rounds of applause; but the performance fell as dead as his unhappy offspring. On his return to Rome he was universally cut by the young men, who were peculiarly alive to a penalty that might be the death of any one of them. The remains of young Manlius were collected into a dreary pile, and the trophies he had illegally won were added as the materials for a bonfire. His obsequies were the first of the same kind among the Romans that we have been able to meet with, after a truly industrious analysis of every hole in which the dust of ages might be found, and a careful sifting of the ashes of antiquity.

The two armies were still standing, when Decius Mus, who was most anxious to distinguish himself, and was watching intently to discover which way the cat would jump, observed a backward movement among his spearmen. His opportunity for glory had now arrived, and the gallant Mus, rushing recklessly to the scratch, behaved himself less like a mus than a lion in the conflict. He fell under a perfect shower of javelins, and lay on the field literally *piqué* with the pikes of his enemies. The latter were dismayed, and his own friends animated by what had taken place; but the rule of contraries must here have prevailed, for the death of an adverse general should not have disheartened the Latins, while the sacrifice of their own chief was, if looked at in a proper light, but poor encouragement for the Romans. They, however, grew bold; but it was scarcely necessary for them to strike a blow, as the Latins yielded under the stroke of a panic. They fell in such numbers, that three parts are said to have perished, and only a fourth of the army remained to tell of the little quarter allowed them by the enemy.

The Latins suffered so severely from the victory of Decius Mus, that like rats running from a tottering house, their allies, one by one, fell away from them. Numisius, the Latin commander, did his utmost to stir up the spirit of the nation; but the spirit was so thoroughly weakened by cold water, that it was the act of a spoon to endeavour to agitate so feeble a compound. He succeeded in raising a slight ferment-ation, but what little spirit remained, went off by speedy evaporation in the process of warming up, under the influence of patriotic fire. A small and disorderly band, which could not act in concert, was brought into play, but produced no effect, though it was conducted by Numisius with considerable energy. The Romans succeeded on every side, the Latin army was broken down, the confederacy broken up, and one town after another showed a preference for the better part of valour by surrendering at discretion. The land taken from the conquered was distributed among the Roman people; but the word " people " has frequently a very contracted meaning when profits are being shared, though the term is comprehensive enough to take in a whole nation when the services of the " people " are required. It is to be feared the people who went out for the fight were far more numerous than those who came in for the spoil that had been got by it.

The beaten Latins had the additional mortification of having to pay their successful assailants; an arrangement as provoking as it would be to the victim of an assault to be obliged to discharge the amount of the penalty, in addition to suffering the inconvenience of the outrage. Thus was Capua compelled to pension 1600 Campanian knights; and this pension the Capuans had to give to the knights, simply because the knights had, in a different sense, given it—severely—to the Capuans. It is doubtful whether the Samnites took anything by the general adjustment—if that can be called an adjustment in which justice had little share; but that they left much behind them is quite notorious.

Among their equipments for battle had been several gorgeous gold and silver-mounted shields, in the shape of a boy's kite, and as the Samnites ultimately protected themselves by flying, the kite-like form of their shields was thoroughly appropriate. Their breasts were covered with sponge, which gave them a soft-hearted air; and the sinking of their bosoms under nearly every blow, was clearly perceptible. They wore a shirt of mail, composed of brazen scales, and the display of so much metal in their shirts enabled them to present at times a bold front to the enemy. They had greaves upon their legs, which were a grievous impediment to their running away; and their helmets, adorned with lofty plumes, only served to render more conspicuous in defeat their crest-fallen condition. They wore tunics or coats of cotton next their skin, and put on their shirts outside; but between these, was a short garment of wool : so that the only idea we can give of the mode of making a Samnite *toilette* is by asking the reader to begin by putting

I

on his coat; to place over that his flannel waistcoat, and to add his shirt by way of finish.

Among the other spoils of the war with the Latins, were the ships taken from the port of Antium; but the Romans, who were not a nautical people, had so little idea of the value of a fleet, that they carried the beaks or prows of the vessels to Rome, and fixed them in the Forum, as pulpits for their orators.* How the ships could have kept above water when subjected to mutilation, it is difficult to conceive; and indeed it would appear probable that having been deprived of their heads, they must have gone down, as a matter of stern necessity. We must, however, do the Roman people the justice to add, that two officers had been appointed to the superintendence of naval affairs; and some will declare they see in the mere existence of an Admiralty Board sufficient to account for much extravagance, and all sorts of blundering. Rome had hitherto been in the condition of a house divided against itself, or rather of the adjoining houses pulling against each other, and every widening of the breach must of course have been attended with danger to both of them. The cessation of war with the Latins enabled Rome to draw closer the neighbouring social fabric, and many of its inhabitants were invited to join, and make themselves part of the family of the Romans. The latter also began to see the impolicy of keeping up certain distinctions between class and class, which have the same effect upon a nation, as the bitter feuds between separate floors are likely to produce upon the happiness and comfort of a lodging-house. When an upstart one-pair-front sneers at its own back, or looks down upon an abased basement; when a crushed and crouching kitchen, waiting in vain for its turn at the only copper, revenges itself by cutting the only clothes-line—if the line is drawn only for the good of those in a higher station, instead of its being a line drawn, as every line should be, for the good of all;—when a household is in such a state, we may see in it the type of a badly ordered community. Such had been long the unhappy lot of Rome, until it began to strike on the minds of a few influential men, that no nation can be really great while the mass of its people are in a state of abject littleness. The majority of the patricians fortunately took an equally sensible view of their case, and arrived at the wise conclusion, that moderate privileges fairly held, and freely conceded, are preferable to any amount of exclusive advantage, improperly assumed on the one hand, and impatiently submitted to on the other. Happily for the patricians, they had among them a man bold enough to incorporate in a law the opinions of the main part of his own order, and strong enough to prevail over the weakness and prejudice of the meaner members of the body.

The name of this patrician reformer was Q. Publilius Philo, who introduced three laws calculated to extend the basis of political power.

---

* From this circumstance, the word Rostrum, which means the prow of a ship, has been derived, and has got into such universal use as to describe the box from which an auctioneer launches his eloquence.

By the first, the *curiæ*, consisting of patricians only, were compelled to confirm the laws passed by the centuries in which the two orders were mixed ; by the second, the *plebiscita*, or decrees of the plebs, were to be binding on all Roman citizens ; and the third provided, that there should always be one plebeian censor. These laws, though, perhaps, well adapted to the wants of the age, were not exactly such as we should hail with enthusiasm if they were to be brought forward in our own day by the head of a government. Depriving the curiæ of a veto was a measure equivalent to a proposition that the measures of the House of Commons should not require the concurrence of the House of Lords ; and giving the force of law to a *plebiscitum* was much the same thing as determining that every resolution of every public meeting should at once be embodied in the statute-book. Such an arrangement in the present day would render our laws a curiosity of legislative mosaic work, laid down without the advantage of uniformity or design. If the interpretation of an act of Parliament is sometimes difficult, we may conceive the utter hopelessness of the effort to understand the laws, if they were to consist of a body of resolutions pouring in constantly from Exeter Hall, or Freemasons' Tavern, and, occasionally, from a lamp-post in Trafalgar Square, or a cart on Kennington Common.

With every due respect for the *plebiscita*—or resolutions of public meetings—we doubt whether any party would be desirous of accepting them as a substitute for our present method of law-making. The only chance of safety would be in the fact, that the *plebiscitum* of to-morrow would be sure to repeal the *plebiscitum* of to-day, and the best security for the state would consist in keeping a public meeting always assembled to negative every new proposition.

It was many years, however, before Rome, though it had suffered so much from patrician insolence, was prepared to go to the length of allowing a *plebiscitum* the force of law without being subject to the veto of the senate.* Aristocratic pretension had, however, been carried to such an extent in Rome, that we could hardly be surprised at any amount of democratic license ; for extremes are sure to meet, and it is unfortunate, indeed, for a country that is reduced to such extremities.

---

* The Hortensian Law, carried some years later by Q. Hortensius.

CHAPTER THE TWELFTH.

FROM THE BEGINNING OF THE SECOND TO THE END OF THE THIRD
SAMNITE WAR.

Rome had entered into an alliance with the Samnites; but the
latter became rather suspicious, when they found the former making
friends with all their enemies.   Every one who aimed a blow at
Samnium was forthwith taken into the favour of Rome; and as Samnium
was being attacked on every side, the new connexions of Rome became
very numerous.   Alexander of Epirus, who had come over as a friend
to the Tarentines, thought he might vary the object of his visit by
becoming the foe to somebody else; and he accordingly pitched upon the
Samnites, who might fairly have traced the Roman hand in some of the
hostile demonstrations that were made against them.   There being
some inconvenience in fighting through a third party, to say nothing of
the unsatisfactory nature of such an arrangement to the go-between,
the Romans and the Samnites soon came into direct collision.

One of the Consuls, D. J. Brutus, was sent with troops to Apulia;
but the other Consul, L. Furius Camillus, was in such wretched health,
that he could scarcely hold up his own head, and was quite unfit for the
head of an army.   L. Papirius Cursor, the dictator, undertook the
command himself; but on his way to Samnium he was suddenly
recalled to Rome, in consequence of some blunder with the auspices.
Leaving behind him Q. Fabius, his master of the horse, he desired that
officer to do nothing; for L. P. Cursor having taken a cursory view of
the state of affairs, saw there was a victory to be gained, and wished to
reserve to himself the glory of gaining it.   Q. Fabius, with a natural
reluctance to be shelved, determined to do the work himself; and by
the time his chief returned, had won a brilliant victory.   The rage
of the principal knew no bounds, when he discovered that everything
had been accomplished in his absence; for though there might have
been no objection to the subordinate's actually doing all that was to be
done, there was an unpardonable violation of official etiquette in its
having been got through when the chief was away, and when it was,
therefore, notorious that he could have had no hand in it.   The
dictator was so indignant, that he would have visited his deputy with
all the severity of military law, for having dared to show a capacity to
command, when his capacity was, in fact, subordinate.   It was looked
upon by official men as an act likely to spoil the official market, by
showing that the most highly-paid services are not always the best;
and it was felt, also, that the chief had been ousted of his prescriptive
title to claim, as his own perquisites, all the tact and talent of his
underling.

L. P. Cursor swore vengeance upon the head of Q. Fabius; but the soldiers threatened a revolt in the event of his being punished, and the hero who had put a whole army to flight was obliged to take to his heels for having dared to use his head in the absence of his superior.

The Dictator had rendered himself very unpopular with the troops by his injustice and cruelty to Q. Fabius; but he regained his popularity by allowing them to be guilty of all sorts of injustice and cruelty towards a vanquished enemy. Though their indignation had been raised against him, through the medium of their generous sympathies, he now appealed to their meanest passions, by promising them the fullest license in plundering the foe; and such is the inconsistency of human nature, that he did not appeal in vain; for, urged by avarice, they fought with such determination as to secure a victory. Pillage became at once the order of the day, and a truce was granted for one year, on condition that the Samnites, who had been robbed of everything available at the moment, should become responsible for a twelvemonth's pay to the Dictator's army.

The period of the truce was occupied in negotiation; for it would have been rather too gross a piece of effrontery on the part of the Romans to continuue attacking the very party from whom they were receiving their pay: and having waited till the receipt of the last instalment, they announced that the only terms they would accept would be the unconditional assent of the Samnites to anything that might be proposed to them.

This result was so excessively disgusting to the Samnites, that some actually cried with rage, while others cried for vengeance. A few of the most influential, with tears in their eyes, went to their fellow-countrymen literally with a cry; but amidst all this broken-heartedness, there was a general raising of the nation's spirit. The Samnites felt that the time for action had arrived, and C. Pontius was chosen to act as their general. He at once laid siege to Luceria, when disguising ten of his soldiers as shepherds, he sent them forth with instructions to look as sheepish as they could, and they had also full directions how to act in the event of their being captured. The Romans, commanded by T. Veturius and Sp. Postumius, soon fell in with the Samnite masqueraders, whose real character was not suspected; for it does not appear to have excited any surprise that ten shepherds should be hanging about a neighbourhood in which no sheep were perceptible. With a simplicity more suited to romance than history, the Romans submitted themselves to the guidance of the ten anonymous shepherds, who conducted the whole army into the Caudine forks, as easily as if the veterans had connived at their own betrayal. No sooner were they lost among the forks, than the soldiers learned what spoons they had been, for they found themselves blocked in by the enemy. They fought with considerable bravery, but the Samnites, who lined the surrounding heights, were completely out of their reach, and the Romans, having made a few vain efforts to throw up their spears, suddenly threw up the contest. Of every weapon they hurled, the consequence fell upon their own heads, and nothing was left but to make the best terms they could with the enemy.

Pontius, the Samnite general, was puzzled how to act, and sent to inquire of his father what he should do, when the old man replied, " Release them unhurt ! " and the answer not being quite satisfactory, another messenger was sent, who brought back the brief but expressive recommendation to " cut them all to pieces." Pontius, thinking the old gentleman had gone out of his mind, sought a personal explanation ; but the veteran, who was clearly averse to doing anything by halves, or meeting anybody half-way, persevered in his recommendation to his son, to do one thing or the other. The Samnites were struck with admiration at the wisdom of the sage ; but although all were dumb-founded by the profound philosophy of the advice, nobody thought of taking it. Pontius proposed terms, and having been deceived so frequently by the Romans before, he magnanimously resolved to try and be even with them at last, by putting them and his own countrymen on a perfect equality. He stipulated for the restoration to the Samnites of all the places taken from them ; but the most painful portion of the arrangement to the Romans was their being called upon to pass under the yoke,—a ceremony which was supposed to lower for ever all who had once stooped to it.

Six hundred equites were held as hostages for the due observance of the treaty, and these knights were, in fact, so many pawns, held in pledge for the honour of the Romans. The Consuls, stripped of every thing but their shirts, and looking the most deplorable objects, crawled under the yoke, followed by the whole army in the same wretched undress as their leaders. As they passed through Capua, the inhabitants, touched with sympathy, came forth with bundles of left-off wearing apparel, which was tendered to the humiliated troops ; but their wounds were too deep for ordinary dressing. They walked silently to their homes, through the back streets of the city. All business was suspended on the day of their arrival, and though the Romans had seen suffering in almost every variety of guise, they had never met with it under such melancholy Guys as those that were then before them. The Consuls resigned their offices as rapidly as they could, for their nominal dignity only added to their real disgrace, and they may be supposed to have felt the relief experienced by the broken-spirited cur, whose tail has just undergone the curtailment of the hateful, but glittering kettle.

Rome, smarting under the disgrace of a defeat, brought on by want of resolution in the troops, proceeded to incur a still greater disgrace by a resolution of the Senate. That body having met to consider the agreement entered into with the Samnites, determined not to ratify it ; and, though aware of the fact, that six hundred Roman knights were detained as hostages, in chains, the Senate cared as little for their bonds as for the words of the Consuls, which had been passed for the fulfil-ment of the treaty. Spurius Postumius, who had nothing genuine

in his conduct, was among the first to propose the violation of the
arrangement he had made, and recommended that he himself, as well

The Romans clothed by the Inhabitants of Capua.

as all who had agreed to peace, should be, for the look of the thing,
surrendered to the Samnites. He entered so fully into the deception
about to be enacted, that when the Lictor was tying the cord loosely, as
if conscious of the illusory character of the whole proceeding, Spurius
insisted upon the cords being drawn sufficiently tight to enable him to
declare to the Samnites that his hands were really tied, and that, if
the Senate refused to be bound by his arrangements, he was so
thoroughly bound by theirs as to be utterly powerless. Carrying the
farce still further, he was no sooner delivered up to the Samnites than

he turned round upon the Roman Fecial, and exclaiming, "I am now a Samnite," administered to the proper officer a violent kick, as if to show that he and Rome were to be henceforth on a hostile footing. The Samnite general looked on with contempt at the whole affair; the hostages were refused, and the 600 knights were also sent back; for Pontius had expected the Romans to keep their word, and was neither ready nor willing to be burdened with the keep of several hundred captives. This remarkable breach of their own faith left a more permanent mark upon them than any breach that could have been made by an enemy in the walls of their city; and the fact of their having built a temple to Public Credit, rendered their discreditable conduct still more remarkable.

The Samnites and the Romans were now perfectly agreed in their determination to fall out, wherever they might happen to fall in with one another. A series of small conflicts ensued, of which the accounts are almost as conflicting as the battles themselves; but there is every reason to believe that Fortune showered her favours right and left, by giving them first to one side and then to the other. L. Papirius Cursor, the Roman Consul, seems to have made himself the pre-cursor of his country's ultimate success, for he is said to have led the way to it by recovering Luceria. Hostilities had by this time become so fierce, that it was necessary to take a little breathing time on both sides, and a truce of two years was agreed upon. The war was then renewed under L. Æmilius and Q. Fabius, the dictators, who fought with various results, taking occasionally a city, and at other times being compelled to take what they were not at all disposed to receive at the hands of an enemy. No very remarkable incident occurred at the recommencement of the war, excepting the taking of the town of Sora by treachery; but meanness and deception were so common in the time we write of, that any event involving those despicable qualities cannot be considered unusual. Sora was situated on a rocky eminence, and though secure to a certain extent in its lofty position, it was not above the reach of that low cunning which will stoop to anything for the attainment of its object. A deserter, who appears to have had everything his own way among the Samnites, as well as among the Romans, persuaded the latter to retire some miles off, as if they had abandoned the siege, and then ordered them to have a regiment of cavalry concealed in a wood near the city. What the Samnites were about during these proceedings does not appear; nor is it easy to understand how they could have overlooked an important branch of the forces of the enemy among the trees; but tradition, when she wishes to shut her eyes to a difficulty, never hesitates to shut the eyes of all whose vigilance might have been fatal to the incident about to be related. The inhabitants of Sora may therefore be supposed to have been fast asleep and slow to wake, or to have had their backs turned, or to have taken something which had turned their heads, when the deserter was making his arrangements for the betrayal of their city. Having taken the steps already described, he conducted ten Roman soldiers up a sort of back staircase behind the crags; and the blindness of the inhabitants of Sora had come to such a pass, that the mountain pass was so thoroughly lost sight of as to be left without a single sentinel. Having lodged the ten men in the fortress, he concealed them there until night; but it is difficult to say how the ten stalwart soldiers could have been so thoroughly put away in the day-time as not to be observed, unless tradition, wishing to put her own construction on the affair, has proceeded to the construction of some secret cupboard in the fortress, where the men may have been closeted together until the hour arrived for their being brought into action. Waiting till the dead of night, the deserter desired the ten men to shout as loud as they possibly could, and to keep on hallooing until the cavalry were out of the wood; a movement which was to be effected when the deserter, rushing into the city, had frightened the inhabitants out of it, by running all over the town in a state of pretended alarm, which was to be accounted for by the continued shouting of the ten men in the citadel. Notwithstanding the numerous objections to the veracity of this story, tradition has handed it down to us, and we, as in duty bound, continue to hand it on, though we do not allow it to pass through our fingers without taking the precaution to stamp it with the mark of counterfeit. Tradition proceeds to say that the scheme was perfectly successful: that the citizens, frightened by the shouting of the ten soldiers in the citadel, ran into, or rather on to, the arms of the legions who were advancing with drawn swords to the gates of the city.

The Samnites having become weary of war, and tired of an existence which was passed in continually fighting for their lives, determined to bring matters to an issue as fast as possible. They met the Romans under Q. Fabius at Lautulæ, where Q. was driven into a corner, and ran away, when his army not receiving from him the cue to fight, rapidly followed his example. C. Fabius having subsequently come to the assistance of Q., they united their forces, and being almost two to one against the Samnites, they obtained a victory.

Rome had, however, quite enough to contend against in various quarters; and, among others, the Ausonians betrayed hostile feelings, which were rendered abortive by another betrayal of a very disgraceful character. Among the Ausonians there existed a nominal nobility, whose rank gave them a sort of respectability to which they possessed no moral title. These nobles, by name and ignobles by nature, were mean enough to admit, by stealth, into some of the cities of Ausonia, a number of Roman soldiers in disguise, who, with the cruelty so commonly associated with fraud, commenced a general slaughter of the inhabitants.

It would be a waste of time and patience, both to writer and reader, were we to ask him to accompany us into every little field where a little skirmish may have taken place, at about this period, between Rome and her enemies. To describe the fluctuations of the fortune of war, would be as dry and unprofitable as the minute narration of all the incidents of a long game at heads and tails; nor would the historian have repeated very often the particulars of the throwing up the coin, before the reader would be found throwing up the history. We shall, therefore, content ourselves with giving the heads in a curtailed form, without going into the particulars of the movements of the generals. There was an enormous quantity of putting to the sword on both sides, but without running through the whole, we will submit to the eye of the reader the points best adapted for the use of the pupil. In the north of Samnium, the Romans were surprised by an Etruscan army, and nearly destroyed; but when they were more than half killed, they began to look alive, and completely exterminated the foe, whose survivors, consisting of their cattle, fell into the hands of the conquerors. The Consul, C. Marcius, had succeeded in taking a place called Allifæ; but the Samnites soon afterwards brought themselves completely round, and made him the centre of a circle, which, as he was entirely cut off from Rome, was to him a centre of extreme gravity. Not even a messenger could find a way to take to the city the tidings of the Consul's perilous position; but it seems to have become known, by some means or other, for L. Cursor hastened to the scene, and caused the Samnites to abandon their position. Beginning to despond, they sought a truce, for which they had to pay a most exorbitant price, in cash, corn, and clothes; for they had to pay, feed, and clothe for three months the troops who had paid them off, in another shape, and submitted them to a long series of thorough dressings. They, however, still held out against acknowledging the sovereignty of Rome, and thought themselves exempt from humiliation in making themselves the slaves in fact, as long as they remained independent in name, of that ambitious power. The main point of dispute remaining still undisposed of, more fighting ensued, until Samnium was at length so thoroughly reduced as to be obliged to confess itself beaten at last; and the Samnites, who had by degrees parted with everything they possessed for the luxury of maintaining that they were free to do as they pleased with their own, acknowledged Rome to be their master. Rome also needed relaxation; for her energies had become relaxed by a war of twenty years; and both parties having done each other all the harm they could, ceased only because the power of mischief had become completely lost on one side, and seriously impaired on the other.

So inveterate was the hostility between Samnium and Rome, that any pause in their actual conflict was filled up by preparations for a renewal, the first opportunity for which they were eagerly expecting to take advantage of. The third Samnite war was commenced by an attempt on the part of the Samnites to recover Lucania, and for that purpose they stupified the Lucanians by a series of severe beatings, which deadened the sense of the inhabitants to their danger. The nobles, who seem to have had the instinct of self-preservation in a higher degree than the virtue of patriotism, were quite prepared to obey a master who would purchase, rather than resist an enemy who would harass, them. They accordingly offered their allegiance to Rome, on condition that Rome would save them the trouble of defending them selves against Samnium. Roman envoys were despatched, in compliance with this arrangement, to call upon the Samnites to evacuate Lucania; but the envoys were unceremoniously ordered off, and betook themselves to a very quick return, unattended by the smallest profit. After a few minor encounters, the two Consuls, Q. Fabius and P. Decius Mus, the son of old Mus, already alluded to, led their combined forces into Samnium, and went different ways, though they fully purposed pulling together. Q. Fabius met the whole of the Samnite army, and a battle commenced, in which each was rapidly destroying the other's soldiers in about equal numbers, without any good to either, beyond the very melancholy satisfaction of being even with each other in the losing game that both sides were playing. This would probably have continued until the chances of war had degenerated into a game of odd man, in which the sole survivor would have been the victor, when a Samnite soldier, rather more far-seeing than the rest, espied what he supposed to be the army of Decius. That there are some things to which it is better to shut one's eyes, was proved on this occasion; for the long-sighted Samnite had no sooner espied a body of men in the back-ground, who were in reality the reserve of Q. Fabius, than he frightened himself and his fellow soldiers, by spreading a rumour that Mus was creeping slowly, but surely, up to them. The Samnites were at once struck with a panic, the blow inflicted by which is always more fatal than that of the sword, and the loss of spirit led to the destruction of nearly the whole body. Decius having joined his colleague, the two Consuls hunted the country of the Samnites, making game of everything that came in the way, while Appius Claudius carried on the war in Etruria. We should be curious to see the population returns— if any such existed—in relation to the Samnites, who were, according to tradition, being continually cut to pieces, routed, ravaged, and otherwise destroyed; but who, nevertheless, were, according to tradition, continually taking the field again in large numbers, as if nothing had happened. L. Valerius had just returned from assisting his colleague, Appius Claudius, in Etruria, when the Samnites turned up rather abundantly on the Vulturnus, and being at once attacked, were again cut to pieces, for by no means the last or only time on the great stage of history.

At about the same time, when the news of this victory reached Rome the Gauls were expected, and though it was against the law that the same Consul should be elected twice in ten years, the Romans, altering the constitution, without the trouble of revision, suspended the law for the purpose of securing the services of Q. Fabius.

He was re-elected with his colleague Decius Mus, and before setting out for battle, they consulted the augurs, who evinced their usual readiness to interpret the omens in the most favourable manner. On coming to the fortified camp of Appius Claudius, Fabius found the soldiers collecting wood, to form a stockade, which drew from him the remark, " It is not by cutting sticks you can succeed, but by showing a bold front to the enemy." The soldiers, animated by his words—which, to say the truth, do not appear to have anything particularly invigorating about them—were suddenly roused into lions, after having been in a lamb-like or sheepish condition, and instead of cutting any more wood, or pulling up the trunks of trees, began to pluck up a proper spirit. The Romans had now about 90,000 troops in the field, if we adopt the round numbers handed down to us, which do not always square with probability; but the historians wisely provide, as far as possible, for any deficiency that may arise in the course of the various cuttings to pieces, annihilations, and other contingencies which are at one time or other the alleged fate of nearly every army. The vast necessity for a surplus that may be boldly dealt with, can perhaps be understood from a cir- cumstance recorded with reference to a legion led by L. Scipio. It had been stationed near Camerinum, and had in an engagement with the foe been cut to pieces without having been missed ; nor was the loss discovered until their own countrymen recognised their heads carried on the lances of the advancing enemy. When the fact thus frightfully stared them in the face, the countenances of the Romans fell with sympathy at the fate of their comrades, which it must be confessed presented some very horrid features.

At length the hostile armies met near Sentinum in Umbria—the Romans mustering in considerable force, and the Samnites, in spite of much pruning, which seemed only to have the effect of increasing their growth, forming a highly respectable remnant. The latter had also a considerable accession in the shape of Gauls, Umbrians, and Etrurians ; for tradition, when it desires to give interest to a battle, is always prepared to scrape together from all quarters a sufficient number of soldiers, on both sides, to equalise the chances of victory. While the armies were drawn out in line before each other, they are said to have been suddenly occupied in the contemplation of the following rather remarkable incident. A deer, pursued by a wolf, ran rapidly down the middle, and the two animals were on the point of going up again, when the deer, apparently changing its mind, ran among the Gauls, who, without hesitation, converted it into venison. The wolf, with a cunning worthy of the fox, declined venturing on an experiment that had been so costly to the deer, and turned in among the Romans, who, perhaps, fearing that the wolf might have a taste for calves as well as for sheep, took the precaution to save their legs, by making as wide an opening as possible. No sooner was the wolf out of the way, than the Romans began to boast that fear had gone to the foe in the shape of a deer, while valour had come to their side in the person of Mars, whom they declared they saw hidden under the hide of a wolf, his favourite animal. The battle at length commenced, and the day being ex- ceedingly warm, added, in one sense, most inconveniently to the heat of the contest. The Gauls created immense consternation among the

Romans by rushing down upon them in chariots armed with scythes, at the sight of which they were terribly cut up, and unmercifully cut down, before they had time to recover from their astonishment. Not wishing to be left as a wretched harvest on the field, the Romans were about to fly, when they were once more saved by a Mus, who on this occasion will be thought by some to have deserved the epithet of "*ridiculus*." Recollecting the example of his father, he resolved to sacrifice himself for the benefit of his country, and, calling upon the pontiff, he caused his vow to be regularly registered. The ceremony having been gone through, in due form, he put spurs to his horse, and rushing in among the foe, he became, as it were, a scabbard for the swords of all who could get within reach of him. The Gauls were so completely stupified by what they saw, that they were literally lost in wonder; for, while they stood staring with astonishment, the Romans fell upon and massacred nearly the whole of them. Gellius Egnatius, the Samnite General, was slain, together with many thou-sands of his own countrymen, who are described by tradition as having been once more cut to pieces, though these pieces are not the last in which they are destined to make their appearance. History, with a natural anxiety to keep a stock of Samnites on hand for future use, suggests that 5000 ran away, though the Romans were too much reduced to run after them, and as the fugitives lost a thousand of their number by fighting, during their retreat, it must be presumed that, in their extreme nervousness, they began attacking each other.

Q. Fabius led back his army into Etruria, which had recently been thoroughly ravaged by Cn. Fulvius; and the Etruscans, who had already been beaten once, were thoroughly beaten again, so that any residue of strength might be effectually knocked out of them. The retreating Samnites had by this time arrived at the valley of Vulturnus, where the country was in such a state that they could find nothing to eat; but, for a people who were accustomed to survive the constant infliction of the sword, the absence of food was a very subordinate grievance. Volumnius and Appius Claudius fell upon them with their united forces, and the Samnites were once more cut to pieces; but, notwithstanding their fragmentary condition, they were able to appear collected and calm, before the end of the following year, in Etruria. They, at length, mustered all their strength, and determined on making a desperate effort against the Romans, who were in great force under Papirius Cursor, near Aquilonia. Papirius sent for an augur, who kept a small brood of sacred chickens, for the purpose of hatching up something to say to those who consulted him. The augur declared that the omens were favourable, for the chickens had eaten a hearty meal; but an officer, who had watched the birds at breakfast, and had been struck by the extreme delicacy of their appetites, came forward to impute foul play to the augur. Papirius immediately ordered the soothsayer to be placed in the front of the line of battle, where the poor old man, who was no chicken in age, whatever he may have been at heart, was made to answer with his life for having failed to answer with truth the questions proposed to him.

The Samnites paid no attention to omens, but bound each other by awful oaths to undergo their usual fate of being cut to pieces rather than surrender; and it must be admitted that they bore the penalty of defeat with a coolness that can only be accounted for by their being thoroughly used to it. No less than 16,000 took the oath, and kept it so well that the whole 16,000 were found in bits precisely where they had taken their places in battle. We might express our doubts upon this subject, were it not that the sage critics, who are averse to any departure from the gravity of history, would perhaps accuse us of levity in refusing credence to Livy, on whose authority the tale is told, though dulness itself will probably be roused to a stare, if incapable of a smile, at the remarkable dish of hash which the serious historians call upon him to swallow.

Samnite Soldier.

The victory of Rome was complete, and the Samnites, whose riches seem to have been almost as inexhaustible as their numbers, yielded up spoil that might appear fabulous in the eyes of any but those who are so thoroughly matter-of-fact as to be incapable of distinguishing a matter of fiction. To swell the triumph of the conquerors, Papirius is said to have given crowns of gold and silver to officers and men, with collars and bracelets of the same precious material; from which it would seem that the Samnites had abandoned their ornaments in running away; for metal, though current on ordinary occasions, goes a very little way in the hands of those who are groaning beneath the weight of it.

Once more the Samnites poured themselves as copiously and mysteriously as the streams that flow from the inexhaustible bottle of the conjuror over the greater part of Campania, and Q. Fabius Gurges took the command of the Roman army. The Samnites were led by C. Pontius, an aged prodigy, who had seen much service, which had been of no service whatever to his countrymen, for they had not even learned to profit by the lessons of experience. C. Pontius combined, in a remarkable degree, the imbecility of age with the rashness of youth, and presented the sad spectacle of juvenile and senile indiscretion combined, or the junction of the characteristics of an old fool and a young fool in the same individual. Q. Fabius, however, reckoned too confidently on success; and seeing a detachment of the Samnites executing a manœuvre, he thought it was the whole body in the act of retreat, which caused him to proceed so carelessly, that he was himself defeated, and would have had his army utterly destroyed, but for the feebleness of his antagonists.

The news of the defeat of Fabius excited much dissatisfaction at Rome, and the General was about to be recalled, when his father, in an uncontrollable fit of nepotism, implored the people to allow the young man to keep his place—a request that was at length granted. The impolicy of overlooking the incompetence of the son at the request of the father, was nearly being exemplified in a fatal manner; for the younger Fabius was on the point of another failure, and an alarming sacrifice of all his army, when Fabius Maximus came up with a reserve, which turned the fortune of the day, by the cutting to pieces of 20,000 Samnites; while 4000, including poor old Pontius, were made prisoners. It will be seen that tradition, while dooming 20,000 Samnites to the sword, reserves 4000 in captivity as a surplus to supply future contingencies. Although the better authorities consider that in the last-mentioned battle this people, who were almost as endless as their hostilities were aimless, must have been used up, there are still a few skirmishes to be met with on the borders, if not within the verge of truth, which require that a few thousand Samnites should be kept as a reserve for the purposes of the historian.

C. Pontius was led as a prisoner in the triumph granted to the Fabii; but this triumph, and everything connected with it, was converted into a disgrace by the beheading of the poor old Samnite chief, who, if he had been weak enough to place himself in opposition to Rome, had after the battle of the Caudine forks, evinced an amiable weakness towards the captives that had fallen into his power. Fabius Maximus having died soon after, tradition, who is much addicted to returning verdicts in the absence of evidence, declares the cause of death to have been a broken heart; and, as it would certainly have been proper under all the circumstances that he should have done so, we have no inclination to disturb the rather doubtful decision.

Some authorities,* finding they have a Samnite surplus to deal with, describe the Samnites as being again defeated by M. Curius Dentatus, who seems to have been a curiosity in his way; for, having been offered a house with seven hundred jugera as his share of booty, he refused to accept more than seven, which was the portion allotted to his comrades. Those who are accustomed to read of, and admire, the system on which prize-money is apportioned in modern times,† will probably set down Curius Dentatus as a remarkable fool; and indeed, though his self-denial smacks of patriotism, we are not sure of its justice; for, if he had performed his duty as a general, his services to his country must have been more valuable than those of the ordinary soldiers under him. It may be, however, that he knew best what he had done, and what he deserved; nor must we forget the great fact that in taking a man's own estimate of his own merits, we run very little danger of underrating them.

* Eutrop. ii., 5.

† A reference to any Gazette containing the announcement of an appropriation of prize-money, will introduce to the reader's notice such items as the following, which are extracted from a very recently-published document, stating the proportions of prize-money granted on the seizure of a slave-vessel :—Flag, £87 12s. 3d.; Lieutenant commanding, £164 5s. 7d. The proportions then diminish rapidly through several classes down to the tenth, which is adjudged to receive £2 13s. 3d. The ratio may be all fair enough, but we must confess the large sum always wrapped up in the flag seems somewhat of a mystery.

CHAPTER THE THIRTEENTH.

ON THE PEACEFUL OCCUPATIONS OF THE ROMANS. FROM SCARCITY OF
SUBJECT, NECESSARILY A VERY SHORT CHAPTER.

Æsculapius.

T is with sincere satisfaction that we turn from the monotonous details of war to the arts of peace; and though it is usually said that the stain of blood can never be wiped out, we are glad to find that the marks and traces of discord are doubtful and few, while the evidences of the nobler pursuits of man are numerous and genuine. Among the most 'enduring monuments of the art and industry of the Romans, may still be traced the remains of the celebrated Via Appia, or Appian Way, the secret for the formation of which would be invaluable to the inhabitants of our large towns, and particularly to the Paving Boards of the Metropolis. While parts of the Via Appia remain perfect after upwards of twenty centuries, the streets of London are torn to pieces year after year; and it might melt a heart of stone —if stone possessed a heart—to see the granite continually disturbed by the remorseless pickaxe. The Via Appia was constructed of large blocks placed very closely together; and though modern Paving Boards have done their best by laying their heads together to imitate the plan, success has never rewarded their labours.

Not less wonderful than the road of Appius, was the aqueduct that bore his name, and which had solved the question so apparently incapable of solution in our own times, of the means of securing a supply of water to a great Metropolis. Though water was not commonly drunk by the Romans as it is by ourselves, and though the Tiber was purity itself compared with the Thames, the liquid was so clearly or rather so thickly undrinkable, that a supply was brought from a distance of eight miles, in the manner we have mentioned.

While all admit the grandeur of the aqueducts of ancient Rome,

K

objection has been made to their construction as a needless expense; and it has been said, that their lofty arches proved only the height to which folly and extravagance could be carried. Pipes have been suggested as capable of answering every useful purpose; but considering the difficulty of obtaining them sufficiently large, of keeping them always free from obstruction, and other obvious disadvantages, it is doubtful whether the pipe, after payment of the piper, would prove so economical in the main. The aqueduct, indeed, has been recently adopted on a large scale, by a people not likely to retrograde in arts and sciences, though the rapidity with which they go a-head may cause them to run through the whole circle of ingenuity, till the most modern invention, arriving at the same point as the most ancient, affords an illustration of the meeting of extremes. New York now receives its supply of water through an aqueduct,* carried on solid masonry, over valleys and rivers, under hills and tunnels, for a distance of forty miles; a proof that when a city has the will to obtain pure water, there is always a way—though it may be forty miles in length—for getting what is required.

In Rome, it had been customary to bore a well where water was wanted, but the water was so impure, that it soon became necessary to let well alone. The science of engineering, aided by that great moral engine, their own energy, enabled the inhabitants to bring their supplies from a considerable distance, and as the aqueducts were gradually sloped, the water followed, as it were, its own inclination in coming to Rome. Filtration was ingeniously provided for, at convenient distances, by reservoirs having two compartments, into one of which the water fell, and passing into the other before returning to the main body, there was time for the deposit of all impurities. Every precaution was taken against the intrusion of those unhappy families of animalculæ, which are continually tearing each other to pieces in every drop of the London element, and whose voracity seems to hold out a faint hope that, as they are continually demolishing each other, they may be all mutually swallowed, before the supply of the Metropolis with pure water is achieved.

During the Censorship of Appius Claudius, the cause of literature, or at least the dignity of the profession of a public writer, was advanced —though, perhaps, we ought rather to say, that official employment was honoured—by the promotion of Cn. Flavius, a scribe, to the Curule Ædileship. This individual appears to have possessed the happy gift of investing dry subjects with the garb of popularity; and he had won considerable reputation by giving the forms of legal actions in a shape that rendered them comprehensible to the general reader. He made law legible in his work on *legis actiones*, and had assisted the spread of information by an almanack or calendar, in which the *dies fasti* and *nefasti* were marked down, and other information afforded which could only have been obtained previously from the pontiffs.

---

* The Croton Aqueduct, commenced in 1837, and finished in 1842, for conveying water from the river Croton to the City of New York.

The lawyers and the priests, who were less liberal in those days than in our own, were both enraged with an author who had laid open the mysteries of both professions by a few happy touches of his pen; and on his being called upon to give the public the benefit of his services as a curule ædile, they appealed to the miserable prejudice existing against a man who had shown talent in one line, when called upon to exert his abilities in some new direction. The nobility were especially affected at the prospect of the public service being thrown open to merit alone, instead of gentle or gentile dulness being allowed the sole use and abuse of official honour and emolument. Exclusiveness and illiberality could not, even in those days, wholly prevail, though the opponents of the public writer succeeded in causing him to abandon not only his literary pursuits, but to give up all his books, and thus render himself emblematically on a par with themselves in ignorance, by divesting himself of the types of knowledge on his acceptance of office.

At about the same period other and more important measures were adopted for infusing into the service of the State some of that intellectual vigour which is to be found most abundantly in the main body of the people. The pontiffs and the augurs had been hitherto chosen from the patricians alone, when by the Ogulnian law, passed in the tribuneship of Q. and Cn. Ogulnius, it was enacted that four pontiffs out of eight, and five augurs out of nine—at which the numbers were then fixed—should be plebeians. The science of augury certainly required no particular talent; but, as its professors were held in very high repute, the introduction of the plebeian element into the body, was a triumph for popular principles. The divining rod in an age of superstition was also a very powerful rod in the hands of those who held it; and the privilege of reading or rather interpreting the signs of the times according to the wish of the interpreter, was a source of so much influence among a people guided by omens, that the admission of the plebeians to the exercise of these functions was equivalent to allowing them an important share in the government.

The science of augury is intimately connected with the history of the Romans, for they never took a step of a private or a public nature without consulting the soothsayers, who were, in fact, the fortune-tellers of antiquity. That a nation should place its destinies in such doubtful hands, seems in the present day as absurd as if the Prime Minister, before arranging his measures for a session, were to take counsel with Dr. Francis Moore, and the Opposition were to frame their tactics on the advice of Zadkiel. A glimpse at the nature of the art of augury will demonstrate to the student the ease with which the seer could see exactly the thing he wanted. The subjects of his observation were, first, the clouds, which afforded ample opportunity for obscurity; secondly, the birds, which, when seen to the right, meant exactly opposite to that which they indicated when seen on the left—thus allowing for a good deal to be said on both sides; thirdly, the chickens, who were supposed to give a favourable omen if they ate abundantly— a theory which gave rise to many a tremendous cram; fourthly, the quadrupeds, from which the augurs could easily draw a deduction at all fours with their own wishes; and, fifthly, and last, a miscellaneous class of signs, or incidents, comprising a sneeze, which enabled the augur to lead the sneezer by the nose, or a casualty, such as a tumble, which, in the absence of any other more important sign, the soothsayer was always willing to fall back upon.

A remarkable instance of ignorance and superstition was afforded by the conduct of the Romans, when the city, being in about its four hundred and sixtieth year, was visited by a pestilence. Recourse was had to the Sibylline books for a prescription to get rid of the plague, when the augurs, like a doctor who, unable to cure his patient, orders him abroad, declared that the only thing to be done was to go to Epidaurus, a town in Greece, and bring to Rome the god Æsculapius. Ten ambassadors were despatched on the mission; but after looking in all directions for Æsculapius, they happened to stumble over a stone, in which they were told he was resident. Having been induced to purchase the article at a high price, they were taking it on board their ship, when they fell in with the proprietor of a small menagerie, who, directing their attention to a tame snake in the collection, offered it to them a bargain as the identical Æsculapius they were looking for. The Roman envoys, thinking there might, after all, be nothing in the stone, concluded there might be something in the snake, which began to twine itself affectionately about them; and having been bought and paid for, sagaciously glided through the town, made for the Roman vessel, and coiled himself up like a coil of rope in the cabin of the ambassadors.

On their way home, a storm caused them to put in at Antium, when the snake, who might have been a very good snake, but was a very bad sailor, went ashore, took a turn or two round a palm-tree, hung out there for three days, and then went back to the vessel. On the arrival of the ambassadors at Rome, they began describing at some length the result of their journey, when the snake gave them the slip, and while their tongues were running on, managed to run off to the island in the Tiber. Having looked in vain for the snake in the grass, they built a temple on the spot, in honour of Æsculapius, and the serpent glided on —no one knows where—to the end of his existence.

The wars which had been so exhausting to the almost inexhaustible Sabines, had been scarcely less ruinous to the Romans, and indeed the opening up of so many bones of contention had, to use the words of a recent writer, consumed "the very marrow of the nation." * In spite of all their conquests, the people were miserably poor; for destruction, in- stead of production, had been their occupation during a series of years; and though their wants had been supplied for a time by plunder, scarcity was sure to ensue at last, from a stoppage of the very source of all

* Dr. Schmidtz, p. 223.

wealth, the peaceful exercise of industry. The tide of adversity which, in the first instance, overwhelms only the lower ranks, rises, with

The Ambassadors purchasing Æsculapius.

unerring certainty, until even the highest are absorbed, and few are able, in the end, to keep their heads above water. When circumstances appear hopeless, remedies become desperate, rash legislation ensues, and thus, during the distresses of Rome, the plebs having seceded, a proposal was adopted, in the shape of the Hortensian Law, to allow them to do just as they liked, in order to tempt them back again.

This was, happily, the last secession of the plebs, who, in their dignified withdrawal, remained completely within the pale of the law, while passing beyond the gates of the city. The intention of the seceders was to get on as they could without the patrician class, leaving the latter to do their best by themselves—a proceeding that had speedily the effect of showing that there is a mutual dependence between all ranks, and that one cannot exist in comfort without the association and support of the other. In Rome, the patricians had played the dangerous game of exercising the rights of their position without fulfilling its duties ; and the plebeians finding themselves deprived of their share of the profits of the connection, were quite justified in cutting it. After the passing of the Hortensian Law, the invidious distinction between the patricians and the people was at an end, and the word *populus* was applied to the whole body of citizens ; but with the natural tendency of all classes to level only down to themselves, the Romans who were well to do in the world continued to use the term *plebs*, or *plebecula*, in a depreciatory sense, to denote the multitude.

It is true, that some works of great utility were accomplished during the unhappy period to which we have been alluding ; and the aqueduct as well as the Via Appia, to both of which we have already referred, were executed at the time stated. Instead, however, of being the result of the free industry of the nation, these undertakings were extorted chiefly from the labour of the Samnite prisoners; so that the Romans may be said to have watered their city with the tears, and paved their road with the sighs,* of their miserable captives. The arts made considerable progress, notwithstanding the general poverty, and perhaps the fact, that necessity is the mother of invention, may account for the stimulus given to the skill and ingenuity of the nation. The still existing figure, in which two bronze babies are represented in an attitude of playful satisfaction, deriving sustenance from a bronze wolf, who looks as easy as the hardness of the material will allow, has been assigned to the age alluded to, and the Sarcophagus of Scipio Barbatus, complete even to the ancient funeral verse, which the irreverent might estimate at the value of an old song, belongs, probably, to the same period.

* The sigh of a pavier is really a very formidable matter. We always fancy the heart of the poor fellow is in his mouth, whenever we hear him at his labours.

CHAPTER THE FOURTEENTH.

FROM THE END OF THE THIRD SAMNITE WAR TO THE SUBJUGATION OF
ALL ITALY BY THE ROMANS.

ROME was for a time at rest; but its repose was broken by the alarm-bell of war still ringing in its ears, while dissension, hanging over it like a nightmare, placed a weight upon its chest, and became a constant burden on its resources. As if the Romans had not enough troubles of their own, they became involved with the disputes of their foreign relations, who were, most of them, very poor rela tions indeed—a sort of connexion which nations, as well as individuals, are apt to find extremely burdensome.

A number of petty states began urging each other to do something that would embarrass Rome, and many who had not the courage to strike were desirous of seeing others display their valour. The Taren tines and the Volsinians being anxious to fight their own battles with other people's arms, succeeded in making cats'-paws of the Gauls, who were induced to pounce upon Arretium. The Romans were appealed to for assistance, and they immediately sent an army just large enough to be too little. Defeat ensued, as a matter of course; and L. Cæcilius, the leader, being slain, M. Curius was despatched to head the troops; but on his arrival, he found there was no body to which he could serve as a head, for the army had been either killed or captured.

In this disagreeable dilemma, he sent ambassadors to know the terms on which the prisoners would be given up; but the ambassadors —like good money sent after bad—never came back again. The Romans perceiving at last that they were only cutting their army into convenient pieces for the enemy to swallow up, despatched, at length, a force large enough to put a stop to any further consumption of such valuable material. The Romans were now decidedly successful, and the Senones were, according to certain authorities, "just annihilated;"[*]

* Polybius.

but as the Senones are frequently met with again, it must be presumed that the assertion, *ex nihilo nihil fit*—" nothing can come of nothing "—is unacknowledged by the writers of classical history.

Foreign intervention seems to have been quite the order of the day; for the Boians rushed forward to show their sympathy at the fate of the Senones, which, if it consisted of annihilation, must have been nothing to the parties themselves, and should have been, *à fortiori*, nothing to others. Touched with a similar infection, the Etrurians began to sympathise with the Boians, and having met the Romans near Lake Vadimo, the sympathisers were "cut to pieces," if we are to believe report; but we know not whether to the scissors of the reporters or the shears of fate, the cutting to pieces in question may be attributed. The Etruscans, at all events, were able to return to Etruria* in sufficient force to render them a still formidable foe to the Romans, who were eventually glad to grant a peace on very favourable terms; and, putting all things together, we are inclined to believe that the Etruscans were not in that very piecemeal state to which tradition is fond of reducing them.

A quarrel between the Lucanians and the Thurii caused another call on the intervention of Rome, who was a thorough polygamist in espousing the quarrels of others. C. Fabricius was sent to the relief of Thurii with an army so small, that it began to shrink from the encounter, and thus increase, as it were, its own littleness. The spirit of the Romans had something, however, of the caoutchouc in its composition; for it could be drawn out as easily as it gave in, and a trifling circumstance showed its elasticity on the occasion of the attack on Thurii. A gigantic lad, with a ladder in his hand, was seen approaching the ramparts, which he proceeded to mount, and by this simple act of scaling the wall, he turned the scale of victory.

The opposing general was taken prisoner, and numbers were left dead on the field, including several of the Samnites, who in devoting themselves to glut the appetite of war, appear to have formed the great *pièce de résistance* of the period. The feast of carnage seems never to have been complete in these days, without this very substantial dish, which seems to have formed literally an instance of "cut and come again," for we find a supply of Samnites always ready for fate's relentless carving-knife. The treasure taken by Fabricius, the Roman general, was immense, and much of it was derived from the inexhaustible Samnites, who, though constantly being cut up like the goose with the golden eggs, possessed one extraordinary advantage over that auriferous bird, for they could bear the operation as often as avarice itself could require. The booty was wonderful in amount; but the mode in which it was disposed of, was more marvellous still; for the general, instead of following the general custom, by pocketing all he could, distributed a large portion of it among the soldiers, reimbursed the amount of a year's taxes to the citizens, and sent a handsome surplus to the treasury.

* Polyb., ii. 20.

It is to be regretted that we have no such examples of justice and generosity in the present age; for if every man were to return as conscience money to the Exchequer all that he did not fairly earn, the National Debt might soon figure—without any figures at all—as a myth in our financial annals.

Thurii received a small Roman garrison, which not being strong enough to defend itself, was *à fortiori*, or rather *ab impotentiori*, too weak to protect those for whose safety it had been appointed. Rome, therefore, despatched ten ships to its aid, in defiance of a treaty with Tarentum, that no armed vessel should proceed beyond a certain point. The people of Tarentum, who happened to be at the theatre, which commanded a view of the sea, and who were evidently looking at the ocean as a much finer spectacle than the play, observed the approach of the ships, and leaving the actors to finish their performance to empty benches, they rushed out to meet the enemy. The commander of the squadron was not prepared for an audience that would hear nothing he had to say, the sailors were alarmed at finding themselves suddenly assailed, and the poor rowers were completely overawed at their unexpected position. Only five ships escaped, the remainder being sunk or captured, with all their crews and cargoes. The Tarentines fell upon Thurii, whose cause was now completely undefended; but the Roman garrison, instead of being despatched by the sword, was generously despatched home by the earliest means of conveyance.

The Romans, having lost a considerable number of men, thought it better to recruit themselves by peace, as they were unable to find recruits for their army. It was accordingly determined to try the effect of an embassy upon the Tarentines, and some Feciales were employed to propose—what Rome considered—very moderate terms of arrangement. L. Postumius is said to have been one of the envoys, and it is added that upon his commencing a speech in bad Greek, there was a burst of laughter at his mistakes in grammar, orthography, and accent. He had been selected for the charm of his eloquence, but the spell was broken by the spelling, and in the confusion of his nominatives and datives, he was unable to make out a case of any kind. The Senators gave way to bursts of laughter—those bursts of nature which it is often difficult to control—and a buffoon, encouraged by the bad example of his betters, played some practical joke upon L. Postumius. The insulted emissary immediately held up his toga, which had been soiled by the jester, whose wit seems to have consisted in throwing dirt; but a shout of laughter was the only reply that the complaint of Postumius elicited. Desiring them to laugh on, he made an allusion to the possibility of the operation being transferred to the other side of the Roman mouth, and he added that a lavatory supplied by their blood was the only wash to which he would send his toga. Returning to Rome, he pointed out the stain that had been thrown upon him, and the Senate declared war on the spot the moment the spot was exhibited. An army was accordingly sent against Tarentum, but the leader, L. Aemilius Barbula,

—so called probably from his being the little-bearded or the downy one—
offered peace a second time. The Tarentines, thinking the Romans were
afraid of fighting, refused to come to terms ; but seeing that the latter
did not retire, it became necessary to seek assistance in meeting them.

It appears that in these early days there were a set of persons willing
to undertake butchery as a trade, by hiring themselves, or rather
lowering themselves, to fight for any one who would pay them.   Among
these, one of the most respectable was Pyrrhus, king of Epirus, whom
we may almost regard as a professional spiller of blood, for he took care
to turn his labours to a profitable account, by bleeding those on whose
side he fought, as well as those he fought against.   According to some
writers, Pyrrhus was no mercenary, because in agreeing to lend his
arms to the Tarentines, he had in view a kingdom, rather than cash, or,
in other words, he did not propose to be paid by those whom he assisted,
because he intended to appropriate to himself everything out of which
they would have the means of paying him.   Pyrrhus, in fact, can only
be excluded from the order of mercenaries by transferring him to the
catalogue of thieves, and of this arrangement we have no objection to
give him the benefit.

Though he lived in an age when the education of sovereigns was
sadly neglected, he possessed a fair amount of information, and he had
the fortunate habit of listening to good advice, so that he got credit for
being wise on the strength of the wisdom of his counsellors.   His tongue
was no less polished than his sword, and his manners would have fully
justified their being charged as extras in the bill of any school in which
they may have been acquired.   He was only thirty-seven years old when
he entered Italy with a stud, including no less than twenty elephants
and two thousand horses, though he was, of course, the principal lion of
his great travelling menagerie.   He was accompanied by a vast number
of slingers, whose arms were in their slings, and a large body of bowmen,
who could draw the longest bow with a truthfulness quite astonishing.
An incident connected with the invocation of the aid of Pyrrhus by the
Tarentines has come down to us by tradition, that common carrier who
lays much at the historian's door, that he is not always inclined to
answer for.   It is said that a respectable young nobleman, of the name
of Meto, appeared one day in the Tarentine senate with a quantity of
faded flowers in his hair, as if he had just come home late from a dinner
party, and had passed on his way through one of the markets.   Being
attended by a female with a pipe, the Tarentines were seized with a
sudden desire to cheer, a propensity still evinced by a modern mob in
the presence of any absurdity.

The excitement at length broke out into a general demand for a
dance, and a shout arose similar to the unmeaning cry of " Hornpipe ! "
that is heard in a modern theatre on the first performance of a pantomime.   The young noble, feeling that he might be involved in an
extraordinary caper, seems to have suddenly resumed his senses ; for he
exclaimed with a serious air, " Yes, we must dance and feast now, for

Pyrrhus arrives in Italy with his Troops.

Pyrrhus will soon put an end to all our merriment." The words of
Meto seemed too prophetic; for Pyrrhus had no sooner arrived, than, on

Appearance in the Senate of a young Nobleman, named Meto.

the principle, perhaps, that where there is a great deal of work, there
should be no play, he shut up the theatre of the Tarentines. He stopped
everything in the shape of amusement, and the young noble's prediction
as to the city's dancing days being nearly over, was completely verified.
It would certainly have been better for Pyrrhus in the end had he
listened in the beginning to his counsellor, Cineas, who, according to
Plutarch, talked the matter over with his royal master, in the most
familiar manner possible. "Now, tell me," said Cineas, "supposing
our expedition to be successful, what will be the next step?" a query
which elicited from Pyrrhus a whole catalogue of arduous exploits,
which he had in contemplation. "Very good," said the sage, "and
when all is conquered, what then?"—"What then?" responded
Pyrrhus, "why, then, of course, we can take our ease, drink, and be
merry."—"True enough," rejoined Cineas, "but why not take your
ease, drink, and be merry at once, without all the preliminary toils and
dangers you propose to undergo, and by which you only postpone,
instead of advancing, your ultimate object?" Unfortunately Pyrrhus,
like many others, failed to see the force of this kind of reasoning, and
he continued to encounter immediate peril and fatigue, with the remote

prospect of future repose, which there was nothing to prevent his taking at once if he had really set his head on it.

Though he would not acknowledge himself to be convinced by the arguments of the philosopher, it is probable that Pyrrhus secretly felt the value of the advice that had been given him; for his first step was a proposal to treat; and he even offered a draft by way of preliminary, but the Roman Consul rejected the proffered measure. The armies accordingly met on the banks of the Siris, a small river near Heraclea, and Pyrrhus sent a spy with a spy-glass, to inspect the position of the enemy. The spy was immediately spied out on the other side, and arrested forthwith, so that the look-out of the spy appeared utterly deplorable. Having, however, been shown everything there was to be seen in the Roman camp, as if he had been a traveller in search of information, instead of a sneak traversing a hostile area, the spy was sent back with care—right side upwards, which he scarcely deserved—to his master. This incident elicited from Pyrrhus the remark, that "the barbarians had an exceedingly gentlemanly way of conducting a war;" and the next day being fixed for the battle, he felt that he should have the satisfaction of a gentleman in going out with them.

The attack was commenced by the Romans; and the Consul, resolving either to sink or swim, sent a body of cavalry across the river. Pyrrhus, putting himself at the head of his horse, proceeded to meet the charge, but he soon perceived that his brilliant armour was rendering him uncomfortably conspicuous, and he exchanged his dazzling coat of mail for an old rusty suit worn by his friend Megacles. The latter was perhaps proud to wear the trappings of royalty, but the emptiness of false glitter was speedily exemplified, for Megacles being mistaken for the king, was killed, and the shining armour was carried in triumph to the enemy's camp before the hollow mockery was discovered.

The battle was fought with determined bravery on both sides, but brute force decided it at last, for the elephants of Pyrrhus weighed immensely in the scale of victory. The creatures coming down *en masse*, were more effective than the heaviest of ordinary heavies, and advancing with all their might upon the horses, the latter, though resisting with all their mane, felt their animal spirits rapidly oozing out of them. The carnage committed upon the Romans would have been merciless and complete, had it not been for the humanity of one of the elephants, who, taking a benevolent turn, pulled himself short round, and prevented his own side from continuing the pursuit of the fugitives. Pyrrhus, having laid his hands on everything he could take, proceeded to take everything he could lay his hands upon. A rich harvest having been collected, he, on the day following, went to glean what he could on the field of battle. Perceiving that the Romans had all fallen with their eyes towards the foe, he could not but acknowledge, with so much bravery staring him in the face, the courage of his antagonists. "With such soldiers as these," he exclaimed, "the world would be mine, or, at

all events, it would be theirs if I were their general." He had, however, lost half his own men ; and as they lay prostrate before him, they
seemed to offer a flat contradiction to the congratulations offered to him
on his victory. " Another such a triumph," he replied, " and I should
return to Epirus thoroughly unmanned, for there would not remain to
me a single soldier." He offered to the prisoners employment in his
own army, but they, without exception, refused ; and, considering their
conduct unexceptionable, he had their chains taken off, that they
might feel themselves quite unfettered in their future movements. He
burned the bodies of the dead, out of compliment to their remains,
whose combustion, could they have acted for themselves, would no
doubt have been spontaneous. He made a tolerably fair division of the
spoil, giving some to his allies, and devoted a considerable slice to Zeus
—a piece of devotion of which the priests of the temple got the chief
benefit.

The policy of Pyrrhus was to turn old foes into new friends ; and he
sent his trusty counsellor, Cineas, to Rome, with a suggestion that
all animosity should be buried in the graves of those who had fallen on
both sides. The Senators were beginning to waver, when Appius
Claudius the Blind—who had been carried down to the house by his
four sons—an arrangement that suggests the picture of a veteran
supported by a youth at each arm and at each leg—declared suddenly
that he could see through the whole affair, and called upon the
Romans to open their eyes to the designs of Pyrrhus. The veteran,
who, from infirmity, was unable to stir without assistance, could still
agitate with his tongue ; he urged that the proposals of Cineas should
be rejected ; and the assembly having first carried the motion, carried
home the mover in triumph.

Cineas, on returning to his master, described the city as a temple,
and the Senate as an assembly of kings ; for he could not get the
temples out of his head ; and the magnificent curule chairs kept
reminding him of the dignified setting down he had received from the
Senators.

Pyrrhus, finding his friendly advances repulsed, resolved on advancing
upon Rome in a less amicable spirit. Proceeding towards Capua, he
encountered Laevinius, the consul, whom he had on a previous occasion
beaten ; but he was now not quite so fortunate ; for, after a severe
contest, neither side could say exactly which had got the worst of it.
Pyrrhus, however, marched upon Praeneste, which fell into his hands,
in consequence of the Romans having let it slip through their fingers.
From the acropolis of Praeneste he is said to have seen Rome, at a
distance of eighteen miles ; but he must have seen very little, if so far
off, unless he was accustomed to magnify what he saw in a very remarkable manner. The sight was sufficiently imposing to cause him to
retreat ; and he went into winter quarters at Tarentum, where he spent
his own time, and the money he had taken from the enemy.

While Pyrrhus was thus engaged, or rather disengaged, three ambas-

sadors, named C. Fabricius, Q. A. Papus, and P. Dolabella, were sent
to him from Rome, to negotiate for the release of prisoners. C. Fabricius
was a very superior man; and Pyrrhus, thinking to gain over the
superior man, employed means by which none but a very inferior individual was at all likely to be influenced. Bribery was the first expedient attempted by Pyrrhus; but C. Fabricius showed his contempt for
money by pursing his eyebrows. Having failed in his coarse appeal to

Self-possession of Fabricius, the Ambassador, under rather Trying Circumstances.

avarice, Pyrrhus tried what was to be done through fear; and one day
a *tête-à-tête* between the king and the ambassador was disturbed by the
sudden introduction of a third *tête*, in the shape of the head of an

elephant. The sagacious brute stood concealed behind a curtain, and, with a blow of the trunk on the cheek, he administered a smart box on the ear to the startled ambassador. The animal accompanied the .act with a hideous roar, and threw his trunk over the head of C. Fabricius, who remained for a moment unable to see the clumsy joke that was being played upon him. He, nevertheless, retained his self-possession, remarking simply that neither by throwing gold dust in his eyes, nor by the still blacker job of the elephant's trunk, was he to be blinded to his duty.

Though Pyrrhus would not accede to the terms proposed for ransoming the Roman prisoners, he allowed them to go to Rome, for the season, to be present at the celebration of the *fêtes* of the Saturnalia. These games appear to have included some rather melancholy mirth, the principal fun of the affair consisting in the practice of shouting out " Io ! "—which is equivalent to " Go it ! "—in the public thoroughfare. Presents were exchanged among friends ; and servants were in the habit of offering wax candles to their masters,—a sort of composition, perhaps, which the former came to with their consciences, in memory of the enormities of the grease pot. The domestic was allowed to wear his employer's clothes ; and this portion of the ceremonies of the Saturnalia is still privately observed by the gentleman's gentleman of the family. While the wardrobe of the master remained at the mercy of the valet, the synthesis, or dressing-gown, was the fashionable attire ; and for a period of general relaxation, this loose wrapper was perfectly appropriate.

Having done at Rome as Rome was doing, during the Saturnalia, the prisoners returned to Pyrrhus, who opened the campaign in Apulia, and met the two Roman consuls—P. Sulpicius, and P. Decius Mus— at Asculum. This Mus is the third to which the labours of the historical muse have given birth ; and he is said to have shared the fate of his grandfather and father—if at least that fate can be said to have been " shared," of which each had to bear the whole inconvenience. The battle fought at Asculum was severe, the Romans having lost 6000 men ; for tradition delights in round numbers, with which probability often refuses to square ; and no less than three thousand five hundred and five—for in this case exactness is carried to a degree of excess—are said to have fallen on the side of Pyrrhus.

War was found to be doing its usual work, the sword was cutting both ways at once ; the candle was burning away at both ends, and the litigants were figuratively cutting their own throats, as well as those of their enemies. Each party would have backed out, if he could have seen his way, when an incident occurred that opened the door to a compromise. Pyrrhus had a medical attendant ; who, perhaps, felt that doctor's work might as well be done at first as at last, and offered to poison by one dose, instead of by slow degrees, his illustrious patient. The medical traitor accordingly prepared a draft, which he knew he could persuade Pyrrhus to accept ; but the Romans rejected the idea with scorn, and denounced the scoundrel, who when taken was severely shaken by his indignant countrymen.   The wretch at first denied having written the prescription, and attempted to eat his own words ; but they stuck in his throat, and he died from the physical impossibility of getting them either one way or the other.

Pyrrhus was so pleased with the treatment of the empiric who would have poisoned him, that he sent back all his prisoners to Rome without ransom, togged* out in new togas, and attended by pages, stitched in neat wrappers.   After some negotiation, which was assisted by the returned prisoners, who urged their own new suits in support of that of Pyrrhus, now eager for peace, a truce for four years was agreed upon.   It was stipulated that he should leave Italy, and he took the opportunity to cross to Sicily with the benevolent intention of freeing the people from the Carthaginian yoke ; but, like most foreign liberators, if he took off an old yoke with one hand, he had in the other a new apparatus, which he was anxious to substitute.   His object was to have made himself master of the place ; but after remaining three years, he began to lament the faithlessness of friends, and helping himself to as much booty as he could lay his hands upon, he left the Sicilians to deplore the loss of himself and the treasure he took away with him. He had, in fact, been sent for by the Tarentines, and was on his way to see what he could do for them, when he was met by a Carthaginian fleet, which sank seventy of his ships—as we are told by the same authority that represents him to have started with only sixty,—a fact which leaves little doubt as to which party profited most by the friend- ship between Pyrrhus and the people of Sicily.   He suffered a further loss in the mountain passes, where he had some very narrow escapes ; but he nevertheless continued to keep a balance of 20,000 foot, and 3000 horse for the purpose of meeting any future engagements.

On his arrival at Tarentum, there was such a panic among the Romans that nobody would enlist, until Curius Dentatus announced his intention of confiscating the property of the first who refused to enter the rank that was open to him.   Besides the panic caused by the name of Pyrrhus, an alarm had sprung up in consequence of the head of the god Summanus having been struck off his statue by lightning, and nobody could ascertain what had become of it.   Accident led to its discovery in the bed of the Tiber, from which it had probably been fished by one of those extraordinary hooks which so many of our historical facts are found to hang upon.   The augurs were consulted as a matter of course, and on a case being submitted to their opinion, they advised that the action against Pyrrhus should be carried on ; for, according to the soothsayers, the loss and subsequent finding of the head, proved that after hair-breadth escapes victory would crown their labours.

Pyrrhus in the mean time marched to Beneventum to attack Curius,

---

* The ignorantly squeamish, who may object to the word " togged," will please to observe that it is purely classical—the Latin *toga* being the root of the participle " togged," as well as the substantive " toggery."

intending to surprise the latter by sending, through a mountain pass, some troops and elephants. The idea of a short cut for these massive brutes was absurd, and the unwieldy bulk of the elephants caused a succession of stoppages in the highways and byeways through which they were being driven. The Greek columns got occasionally into a fearful fix, and it was with difficulty they could lug through the mountain pass

Discovery of the Head of Summanus.

their extremely bulky luggage. Instead of completing their journey by night, it was daylight before they had commenced their descent on Curius, who saw them at a distance, and prepared a warm reception for the elephants. He attacked them with burning arrows, and lighted barrels of tar, which were pitched among the poor brutes, who fell back upon their own camp, and every tent was turned into a crush-room. Several elephants were killed, and four, being taken alive, were made to march as prisoners in the Consul's triumph. Pyrrhus reached Tarentum with a handful of horse, and a pocket-full of bread; but, being unable to pay the salaries of his adherents, they soon fell away in the absence of the usual golden rivets. He retired to Greece, where he engaged in all sorts of adventures, till the want of money prevented him from carrying on the war in any shape; and it is said that he had come down, at last, to such very petty disputes, that he died of a blow on the head, from a stone aimed at him in a street-row by an angry woman. On the death of Pyrrhus, those whom he had assisted relinquished all hope of maintaining themselves against such a formidable enemy as Rome, and the Lucanians, Bruttians, and Samnites proceeded to do homage to a power they had been in the habit of

defying as long as they had any one on their side strong enough to
assist them in fighting their battles.   The Samnite ambassadors, who
were entrusted with the humiliating duty of conveying the submission
of their countrymen to Curius Dentatus, found him at his Sabine farm,
engaged in the discussion of a large dish of turnips.   He received the
envoys with no other form than a wooden one, upon which he was
seated, and he continued his vegetarian meal, as he listened to their
overtures.   They offered to bribe him with gold; but, taking up a
spoonful of the mashed turnips, he declared that, as long as he could
make sure of his daily bunch of his favourite luxury, wealth had no
charms for him.

Curius Dentatus refusing the Magnificent Gift offered by the Samnite Ambassadors.

The Samnites made one more desperate effort against Rome, and
Lollius, a runaway hostage, who had escaped to his native mountains,
found life such thoroughly up-hill work, that he resolved to change it, or
part with it.   Having got round him a band of robbers, who were just
the sort of persons to do everything by stealth, he secretly prepared to
attack the Romans ; but they, hearing of the approach of the marauders,
were early in the field, and, securing the leaders of the insurrection,
struck off their heads in order to break the neck of it.

Rome was now mistress of Italy, but her ambition, which, though
always vaulting, knew no bounds, would not allow her to keep her
empire within its natural limits.   In the management of her conquered
possessions she affected much generosity, in professing to admit the

vanquished to a share of her own advantages,—an operation she effected by taking all the advantages to herself in the first instance, and then conveying a small moiety back to those from whom they had been wrested.

The Colonial system pursued by Rome was peculiar, for instead of selecting uninhabited places, she preferred a population ready made, possessing wealth already acquired, of which she usually helped herself to a full third in exchange for a Government, which she supplied from her own large stock of persons in want of places. The relationship between Rome and her colonies has been compared to that of parent and child; but considering the stripping process to which Rome had recourse, she seems to have acted less as a mother than a kidnapper. The Roman Constitution, like the Roman cement, was an excellent compound, of which it is impossible to describe the ingredients; and, indeed, it is found that the best Constitutions—like our own British— are those which cannot be defined by a written prescription, or made the subject of a perfect analysis. There was a judicious spreading of political power over a considerable surface, and thus—to use a figure from the chemist's shop—a plaster was always ready to be applied to the sores, or even the trifling eruptions that might make their appearance on any portion of the great body of the nation.

As in our own admirable form of government, there were three estates, comprising the people, the senate, and the executive; but the want of a permanent and universally recognised head of the state, kept the country continually exposed to agitation on the part of designing demagogues.

As the sword, unfortunately, cuts the most prominent figure in the early history of Rome, we must not omit to speak of its military organisation, which was very complete; for in early times there seemed to be an impression that neighbours ought to be approached with the arm of war, rather than with the hand of friendship. Every Roman citizen was a soldier, and was liable at any moment to be called upon to turn his ploughshare into a sword, though when his special service was over he was at liberty to turn his sword back again into a plough-share. This transformation was not effected without damage to the instrument, and the ordinary operations of agriculture were frequently interrupted by calling the labourer from the garden to the field, and forcing him to drill when engaged in sowing broad-cast. We have in a single chapter of Livy* an account of what a Roman army consisted of during the great Latin war, and though learned writers† have snarled and quarrelled over the materials, like dogs over a dry and meatless bone, we quietly walk into the midst of them, and deliberately extract the marrow. An army may be described in half-a-dozen lines, though it consisted of five, which were termed respectively, *Hastati, Principes, Triarii, Rorarii,* and *Accensi.*

* Livy, viii.—8.   † Lipsius and others.

The *Hastati*, so called from their carrying the *hasta* or spear, consisted of youth in the bloom of early manhood, and who went in front, that their early bloom might encounter the first blow of the enemy. The next row was formed of the *Principes,* or men in the vigour of life, distinguished by the abundance and splendour of their shields, arms, and accoutrements, and comprising what may be termed the heavy swells of the army.   Next in order came the *Triarii,* a body of veterans, selected for their past experience—a quality which, however valuable in council, may be often useless in war; for though experience might have told a veteran that he ought to run for his life, his heels, being as old as his head, might have refused to do the latter's bidding. The fourth rank was composed of *Rorarii,* from the word *Rora,* dew, who sprinkled the enemy with various missiles, and who standing behind the *Triarii,* must occasionally, by aiming short of the foe, have given more than their due to the veterans immediately in front of them. Last in order came the *Accensi,* or supernumeraries, whose courage and fidelity were not of the highest class, and who either brought up the rear or left it behind, as their resolution urged them on, or their want of it kept them back, while there was always an opening left in case their fears should run away with them.   It was frequently the practice of the *Accensi* to reserve the vacant back-ground as a sort of race-course, in which races between their valour and their discretion were being continually run, and in the majority of cases the latter got by far the best of it.

The habits of the early Romans were extremely simple ; agriculture was their most honoured employment ; and it was thought high praise to say of any man, that he was a good husband, and a good husbandman. Their food was chiefly corn ; and many a happy family afforded an illustration of the fact that love, notwithstanding the assertion of the song writer to the contrary, can sometimes live on flour.   Wine was so precious, that, in libations to the gods, it was poured out drop by drop, to prevent their getting a drop too much ; and, indeed, so scarce was it in the early days of Rome, that Romulus is said to have used milk in his sacrifices ; while Papirius, at a later period, vowed, in the event of his victory over the Samnites, a small glass—or *petit verre*—to Jupiter.

Long beards were worn by the Romans until the arrival of a Greek barber from Sicily ; and he is said to have plucked out, with a pair of tweezers, the beard which had grown for four centuries and a half into a rooted habit.   On some he employed the razor, and he was able to reap an abundant harvest from the chins of a people who had never yet worn a smooth-faced aspect.

The invasion of Pyrrhus caused the adoption at Rome of many Grecian luxuries, and among others was the luxury of substituting a silver coinage for copper, which had been found so inconvenient that a rich man had been obliged to use a wagon instead of a purse, if he wished to take his money about with him.   Silver was, however, so scarce, that one Cornelius Rufinus was turned out of the Senate for having on his sideboard more than ten pounds of plate ; for it was believed that he could not have come honestly by so much of it, and he was regarded as either a thief, or at least as a receiver of stolen property.

So humble were the pretensions to display in those early days, that a silver cup and a salt-cellar formed, usually, the entire contents of a Roman noble's plate-basket.   Music, among the early Romans, was at the lowest possible pitch, and the only professors were flute-players, of scarcely any note, from Etruria.   Their strains were so dismal as to be employed only at a sacrifice or a funeral, when extreme melancholy was required.   On one occasion the band is said to have struck, and retired to Tibur, when the musicians were only brought back by being made helplessly drunk,—a weakness to which some of those hirelings who assist at the performance of funerals are in our day liable.

CHAPTER THE FIFTEENTH.

THE FIRST PUNIC WAR.

A LL Italy now belonged to Rome, but the thirst for conquest was not quenched even by the sea itself, beyond which the Romans prepared to extend their power. Among those who made a business of bloodshed, by lending themselves out as soldiers to any one who paid them, the Campanians enjoyed—if there could have been any real enjoyment in the matter—a bad eminence. They had followed the trade of human butchers for about fifty years; and, among other sanguinary engagements, they had accepted a job from the tyrant * of Syracuse.

The Campanians had done their work of devastation; and there being no further use for them, they had received notice to quit; but instead of returning home, they resolved to stay, and perpetrate a little plunder for their own exclusive benefit. They accordingly surprised the town of Messana—if any enormity may be considered surprising, when committed by such a set—and calling themselves the Sons of Mamers, or Mars, they established themselves under the title of the Republic of the Mamertines. From this point they carried on their trade of robbery and murder, which they put in practice right and left, upon most of their neighbours. On the unerring principle, that wrong never comes right, the rulers of Syracuse, who had, for their own bad purposes, introduced the Campanians into the place, became, in turn, the victims of that lawless band of freebooters. At length, Hiero, a king of Syracuse, determined on getting rid of the nuisance which his predecessors had established, and fell upon the Mamertines with such effect, that they were on the point of being crushed, when they were saved by the interference of a Carthaginian Admiral. The Mamertines being themselves faithless, were suspicious of every one else, and were as false to each other as they were untrue to all besides; so that they looked distrustingly on the offer made, and were unable to agree as to the

---

* The word "tyrant" meant, originally, nothing more than a sovereign who had arrived at supreme power by rather irregular means; but, as power thus obtained was most commonly abused, the words "tyrant" and "tyranny" became universally odious.

policy of accepting it. They were speedily in the position of a house divided, for some were ready to receive the protection of Carthage, while others sent for help to the Romans, who, to their utter disgrace, passed a decree, pledging themselves to an alliance with the Mamertine miscreants. It must be stated, to the honour of the Senate, that a majority of that body rejected the humiliating proposal with scorn ; but the Consuls, desirous of giving *éclat* to their term of office—an evil incidental to the system of having a temporary, instead of a permanent, head to the state—did all they could to plunge the country into a war, and brought the question before the assembly of the people.

The lower passions of pride and avarice are soon aroused among the mass by specious promises of glory and conquest ; and though each man might, for himself, have spurned an alliance with the Mamertine mercenaries, the result proved the truth of the saying, that " a corporation will do what an individual will shrink from with shame ;" for the Comitia Tributa voted that the disgraceful compact should be formed.

Appius Claudius, the son of the blind Consul, was sent to Messana with a fleet of TRIREMES, or vessels with three ranks of oars, which had been borrowed from the Greek towns of Italy ; for the Roman Admiralty, in the true spirit of a board, though continually building ships, was unable to produce an effective navy. Appius Claudius was not seaman enough to carry his TRIREMES to Sicily, and his rowers were not so expert as they should have been in the management of the oars, which were placed in ranks, one above the other, to a considerable height, so that a long pull, a strong pull, and a pull altogether was extremely difficult.

Having at last got near enough for a parley, he invited Hanno, the Carthaginian general, to a conference ; and, finding him a weak and nervous person, he seized him by the neck, and fairly shook the whole of his resolution out of him.

Hanno was frightened into delivering up the citadel, and returning to Carthage, he was hurried off to speedy execution, for having failed in the execution of his duty. King Hiero, being deprived of his Carthaginian aid, was completely beaten, and was glad to offer peace, or rather he was glad to get it, on any conditions, for his own condition was truly deplorable. He paid down 200 talents in ready money, which was equivalent to about fifty thousand pounds of our modern coin, to prevent the sacking of Syracuse, and by sacrificing all his cash in hand, he was able to save his capital. From this period may be dated the commencement of the first Punic War ; and as a feeble-minded reader may be dwelling on the word Punic, in the silly expectation of a pun, we, by explaining that it is derived from Phœnicia, whence Phœnic or Punic, at once check the morbid appetite. The city of Carthage is said to have been about one hundred years older than Rome ; but cities, like ladies beyond a certain date, baffle all attempts to reduce their age to a matter of certainty. Tradition assigns the foundation of Carthage to Dido, who, having been converted into an unprotected female by the murder of her husband, fled from Tyre, and when completely tired out, sat down to rest on the coast of Africa. Here she agreed to take, on a building lease, as much land as could be covered with a bull's hide, when, to the astonishment of the lessor, she produced a skin cut up into thongs, and acting as her own surveyor, she claimed to be monarch of all she surveyed, by putting this new species of leathern girdle round as much earth as possible. There was certainly less of the princess than of the tradeswoman in this transaction, which, however, was characteristic of the future city, for it became famous for its business and its bargains, as well as infamous for its bad faith ; the term *Punica fides* having become a by-word to express the grossest dishonesty. Her devotion to commerce led to the establishment of a powerful navy, and her citizens having something more profitable to do than to fight, her army was always hired from abroad when occasion required. Rome, on the other hand, had made war her chief pursuit, and the consequence was, that she had plenty of soldiers, but no ships, except a few she had taken from her foes ; and her occupations being mostly of a military or destructive kind, she had no resources but her valour to rely upon.

The Romans remained in Sicily, where several powers claimed their protection ; but Hannibal Gisco, anxious to preserve Agrigentum, threw himself and sixty elephants into it. Here he was besieged for seven months with an army of 50,000 men, who, of course, consumed daily a large quantity of food ; but there was something utterly irrational in providing daily rations for sixty elephants. It was arranged, therefore, that Hanno should proceed to the relief of Agrigentum, but he was defeated with the loss of thirty elephants, left dead on the field—a field which must have been necessarily a very wide one for conjecture. Hannibal Gisco's army consisted of a medley of mercenaries, including some Gauls, who, having much money owing to them, refused to strike, except for their pay, and who intimated that they would not draw their swords until they had drawn their salaries. Their general, unable to settle with them in cash, chose a more treacherous way of paying them off ; for, getting them into an ambush, he caused a volley of missiles to be aimed at them, and the discharge was in full of all demands, for it effectually stopped all further clamour.

Agrigentum was plundered by the Romans, who sold 25,000 of the inhabitants for slaves—at least, according to tradition, who usually deals in round numbers, amounting often in value to the sum which a perfectly round number or figure indicates.

Though the Carthaginians had failed on land, their fleet gave them advantages at sea, for there the Romans were completely out of their element. The latter, however, resolved to have a navy of their own, and the Board of Admiralty set to work in good earnest, with the co-operation of the Woods and Forests, which supplied the requisite timber. The difficulty now felt, was to obtain a design upon which to build, and instead of trusting to official surveyors, who might have shown plenty

of cunning, without producing any craft, the Romans took for a model
a Carthaginian quinquereme that had come ashore on the coast of

Roman Man-of-War, from a scarce Medal.

Bruttium. Being relieved from the supervision of the professional
architects, the ship-building progressed rapidly, and within sixty days
after the trees had been felled, one hundred and thirty ships were built;
though the builders must have been as green as the wood, and as crazy
as the craft, to have imagined that such a fleet could have any but the
most fleeting existence. While the vessels were being got ready, it
occurred to the authorities that crews would be required, and as
the Romans had as yet neither ships nor sailors, a few scaffolds
were erected on land, that the intended tars might try their hands
at naval tactics.

Matters went smoothly enough on shore, till the would-be seamen, having ventured out to sea, found themselves as ignorant as babies, when rocked in the cradle of the deep; and as the waves washed over them, they perceived they had learnt nothing of their new art but its driest details. With seventeen of these queer quinqueremes, each with 300 rowers, who by their misunderstandings kept up a continual but useless row, the Consul, Cn. Cornelius Scipio, sailed for Messana, when the Punic Captain Bugud, a regular Carthaginian tar, sent him flying, with half his timbers shivered, into a port of the Lipari. The crews, most of them half dead with sea sickness, scrambled as well as they could on shore. Their commander, Cn. Scipio, was taken prisoner, and so ridiculous had been the figure he cut, that his countrymen conferred upon him the name of Asina—or the donkey—a character that might in these days have qualified him for an appointment to a jackass frigate.

After this ludicrous defeat, the command of the Roman navy was taken by the other Consul, C. Duilius, who determined to wash out in the ocean, as well as he could, the stain thrown upon his countrymen. He felt that naval tactics were out of the question among those who were, in one sense, sailors of the first water, for they had never been on the water before; and as to rowing, he knew it to be so impracticable that he resolved to throw the oars overboard. He hit on an expedient for making a naval engagement resemble as much as possible a fight on shore; and by overcoming in some respect the inequalities of the waves, he put his own men on nearly the same footing with the enemy. He constructed boarding bridges, capable of holding two or three persons abreast, and these bridges being thrown on to the enemy's ships, enabled the Romans to walk into them.

The Carthaginians who were not prepared for such close quarters, and had trusted rather to the roughness of the sea, to deprive their opponents of an even chance of success, were so thoroughly taken by surprise, that they suffered their ships to be taken one after the other. C. Duilius was handsomely rewarded for his victory; he was hailed as the first naval hero that Rome had introduced, and as if the festive propensities of a sailor on shore had been foreseen, he was allowed the curious privilege of being accompanied home at night from banquets by an attendant with a torch—in which we see a foreshadowing of the policeman and the bull's-eye. He was further honoured by a *columna rostrata*, a sort of Nelson Column, adorned with the beaks of ships—a short stumpy looking affair, of which the museum at Rome contains an imitation from the hand of Michael Angelo,*—who has afforded us a fair copy of one of the columns of the Times, in which the deeds of great men were advertised.

This nautical exploit of Rome was followed up by minor successes,

---

* The curious reader, who is disposed to go over to Rome, will find the work of art alluded to in the text at the southern extremity of the vestibule, just at the foot of the staircase leading to the upper apartments, and close to a marble statue of Augustus.

and L. Scipio made an attack upon Corsica, where he was opposed by a Carthaginian fleet, under the command of Hannibal Gisco, who was killed by his own men, but honourably entombed by the Romans, who nobly buried their former animosity.

Carthage and Rome were mutually suffering by their hostilities, and each nation lost its thousands alternately, according to what is called the fortune of war; but which, like the fortune of the gaming-table, must end in the ruin of both sides, for the sole profit of the grim enemy. While the forces of Rome were being diminished nearly every day, her enemies were multiplying; and that inextinguishable race, the Samnites—the increase of whose population would present a most startling series of returns—appeared to the number of upwards of 4000, who had been enlisted into the Roman navy. Their intention was to set the city on fire, but their own leader threw cold water on it before it was even lighted, by making himself an engine of communication with the Roman Government.

In Sicily the Romans were continually in motion, but they took little by their motion beyond a few small towns. At length they determined on one grand naval effort, and they prepared 330 quinqueremes, which were placed under the Consuls, L. Manlius and M. Atilius Regulus, who were probably selected as the most likely to be able to command a fleet because they had never tried. The Carthaginians went to meet them with 350 quinqueremes, in which were—according to tradition—150,000 men; an instance of overcrowding which would have qualified the commander, Hamilcar, for the captainship of a Thames steam-boat. The collision between the two fleets was as destructive as might be anticipated. Thirty ships of the Carthaginians went to the bottom; and, considering their cargo, we can only wonder how they remained at the top. The Romans lost comparatively little, for with them matters went on pretty swimmingly. Regulus was so elated that he sailed for Africa, and, having taken Clupea, the neighbourhood of which was cultivated like a garden, he sat down to enjoy the fruits of success. He took the pick of everything he could lay his hands upon, and he pounced upon the cattle wherever a herd was to be seen. At the end of the year his colleague, L. Manlius, returned to Rome, with a portion of the fleet, and 27,000 prisoners—an arrangement that savours of an enormous cram—and left Regulus alone in his glory, which was destined to become his shame.

Early in the year of the city 498, Regulus, having the field to himself, went into it with great confidence. He laid siege to the town of Adis, which the Carthaginians tried to relieve; but getting among the mountains with their elephants, they were unable to turn round, and found themselves encumbered by the trunks as well as the bodies of these ponderous animals. Regulus took Tunis, and several other places, though in the course of the campaign he is said to have encountered an unexpected enemy in the form of a snake in the grass—a species of serpent one hundred and twenty feet long, which swallowed up his soldiers by hundreds—swords and all—though the reptile ran the risk of cutting its own throat by such extreme voracity.*

The Carthaginians were anxious for peace, and sent ambassadors to the Roman camp to negotiate, but Regulus, in his proposal of terms, exceeded all reasonable limits. He pretended to act on the principle of give and take, but the giving was to be all on one side, and the taking all on the other. The Carthaginians returned no answer to these insolent demands; but it is probable their silence must soon have been construed into consent, had it not been for the valour of a Spartan of the name of Xanthippus. This individual was a mere mercenary, who put other people to death for his own living; but he was, at all events, a working man, and infused his own spirit of energy into the Carthaginian army. He personally superintended the training, not only of the men, but of the elephants, and taught the soldiers how to wield as a power those hitherto unwieldy animals. Taking a hundred under his immediate tuition, he brought them into such a state of docility, that when turned out for exercise, they formed a stud worthy of the zoologist's attentive study.

With these sagacious brutes, and a large number of troops, he went forth against Regulus, whose army amounted to 30,000 men ; but the soldiers of Xanthippus fought with the courage of lions, which, backed up as it was by the firmness of the elephants, gave them a decisive victory. More than 30,000 Romans perished, if the accounts handed down to us are to be believed, and 500 were taken prisoners, though, if the same accounts are to be believed, the Roman army was only 30,000 strong; so that the 500 captives must have been supplied from some of those exclusive sources which are open to none but the historian. 2000 more are alleged to have escaped, but we must leave the reader to solve the difficulty as he can ; for as two into one will not go, so 33,500 out of 30,000 will not come by any process we are acquainted with. Xanthippus, the mercenary, had made it worth his while, for he was highly paid, and received rich presents, with which, as he dreaded the envy of the nobles, he thought he had better make himself absent as speedily as possible. He returned, therefore, to Sparta, to astonish the natives of his own city with the wealth he had acquired.

The Consuls of the year, Ser. Fulvius and M. Aemilius, were now despatched with the whole of the Roman fleet, amounting to about 300 ships, to Africa, where, after destroying the whole of the Carthaginian fleet, it went ashore on the southern coast; and this fleet of 300 ships lost, according to the authorities,† 340 vessels. The Carthaginians, whose army on land amounted to about 18,000, managed to lose about 30,000 at sea; but an abundant population was still left for the historian to deal, or rather to cut and shuffle, with. We must confess ourselves wholly incompetent to grapple with the arithmetical problems

---

* The tale of this serpent has come down to us from Livy, and would, no doubt, form a very suitable companion to the sea serpent, if the latter could be found.

† Diodorus.

that continually present themselves to us in the course of our re-
searches, and we therefore postpone all attempt at a solution of the
difficulty until the universal solvent shall be discovered.

The Romans and Carthaginians, instead of being overwhelmed by
their own misfortunes, were in high spirits at the disasters of each other,
and both parties proceeded to repair the damage done to themselves, in
order to qualify them for doing further injury. At Rome the Senate
ordered a new fleet to be built, which took several Carthaginian towns,
and Carthage ordered a fresh army to be levied, which took nearly all
the Roman vessels.

Shortly afterwards another naval force was despatched under the
Consuls, Cn. Serulius Cæpio and C. Sempronius Blaesus, who had got
together 260 ships, with which sundry ravages had been committed on
the African coast, when the sea, with its insatiable appetite, swallowed
up at a few gulps the greater part of the squadron.

Rome was now thoroughly sea-sick, and determined to have nothing
more to do with the water, but to wash her hands of it. She was,
however, still powerful by land, and encountered the Carthaginians at
Panormus, where the pro-consul, L. C. Metellus, gained a decisive
victory, by turning the elephants against their owners, and fighting the
latter as it were with their own weapons. This defeat led to a desire
on the part of Carthage for peace, and an embassy was sent to Rome,
accompanied by Regulus, who had been a prisoner five years, and who
agreed to consider himself morally in pawn, pledging himself to
return, if the terms proposed by Carthage should not be acceded to by
his countrymen. The conduct of Regulus seems to have been dictated
by a strong love of histrionic display, for he appears to have been
acting a part in which he sought to make as many effective points as
possible. In the first act we find him at the gates of Rome, refusing
to come in, although he had left Carthage for the purpose of doing so.
His wife and two children having gone to meet him, he looked at
them as strangers ; but this piece of dramatic effect may be accounted
for as springing from various other motives than those affecting the
patriot.

Having been invited to take his seat in the Senate, he at first refused,
but he yielded after a considerable amount of pressing ; a proof that his
refusal was founded on no fixed principle. When asked for his
opinion on the Carthaginian question, he spoke against the arrangement
he had been sent home to further, and the noble Romans strongly
urged him to stay behind, though he had pledged his honour to return,
and the Pontifex Maximus, the head of the religion of the nation, devised
a dodge by which Regulus might have evaded his promise. It must,
however, be stated, to his credit, that he kept his word to the Carthaginians, and returned among them ; but instead of being hailed as a hero,
he was denounced as an impostor, and put to death in the most cruel
manner. The stories told of his being corked up in a cask filled with
nails and serpents, are altogether false ; for, after carefully looking into

the matter, we are glad to be enabled to knock the cask to pieces by the gentlest tap possible.

Rome, having refused to make peace, was compelled, in self-defence, to go to war, and ordered 200 new ships with the recklessness of the spend-thrift who, calling on his coachmaker, desired that "some more gigs " should be immediately sent home to him. The Carthaginian fleet was in the harbour of Drepana, when P. Claudius Pulcher—son of Appius the blind, and who seems to have wilfully shut his eyes to the danger he ought to have seen—determined to surprise the enemy. Every attempt to dissuade him from his rash purpose was vain, and he persevered in spite of the auspices, which were declared to be unfavourable ; for the sacred chickens were completely off their feed—a fact he set at defiance, by observing that, if the birds would not eat, he would at least make them drink ; and he threw them all neck and crop into the water. The fate of the chickens went to the hearts of the Roman soldiers, who became thoroughly chicken-hearted, and fought so languidly, that they allowed themselves to fall by hundreds into the hands of the enemy. The Senate recalled Claudius to Rome, where a charge of high treason was preferred against him ; but a thunder-storm interrupted the proceedings, which were never resumed, for the thunder seems to have cleared the air of all the clouds impending over him. As he must have ultimately died in some way or other, and as there are no records of his having been put to death, history has returned an open verdict, which is equally adapted to the suspicion that he came to his death by his own hands, or that it was brought to him by the hands of his fellow countrymen.

The reverses of Rome by sea were a second time the cause of her giving up her naval establishments, and she sold her marine equipments to the dealers in marine stores, at a ruinous sacrifice. Carthage, therefore, became mistress of the seas ; but the mistress being unable to pay the wages she owed, began borrowing money of her neighbours. Ptolemy of Egypt was applied to, but he civilly laid his hand on his heart, declaring he had nothing to lend, and kept his money—if he had any— in his pocket. In this dilemma, the command of the Carthaginians fell upon Hamilcar, surnamed Barca, or the lightning, from his being one of the fastest men of the day ; and though any general, equal to the general run, might head a force with plenty of money to pay the troops, a genius was required to keep an army going, or rather to keep up a standing army, with empty pockets. He found the mercenaries in a state of insubordination for want of their customary emolument ; but, having no money of his own, he made Bruttium and Locri his bankers, and gave his soldiers a general authority to draw, with their swords, for whatever they required. Taking his position on Mount Hercte, now the Monte Pelegrino, he maintained himself and his army for three years, enabling his troops to carry out the principle of **spending** half-a-crown out of sixpence a day—the sixpence being their own, and the half-crown being anybody else's, from whom it could be most conveniently taken. After remaining three years at Hercte, he removed to the town of Eryx, intending to tire the Romans out; but like many others who attempt to exhaust the patience of others, he found his own stock rapidly diminishing. He was drawn into an engagement, in which he lost so many of his soldiers, that he was obliged to ask for a truce to bury the dead; but the Roman general would give him no undertaking not to proceed during the funerals. A short time afterwards, when the fortune of war had changed, Hamilcar was asked to give a similar permission, and, by allowing the burials to proceed, he has raised a monument to his own magnanimity.

The Romans, who were as fickle on the subject of a fleet as the element to which it was destined, resolved a third time to have a naval force; but ships were out of the question, when raising the wind was quite impossible. The state being without funds, appealed to the merchants, who consented to sink a large sum in an entirely new navy, with the understanding that if the tide of fortune should turn in their favour, they were to receive their money back again. The Romans had by this time become better sailors than before, while the Carthaginian tars had greatly deteriorated for want of practice. The ships of the latter were so heavily laden with corn that they could not' proceed like chaff before the wind; and the sailors, encumbered by the cargo, found themselves going continually against the grain in attempting to work the vessels. The Romans obtained an easy victory, but it could not have been so easy to dispose of its results; for, after killing 14,000 men, they found themselves still saddled with 34,000 prisoners. A peace was concluded; one of the conditions being, that Carthage should pay to Rome 200 talents by instalments extending over twenty years—an arrangement equivalent to the discharge of a liability at the rate of one shilling per annum in the pound, and the extinction of the whole debt by simply paying the interest.

The first Punic War was now at an end, and it was high time it should be, for the losses sustained on both sides were enough to have exhausted the Roman as well as the Carthaginian population; and our history would then have come to an abrupt termination, like the tragedy of the youth, who was obliged to drop his curtain in the second act, in consequence of his having killed all his characters. It is fortunate, therefore, that the classical authorities, after " cutting to pieces " their thousands and drowning their hundreds, in a day, should have paused in their career of devastation just in time to leave something to go on with, to the conscientious historian.

While, however, war killed everything else, it kept itself alive in the most extraordinary manner; for though brought to a temporary pause by having swallowed up all its usual articles of consumption, fresh food was speedily found, and the jaws of destruction were again on active service.

The Romans having subdued Sicily, proceeded to prepare a constitution, or, in other words, having rendered the place subservient to themselves, they took measures for supplying a livery. Being tired of the old pattern, they devised something new, and produced an article of the following fashion :—They made Sicily a province ; but those whose province it is to say what a province was, have left us in some doubt as to its precise meaning. The best definition is that which derives the word from Providentia, a duty, or a thing that ought to be done, and the provinces of the Romans were sometimes done indeed, though in a sense more modern and familiar than classical. A province, instead of becoming a part of Rome, retained its national existence, though such existence was scarcely worth having, for it was accompanied by a loss of sovereignty,—a condition that may be compared to that of a body living after its head was off.

A governor was sent annually from Rome with a long train of officials, and the appointment being only for a year, leaves no doubt that the holder for the time being made the most he could of it. His staff included two Quæstors or tax-collectors, and a number of Præcones or auctioneers, who were always ready to sell off, in the event of a seizure. Sicily was, in fact, in a state of complete servitude to Rome, the only anomaly in the relationship consisting in the fact that the master, or rather the mistress, received the wages, instead of paying them. The amount was fixed at one-tenth of the wine, the oil, the olives, and other products of the soil ; so that much of the fat of the land became the perquisite of the mistress of Sicily. These tenths were called *decimæ*, and so ruinous was their effect on the place whence they were drawn, that the words decimation and destruction have become nearly synonymous.

The constitution of Rome had remained much the same during the period to which the present chapter refers, though the aristocracy of birth was beginning to give way to the far more objectionable aristocracy of money. Such was the influence of wealth, that the Quæstors or tax-collectors became members of the Senate as vacancies occurred, and the enormous riches of these persons proved how much of the public money, of which they had the entire handling, stuck to their fingers.

CHAPTER THE SIXTEENTH.

SOME MISCELLANEOUS WARS OF ROME.

ROSTRATE greatness always offers an inviting mark to upstart littleness; and the story of the Lion *couchant* kicked by the Jackass *rampant*, is as old, at least, as the days when Rome, exhausted by her wars with Carthage, was attacked by the imbecile inhabitants of the feeble city of Falerii.

Had the Faliscans dashed their heads deliberately against a brick wall, they could not more effectually have shown how few brains they possessed; and, to carry out the figure of the Lion and the Ass, a switch of the former's tail soon told the latter's story. A few days sufficed to lay the Faliscans in the dust they had so foolishly kicked up, and in the clouds of which we very rapidly lose sight of them.

The Carthaginians had been compelled to evacuate Sicily, and the mercenaries were of course to be paid off in one way or the other. On a former occasion, some of the hired soldiers who had demanded their money were taken to a bank—which proved to be a sand-bank in the sea—where, at the rising of the tide, they, instead of their claims, were subjected to immediate liquidation.* The army from Sicily took, however, a firmer stand, and proceeded to Carthage with a determination to do business in the city. It contained, as they knew, the spices and luxuries of India on which they loved to live; the purple of Tyre, which taught them how to dye; and the ebony and ivory which proclaim in black and white the wealth of Ethiopia. The persons who poured into the place formed an assemblage less pleasing than picturesque, for the group comprised all sorts—except the right sort—of characters. Among the mass might be seen the almost naked Gaul, who was outstripped in barbarity by some of the other tribes; the light cavalry of dark Numidians, and men who had their arms in slings; for such were the weapons of the Balearic slingers. The mercenaries, immediately

* Diod. 5.

M

on their arrival in Carthage, proceeded to the Treasury, where they found
nobody but Hanno, who in an appropriately hollow speech, announced the
emptiness of the public coffers. He regretted the necessity for appearing
before them in the character of an apologist; but while admitting how
much Carthage owed to the troops, he announced the impossibility of
paying them. The State, he said, was heavily taxed, and, he added, with a

Hanno announcing to the Mercenaries the emptiness of the Public Coffers.

feeble attempt to be facetious, that he must lay a small tax upon their
patience, by getting them to wait for their money. The speaker was
at once assailed with imprecations in ten different languages ; but he
stood firm under the polyglot uproar. The cry of " Down with him ! "
reached his ears in nearly a dozen different tongues ; and when he tried
to remonstrate, through the medium of interpreters, the worst inter-

pretation was put on all that was said, and a good understanding seemed quite impossible.

An attempt was then made to stop the mouths of the mercenaries with food ; and provisions were sent in abundance ; but the only reply was, an unprovisional demand for the money owing. At length the pay had been got together, and was about to be distributed, when an Italian slave, named Spendius, who had probably spent by anticipation all he had to receive, advised his companions to decline the offer, on the ground that if they refused what was due, their policy might obtain for them a large additional bonus. The suggestion was popular with the mercenaries, who held a meeting to discuss the point, and who, to save the time of the meeting, overwhelmed with a shower of stones anybody who rose to speak on either side. The resolution was soon carried ; but it was by the aid of what may be termed the casting votes of those who sent up, in the impressive form of a plumper, the first missile they could lay their hands upon. For three years these intestine disturbances raged in Africa, and reduced it to the lowest point of exhaustion, till at length the malady wore itself out, though Hamilcar Barca, by intercepting the supplies of the rebels, assisted greatly in depriving treachery of the food it lived upon.

The pecuniary panic of Carthage spread in nearly every direction, and the mercenaries at Sardinia, affected by the tightness of money, called upon the African colonists to pay with their lives the debt they could not discharge with their pockets. While the Sardinians and Carthaginians were reducing each other to a state of such weakness that neither could make any further effort, Rome stepped in, and like the lawyer between the exhausted litigants, carried off the whole of what they had been fighting for. Sardinia became a Roman province ; when Carthage, whose bad faith has passed into a proverb, complained bitterly of the treachery of Rome : for we find the story of the kettle accused of blackness by the pot, is as old as the earliest pothooks employed in the writing of history. Hamilcar, who was the patriotic mouthpiece of the day, declared that he would raise his country ; and it must be admitted, to his honour, that he did not take the means employed by self-styled patriots, who pretend to raise a country by stirring it up from the lowest dregs, but he tried to elevate it by all the honourable means in his power.

Rome had at this time her hands tolerably full, and found employment for her arms in all directions ; when, to add to her embarrassment, the Cisalpine Gauls were set in a flame by one of the many irons that she had in the fire. An Agrarian law, proposed by the tribune, C. Flaminius—whose name savours of the firebrand—was the cause of the outbreak. The measure enacted, that the land taken from the Gauls should be distributed among the Romans ; and accordingly some settlers were sent out, who unsettled everything. The Cisalpines commenced negotiations with their Transalpine allies ; but though the negotiations were carried a very long way, they eventually came to nothing.

M 2

Rome was so occupied with foes, that she had scarcely time to turn round ; but when she did turn round, she discovered that some very objectionable proceedings were being carried on behind her back by a set of people called the Illyrians.   These persons picked up a dishonest living as pirates, and had plundered, among others, some Italian merchants who supplied the Italian warehouses of Rome and its neighbourhood.   The Illyrians were ruled over by a woman, named Teuta, who, when applied to for reparation, observed that she was sorry for what had occurred, but that piracy was what her subjects got their living by, and she did not see how she could interfere with the manners and customs of her people.   The Roman ambassadors answered, that the custom of their country was to protect the injured ; but on this occasion, at least, the country failed in its Protectionist principles, for the ambassadors were slain before they could get home again.   When their death was known at Rome, every exertion was made to afford them that protection which came too late to be of any use, and a large army was sent into the country of the Illyrians.   The Roman arms were perfectly successful, and Teuta was glad to obtain peace by promising to put down piracy, and by actually putting down a very large sum of money by way of tribute.   Rome had done considerable service to the Isles of Greece by checking the disreputable trade of piracy ; and as the Romans took evident pride in being noticed by the Greeks, the latter paid the former for their military aid, by some of those civil attentions which cost nothing.   At Athens, as well as at Corinth, Roman embassies were received ; and though the ambassadors might be considered rather too venerable for sport, they were allowed to take part in the Isthmian Games, as well as in the Eleusinian Mysteries.

The Isthmian Games were the same as those at Olympia, of which we furnish a brief outline for the information of those who feel an interest in the sporting annals of antiquity.

During the first thirteen Olympiads, the only game was the foot-race, of which the spectators and the competitors, but especially the latter, if they selected it as their walk of life, must have been at last thoroughly tired. Wrestling was next introduced under the name of πάλη, or Lucta; and though wrestlers have for centuries been endeavouring to throw each other, they have not yet fallen to the ground, for they still maintain a footing in the sports and pastimes of our own people.   Next came the Pentathlon, a sort of five-in-one, which comprised, in addition to the foot-race and wrestling, the practice of leaping, in which much vaulting ambition was displayed ; and throwing of the discus, as well as of the spear—an exercise that required the utmost pitch of strength and dexterity.   Subsequently boxing was introduced, under the name of Pugilatus, and it seems to have resembled pretty closely our own pugilistic encounters ; for in ancient works of art we find the boxers represented with faces whose indentures witness their apprenticeship to the degrading trade they followed.   The physicians of the period are said to have recommended boxing as a remedy for headache ; * but this application of the theory of counter irritation is not adopted in modern practice.   Another feature of the Olympian and Isthmian Games was the Pancratium, a contest calling for all the powers of the combatant.   In this exercise biting and scratching were allowed—a disgraceful license which leaves us in no doubt as to the classical source whence the vulgar phrase of " going at it tooth and nail " is derivable. Horse and chariot races were also introduced, as well as contests of trumpeters, who dealt out blows of the most harmless description against each other.

Early Roman Gladiator and his Patron.

Such were the games in which the Róman visitors to Corinth were allowed to take part ; and we will now proceed to confer on the reader the privilege once peculiar to the inhabitants of Athens, by initiating him into the Eleusinian Mysteries.   Their celebration lasted several days, the first of which was occupied in getting together the mystæ, or initiated, whose qualification consisted in their having sacrificed a sow —an act less worthy of a priest than of a pork-butcher.   On the second day the mystæ went in solemn procession to the sea-coast, where they took a bath, by way of wetting the public curiosity.   On the third day they went through the interesting ceremony of a fast, which, to the looker-on, must have been a somewhat slow process.   The fourth day was devoted to the carrying about of a basket containing poppy seeds ; and this literally seedy procession was closed by a number of women, each holding in her hand a mystic case, the contents of which were in no case allowed to be visible.   On the fifth day the mystæ went, with lighted torches, to the temple of Demeter, at Eleusis, where they spent the night ; but the torches throw no light upon what they were looking for.   The sixth was the grandest day of all, and was employed in carrying about a statue of the son of Demeter ; in whose honour the mysteries were held ; because, when wandering about in search of her daughter, she had supplied corn—though nobody can say how she carried it about with her—to the inhabitants of Athens.   During the night of this important day the mystæ were taken, in the dark, to see what nobody appears to have seen at all ; and we are therefore spared the trouble of describing it.   On the seventh day the initiated returned to Athens, and stopped on their way at a bridge over the Cephisus,

* Aretæus de Morb. diut. Cur. i.

from which they indulged in jests at the passers-by; and the obscurity of the jokes would, no doubt, if they had come down to us, have been thoroughly in keeping with the mysteries they were intended to celebrate.

Such were the games and mysteries to which the Romans were admitted in Athens and Corinth, though they had, at about this time, established among themselves a sport exceeding in ferocity the scratchings and bitings of the Greek Pancratiastæ, or the ear-flattening and nose breaking efforts of the Corinthian pugilists.

Until the Punic War commenced, the state had found money for the public games at Rome; but war having exhausted the treasury, the expense of amusing the people was thrown upon the Ædiles, who made the matter a medium of corruption, for they vied with each other in their outlays, in order to catch the votes of the people. The Ædile who had carried on the most extravagant games was the most likely to get elected to higher dignities; for popularity has ever been, and it is to be feared ever will be, the prize of those who possess the art of dazzling, rather than permanently enlightening the people. That their taste was degraded by those who sought their suffrages, we learn from the fact, that at about this time the sanguinary conflicts of the gladiators * were first added to the amusements of the populace.

There seems to have existed in almost all ages and countries a morbid appetite, similar to that which formerly gorged itself on the spectacle of human beings " butchered to make a Roman holiday." When the brute-tamer promises to thrust his head into the mouth of the lion, or the " intrepid aëronaut " is about to risk the dashing to pieces which some previous aëronauts have experienced, and from which others have narrowly escaped, the crowds who flock to be present are actuated by the same sanguinary thirst for brutal excitement which filled the Roman amphitheatre when an encounter of gladiators was advertised. The attraction was great enough on ordinary occasions, but an overflow could always be secured by announcing an entertainment *sine missione*, which implied that the lives of the conquered were not to be spared. It is to be feared that many of those who have never been at Rome are nevertheless prepared to do as Rome did on the occasions alluded to; and if the certainty, instead of the mere chance, of a sacrifice of human life were to be announced as an entertainment, the largest place of amusement in the metropolis would, in all probability, be thronged, though the ordinary charge for admission should be doubled.

The early Roman gladiators were either captives or malefactors, and were fed on a particular kind of diet, as brutes in the present day are fattened for the prize-show and the shambles. To give as much variety as possible to the sport, the gladiators were divided into

---

* The first public exhibition of the kind at Rome took place B.C. 244, at the funeral of the father of Marcus and Decius Brutus; but the Ædiles carried out the idea on what they considered a grand scale, and immense numbers of gladiators were sacrificed for the " amusement " of the people.

different classes, and, with an excess of ferocity almost incredible, measures were adopted to give a dash of mirth to the frightful encounters. Some of the combatants, called Andabatæ, wore helmets without any apertures for the eyes, so that "roars of laughter" might be excited at an occasional display of blind fury. Others, called Retiarii, carried nets to throw over the heads of their antagonists, and when caught in these nets, their lives hung upon a thread; for, if the net did not break, their defeat was unavoidable.*

The foes of Rome were just about this time so numerous, that whichever way she looked, she had in her eye the sword of an enemy. The Boians, the Tauriscans, and the Insubrians, with a number of miscellaneous tribes, entered into an alliance, and threatened to enter into Rome itself, where a prophecy was current, that the Gauls and Greeks would take the city. Having consulted the book of fate, the Romans found instructions for burying alive in the forum two Gauls and two Greeks; a proceeding which, but for its connection with the grave, would border on the ludicrous. An army, under the Consul L. Æmilius Papus, was sent to Ariminum; but the Gauls, ignoring the movement, advanced within three days' march of Rome, and ultimately found themselves between the army just mentioned and another army that had been stationed in Etruria. Flight was their only resource; and though the cavalry took to their horses' heels, and the infantry took to their own, forty thousand are said to have fallen on the field; but even imagination, which is accustomed to wander in very wide fields, can scarcely find one sufficiently extensive for such an incident.

It would seem that population in those days partook of the nature of corn; for however thoroughly a people might be cut down and thrashed in one year, there was always an abundant supply for the sword of an enemy to go to work upon in the year following. The Gauls were accordingly to be found in full force within twelve months after their having been destroyed, and the consul, C. Flaminius, killed them all over again; but they still were numerous enough in body, and sufficiently poor in spirit, to acknowledge the sovereignty of their conquerors.

While the attention of Rome had been divided among her numerous foes, the remnant of the Carthaginians had been expanding with the usual rapidity, and had extended to Spain, where, under Hamilcar Barca, a Carthaginian empire was in the course of being established. Hamilcar's policy towards the Spaniards was bold and rather original, for he determined to win their affections by thoroughly beating them. Every blow he aimed produced a favourable impression, and the Spaniards were as ready as so many spaniels to lick the hands that were continually smiting them.

The system of Hamilcar was followed after his death by his son-in-

* It may be hinted to the student that the Dying Gladiator in the Museum at Rome is no gladiator, but a Gaul; and the collar round his neck, supposed to be a mark of disgrace, is, in fact, the Torques, a symbol of honour. The sculpture is Greek, and belongs to a period of Art long previous to the introduction of gladiatorial displays.

law, Hasdrubal, who ruled in Spain for eight years, and who proved so good a ruler, that matters were kept as straight as could be desired. He was, however, assassinated at last by some culprit, who has eluded the vigilance of the historical detectives, for not even Niebuhr, who stands acknowledged as A 1, has been able to lay his finger on the criminal.

Hasdrubal was succeeded by the son of Hamilcar Barca, a young man named Hannibal, whose precocity as a lad was exemplified by an awful oath, which he took at nine years old, under the direction of his father. Whether it was judicious of a parent to teach his son to swear, is a question for the moralist; but whether a child of nine could have understood the nature of an oath, is usually a question for a judge; and any intelligent reader may safely act as a judge in the matter alluded to.

The biographers of Hannibal have endeavoured to prove that he was that precocious nuisance, an infant prodigy, because, at the age of nine, he expressed a desire to accompany his father to the wars; though there is scarcely an infant of those tender years who, if asked "whether he would like to go with his papa," would not answer "yes," as a matter of course, without having the slightest notion where he might be going to. Young Hannibal is said to have learned the art of war in the camp, and to have gone into arms before he could be considered fairly out of them. Before leaving Carthage, his father administered to him a soldier's oath, and the boy swore like a trooper that he would be Rome's implacable enemy.

On succeeding to the command in Spain, he was twenty-six years old —a proof that promotion had been very rapid in his case; and, although merit may have had something to do with his rise, there can be little doubt that he owed much to interest. Adopting the policy of his predecessor, he attempted to engrave his name in the hearts of the Spaniards by the agency of the sword; and he may be said to have literally thrust himself upon them, though they were often bored to death by his too pointed attentions. All the South of Spain was under his thumb, with the exception of Saguntum, which had hitherto slipped through his fingers. He proceeded, therefore, to take it immediately in hand, when the Saguntines sent for assistance to Rome, whose Senate resolved unanimously that Hannibal could not attack the place; but when a copy of the resolution reached him, he had already begun besieging the city. He sent word to the ambassadors who brought the intelligence out, that they would display a sad want of intelligence if they ventured to come too near to him; and, as he had no time to go to them, they had better retire. Acting upon his suggestion, they repaired to Carthage, where they demanded that Hannibal should be given up; and there being some hesitation among the Carthaginian Senate, Q. Fabius, one of the Roman ambassadors, made a fold in his toga as if he had some mystery wrapped up in it. "Here," he exclaimed, "is either peace or war, whichever you prefer;" to which the Senate, in a

Hannibal, whilst even yet a child, swears eternal hatred to the Romans.

spirit rather military than civil, replied, "Whichever you think proper."
Fabius, throwing back his toga, and assuming an imposing attitude,

His Excellency Q. Fabius offering Peace or War to the Carthaginian Senate.

exclaimed, "Then I offer you war;" when the Punic Senators, taking
up his last word, raised through the senate-house a shout of "War,"
which, vibrating through every pillar, was conveyed by every post, and
echo sent back an immediate answer.

This was a declaration of that Second Punic War, for which Hannibal
began to prepare when Saguntum, after having held out for eight
months, was starved into submission. Though rich in the precious
metals, and particularly in silver, the Saguntines experienced the bitter

truth, that to be born with a silver spoon in one's mouth, is but an empty gratification, after all, when the spoon has nothing in it. Hannibal sacked the city, and converted into baggage all the loose silver he could find, which he kept in hand for the purpose of glutting the avarice of his troops, whose valour depended materially on other people's metal.

The battle of Saguntum was signalised by the introduction of a weapon called the Falarica, which was in one respect a species of fire-arm,—for its point was covered with flaming pitch and tow, that, when pitched with effect, carried fire into the ranks of an enemy. It was, perhaps, fortunate, that inventive ingenuity had not gone very far among a people who seemed only disposed to throw away the little they possessed of it, in the form of destructive missiles.

CHAPTER THE SEVENTEENTH.

THE SECOND PUNIC WAR.

WE have now arrived at the great historical drama of the Second Punic War, which some authorities have divided into five acts; the principal part being undertaken by Hannibal, and the scenery being laid in Italy, Spain, Sicily, and Africa. The first act opens with the passage of Hannibal over the Alps, which forms one of the most remarkable passages in the life of that renowned soldier. In the second act we arrive at the taking of Capua; and in the third, we see Hannibal on the look-out for reinforcements, which never arrive from his brother Hasdrubal. The fourth act brings us to Italy, from which the Carthaginian commander makes a forced exit; and for the last act of all, the scene is changed to Africa, when the curtain and 20,000 Carthaginians fall together.

Hannibal having resolved on the part he was about to play, called together those who were to act with him in the stirring scenes in which he intended to figure. His company consisted of 90,000 foot, 12,000 horse, and an unrivalled stud of 37 elephants. With this troop he crossed the Pyrenees, by means of slopes, which nature had kindly provided, instead of platforms. The first incident of importance which happened on the way, was a mutiny among those, who, when they arrived at the foot of the mountain, protested against being brought to such a pass; and Hannibal wisely sent the discontented back, that the insubordination might go no further. Forty thousand foot retraced their steps, and 3000 horse backed out, on the opportunity being offered them. With the rest of his army, he reached the banks of the "arrowy Rhone," which he found particularly arrowy when he made an effort to cross; for he did so under a shower of darts from the Gauls, who thus pointedly objected to his progress. The hostility manifested towards the invaders was not simply on account of their appetite for conquest, but their appetite for food was productive of a most inconvenient scarcity. To provide every day for 60,000 soldiers was difficult enough, but there was something awful in the idea of the daily dinner-party being increased by 9000 hungry horses, and nearly 40 healthy elephants. The passage of the Rhone was a matter of considerable difficulty; for the horses stood plunging on the banks of the river, instead of plunging boldly into it. The elephants were still less tractable, and were, after much trouble, pushed or persuaded on to a raft, covered with earth and bushes, to make it resemble dry land; but it no sooner began to move, than the unwieldy animals felt themselves and their confidence seriously shaken. This caused them to crowd together to the edge; and, while taking this one-sided view of their position, they turned the matter over so completely, that they all fell in with one another, and most of them came to the same conclusion. Continuing his journey, Hannibal arrived at the bottom of the Alps, and, coming to the foot of St. Bernard, he extracted from the foot all the corn he could lay his hands upon. The weather was, unfortunately, so severe that the cold nearly broke his army up into shivers; while provisions were so scarce that at one time there seemed to be no chance of anything to eat but ice, and though the air was thoroughly gelid, it was impossible to live on it. Tradition tells us, that when Hannibal came to this point of his journey he found two brothers in the middle of a fight for a crown; but what was the country to which the crown belonged, or whether the article was a mere bauble that had been picked up in the road, or whether the crown was a sum of money representing the stake for which the brothers fought, we have no means of determining. The combatants, at all events, agreed that Hannibal should arbitrate between them; when, adopting the principle of "Age before honesty," he adjudged the article in dispute to the elder of the litigants. The decision did not involve any very remarkable acuteness on the part of the umpire, who seems simply to have sided with the big brother against the little one. The successful claimant was so delighted with the judgment delivered in his favour, that he placed a large stock of clothes, for the army, at the disposal of Hannibal. Some fearful misfits arose from this neglect of the wholesome maxim, "Measures, not men," for there was not a man whose measure could have been properly taken.

It was now time to undertake the ascent of the Alps, and to commence operations on a scale so grand, that all former experience in scaling a height, was little better than useless. Many of the soldiers at the sight of the mountains, instead of rising with the occasion, sunk with it into a fainting state; and others objected to venture into the snow, on the ground that they did not understand the drift of it. Hannibal represented the whole affair as a mere nothing; and added, that the passage over the Alps was not such very up-hill work after all, for that men, women, and even children, had often been quite up to the work he now proposed to cut out for his army. "Soldiers!" he exclaimed, "you have no choice, except between certain famine on one side of the Alps, or fertile plains, which you may see plainly enough in your mind's eye, on the other." Hannibal having made this brief speech, was rewarded with loud cheers; the army followed him, and proceeding to the passes, he found them lined with Gauls; but he tore the lining out in the most merciless fashion.

On reaching the Valley of the Tarentaise, Hannibal was offered guides, whom, however, he distrusted; and refusing, therefore, to be led away by specious promises, he sent his baggage by way of experiment; intending, when he heard of the safe arrival of his soldiers' trunks, to despatch by the same route their entire body. When the elephants came within a stone's throw of the Gauls, the latter hurled down rocks in vast masses on the affrighted beasts, and snowballed them with the snow from the loftiest part of the mountains. The assailants, however, completely missed their aim, for Hannibal threw himself upon them, and succeeded in completely crushing them.

It was a fine October morning when the Carthaginian general set out to cross the Alps by the road over the Little St. Bernard, and after a nine days' march, which was at that time a nine days' wonder, he reached

Hannibal crossing the Alps.

the top of the mountain. The fatigue endured by Hannibal and his army cannot be described, and the toils of the journey were aggravated by the chance of their falling into the toils and snares of the enemy. Little passed their lips in the shape of food, and very little passed their lips in a contrary direction, for they were afraid to speak, lest their words should disturb the impending avalanche. The way was rugged, save where it was carpeted by the snow; but even where it was trodden hard enough to serve as a sort of track or guide, they could scarcely trust to it, for it gave them the slip every now and then in the most unsatisfactory manner. On the tenth day they began their descent; and they, perhaps, little thought at the moment that in quitting the top of the Alps they were coming down to posterity. The two first days slid away merrily enough over the ice and snow, but on the third they arrived at a point where the ground had slipped out of its place, and left to the enterprising travellers a far from eligible opening.

The shifting of the earth had, in fact, put them to the most perplexing shifts, for the old road had perversely gone out of its way to baffle the travellers, and lay at the distance of 1000 feet below them. As Hannibal looked down upon the chasm, his spirits fell for a moment; but he speedily rallied, and determined, rather than allow his army to perish with cold, that he would make a way with them. Nature, however, opposed him by means of a mass of rock; and as he and Nature were at variance, he began to think how he could best split the difference. How he made his way cannot be confidently stated, though several of the learned *, who have gone deeply into the subject, have come out of it in opposite directions; and the authorities cannot be said to clash, for they are as wide apart as possible. Tradition, who never fails to take a trenchant way of getting through a difficulty, settles the point at once, by attributing to vinegar the success of Hannibal's scheme; but the vinegar must have been sharp indeed to have cut asunder the rocks which barred the progress of the illustrious traveller.

It is difficult, also, to conceive how he could have carried with him the liquid in sufficient abundance to enable him to accomplish the object he had in view, and we are inclined to the belief that it was by continued assiduity, rather than by a mere acid, that the wondrous task was effected. A good-sized cruet full of vinegar would produce no impression on a common pebble, and when we imagine how many hogsheads after hogsheads must have been necessary to moisten the rocks through which Hannibal passed, it can only be the sheerest pig-headedness that would still obstinately adhere to the supposition we have stated.

The passage of Hannibal over the Alps may be regarded literally as one of the grandest passages in history. Though subsequent generals have, in some degree, generalised the achievement, the special merit of it belongs to the Carthaginian leader, whose superiority over his followers consists in the fact that they did but find the way, while he might have claimed the credit of making it. The exploit of Napoleon has been compared to that of Hannibal, though the former, after all, did but follow what had been, for two thousand years, a beaten track; the latter being the individual who beat originally a track for himself, and thoroughly vanquished every obstacle.

At length, after having nearly lost himself in the Alps, Hannibal found himself, at the end of a journey of fifteen days, in the plain of Turin. On mustering his army, he discovered that considerable reductions had taken place in it; for the foot, which had stood at 50,000 when he crossed the Rhone, had now dwindled to less than half the number. He had lost 3000 horse, and his stock of elephants had materially diminished—the few that remained having become so thin, that there was a striking falling off in the material as well as the numbers of the body. So little had his visit been expected, that the Romans were not prepared for it; and Scipio, who ought to have been waiting at the foot of the Alps, did not arrive at Pavia until Hannibal had had time to recruit himself after his late fatigue. Here both armies met, and Scipio gave battle; but Hannibal's cavalry gave it to him in a sense more familiar than satisfactory. In the course of the engagement, the Roman general received a wound, which wound him up to the highest pitch of rage; and he would have exposed himself to certain death, if his son had not valiantly rushed between him and the enemy.

The Romans now began to rate each other for having underrated the strength of the foe; and Tib. Sempronius was recalled from Africa, where he was wasting his time by wasting the coast in the most unprofitable manner. Hannibal pitched his camp on the banks of the Trebia, where, among the bushes, he found for his army a convenient ambush. Sempronius had by this time joined Scipio, who was still a great invalid, and being generally indisposed, was not at all disposed for battle. Sempronius, on the other hand, thinking he should obtain all the glory that was to be acquired, felt eager for the fight; and Hannibal, from the other side of the river, assumed the most provoking attitude, in order to tempt the Romans to come after him.

At length, some of the guards became so irritated, that they volunteered into the cold-stream, and plunged into the icy river. There happened to be at the moment a fall of snow, which was taken by the wind into the faces of the soldiers, who, nevertheless, fought with bravery, though in appearance they seemed to exhibit a mass of white feathers. The Romans, though nearly frozen to death, were not only cool and collected, but eagerly sought, in the hope of warming themselves, the heat of the battle. They were, however, completely beaten, and retired to Placentia, from which the Consuls, with much self-complacency, sent to Rome an account of the battle, in which they attributed to the wind the blow they had sustained, and, plausibly suggesting the ice as the cause of their failure, they endeavoured to slip out of it.

Hannibal determined to pass the winter as quietly as he could, but he appears, according to the authorities,* to have indulged in a little masquerading, for the purpose of deceiving the Cisalpine Gauls, who more than once conspired to kill him. He would frequently change his dress; and he appears to have had a large assortment of wigs, in one or

Hannibal disguising himself.

other of which he was accustomed to disguise himself. Sometimes he would appear in hair of the richest brown, and at other times it was of the reddest dye; so that the people were puzzled to understand how the same head could, on one day, appear covered with the luxuriant chestnut, and on another day, disfigured with an untidy bunch of carrots. On one occasion, when a conspiracy against him was ripe, he came to the council with a limping gait, and thus saved himself from a much more serious hobble.

In the spring of the next year, the Consul, C. Flaminius, was sent to Ariminum with an army, and Hannibal started for Etruria. This expedition—if expedition is the proper term for an affair so extremely slow—lasted three days and three nights; the soldiers proceeding through marsh and morass, through thick and thin, to the end of their journey. The Spaniards went first, who picked their way, followed by the Gauls, who stuck in the mud, and were spurred on by the swords of the Numidians, who followed. All the horses were knocked up, and

* Polybius, 3. Appian, c. 316. Livy, 22.

Hannibal, to whom all the glory of the march has been given, endured the least of the fatigue, for, while the common soldiers were wading through the mud, their chief was elevated on the back of the only surviving elephant.

The advantages of a high position were, in this instance, strikingly exemplified, for if Hannibal had moved in the humbler walks on this occasion, the probability is, that he could not have walked at all; but that, sinking in the marshes, he would have gone down—in a swamp—to posterity. He, himself, lost the use of one of his eyes, though, indeed, he exhibited throughout this disastrous affair an unusual amount of shortsightedness. After reaching Fæsulæ, now Fiesole, near Florence, he made for Rome, and Flaminius made after him as far as Cortona; but Hannibal, turning sharp round the corner of the Lake Trasimenus, ran unperceived up the heights, getting round to the rear of the Roman general, who thought the foe was still in front of him. While Flaminius was pressing forward, Hannibal and his forces fell upon him right and left, as well as behind, and a fog coming on at the time added to the perplexity of the Consul, by preventing him from seeing his danger. A fight in a fog is one of the most dismal pictures that can be described, if, indeed, it can be called a picture at all, when nothing can be seen, and the whole is a mere daub, caused by a fearful brush between two conflicting armies. Such was the fury of the fight, that it is said an earthquake, which happened at the time, was unperceived by the combatants; and, indeed, so shocking was the carnage, that a shock of nature might have sunk by its side into comparative insignificance. 15,000 Romans were slain, and those who are always ready to prophecy after an event, began to see clearly in certain omens that had happened some time before, the cause of all that had lately happened.

A shower of stones had fallen at Picenum, but it does not appear whether those who told the story of the stones had a hand in throwing them. In Gaul a wolf had swallowed the sword of a sentinel; and in Cœre the answers of the oracle were suddenly written in smaller characters—a proof only that the oracle had got from text into round-hand—the ordinary result of improved penmanship.

The battle had undoubtedly been fearful in its results, for Flaminius himself was slain; and 15,000 Romans having been cut to pieces, were thrown into a brook, which still bears the name of Sanguinetta, from its being turned into the colour of blood, though the statement is too extravagant to have the colour of probability. The horrors of the war were great enough without the aid of exaggeration, and though the instances of suffering were no doubt great, we are inclined to doubt the story, that the Numidians went without their allowance of wine, in order to wash the feet of their horses; for, though the animals might have been unable to do without their hock, they could surely have dispensed with their Falernian.

On the news of Hannibal's victory reaching Rome, the prætor

announced the distressing circumstance to a numerous meeting of the people, who, in the absence of the Consul, took upon themselves to appoint a dictator. Q. Fabius Maximus was chosen, and the mastership of the horse was conferred on M. Minucius. Hannibal was expected at Rome, but, like a wise general, he defeated general expectation, and proceeded to Spoletum, a Roman colony, which he hoped would have held out great advantages ; but it held out with great spirit against him. Wishing to avoid the inconvenience of a siege, and of sitting down before the city with nothing but a marsh to sit down upon, he marched into Picenum, which contained abundance of everything necessary for the support of his army. His soldiers were afflicted at this time with a cutaneous disease, and, though this annoyance was only skin-deep, he feared a general breaking-out, if he had detained them against their will in an unhealthy country. From Picenum he passed into Apulia ; and though he was disappointed in the hope that the inhabitants would join him, they were too weak to resist, and he turned every Italian city into an Italian warehouse for the supply of the comestibles he required. The dictator Fabius followed at a short distance, but always taking the high ground, by hovering about the hills and keeping the upper hand of Hannibal.

His intention was to proceed to Casinum, but by some stupid misunderstanding, the general led the way to Casilinum, and the result was, that Fabius got ahead of him. On the mistake being discovered by Hannibal, he got 2000 oxen—but where he got them from does not exactly appear—and, having procured several thousand bundles of wood, he tied them to the horns of the animals. Having set the wood on fire, he turned the oxen out among the Romans, whose quarters soon were thrown into the sort of confusion prevalent in a London thoroughfare on a Smithfield market-day. In order to inflame the oxen, their horns had been covered over with pitch, which gave them an inclination to toss, and the poor creatures were running about in all directions, under the influence of fear and fury. Fabius is said to have mistaken the cattle for the Carthaginians, and to have rushed forwards, sword in hand, resolved on butchery. The Romans were thus drawn out of their favourable position, and Hannibal slipped into it, leaving the bulls to decide by a toss-up, if they pleased, the chances of victory over their aggressors. On the mistake being discovered by Fabius, he backed out as well as he could, and ventured on a few skirmishes, in which he met with some success, but he continued his policy of trying to tire out the enemy.

The plan he adopted was to continue always in an imposing attitude but to be ready to slip away, so that, when his antagonist gathered up his strength to make a hit, the force was always expended on vacancy. The Romans grew extremely impatient of a series of tactics which showed no immediate result ; and Fabius, having occasion to return to Rome, was insulted by having the epithet of Cunctator, the dawdler, or the slow-coach, applied to him. One of the tribunes even went so far as to charge him with treachery; to which he made, what is usually called, the "noble" reply, "Fabius cannot be suspected."

It seems to have been extremely easy to get a reputation for "noble" replies among the Romans, since the mere denial of a charge, amounting to the commonplace plea of "not guilty," is frequently cited by the historians as a noble reply, because an individual in a toga happens to have uttered it. For the purpose of annoying Fabius, or the "slow coach," the people conferred on Minucius, who, for the sake of distinction, may be appropriately termed the "fast man," an equal share of power with the dictator himself, and half the command of the army. On the return of Fabius to the camp, Minucius proposed that they should command on alternate days, a course that would have been extremely inconvenient; for if Minu-

cius had ordered the army to take a week's march, it is possible that on the day ensuing, Fabius would have ordered the army back again. The latter, therefore, proposed that each should take a separate half; but an army, like a house, cannot be divided without weakness being the inevitable consequence. The ill effects of the separation were soon shown; for Minucius, who was hot and hasty, was soon provoked by Hannibal to make an attack, and the Carthaginian general, who had been accustomed to talk of the Romans hanging over him like a cloud, declared that they had now come down upon him in a weak and watery shower. Minucius and his army would certainly have been absorbed, or, to use a more powerful figure, they would have been effectually wiped out, but for the generous intervention of Fabius. The latter saved the former from destruction, when Minucius, who was no less mawkish than rash, followed up the allegory of the rain by bursting into tears, and throwing himself on the neck, as well as on the generosity, of Fabius. Minucius resigned the dictatorship into the hands of his colleague, who leisurely wound up the campaign; and having resigned his power, has to this day reigned supreme as the example of the slow-and-sure principle in the theme of every schoolboy.

Hannibal was now beginning to feel the effects of the policy of delay, for he was getting out of heart, and was terribly out of pocket. The harvest had been all gathered in before he could lay his hands upon it; and he felt it would be idle to take the field, unless he could take the corn that had grown in it. His army was clamorous for food; and complaint is never so open-mouthed as when hunger is at the bottom of it. The Romans began to think the time had arrived for a decisive blow, and had chosen as one of the Consuls of the year an individual named C. T. Varro, whom Livy has described as an eloquent meat salesman.*   He had been in the habit of going from door to door in the service of his father, collecting orders for meat in the morning, and taking it round in the afternoon; but he was determined that his voice

Young Varro.

should be heard in something more impressive than a cry of "butcher," at the door-ways of the citizens. His first flights of eloquence were in the market-place, where he interlarded his ordinary exclamations of "Buy, buy," with sarcastic inquiries how long the people would consent to be sold by those who professed to be their friends and rulers.   By degrees, he quitted the shambles for the platform, and he began attending public meetings as a professional demagogue. Like those who pursue patriotism as a trade, he accepted the first offer of a place that was made to him; and he became in succession a quæstor, an ædile, and a prætor. At length he was elevated to the consulship, or rather the consulship was lowered to him; for though the name of Varro became afterwards truly illustrious, we cannot allow to C. T. the title of respectable. His colleague, as Consul, was L. Æmilius Paulus, a patrician, who is said to have cherished a profound hatred of the people;

---

* Polybius says nothing about the origin of Varro; and as there was no directory in those days, we are unable to decide whether the omission of Polybius, or the assertion of Livy, is more to be relied upon.

but why he is said to have done anything of the sort—except it is in slavish subjection to the old prejudice, according to which all the patricians are supposed to hate all the people—we are at a loss to discover. The two Consuls were at daggers drawn between themselves, which prevented them from agreeing as to the proper time for drawing the sword against the enemy. C. T. Varro, the ex-butcher, was for cutting and slashing at the Carthaginians off-hand; but Æmilius Paulus, having consulted a poulterer, declared the sacred chickens to have lost their appetites, which some considered a foul pretext, and others a fair excuse, for avoiding a battle. The Consuls had, however, set out with 80,000 foot, and 6000 horse, which were encamped on the river Aufidus; their stores being packed up in baskets and cans at the little town of Cannæ. Hannibal, who was completely out of elephants—there being not even one left for the saddle for his own especial use—was compelled to ride the high horse—the highest he could find among his cavalry— as a substitute. He took Cannæ under the very eyes and Roman noses of the consuls, one of whom, Varro, would have fought, but Æmilius Paulus, the other, had taken the sacred chickens so much to heart, that he had not courage for anything.

At length, on the 2nd of August, Hannibal, whose pockets were empty of cash, and whose baggage was bare of provisions, determined to provoke the Romans to a battle. Had the policy of Fabius Cunctator, "slow coach," been pursued at this stage, the defeat of the Carthaginians was certain, for they were an army of mercenaries without pay, and in ten days there would not have been a bone for the dogs of war to feed upon. Hannibal, who had always much tact in discovering which way the wind blew, was taking a walk in the morning, when his eyes getting suddenly filled with dust, caused him to see a point that had hitherto escaped him. It occurred to him at once that, by placing his army with its back to the wind, the Romans who faced him would have to face a blow which might prove very embarrassing. He knew that the dust would set the Romans rubbing their eyes, or even if they did not raise a hand against the inconvenience, they would, at all events, be compelled to wink at it. In order to increase the annoyance, he ordered the ground to be thoroughly well ploughed, and though he had not the advantage of shot, he found the dust a very good substitute for powder. He had placed the Gauls in the middle, supported by Africans on each side, and the Romans having first attacked the centre, which gave way, were enclosed between the two wings; a position in which they were so hard pressed, that they could not get out of the claws of the enemy.

The slaughter was, as usual, tremendous, 45,000 being left dead on the field, or rather, in conformity with the excess of caution used in those days to prevent the return of an adversary to life, being "cut to pieces." Æmilius Paulus, the patrician, who had been reluctant to fight, was killed while boldly combating with his sword in his hand, but Varro, the patriotic butcher, who had been all ardour and enthusiasm to strike the decisive blow, ran off as fast as his horse's heels could carry him. He reached Rome in safety, and such a perfect master was he of the demagogue's art, that he succeeded in obtaining the thanks of the Senate for his services. It was true that he had shown boldness, amounting to rashness, when the security of the army was at stake, and he had exhibited caution amounting to cowardice, in taking care of himself, by running away when the battle was lost; but he had got the character of the "people's friend," and the people are often a long time in finding out, and casting off, those who are in the habit of duping them.

Among other instances of gross popular delusion which occurred about this time, was the sending of Fabius Pictor as ambassador to Delphi, to consult the Oracle. Fabius was the historian of his age, and was supposed, therefore, qualified to record all sorts of falsehood; for history in those early days had not been dignified by that conscientious accuracy which is in our own time indispensable. His second name of Pictor was acquired rather by his industry as a house-painter, than by his talent as an artist, for he had done the whole of the painting of the Temple of the Goddess of Health; and he probably devoted himself rather to the pound brush than the pencil. As a writer of history, there was something of the painter in his labours; but he was unfortunately in the habit of employing very false colours. On his return from Delphi, the public seemed to have derived very little instruction from his journey; for the sacrifice of two pairs of human beings, a male and female Greek, and a male and female Gaul, was the principal result of the information he brought home with him.

As it may be interesting to the student to be told how the Oracle was worked in those days, we furnish a few particulars. The office for making inquiries of the Delphic Oracle was in the Temple—dedicated to Apollo—where a fire was continually burning, fed with the wood of laurels, which typifies the ever-greenness that deception lives upon. In the centre of the Temple was a small opening which emitted intoxicating smoke, and, as the Pythia sat immediately above it, she was rapidly reduced to a state in which she fell on the floor and uttered incoherent sounds, which were said to be inspired. A prophet was in attendance to write down the pith of what the Pythia was supposed to say, and the purport of these drunken ravings was accepted by nations and individuals as a guide to their conduct in cases of the most serious interest.

Originally the Pythia was always a young girl, but, subsequently, a law was passed, limiting the office to those who had passed their fiftieth year; and there is no doubt that intoxication being the chief duty, rendered the place peculiarly eligible to the old women. At first there had been only one female employed, but when the business increased, a second, and subsequently a third, was appointed, so that there might always be one at hand to perform the duty, while the other was drunk and incapable. Of course, a fee was exacted from all who came to consult the Oracle, which was entirely in the hands of a few aristocratic families of the place, who made a double profit, by taking money, and giving only such advice as was calculated to promote their own class interests.

CHAPTER THE EIGHTEENTH.

CONCLUSION OF THE SECOND PUNIC WAR.

HANNIBAL was now strongly urged by one Maharbal, the commander of the cavalry, to march against Rome, and the gallant general went so far as to promise that if he had permission, he would go and take it so easy, that in five days they might sleep in the Capitol. "The idea is indeed a good one," said Hannibal, with an incredulous smile, "but the only objection to its being carried out, is that it's utterly impossible." Maharbal persevered in his recommendation; but finding his advice rejected, he grew sententious and sentimental, which is often the effect of a snubbing. "Alas!" he exclaimed, with that anti-colloquial style of expression, which characters in history—but not in real life—are so fond of assuming,—"Alas! thou knowest how to gain a victory, but thou knowest not how thou oughtest to use thy victory when thou hast gained it." If this was the ordinary mode in which Maharbal expressed himself, it is not surprising that Hannibal preferred his deeds to his words, the use of his sword to the abuse of his tongue, and his hand in war to his advice in council.

The object of Hannibal had been to attach to himself the Italian towns, but they naturally repudiated an attachment, which consisted in his fastening himself on to them with an army which they were made to support at a ruinous sacrifice. He had, however, succeeded in winning over Capua to his designs, for it was inhabited by a contemptible race, who lay continually in the lap of luxury, where the lapse of all the better qualities would seem to be unavoidable. Not satisfied with treachery to the parent state, the Capuans added cruelty to their other vices, and stifled in their hot baths all the Romans who were living among them—an enormity which sends the blood immediately to boiling heat, to contemplate. The faithless inhabitants stipulated that they should be allowed to break all their engagements with Rome, on entering into new engagements with Carthage,—an arrangement like that of a dishonest servant, who, having robbed a former master, stipulates for impunity for past roguery as the condition of future fidelity. Hannibal was weak or politic enough to enter into terms with this contemptible set; but he incurred the unfailing penalty of wrong, for his own army became corrupted by contact with the Capuan crew, and his fortunes began to decline from the time of his alliance with this degraded people.

The exertions of Rome to repair her reverses were extreme after the battle of Cannæ; and though nearly every family had lost a relative, the period of mourning was limited to thirty days, while a law was passed prohibiting all women from weeping in the streets, for they had been found a crying evil. Sparing no expense, the state performed an operation of a rather curious kind, for 8000 slaves were bought on credit —the Government thus making a large purchase without any money at all—and freeing these slaves, made them fight; thus retaining them actually in bondage, while nominally giving them their liberty. Even gladiators were allowed the valuable privilege of fighting the foe instead of each other, and of falling in the field instead of falling in the circus.

Hannibal having used up nearly all his men and materials, was compelled to send to Carthage for fresh supplies, when his old rival Hanno exclaimed in the senate, that if the Carthaginian general had been unsuccessful, he deserved no help, and if he had been victorious, he could not possibly need any. The speech of Hanno on this occasion would have done credit—or discredit—to a political partisan of the present day; for it was essentially the language of a disappointed leader of the opposition. " If," said the honourable—or dis-honourable —member (for in mere party dissensions it is difficult to distinguish one from the other), " if Hannibal has conquered all our enemies, why does he send to us for soldiers ? If he has reduced Italy—the most fertile country in Europe—why does he ask us for corn ? And if he has obtained such rich booty, what on earth can he want with money ? The truth, I suspect, to be, that his victories are sham—his territorial acquisitions sham—the riches (of which he has sent us specimens, in the shape of a few rings,) sham,—while his necessities, and the burden thrown upon us in supplying them, are the only things that are real."

This argument, though specious, did not altogether prevail, for the senate decreed him four thousand Numidians and forty elephants, the men and the brutes being looked upon as equally articles of consumption in the game of war that had been so long playing. The Romans began to act with increased determination, and blockaded Capua, which was left to its fate by Hannibal, though an attempt to relieve it was made by a detachment which received a severe beating at the hands of Tib. S. Gracchus.

This period is rendered additionally remarkable by the siege of Syracuse, which eventually fell into the hands of M. Claudius Marcellus, whose efforts had long been thwarted by the genius of Archimedes. This illustrious inventor lived to the good old age of seventy-five ; but how he lived so long is a matter of almost as much wonder as some of his inventions, for his biographers tell us that he always forgot to eat and drink ; nor could he ever be persuaded to take a bath, except when his friends pushed him into one. Even when this was accomplished, he was sure to be found under the ashes of the fire-places, writing problems among the cinders, and endeavouring to sift some important point ; so that a bath was really thrown away upon the great philosopher. In a visit to Egypt, he became anxious to elevate the Nile to a certain point ; but he remained in Egypt until all his money was spent, for the philosopher had never thought of raising the wind while intent on raising the water. He invented a screw, which still bears his name; but he is said to have amused himself, during the siege of Syracuse, by sitting at the window and inventing all sorts of missiles to hurl at the ships of the enemy. One day he might be seen throwing stones from a newly-invented sling, and a few days after he was found casting out chains, to pull—with a tremendous hook—the ships of the foe completely out of the water. He was so intent upon everything he came near, that he gave a lift to enemies occasionally as well as to friends, as in the instance just recorded, and he declared his ability to give the whole world a lift if he could only find a convenient spot in the neighbourhood for himself and his lever to rest upon. That in one sense he carried out his boast, we are willing to admit; for he undoubtedly elevated the world by raising the standard of science, and he exalted the whole of civilised humanity by his great discoveries. The part he took in the siege of Syracuse has been underrated by some, and exaggerated by others; for though the story of his pulling the ships out of the sea requires a length of rope, and other apparatus, which none but the greatest stretch of imagination can supply, his destroying the vessels by burning-glasses is perfectly credible. He is supposed to have used very powerful reflectors, capable of taking effect within the distance of bow-shot; and though for some time the moderns insisted that the long-bow had been pulled for the purpose of increasing the space, the powers of the burning-glass are now familiar to every schoolboy.

On the fall of Syracuse, orders were given by Marcellus, the Roman general, that the philosopher should be respected; but he was so absorbed in a problem, that the soldier who was sent after him not being able to solve the problem of who he was, or what he was about, fell upon and slew him.

It is of the great man we have been noticing that a story is told, which proves that the pursuit of the laws of gravity may sometimes be associated with the ludicrous. King Hiero, of Syracuse, had handed over a good lump of pure gold to a working jeweller to be converted into a crown, with the distinct understanding that the true metal only should be used, and that there might be no alloy to the pleasure his Majesty would feel in wearing it. The goldsmith brought back an article of the proper weight; but the king, after trying it on his head, turning it over in his mind, and revolving it beneath his eyes in the sun, declared his suspicion that the metal had been tampered with, and a base imposition had been practised. He consulted Archimedes as to the means of detecting the imposture; and on one of those days when the friends of the philosopher had forced him to take a bath, he became immersed as deeply in speculation as in the water.

The bath into which he plunged having been full to the brim, the apartment was soon flooded by the water he displaced; and looking at the wet floor, he thought only of the dry facts of science. It occurred to him that any body of equal bulk would have done exactly the same thing; and he immediately thought of his royal master's crown, which, if all the gold sent for its construction had been fairly used up, should displace as much water as a piece of pure metal equal in weight to that which the crown ought to contain. The moment the idea struck him he jumped out of the bath, and thinking of nothing but the bare facts,.

εὕρηκα

Archimedes taking a Warm Bath.

he ran through the streets, perfectly unconscious of the naked truth of his own condition. His shout was εὕρηκα *—I have found it; but everybody thought, when they saw him, that whatever he might have found, he had certainly lost his senses.

There is, no doubt, much exaggeration in the absurd stories told of Archimedes; but we may excuse a little oddness in a great man whom none was even with. He ran so far in advance of his age, that eighteen centuries had nearly elapsed before any one came up to him, and then it was chiefly by following the track marked out by his footsteps.†

* The term εὕρηκα has lately been applied to a newly-invented shirt; but the term is extremely inappropriate, for the philosopher had no shirt on when he proclaimed his great discovery.

† Stevinus, the Flemish mathematician, and Galileo, both of whom were born about the middle of the sixteenth century, were the first who came after Archimedes in any great mechanical discoveries.

We must now leave the nobler instruments of science, to return to the engines of war, which were as usual in full play, and had been employed in the total dissolution of the already too dissolute city of Capua. The dissipated nobles, palsied by their excesses, and paralysed by their fears, fell by their own hands ; for they had neither the courage to fight for the chance of success, nor the nerve to meet the consequences of failure.

It is stated that one Vibius Virrius, the chief of the Senate, on the eve of the opening of the gates, gave a sort of legislative supper to twenty-eight of the members, and, at the conclusion of a hearty meal, he produced a cup, with the contents of which he proposed that every one present should poison the remainder of his own existence. The deadly potion was poured out into twenty-nine different vessels, and, with faces more or less wry, the Senators swallowed the fatal mixture. On the surrender of the place, the citizens were sold for slaves ; and it must be admitted that they had shown themselves fit for little better than the fate assigned to them.

In the year previous to the fall of Capua, Hannibal had taken Tarentum ; but, three years later, the stupidity or treachery of the general in charge, or man in possession, had allowed Q. Fabius Maximus to take it back again. Hannibal was thus daily losing territory, and his cause was consequently losing ground. Many small states which had adhered to him because they believed him to be strong enough to assist them, withdrew from him directly he appeared as if he could not help himself.

Hasdrubal, the brother of Hannibal, had been harassed in Spain by the two Scipios—Cn. C. and P.—when fortune cleared the stage for him, by killing both within a month, and annihilating both their armies. The fate of the two leaders had such an effect in Rome, that when those eligible to command had heard the particulars, they had no inclination to act as generals. Every one seemed to fear that if he went to head the army in Spain, he should be simply going to his own funeral, and every one naturally shrunk from such an undertaking. At length young P. C. S. A. M.—or, to give his name at full length, Publius Cornelius Scipio Africanus Major—who was only twenty-four years of age, though he had entered the army at seventeen, and had been present, or rather absent, at the battle of Cannæ, where the only survivors were those who ran away—volunteered to supply the places of his deceased relatives. An objection was, at first, made to his age—or rather to his want of age—but, as there was no older candidate for the post of honour and of danger, he was permitted to step into it. His popularity was, in some measure, owing to his having acquired the character of a serious young man ; for ever since he had assumed the toga virilis—an assumption something like the modern practice of going into stick-ups —he had been in the habit of passing his mornings in the Temple of Jupiter. He proceeded to Spain, with the title of Pro-consul, and an army of about 11,000 men, at the head of whom he proceeded to

Carthagena; where he knew the enemy kept the greater portion of
their cash, their corn, and their captives. He was accompanied by his
friend Lælius, who commanded the fleet, and who was sent to make an
unexpected attack from the sea; for Scipio, who was very deep, had
ascertained that the water was very shallow. The defenders of New
Carthage had relied upon the ocean as a defence; but they had, in
reality, built their hopes on sand, which, during the prevalence of a
particular wind and tide, afforded easy access to the city. The place
speedily fell into his hands; and his gallantry—in a double sense—
made him with the brave and the fair an equal favourite. Towards the
ladies he was particularly amiable; and he not only sent back to her
lover an interesting young girl, but he returned to her husband a

Considerate Conduct of Scipio Africanus.

maudlin old woman. The latter was the aged wife of the chief Mardonius, who weepingly implored that her sex might be treated with respect; when the young soldier, hiding his face in his sleeve, either cried or laughed in it.

Hasdrubal now turned his attention to Italy, while Scipio continued his conquests in Spain, and, among other places, took Astapa, which, if tradition tells the truth, he must have found without a single inhabitant. It is said that the place was defended with such valour that only fifty men remained alive, and these became impressed with the feeling that when a thing must be done, it is better to do it oneself than to leave it to be done by others. They came to the resolution that they were sure not to be spared, and they had, therefore, better get rid of one another. They accordingly proceeded to the sanguinary task of mutual destruction; though, as one must have remained to the last, and there would have been some difficulty in disposing of him, it is probable that he survived for the purpose of acting as his own reporter of the dreadful incident. The graver historians insist that not one was left alive in the city; that the last fifty soldiers, having first killed all their women, and all their children, made away with all of themselves; a state of things which induces us to ask how the particulars have come down to us. If, however, we were to indulge this spirit of inquiry to any extent, we should, we fear, be compelled to throw a doubt upon many of those interesting particulars which form the most agreeable portions of history.

Hasdrubal resolved to make a grand effort, and assembled an army, which including some Iberians, under his brother Mago, as well as some Numidians, headed by Masinissa, their king, numbered 75,000 men, and six-and-thirty elephants. Scipio, though objecting to attack a power more than twice his size, was compelled to do so, by a want of provisions, for he had so little food that his army could not even have grubbed on for a month or two. He was again victorious, and Hasdrubal proceeded to join his brother Hannibal; but the letters written by the former to apprise the latter of his coming, instead of going regularly through all the military posts, fell, by some misdirection or indirection, into the hands of the enemy. The Consul Livius Salinator went into the neighbourhood of Sena Gallica—now Senigaglia—and was joined by his colleague, C. Claudius Nero, who came, under cover of the night, with a large army; and it would appear that the forces of Hasdrubal kept such very early hours, that they had all gone to bed, and knew nothing of the reinforcements that had been sent against them. Hasdrubal, however, saw among the Romans, on the following morning, some soldiers, whose faces were so sun-burnt, as to give a strange complexion to a part of the troops, and he concluded that they had recently been on a journey. After having indulged in an inquiring look, he commenced a patient listen, and he fancied he heard two trumpet calls in the hostile camp, when, without considering whether the second might have been the mere echo of the first, he resolved, in his own mind, that the armies of the two Consuls had joined together. He accordingly determined to fly, and began by trying to swim across the river Metaurus, which is usually shallow enough; but the rains had swelled it to such a torrent that he was soon plunged into the depths of misery. His guides, following the impulse of their own cowardice, ran away as fast as they could, and he, in perfect ignorance of the country, found the river rising and his spirits sinking in about an equal ratio. The Romans came up with him in time to find his army completely damped, and his troops were, according to the military practice of the period, cut, at once, to pieces.

Hasdrubal, who had lost heart early in the battle, seems ultimately to have lost his head, for rushing into the midst of a cohort, he was decapitated by a Roman soldier. It is said that the head of Hasdrubal was afterwards brutally thrown into the camp of his brother Hannibal; but happily for the credit of humanity, this story of the head is absurd on the very face of it.

Spain was now subject to Rome; and Scipio, after quelling an insurrection in his army, paid a visit to Syphax, who was king of a portion of Numidia, and who was desperately in love with a young lady, named Sophonisba, the daughter of Hasdrubal Gisco, a Carthaginian general. Sophonisba was one of those troublesome persons, known as fascinating creatures, who, by attracting the eyes of mankind, set them very often by the ears, and lead to much calamity. This too interesting individual had also won the admiration of Masinissa, another king of another part of Numidia, when her father, irrespective of any attachment she might have formed, gave her hand to Syphax, by way of attaching the latter to his interests. Masinissa, in a fit of jealousy, went over to Rome, leaving Syphax and Hasdrubal to fight it out with Scipio.

The Africans and Carthaginians were, to a certain extent, people of straw, which was the material they used in constructing their tents, and Scipio, basely pretending that he desired to negotiate a peace, sent a set of firebrands, under the garb of envoys, into the camp of the enemy. These hypocritical incendiaries carried fire among the foe; and, though the elephants fought like lions, the Carthaginians behaved like lambs, for the poor creatures, thinking the burning of their tents was accidental, looked on with simple bewilderment. 40,000 Africans were cut to pieces on the spot; and Syphax, who had managed to escape, was ready immediately with 30,000 more, to engage Scipio in the neighbourhood of Utica. Syphax was urged on by his wife, who is described as a woman of remarkable spirit—a character equivalent to that of a very troublesome body. Poor Syphax did all he could against a very superior force, but he was ultimately taken prisoner, and sent to Scipio, while Sophonisba remained at home to receive Masinissa—like a woman of spirit—at the gates of her husband's palace.

The lovely creature, admitting that she was vanquished, and declaring that further opposition would be vain, appealed, in the character of an unprotected female, to the generosity of Masinissa. Expressing the utmost horror at being placed as a captive behind the car of Scipio, she entreated the protection of her husband's conqueror ; and Masinissa, not knowing exactly what to do, politely offered to marry her. She at once consented ; and, after a widowhood of a few hours, she was presented to Lælius, the Roman Consul, in her new character.

Syphax, not being dead, was of course rather painfully alive to the conduct of his wife, and having hinted to Scipio that she might be the cause of further mischief, an order was immediately sent to Masinissa to send her back by the bearer. This her new husband was unwilling to do, but he forwarded her a cup of poison, which she drank off with the air of a tragedy queen, and died with a clap-trap in her mouth, which was almost as nauseous as the stuff that she was called upon to swallow.

The Carthaginians now began to feel that every thing went wrong in the absence of Hannibal, whom they invited home, and on his arrival he was really anxious for peace and quietness. Scipio felt much the same, and the two generals, having met, looked at each other for some time in silent admiration. It may be doubted whether they got any further than this point, for even if they had a few words, it did not prevent them from ultimately coming to blows at the great and decisive battle of Zama. Hannibal brought into the field 50,000 men, and about 80 real elephants ; but his soldiers were most of them raw, and liable to be roasted on the ground of extreme awkwardness. He put the Moors, the Gauls, and Libyans in front, the Carthaginian cowards in the centre, for they were but a middling set, and he brought up the rear, with a few of his best soldiers. Scipio exhibited some very skilful generalship on this momentous occasion, and by a clever arrangement of his forces, he left room for the elephants to run through the ranks without coming into contact with any of his soldiers.

The success of Scipio was complete; and Hannibal returned to Carthage after an absence of thirty-six years ; having so far forgotten the manners and customs of his country, that, during a debate in the Senate, he dragged a noble—whose sentiments did not exactly coincide with his own—by force from the tribune. On being called to order, he explained that he had forgotten the forms of the house ; and the discussion proceeded as if nothing particular had happened. Carthage made peace with Rome, on very advantageous terms to the latter; and Scipio, who took the name of Africanus, enjoyed the honours of a triumph, at which poor Syphax—who appears to have been everybody's victim—was obliged to figure in fetters.

The terms imposed upon Carthage were very severe; for she was to deliver up, without ransom, all the Roman prisoners : to surrender nearly all her ships ; and to part with all her elephants. She was also to pay over a considerable sum in cash,—a stipulation which set the Senate off into a roar of anguish, and caused Hannibal sneeringly to exclaim that " the only thing to draw tears from their eyes was to draw money from their pockets." *

* Livy, xxx. 44.

Though Rome had been victorious, so fatal is war to all who engage
in it, that her successes had brought her almost to the verge of
ruin.   Scenes of cruelty had dyed the country with blood, and left a
stain upon it which could not easily be effaced; and wherever the
sword of war had been brandished, nothing else had flourished.   Troops
had been raised merely to be cut down; the country had been wasted
on all sides; and there had been a still more terrible waste of human
existence.   While life was being made so cheap, the means of supporting it were getting dearer every day; for provisions rose to an enormous
price under the influence of a system which converted the ploughshare
into the sword, and turned what should have been fields of corn into
fields of battle.   To meet the expenses of the war, the public had been
obliged to run into debt; and there is no process to which the term
running is more properly applied, though the opposite movement is
always slow, and often impossible.

The Carthaginian fleet having been destroyed, Rome became
nominally mistress of the seas; but, for want of means, she made a
very bad mistress, and the sea might be said to maintain a mastery
over her.

War, however, had been in some degree productive of good; for it
had led to the recognition of the great principle that the public service
was not to be monopolised by the privileged few, inasmuch as where
there is real work to be done, there is scope for the talents and energies
to be met with among the many.   Wealth, however, had become a
passport to public employment; and the door could be opened by a
golden key, which has, in modern times, served most appropriately as
the emblem of office.

The drain upon the resources of the nation was so considerable, in
consequence of the frequent wars, that the Senators sent their plate to
the treasury, and received bank bills instead,—an arrangement as
satisfactory as exchanging silver dishes for silver paper.   The merchants
supplied dresses for the troops on the same terms, and accepted
printed rags for comfortable clothing.

Superstition also sensibly—or rather foolishly—increased during the
wars against Carthage; and the Sibylline books were consulted from
time to time, though usually with no other result than the recommendation of a job, to be performed by Government Commissioners.   On one
occasion the books were declared to require that Cybele should be
brought to Rome; and ambassadors were appointed, at a considerable
expense, to go to Phrygia, for the purpose of fetching her.   They professed to find her, and bring her home; but upon their arrival, they
produced nothing but a large black stone, which the people welcomed
as a most precious stone, and which they were contented to receive as
the goddess they required.

CHAPTER THE NINETEENTH.

WAR WITH THE MACEDONIANS.   PROCLAMATION OF THE FREEDOM OF
GREECE BY FLAMINIUS.   WAR WITH ANTIOCHUS.   DEATH OF HANNIBAL,
AND OF SCIPIO AFRICANUS.

AR being still
the theme of
our history, we
are obliged to
ask the reader
to accompany
us into the
field, though
we are aware
that battles,
and their
deadly details,
cannot inspire
a very lively
interest.

Philip of
Macedonia
had become
jealous of the
power of
Rome, which
had now got a
footing in the
boot of Italy;
and, as Greece lay nearly under the heel, it was natural that the
Grecians should prepare to resist being trampled on.   Philip, therefore,
concluded a treaty with Hannibal, and sent ambassadors with the
document ; but, instead of delivering it into the hands for which it was
designed, they themselves fell into the hands of the Romans.

Rome at once despatched to Illyricum a fleet of 50 sail, when Philip,
observing that the vessels were being wafted over by a favourable
breeze, saw there was something in the wind, and resolved—whatever
the blow—to be prepared for it.   This was the commencement of the
Macedonian War, which became extremely unpopular with the Romans ;
for the people at large regarded it as a bitter cup, though the nobles
desired it for the sake of the " bubble reputation " that the few might
find in it.   In vain did the tribes protest against the proposed war,

declaring they were no enemies to Philip, for the Senate insisted he was an enemy of theirs, and that it was accordingly their duty to fight with him.

The campaign was opened by P. Sulpicius Galba, who crossed the Adriatic, but did little, and was succeeded by Villius Tappulus, who did nothing. Fortune had hitherto observed a sort of stiffness towards both sides, leaning neither to the right nor to the left, when she suddenly took a turn under the consulship of T. Quinctius Flaminius. This individual was, comparatively, young in years, but superlatively old in cunning; and he possessed in an eminent degree the low arts of deceit which are usually held to constitute the high art of statesmanship. He could electrotype falsehood with the external appearance of truth, and he had no lack of that lacquer which brazens out a fraud with the brass of impudence. Everything in the shape of rust had been rubbed off his manners, which had become smooth in the extreme, and had acquired that high state of polish which is frequently associated with a very slippery character. He slid, as it were, into the confidence of all, with the easy lubricity of the serpent, and with not a little of its wiliness. His smile won, or rather lost, those whom he wished to deceive, and he tried its fascination with such effect on some of the Greek chiefs, that they permitted him to enter Thebes, and either did not see what he had in his eye, or were induced to wink at it. He pretended that he wished to parley with the authorities; but, when the citizens were waiting to see what would take place, they found the place itself quietly taken by Flaminius.

Thessaly now became the scene of war, and the Romans met the Greeks near a line of small hills, called, from their shape, the Dogs' Heads, or Cynocephalæ. Here both parties fought with a dogged obstinacy, which was quite in character with the place, until the Greek phalanx, or Macedonian heavies, gave way before the Roman legions. The principle of the phalanx was to pack the soldiers so closely together that their shields touched, and their spears being upwards of twenty feet long, the arms of the rear ranks leaned on the shoulders of those in advance, so that they went forth arm in arm, as it were, to meet the enemy. The Romans, on the contrary, preserved a sort of open order, in which there was room for the exercise of their limbs: while the Greeks, if they were able to raise their arms at all, were very likely to lift them against each other. If the Romans were in need of assistance, there was space left in their ranks for reinforcements to come up. But, amidst the density of a Greek phalanx, nothing could make its way except a panic, which will always find room to run through an entire army. Though presenting, by these means, a formidable front, their line was no sooner broken than they offered a most unprotected rear to an active foe, and the Greek files on the occasion in question bore marks of a special endorsement at the hands of the Romans. Having been packed as closely as cards, 8000 Macedonians fell upon the field, or rather upon one another, and Philip fled to Tempe, as if he was

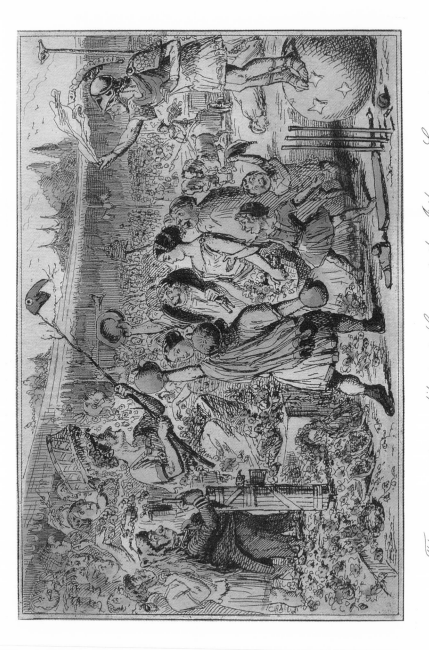

Flamenus restoring liberty to Greece at the Isthmian Games.

desirous to hide his face in its well-known vale after his discomfiture. Here he negotiated an arrangement, which may be termed the peace of the valley, though it was a kind of peace with which he could scarcely be contented, for it stipulated that he should give up all his ships except five; but he was, nevertheless, permitted to retain 500 men of war in the shape of that number of heavy-armed soldiers.

He was also to pay 1000 talents, which would have taken every talent he possessed, and put him to his wit's end at once, if he had not been allowed ten years, within which to find the money. He was furthermore compelled to send his son Demetrius to Rome for his education—a stipulation, of which the object is not particularly clear, unless it was thought that while the offspring was being schooled, a lesson was also being given to the father. Flaminius, laying aside the character of the warrior, proceeded to Greece as a tourist; and, though in private life he was as gentle as a lamb, he was everywhere received as a lion. Having visited the Isthmian games, he interrupted the herald who was about to open the proceedings with the usual proclamation, and putting into the hands of the officer a scroll, desired him to " read it out " before proceeding with the programme. The document was an announcement of the freedom of the Greek cities over which Macedonia had domineered; and the people, finding that Flaminius had made them free, resolved on making him welcome. Frantic with joy, they nearly deafened him with cheers, and almost buried him in flowers; nor could he keep at bay those who pressed forward to crown him with laurel. So dense was the throng, that he must have felt a smothered satisfaction, if he felt any at all; and even if he could have found words to return thanks, he could find no breath to give them utterance.

In order that the Greeks might be shown the use of their new freedom, Flaminius remained behind, to give an illustration of the method of taking a liberty. Calling to his aid ten commissioners from Rome, he proceeded to apportion the free cities of Greece in the manner most agreeable to his own views; for it is a peculiarity of all freedom imported from abroad, that it must be a freedom in conformity with the taste of the importers, and not of those for whose use the article is required. It thus frequently happens that what is recommended as a luxury from abroad proves far from palatable to a people not accustomed to the new commodity; and, though efforts may be made to force it down their throats, at the point of the sword, the morsel is not easy of digestion, and is only revolting to those whom it may have been intended to satisfy.

After completing the independence of Greece, by forcing republics on some of its cities, taking possession of some others, and establishing internal discord in nearly all, Flaminius returned to Rome in the year of the City 559, and enjoyed the honours of a triumph.

As no one is at times louder in his denunciations of dishonesty than the practised rogue, so the Romans, who were for enslaving and plundering

all the world, found it convenient, occasionally, to protest against the rapacity of such as were rivals in the game of conquest. Philip had already
been dealt with on the principle that it is impossible for two of a trade to
agree ; and a quarrel was now picked with Antiochus, who was doing a
somewhat extensive business as a wholesale appropriator of what did
not rightly belong to him. Flaminius, therefore, while declaring, after
his own fashion, the independence of Greece, stipulated that freedom
should be restored by Antiochus to all the Greek cities in Asia,—an
arrangement that would have left the cities at liberty to be made free
with by Rome in her usual manner. Antiochus justified his own wrong
by denying the right of any one else to interfere, and continued appropriating to himself other places to which he had no legal or equitable title.
He seized on the Thracian Chersonesus, on the ground that one of his
ancestors had seized it once before,—a principle about as just as if the
grandson of a thief, who had been transported for stealing a watch,
should, on the strength of his ancestral crime, rob the owner anew of
the same property.

Finding Lysimachia deserted, he took it as his own desert ; when the
Romans, growing jealous of his success in the predatory line, declared
that they should regard, as a direct opposition to Rome, any further acts
of plunder.

While matters were in this state, Hannibal was living in scarcely any
state at all, as an ordinary member of the Carthaginian Senate. He
had taken the opposition side of the house ; and though he was a pro-
poser of many useful reforms, he was frequently coughed down, and in
a minority always. Finding little sympathy amongst his own countrymen, who were all for peace and quietness, he entered into a negotiation with Antiochus, for the purpose of ascertaining whether they could
arrange to create a joint disturbance, and thus weaken the Roman
power. Treachery was, however, going on in all directions ; for, while
Hannibal was plotting with Antiochus against Rome, some of the
Carthaginians were plotting with Rome against Hannibal ; and a
further breach of trust in some other quarter made him acquainted with
his danger. He accordingly resolved to escape ; and having a small
tower—or marine residence—on the coast, he sent orders that a ship
should be ready to sail, and a berth secured for him. He walked about
the streets of Carthage all day, as if nothing had happened, and nothing
was likely to occur ; for the Roman ambassadors were continually
dogging his footsteps ; and he led them about so perseveringly all day,
that when the evening arrived they had scarcely a leg to stand upon.
Hannibal had, however, ordered his horse, which flew with him across
the country to the spot where the ship was in waiting ; and, after
a difficult passage, by land as well as by sea, he arrived at the Court
of Antiochus.

True to his infantine oath, Hannibal did his utmost to excite hostility
against the Romans ; and asked Antiochus to lend him a trifle, in the
shape of 10,000 men, as if they were so many counters, that the

game of war required. Antiochus, however, like a boy jealous of his
toys, refused to hand over the 10,000 men, whose lives might be

Hannibal leads the Ambassadors rather a fatiguing Walk round Carthage.

required as playthings for himself; and he was not long in making use
of them.

The Greeks, being unable to appreciate the sort of independence
they had received at the hands of Rome, sent an invitation to Antiochus;
for it is the characteristic of slavery, as a moral disease, to seek relief
from the existing cause of oppression by the introduction of some
more violent form of the same malady.*

* This is, in fact, the homœopathic principle applied to politics; the counteracting of
like by like, *similia similibus*.

As the interference of strangers will usually lead to family quarrels, so the effect of foreign influence on Greece was to keep the people continually involved in disputes with each other. Part of the population would have welcomed Antiochus warmly, while others received him coldly ; and the king, who had penetrated into Thessaly, had sufficient penetration to see that he had better go a considerable part of the way back again.

By way of narrowing the ground of dispute, he took his position in the Pass of Thermopylæ, and had, for some time, maintained an advantage over the Romans, when M. Porcius Cato, ascending the heights, ran round to the rear, and, by a decisive blow on the enemy's back, changed the whole face of the engagement. Antiochus fled in dismay, and never stopped to look behind him, until he reached Asia Minor, when he sat down, and took a gloomy retrospect of all that had happened. While he met with reverses on land, he heard of the reverse, or rather the same thing, that had happened to his fleet at sea ; and he fairly gave up, not only his cause, but the Chersonesus, Lysimachia, Sestos, and Abydos, with all their contents and non-contents ; the latter of which included the inhabitants.

Antiochus, though subdued in spirit, was not quite beaten in form ; and a large army was sent to Asia, under the command of the two consuls, L. Cornelius Scipio and C. Lælius. L. C. Scipio, though without any acknowledged merit of his own, had the good fortune to be the brother of the celebrated Scipio Africanus, who got him the place ; but it is manifest that such an illegitimate step to an appointment will often end in a grievous disappointment of one kind or another. To provide against the ill consequences of this flagrant job, the celebrated Scipio went out in the capacity of legate, to counteract the consequences of his brother's general incapacity in the capacity of general. The Romans had 20,000 men, who, having arrived in Asia, met 70,000 soldiers of Antiochus, at Magnesia, where the latter received a dose from which they never recovered. Peace was granted to them on very humiliating terms ; but, however bitter the cup prescribed for Antiochus, so disagreeable was the recollection of Magnesia, that he was obliged to swallow almost anything that came after it.

Rome continued her system of giving independence to various places and people, many of whom seemed so little to appreciate the proffered boon, that in some cases money was tendered and accepted as the price of exemption from the proposed advantages. The Cappadocians were so alarmed at the prospect of their new freedom, that, being still free to confess their dislike to it, they sent 200 talents to the Romans, who, no doubt, mentally impressed with the proverbial baseness of the " slave who pays," quietly pocketed the money.

While the principles of independence were being promulgated in the East, the Romans were also employed in carrying their notions of emancipation into the North, where several tribes were cut to pieces, in order that they might feel the interest which Rome condescended to take in them. In some places the old inhabitants were rooted up like old trees, while the younger branches were transplanted to other soils; and a large quantity of Ligurian offshoots were carried off from their parent stems to fill some vacant ground at Samnium. Many places were thoroughly destroyed; and among others, Cremona was so unmercifully played upon, that it was utterly broken up, and the lamentations of its inhabitants were regarded no more than the moanings of a set of old fiddle-strings.

Not satisfied with being the masters of Italy and the tyrants of Greece, the Romans aimed at establishing their dominion in Spain, which was partly achieved by the treachery of some of the inhabitants, and the cowardice of others. Some of its most powerful men entered into an alliance with Rome, and were treated as insurgents or rebels, when they dared to revolt against the foreign authority that had either cowed or corrupted them.

The subjugation of Spain was mainly effected by M. Porcius Cato, who took a rather remarkable way of reducing the country to submission; for he induced several places to commit a sort of moral suicide; and after condemning them in his own mind, he arranged that they should become, as it were, their own executioners. He sent circulars to a large number of fortified towns in Spain, with instructions that the communications were not to be looked into before a certain day; and the inhabitants of every town experienced the agony of suspense, in the fear that their doom was sealed in a letter they were not allowed to open. At length, when the day arrived for penetrating the envelope in which the mystery was enclosed, every circular was found to contain a command that the walls of the town to which it was addressed should be razed to the ground, or, in case of disobedience, that the heaviest punishment should light on its inhabitants. The authorities not being able to communicate with each other, fancied their own town the only one that was doomed, and proceeded to pull the place about their own ears, until it was reduced to a heap of dry rubbish.

When the mischief was done, it was too late to discover that it need not have been done at all; and though unity is in ordinary cases strength, the unity with which the Spaniards had acted in demolishing their own towns, had reduced them to a condition of utter feebleness.

For some time they lived in peace, though their homes were knocked to pieces; but a war broke out again, in the year of the City 572 (B. C. 181). The Spaniards, however, were not thoroughly reduced until four years after, though they were being continually killed, beaten, cut to pieces, and otherwise dealt with, in a manner from which their reduction would seem to flow as a natural consequence. It was Tib. Sempronius Gracchus—the father of the two great Gracchi, of whom we shall have something to say hereafter—that concluded peace with several of the Spanish tribes, who were brought down so low, that their being otherwise than peaceable was almost impossible.

The Romans continued to intrude themselves and their system on different parts of Europe, and planted a colony at Aquileia, in Istria, which caused the Istrians to try and put a full stop to the disposition which Rome had shown to colon-ise. A war ensued, which resulted in the loss of three towns and one king, when the Istrians came to the conclusion that they had had enough of it, and immediately submitted to the Roman authority.

Having, for a time, lost sight of the illustrious Hannibal, we begin to look about for him once more, and find him living in a Court, kept by one Prusias, the greedy and needy king of Bithynia. After the treaty made by Antiochus and the Romans, Hannibal had fled to Crete, where he could not long remain ; and, though history is silent as to the cause, we may conjecture something from the fact, that he effected a clandes-tine removal of all his wealth, though he pretended to leave behind him a vast amount of treasure. Tradition states that, having procured a number of earthen jars, he filled them with lead, and, strewing a little gold, or loose silver, over the top, he carried them to the temple of Diana, and requested the Cretan priests to become his bankers, for the purpose of his entrusting to them this valuable deposit. The priests

Hannibal requesting the Cretan Priests to become his Bankers.

assured him, with many protestations, that he would find it all right on his return ; and Hannibal, having previously packed all his real gold into the hollow insides of some statues of brass, which he pretended to carry with him, in his character of an admirer of the arts, got clear off with all his money.

He continued to travel from place to place, and had spent the contents of nearly all his statues, except a small one, so that his means had
literally come down to the lowest figure. In this dilemma he found
himself at Bithynia, where Prusias gave him house-room for a short
time ; taking advantage of the visit, to render his guest useful in a
war that was being carried on against Eumenes, king of Pergamus.
Hannibal, however, could not persuade the parsimonious Prusias to go
to the expense of conducting hostilities in an effective style ; and,
indeed, there being no money to carry on the war, it was impossible to
do so with credit ; for nobody would make any advance on the security
of a bad sovereign. The Romans regarding Hannibal as a dangerous
agitator, which he had indeed proved himself to be, required that he
should be given up ; but Prusias, declining to be at the expense of
carriage, intimated that whoever wanted Hannibal had better come for
him. The Carthaginian general, foreseeing his fate, endeavoured to
make his escape by one of seven secret passages leading from his
house ; but his enemies had found them out, and were therefore certain
of finding him at home ; for they had taken care to bar his egress.

Though possessing all the courage of a soldier, he was miserably
destitute of a superior kind of fortitude, and he always carried a
bottle of poison about with him. Finding escape impossible, he drew
the fatal phial from his pocket, and, as he shook it up, he indulged in

Hannibal makes the usual neat and appropriate Speech previous to killing himself.

one of those speeches which are usually attributed by classical historians to men on the point of suicide. " I will," he said—or is said to have said, for nobody could have heard him, as he was quite alone, and nobody could have been listening, or the bottle would have been snatched out of his hand ; " I will deliver the Romans from the dread which has so long tormented them, since they think it too long to wait for the decease of a worn-out old man." Here he may be supposed to have paused ; and, after giving the bottle another final shake, to have continued as follows : " Flaminius's victory over a foe, unarmed and betrayed, will not redound much to his honour ; " and, with a mental once, twice, thrice, and away, the wretched Hannibal may be imagined to have raised the nauseous draught to his lips, and to have tossed it off with desperate energy.

Hannibal had certainly, in his lifetime, shown proofs of greatness, though, in the manner of his death, he gave evidence of lamentable littleness.   On the admirable principle of " look to the end," we are unable to agree with those classical enthusiasts who regard Hannibal as one of the most illustrious of mankind, because he was more daring and more skilful in the art of exterminating his fellow-creatures than many of his competitors.   His personal ambition brought misery on his own, as well as other countries, and his obstinate hatred to Rome was not justified by his juvenile oath, for the taking of which he deserved rather the birch than the laurel.   The first public act of his life was to swear when he was too young to have known what he was about, and the last act was to poison himself at the age of sixty-two, when he was quite old enough to have known better.   He made a bad beginning, but a worse ending, and he proved that, though aspiring to rule over others, he was unable to command himself, and was in nearly every respect a melancholy specimen of ill-regulated humanity.

Within about a year of Hannibal's death, Scipio Africanus also died in exile.   This great man, as it has been customary to call him, because he was a large destroyer of the human race, was taken up before the Senate on a charge of embezzlement.   The case happened to be appointed for hearing on the anniversary of some battle he had won, when he declared the day was ill-suited for litigation, and the people, who are always ready for an excuse for a holiday, immediately agreed with him.   His brother Lucius was involved in the same accusation, which he met by producing his accounts ; but, the popular idol seizing the books, declared it was shabby for a nation to be too particular with those who had served it so well, and tore up the whole of the financial statement.   Lucius Scipio remained in Rome ; but Africanus ran away to a villa in Campania, leaving his brother to undergo the confiscation of the whole of his property.   The innocence of Lucius was subsequently established, and, though no " money returned," is generally the motto of the law, he succeeded in getting back a part of what he had been unjustly deprived of.   He, however, having lived without his income, had no sooner got the means restored to him of living within it, than he died, with the melancholy satisfaction of having had justice done when it was too late to be of the smallest earthly use to him.

The merits and demerits of Scipio Africanus have been differently estimated by different authorities; and though it is charitable to give to any man the benefit of a doubt, no one would be thankful for the admission that his was a doubtful character. Scipio Africanus was a great patron of letters; but he seems to have been a despiser of figures, if the story relating to his contempt for the accuracy of his accounts is to be relied upon. Cicero has spoken eloquently of the simple habits of Scipio Africanus, in his marine retirement, throwing stones into the sea, and skimming with them the surface of the water; but this innocent pastime does not relieve him from the accusation of making " ducks and drakes " of the public money, which was the charge that Cato had endeavoured to bring home to him.

He is said to have been generous to his relatives; but to help them, after freely helping himself, may have been nothing more than nepotism, under the disguise of a domestic virtue. It is stated that he showed his disregard for wealth by relinquishing to his brother his own share of his patrimony; but there is little merit in his having despised the comparatively mean contents of his family purse, if he was unscrupulous during the time that he had the public pocket to dip into.

CHAPTER THE TWENTIETH.

PUBLIC AMUSEMENTS.   MORALS, MANNERS, CUSTOMS, AND STATE OF THE
DRAMA AND LITERATURE AMONG THE ROMANS.

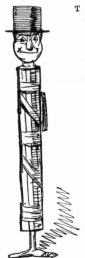

T is customary with the grandiloquent to declare that the page of history is stained with gore; but we limit ourselves to ink, which perhaps, after all, furnishes a decent type of mourning over the deeds we are compelled to chronicle.   It is true that history has too often wars for her principal facts, and the numbers of dead for her figures; but she is apt to speak rather figuratively in estimating the thousands upon thousands who are said to have fallen, sword in hand, or to have been terribly put to it.

The weapon of war cuts, however, both ways; and a nation cannot play with edged tools more safely than an individual can indulge in such dangerous pastime.

The state of war in which Rome habitually lived, had encouraged the worst passions of the people; and nearly every vice had taken an iron hold of them.   By continually fighting, they had become familiar with murder and violence, while the practice of plunder had accustomed them to robbery.   Military stratagem —which was the very essence of strategy—had taught them to regard cunning as a virtue; and he was a hero, in their opinion, who would face the swords and spears of a foe, but sought in poison a cowardly refuge from the "slings and arrows" of his own conscience.   The wealth taken by force was often appropriated by fraud; and a successful leader thought nothing of putting into his own pocket an enormous sum, declaring that it was unreasonable to expect a general to be particular.*   The few became enormously rich, while the many were miserably poor.   The higher orders grasped everything, leaving nothing to those beneath, and the consequence was a state of top-heaviness, which, when existing in the social column, exposes base and capital—but especially the latter—to extreme danger. Money had been acquired by some, who did not know its use; and its abuse was the inevitable result; for the improper employment of gold leads to every kind of guilt on the part of those who are possessed of it.

With the wealth of other nations, foreign fashions were imported, and Roman simplicity was superseded by the art and cunning of the

---

* P. Cornelius Scipio gave no better answer than this to a charge of having embezzled a sum amounting to 36,000*l.* sterling.

Grecian craftsmen. The pleasures of the table were carried to a gluttonous excess; and a slave who, in the capacity of a cook, could set before his master an agreeable kind of sauce, was often allowed impunity for insolence.

Extravagance began to prevail to such an extent among the Roman women, that those females whose wardrobe was of a gaudy hue, were virtually condemned to dye, for a law was passed by the tribune Appius, prohibiting them from wearing dresses of a gay colour. The same law limited them to half-an-ounce of gold; but this was unnecessary; for the extravagantly-disposed would spend all they had; and they were further restricted from riding at or near Rome, or any other city, in a carriage drawn by two horses; for it was considered that with one the road to ruin could be quite rapidly enough travelled. This law occa-

Roman Lady " Shopping."

sioned some violent agitation among the Roman women, who manifested the force of female influence so effectually, that in a few years the law was repealed.

The stern necessities of historical truth compel us to attribute to what is termed the gentler sex, the introduction, among the Romans, of some vices so foul, as to be at variance with all our notions of the fair. One of the worst of these enormities was the celebration of the Bacchanalia, introduced from Etruria; and recent discoveries* in that locality have initiated us into the secret of what are usually termed the

* *Vide* " The Cities and Cemeteries of Etruria," by Dennis.

Bacchic mysteries. The mystification of the votaries was accomplished by drink ; under the influence of which they wound up their festivities with a reel, such as may be traced in ancient paintings ; and round every such reel there is twined some important thread of history.

Imitation is seldom respectable in any case ; for even merit loses half its value when it is not original ; but nothing can be more contemptible than a people putting on bad habits at second-hand. Such, however, was the practice of the Romans, who borrowed nearly all their iniquities from Athens or other cities, and who wilfully brought upon themselves the moral stain of Greece. Cruelty, which goes hand in hand with depravity, had reached such an infamous excess, that it was practised openly by those whom the people delighted to honour. Among other instances, may be cited the example of the Consul L. Quinctius Flaminius, who, while encamped in Gaul, happened to be feasting with one of his degraded creatures, when the latter lamented he had never seen a gladiator killed. A noble Boian entering at the moment, to ask for shelter, Flaminius observed that, though unable to treat his friend to the sight of a dying gladiator, he might satisfy his appetite for cruelty by the exhibition of a dying Gaul. The " creature " had no sooner expressed his readiness to accept the lighter relish as a substitute for the more substantial meal, than Flaminius, drawing his sword, smote the unfortunate Boian on the head, and ran him through the body. So brutalised had the people become by continual war, that no notice was taken of this occurrence until eight years afterwards, when Cato, the Censor, brought up the charge, with a variety of others, more or less weighty, against Flaminius, and caused his expulsion from the Senate.

The name of Cato the Censor, naturally induces a few observations on the character of this ancient specimen of the

" Fine old Roman gentleman all of the olden time."

He was the son of a respectable Sabine farmer, and passed his earliest years in the country, where he followed the plough—a peaceful pursuit, which imprints no early furrows on the forehead, but leaves many on the earth it at once improves and lacerates. At seventeen, every Roman became, of necessity, a soldier ; and though in the game of life fortune had dealt him a spade, he was obliged to throw it out of his hand. Such was the lot of young Marcus Porcius Priscus ; for that was in reality his name, though he afterwards had the title of Cato, or the " knowing one," bestowed on him. His military duties were performed with credit, though he preferred cultivating any other seeds than the seeds of dissension ; and he was more at home in a trench dug for celery, than in one designed for undermining a fort.

After returning from the wars, he took some ground adjoining that which had been occupied by Dentatus ; and regarding that individual as a model farmer, Cato tried to make his own a model farm. So thoroughly did he throw himself into his agrarian occupation, that he may be said to have buried himself in his land. He wrote a work on Agriculture,* which included much miscellaneous information, from the mode of buying an estate to the art of making a cheesecake, the curing of a side of bacon, and the setting of a dislocated bone. While attending to his own business, he found leisure to attend to that of his neighbours ; and in all their petty disputes before the local tribunals, he was in the habit of attending the hearing of summonses for and against his friends. He had a word of advice or a maxim to meet every circumstance in which his advice was asked or offered ; and he could always cut through a difficulty with one of his wise saws. Some might be disposed to term him a busybody and a meddler ; but at all events a young patrician, named Valerius Flaccus, considered him to be a meddler well worth transplanting, and persuaded him to go to Rome, "as," in the language of Plutarch, "a plant that deserved a better soil." Here he "put up" for various places in the public service, and we find him climbing successively to several very high posts, where the example he set by his externally virtuous mode of living, formed a decent contrast to the undisguised vices of the age.

Such was Cato in his earlier years ; but the melancholy fact must be stated, that, though flattery paints only one side of every picture, there is none to which truth may not be called upon to add a reverse. In his youthful days Cato had worked with his labourers ; had partaken of the same fare with them at the same board, and drank nothing stronger than water ; but, in after-life, he contracted a disreputable marriage, and, giving himself up to the dissipations of the table, might have found himself occasionally under it. So thoroughly utilitarian was he in his political philosophy, that he looked upon a labourer as a mere machine, which, when worn out, he contended ought to be got rid of as speedily as possible. Cato the Censor owes much of his reputation for morality to the fact of his having set himself up as a professional moralist. Though he was useful as a castigator of the vices of his age, there was nothing very amiable in the rancorous and uncharitable spirit in which he performed his office. He had a keen appetite for an abuse or a piece of scandal, but, while crime or error excited his hatred, virtue and generosity seemed to rouse less of his admiration than his jealousy. If he had lived in modern times, he would, probably, have been a common informer, a rigid observer of all the outward appearances of virtue, and a discounter of bills ; for it is said of Cato, that he advanced money at exorbitant interest to those whose necessities or recklessness induced them to comply with his terms.

Religion had, at about this period, sunk to a very low ebb in the hands of a crafty priesthood, who used the influence of their position for their own temporal purposes. Prodigies were declared to have happened ; such as the talking of a cow, which was alleged to have "whispered low " in a priest's ear ; statues were said to have wept ; and

* De Re rustica.

the tale was listened to by those who believed that their augurs could, if they pleased, get blood out of a stone.

In literature, though it is customary to speak of Roman characters as an original form of letters, Rome had nothing new, but trusted to what was already known; for she not only copied the vices of the Greeks, but took a leaf out of their books in a more literal manner. She had no writers of her own; but what literary food she possessed was supplied by those translating cooks who make a hash of nearly everything they lay their hands upon.

The earliest Roman dramatist is supposed to have been one Lucius Andronicus, who had formerly been a slave, and who continued his slavish propensities by a servile adaptation of Greek plays, instead of boldly attempting an original production. Like many of the modern translators, he was himself an actor in his own pieces; and it is declared by Livy the historian, that he lost his voice by the frequency with which he was encored by the audience. This statement seems to show that puffs were not unknown when the Roman drama was in its very earliest stage; for the assertion in question could scarcely have been true, since Cicero * has told us that there was nothing worthy of being read or listened to twice, in the plays of Lucius Andronicus.

The greatest comic writer of the period at which our history has arrived, was Marcus Accius Plautus, of whose origin little is known; for the Romans held their wits and humorists in such little respect, that as long as they could raise a laugh, it mattered little who they were, whence they sprung, or what became of them. It was not until after a writer's death that any interest was felt in his life, and such was the case with regard to Plautus, who has been the subject of more invention than is to be found in all his comedies. Conjecture—the author of half the history, and three-fourths of the biography, which the world possesses—describes Plautus as a low-born fellow, made of the very commonest clay, moulded by one of Nature's awkwardest journeymen into a misshapen lump, and whose angular deformities constituted his chief points of humour. Having made a little money as a dramatist, he is said to have embarked it in the baking business; some would say that he might make his own puffs; but his shop failed, and as the public would not, he of course could not, get his bread at it. He next entered the service of a miller and master baker, where he attempted, in grinding corn, to turn at once the handle of a mill and an honest penny. Even in the bakehouse he was unable to forget the flowery path of literature; and while watching the bread, he managed to inscribe on different rolls no less than three comedies. Of these he made sufficient to enable him to quit the oven, which was incapable of warming his imagination; and taking lodgings in Rome, he resumed the life of a dramatist.

What Plautus may have wanted in originality, he made up for by

* Brut., c. 18.

industry, there being still extant twenty of his plays, and he was, according to some, the author of one hundred pieces.

The mantle of Plautus—supposing the dramatist to have died with a coat to his back—may be said to have fallen on Terentius Afer, or Terence. He is believed to have been born at Carthage, and to have been the slave of a Roman senator; for his biographers—who, by the way, were writers themselves—will not hazard the supposition that one of their own order could have been the son of a gentleman. Terentius, however, got into what is usually termed the best society, which had the usual effect of the " best society " on a literary man; for it took what it could never compensate him for—his time; it led him into idle and extravagant habits, and thus brought him, where it will inevitably leave him, if it once gets him there—to ruin. His fashionable friends carried their patronage so far, as to tax his reputation as well as his means, and even claimed a share in the credit of his writings, declaring the best part of them to be their own, though they suffered Terentius to affix his name to them.

Scipio Africanus, who stands convicted of fraud and embezzlement in a former chapter,* had the effrontery to say, or allow it to be said, that he had written portions of the plays in question, or, at least, contributed some of the jokes; but we have nothing to support the claim, except the fact that he might, perhaps, have made a pun, as he is known to have picked the public pocket. The following anecdote, related by his biographer, Donatus, or Suetonius—for the learned are at issue, and have long been stumbling over the two styles—may afford some idea of the treatment to which authors were submitted in the age we are writing of. Having completed his play of " Andria," Terence was desirous of getting it licensed, and applied to the Ædiles, who referred him to Cæcilius, for an opinion on the manuscript. The critic being at dinner, desired the dramatist to take a seat on a low stool, and read his piece, so that Cæcilius might, at the same time, swallow his meal, and digest the new comedy. Terence had read but a few verses, when the critic declared he could not continue selfishly putting good things into his own mouth, while so many good things were coming from the mouth of his visitor. He was requested to put the comedy away until after the dinner, which he was invited to share; and, having done so, the play was finished over a glass or two of wine, which increased the enthusiasm with which the author read, and the critic listened. Both were delighted with each other. Their better acquaintance was drunk; success to the comedy was drunk; their healths were drunk together; and, ultimately, Cæcilius and Terence were drunk separately as well as jointly, before the termination of the evening.

The plays of Terence, though of Greek origin, were moulded after a fashion of his own, and what little of the material he borrowed was almost immaterial to the value of his productions. He received for one

* Chapter xix., p. 202.

of them "The Eunuchus," no less than 8000 sesterces (about £64),
which was, in those days, the largest sum that had ever been paid for a
five act comedy. After having been successful for some years, he

Terence reading his Play to Cæcilius.

embarked, according to some authorities, for Greece—as our dramatists
embark occasionally for Boulogne—to lay in a new stock of pieces for
future translation. Other authorities assert that he went to Asia,
taking a number of translations with him, and was never heard of
again, the ship having been sunk, perhaps, by the weight of his too
heavy manuscripts.

Among the writers of the period, we must not forget to mention
Ennius, a Calabrian, who gave lessons in Greek to the patrician youths,
at a small lodging on the Aventine. He is regarded as the father of
Latin poetry; but Latin poetry could profit little from the paternal
care of one whose devotion to the bottle rendered his own care of
himself frequently impossible. His productions are of a very fragmentary kind; and, indeed, his habits of intemperance prevented him from
making any sustained effort. He was the boon companion of several
patricians, who helped him to ruin when alive, and gave him a monument at his death;—one of them (Scipio Africanus) accommodating
the poet with a place in his tomb, so that the patron might literally go
down to posterity with the man of genius.

While on the subject of the drama, as represented at Rome in the days of Plautus and Terence, we may refer to the fact that masks were worn by the actors, which gave to a theatrical performance some absurd and not very interesting features. There were several sets of masks among the properties of a regular theatre, beginning with that of the first tragic old man, which had a quantity of venerable white worsted attached to it for hair, with cheeks as chalky as grief and tears, strong enough to have washed out the fastest colour, might be supposed to have rendered them. The mask of the second tragic old man was less pale than that of the first, for he was not supposed to have attained to that universal privilege of aged heroism,—a countenance sicklied o'er with a pale coat of whitewash. The mask of the tragic young man, or youthful hero, was remarkable for its luxuriant head of hair, which, from the earliest days of the drama to the present hour, seems to be accepted as the stage indication of a noble character. The tragic masks for slaves embraced some interesting varieties, including a sharp nose, intended to be indicative of many a blow from fortune's hand,—a sunken eye, to bespeak a sorry look-out,—and, occasionally, long white hair, quite straight, which was supposed to convey the idea of the party having seen better days, though the analogy is difficult, unless the lankiness of the locks may be held to show that a favourable turn has in vain been waited for. The mask of a tragic lady had all those signs of a genuine female in distress which are even to this day required on the stage, where long black hair, in terribly straightened circumstances, is the emblem of an anxious mind, which has long been a stranger to curl-papers. When insanity, as well as anguish, had to be represented by the mask, the hair was undivided in the centre, but floated in wild profusion, as if the wearer had gone through a great deal, and as if, whatever she had gone through, her hair had caught in the middle of.

The classical mask of the first comic old man was drawn excessively mild and benevolent, to indicate that propensity for scattering purses among the poor, and bestowing his daughter, with some millions of sesterces, on young Lucius, which were the probable attributes of the Greek and Latin stage veteran. There was also the mask of the testy old man, who was represented perfectly bald, as if he was always taking something or other into his head which had torn all the hair out of it. The masks for comic young men had the ordinary characteristics of stage humour, including red hair, pug noses, broad lips, and raised eyebrows, which are ih these days supplied from those recognised sources of dramatic drollery, the burnt cork, the gum-pot, and the paint-box.

We might enumerate a long list of different masks, without introducing any variety, for they were very nearly the same ; but we have shown enough to prove that the classical taste for which so many clamour without knowing what they talk about, was very little, if at all, above the modern standard. Some authorities * assert that

* Diomedes, iii., p. 486, ed. Putsch.

masks were not worn in the earliest representations of the Roman drama; but some of the oldest MS. of Terence contain figures of the

Light Comedy Man of the Period.

required masks, just as a play of the present day has prefixed to it a list of the costumes of the characters. The admirers of the classical may be grieved and astonished to hear that the taste, for the restoration of which they so much pine, took greater delight in the deadly games of the Circus, than in the lively representations of men and manners.

Historical literature was in a very humble condition, and had much, or indeed all, the prolixity, with little of the accuracy, of a modern report for a newspaper. It is, however, hardly fair to judge the authors severely for writings which we have never seen, and are never likely to see; for they have never come down to us, except in scraps—the result of the various cuttings-up they have encountered at the hands of Polybius and other critics. For the same reason, we are unable to praise conscientiously the "Origines" of Cato, which has long ago been lost, and we are unwilling to adopt the "opinions of the press," which have too often been at the disposal of the member of a clique, or of the purchaser of a puffing paragraph. Oratory always was, and always will be, an important art, except in those countries which are so excessively republican and free, that the people are free for every imaginable or imaginary purpose, except to do as they please, and to say what they think proper. The Romans took the art of rhetoric from the Greeks, but even a good thing is distasteful if forced where it is not asked ; and, when the Athenians sent three professed orators as propagandists of their art to Rome, the foreign agitators were ordered—very properly—to quit the city. As lawyers, the early Romans are entitled to high praise, and they evinced their prudence by making juris-prudence an essential part of their ordinary studies. The Roman youth were required to get the Twelve Tables by heart, or rather, by head, which was supposed to be sufficiently furnished when the whole of the Twelve Tables alluded to were crammed into it.

The science of Medicine was not in very high repute among the early Romans, and physic was, commercially speaking, in very little demand, so that it would have been a mere drug if brought into the market. The aristocratic families generally expected one of their slaves to know something of the healing process, as they usually did of other arts or trades ; and a surgical operation, like a gardening operation, or any piece of merely manual labour, was frequently entrusted to the hands of a simple bondsman. Physic was scarcely known in Rome as a distinct pursuit, until the year of the City 534 (B. C. 219), when the Greek physician Archagathus opened a shop with an extensive stock, and an establishment of baths ; the expense of which would have plunged him into hot water, had not the public come forward to make him a present of his premises. The shops of the doctors were lounging places for the idle, who are always the most profitable patients ; for there is no ailing so troublesome as that of having nothing to do, and abundance of time to do it in. The Romans had made little advance in art, though they professed to show their love for it by robbing other nations of their treasures. On the same principle, the pickpocket, who pilfers a handkerchief, might ask credit for being attracted by the beauty of its design ; and the knave who walks away with a set of silver spoons might pretend to be actuated by a desire to patronise their pattern or their workmanship. Rome, indeed, can scarcely be said to have introduced the arts from Greece, but merely to have introduced a few of the articles on which the arts had employed themselves.

Commerce was looked down upon for a long period as a degrading pursuit ; but from the time of the Second Punic War, the equites, with a total disregard of equity, began lending out money at exorbitant interest. Though they would not condescend to trade for gain, they were prepared to pocket the profits of usury. They would also purchase corn at a low price abroad, and sell it at a dear rate at home ; for they understood and practised all the tricks of the tradesman, though they sneered at and repudiated his position. The slave trade was also carried on to a vast extent by the higher classes, and even Cato is said to have done a little in that way himself, notwithstanding the stiffness of his notions, and the alleged purity of his morals. The patrician principle seemed to be, that the same thing which would be blamable on a small scale, was excusable when practised on a broad basis—that to sell a little was degrading, but to sell a great deal was no disgrace at all; and by a parity of reasoning, they must have held, that so far from its being the same thing whether to be hanged for a sheep or a lamb, it would only be the smaller depredator who would deserve any punishment whatever.

Robbery had greatly augmented the public wealth; but individuals were wretchedly poor, with the exception of the few who had had a hand in the pockets of the conquered nations. Slaves were brought in such numbers to Rome, that at length they would hardly fetch a price; and so many were brought from Sardinia, who were constantly being put up, knocked down at nothing, bought in, and left on hand, that "Sardians to sell!" passed into a proverb to express an unsaleable article. In vain were the poor creatures prepared to do as they were bid, for no one would give them a bidding. The Greek captives fetched a higher price, for they were many of them accomplished men, and became tutors, music-masters, or teachers of painting, in the families of their purchasers. Among the hostages brought to Rome, was Polybius the historian, who got so good a living by giving lessons, that though he had been brought to Rome against his will, he solicited the privilege of remaining there. His "Universal History," in forty books, was a work that ought to be, and would have been, in every gentleman's library, but for the unfortunate fact of its having been nearly all lost: and we may judge of the excellence of the whole, from the knowledge that though what remains of the work is very good, by far the best part of it is missing.

CHAPTER THE TWENTY-FIRST.

WARS AGAINST PERSEUS.   THE THIRD PUNIC WAR.   SIEGE AND DESTRUC-
TION OF CARTHAGE, AND DITTO DITTO OF CORINTH.

PHILIP OF MACEDON had been from time to time waging war with
Rome; but the wages of the troops were so exhausting to his means,
that he was driven to a hollow peace by his empty pockets. He had
agreed to confine his dominion within a certain space; but, as his
ambition had no bounds, he would not be content that his territory
should have any limits. He accordingly fought with and thrashed the
Thracians, who sent ambassadors to Rome for the purpose of showing
him up, as it were, to their common master. Rome punished him by
ordering him to keep within bounds; and threatened, that if he should
be found venturing out of bounds, he should be severely punished.
Philip muttered something about seeking justice elsewhere—a threat
of paulo-post-future revenge which is common with those who, being
engaged in a dispute, have got decidedly the worst of it.

His prospects of ulterior measures were, however, sufficiently remote
to induce him to attempt an arrangement through the intervention of
his son Demetrius. The latter had been educated in Rome, and of
course had a thorough understanding of the Roman character. He
succeeded in his mission, but he obtained his end in a less agreeable
sense; for his existence was brought to a close by treachery. Some
designing persons fomented a feeling of jealousy between himself and
his elder brother, Perseus, who poisoned the mind of Philip with such
fatal effect, that he caused the poisoning—not merely mental, but
physical—of his son Demetrius. When the wretched parent discovered that he had been duped, he became so uneasy in his mind, that
he went quite out of it, and died at the age of three-score, unable to
meet the heavy score that he had run up against himself in the court of
his own conscience.

Perseus was hailed by the Romans as king; but all their hailing
could not render his reign prosperous. He endeavoured to cement his
power by a marriage with the daughter of Antiochus Epiphanes,
for Perseus thought that the aid he would derive from the match,
would render him more than a match for his enemies. He gave his
sister to Prusias of Bithynia, in the hope that the latter, having married
into the family, would feel himself wedded to its interests. Avarice was,
however, the ruin of Perseus; for he did not understand the true use
of the purse, which he used his utmost exertions to fill, and then held
its strings with parsimonious stringency. He had promised to pay
his allies, but their zeal in his cause subsided when they were left
without their subsidies.

Eumenes of Pergamus being among others seized with a panic, went to Rome to ask advice, and on his return nearly lost his life on the highway, by some persons who attacked him in a very low manner. He was passing a narrow footpath near Delphi—from which it would appear that he had walked at least a portion of the way—when some persons concealed in the rocks, hurled down several large blocks of granite, which though not causing his death, brought him within a stone's throw of it. Several huge pieces having fallen upon him, something struck him that all was not right; and he was revolving the affair in his mind, when he found himself rolling down the precipice. He was picked up nearly lifeless, but though very much jammed, he was preserved; and though almost dashed to pieces, he was sufficiently collected, in a few days, to be enabled to go home, by another road, to Asia. It was said that Perseus had had a hand in this disgraceful affair; but he declared that even if he had wished for the death of Eumenes, he would not have been guilty of making such a desperate push for it.

This circumstance gave an impetus to the hostilities between Rome and Perseus, who was driven by the Consul Paulus Æmilius to a place called Pydna, where the two armies came to such very close quarters, that their cavalry were compelled to go halves in the same stream of water. A Roman horse happened to be drinking, when, startled by his own shadow, and not giving himself time for reflection, which would have shown him the cause of his alarm, he ran away into the camp of the enemy. The animal, though goaded on by nothing but the spur of the moment, continued his flight; and some Roman soldiers running after him into the enemy's camp, were speedily followed by so many more, that, though they had come after their own horse, they began attacking the foot of the enemy.

The battle was commenced under such unfavourable circumstances, that Æmilius, the Roman leader, thinking it all lost, declared that it was all one to him what became of him. He manifested his grief by tearing his robe to show how much he was cut up; and beating his foot impatiently on the ground, he stamped himself for ever as a man without strength of mind, in a case where fortitude was required. The Roman cavalry beginning to bear down successfully, the Consul began to bear up; and the tide of fortune being turned, the Macedonians were, according to those grave authorities—which never mince matters, though always mincing men—cut, as usual, to pieces. Perseus flew to Pella; but having omitted to close the gates after him, he was shut out from all chance of escape had he remained in the place, and he went on, therefore, to Amphipolis. There he attempted to address the inhabitants on his own behalf; but he shed so many tears, that he drowned his own voice, and choked his own utterance. He had hoped to rouse the inhabitants by going to the country with a cry; but he damped their enthusiasm with a flood of tears, when they had been looking for a flow of eloquence.

After flying from place to place, like a hunted hare, he felt the game was up, and, retreating to Samothrace, he consigned his weary head to the shelter of Castor, in whose temple he hid himself. He had managed to carry about with him a large supply of treasure, which he was anxious to save, and had hired a mariner to take him to Crete ; but the money having been first sent on board, the crafty seaman, out of curiosity, weighed the gold, and immediately weighed anchor. Perseus having gone down to the beach, to embark, saw the ship in the offing, and, having watched it, he perceived that it was fairly, or rather unfairly off, with all his treasure. As he paced the shore, he felt himself quite aground, and, having no lodging for the night, or the means of obtaining one, he returned to the solitary chambers of the temple. Having a wife and family to provide for, he threw himself on the generosity of Æmilius, who gave him a subsistence, but loaded him with chains, that he might feel the weight of his obligations. The unhappy Perseus was made to walk in a triumph before the car of his conqueror ; and though he had entreated that he might not be so lowered, he was still further let down, by cruel confinement in a subterranean dungeon. His fellow-prisoners are said to have offered him a sword, to end his days, but, on looking at the weapon, he very properly declined to bring his sufferings to a point, by an act of folly and wickedness. He eventually found his way to Alba, where he died in about two years ; his son, Alexander, having adopted the trade of a turner, with the laudable view of turning an honest penny.

Paulus Æmilius exercised the usual privilege of a conqueror, by robbing the vanquished of all they had possessed ; and Macedonia was declared free, in the customary manner, by placing it entirely under the government of its foreign victors.

The triumph of Paulus Æmilius was one of the most magnificent shows that had ever been seen, and lasted three days, during which a perpetual fair was kept up ; for, among the Romans, " None but the brave deserve the fair " was a maxim literally followed. On the first day there was a procession of pictures, showing the exploits of Æmilius in the brightest colours. The second day was devoted to the carrying of the trophies and the silver coin ; but, on the third, which was the grandest day of all, the gold was paraded, followed by 120 bulls, which seem to be suggestive of nothing belonging to war but its butchery. After these came the unhappy Perseus, loaded with fetters, and having about him some other links of a far more affecting kind, in the shape of his three children.

The fame spread by the fate of Perseus was general among the kings of the earth, who flocked like sheep, or rather, crawled like curs, to do homage to the Roman Senate. Perseus arrived with his head shaved, as if to show that he owed not only his crown, but his hair and all, to Rome ; and he wore the tattered garments of a freed slave, as if to prove that he had not a rag to his back, but what he held at the pleasure of his masters.

All who had shown any sympathy with the cause of Perseus were cruelly persecuted, and the unfortunate Rhodians were so terrified with the bare anticipation of their fate, that they began to anticipate it in reality, by making away with themselves and with one another. On the few who remained the hardest conditions were imposed, which made their own condition the more deplorable. Carthage and the Achaian League were the only two powers that seemed to stand in the way of Rome, and of these the latter was thought so contemptible, that some Achaians who had been detained in Italy were saved by a sarcasm of Cato on their feebleness and decrepitude. " We have only to decide," said he, " whether these poor creatures shall be buried by their own grave-diggers, or by ours ; " a cruel pleasantry, which, however, had a humane result, for it was decided that they should be at liberty to go home and yield to their native undertakers the profit—or loss— attendant on their funerals.

The Carthaginians had been for some years at peace with Rome, but had been much harassed by some of her allies, and particularly by Massinissa, their neighbour, in Numidia. It was annoying enough to be subjected to attack, but it was still more provoking to be unable to return the blow, which was the case with Carthage, whose hands were tied by a bond prohibiting her from going to war without Rome's permission. An appeal was addressed to Rome, which sent ambassadors, who were instructed to hear the Carthaginians, but to decide in favour of Massinissa. Carthage at length grew tired of allowing Rome to hold the scales of justice ; for, though the scales might have been true, a false weight was always attached to one side, which gave it a vast preponderance.

The Carthaginians, therefore, took up arms against Massinissa, who, though ninety years of age, fought with great determination ; for he felt, probably, that he was too old to fly, and that his only chance was to make that determined stand so well adapted to a time of life when progress is somewhat difficult. The Carthaginians were worsted, but they were not yet quite at their worst, until Rome was seized with the idea of destroying their city. Cato was especially bent upon this design, or rather he pursued it with unbending obstinacy, for he finished every speech with the words " *Delenda est Carthago*," which may be freely rendered into " Carthage must be smashed." Whatever might have been the commencement of his oration, he always ended with the same words, and whether he spoke in the Senate, the market-place, or his own house, though the premises might be different, he always came to the same conclusion. He went about as a man with one idea, and his conduct was almost that of a monomaniac ; for, if he met a friend in the street, and conversed on different or indifferent subjects, he would take his farewell with the accustomed words, " *Valete ; delenda est Carthago*,"—" Good-bye; we must smash Carthage." During a debate in the Senate he pulled some figs out of his pocket, which he exhibited to some of his brother members as being " remarkably fine." As the fruit was being examined, he observed, that he had " picked them up in Africa; " that " they were capital ; " that " there were plenty more where those came from," and, in a word, he added, " *Delenda est Carthago* "—" We really must smash Carthage."

Rome agreed with Cato, more especially when he pointed out that the place was exceedingly rich; for the Romans, whenever there was anything to be got by robbery, were quite prepared for violence. The Consuls, M. Manilius and L. Marcius Censorinus, assembled with a large force in Sicily, where some ambassadors appeared from Carthage ; but the only result of negotiation was an order that 300 members of the best Carthaginian families should be sent over by way of hostages. The Romans then passed over into Utica, where the Carthaginian ambassadors again tried to treat, but the treatment they experienced was a demand for the instant giving up of all their arms and ammunition. Commissioners were sent into the city to see the orders carried out, which comprised the carrying out of 200,000 suits of armour, and 3000 catapults.* The Carthaginians appear to have lost the use of their heads when they so quietly resigned their arms; but when they were told that they must, in the next place, abandon Carthage, and build another city ten miles off, they began to feel—somewhat too late—that it was time to defend themselves.

The Carthaginian ambassadors proceeded to the usual expression of anguish by tearing their hair out by the roots, instead of trying to pluck up a little courage. Some, who were already bald, rolled themselves in the dust ; and only a few went, like sensible men, to communicate to the Carthaginians the doom with which their city was threatened.

The receipt of the news seems to have deprived the Carthaginians of all their natural intelligence ; for their first step was to maltreat the envoys. An effort was then made to save the city, by shutting the gates ; and the citizens armed themselves with stones, having determined to set their lives upon the cast of these unwarlike missiles. It is impossible not to respect and admire the heroism displayed under the very trying circumstances ; but, unfortunately, trying was of little use, for the chances were all against the Carthaginians. Hasdrubal, who had been living in exile, at the head of 20,000 men—a somewhat large party to remain in banishment—was sent for to take the command, and occupied a post outside the city. The inhabitants, having given up all their ordinary arms to the enemy, supplied fresh ammunition by devoting all their gold and silver to the furnace ; and it was a melting sight to see their treasure sacrificed for this patriotic object. The women cut off their hair, to devote it to the making of crossbows, and the sex took a characteristic pride in furnishing as many strings to a bow as possible. They worked so energetically, that they are said to have fabricated as many as 500 javelins, 140 bucklers, and 300 swords each day ; but this

---

* A catapult was an instrument for throwing arrows to a considerable distance The arrows were called *Tormenta*, not from the torment they inflicted, but from *torqueo*, to twist, because they were made of twisted hair, and perhaps the sight of them was calculated to give a turn to the enemy.

statement seems to involve so much of fabrication, that we find difficulty in believing it.

The resistance of Carthage was obstinate; and the confidence of Rome led to a sort of indolence on the part of the latter, which protracted the siege, until a new life was put into the affair, by the appointment of young P. C. Scipio, the son of Paulus Æmilius, to the Consulship. The Carthaginians also were urged to fresh exertion, and a party of 300 waded through the harbour, with torches in their hands, to burn some engines; but the water damped their efforts, which might be compared to an attempt to set the Thames on fire; and all who were not drowned were glad to make their way back again. The suggestion of the use of flame was an unfortunate one for Carthage, since it seemed to cause the breaking in of a new light upon the Romans, who had recourse to incendiarism in their turn for the accomplishment of their object. Having got within the walls, they ignited several houses, and, carrying fire from street to street, they invested their cause with a glare which is none the less hateful for having been the glare of victory.

After nearly everybody had been killed, 50,000 men and women came forth with olive branches to meet the conqueror; and 900 Roman deserters were still stowed away in the citadel. Hasdrubal yielded; but his wife, who was a strong-minded woman, reviled him in a speech from the ramparts, and, parading her poor helpless children up and down for a few minutes, she threw them before her, and ultimately flung herself into the burning ruins. Preceding historians have expressed their admiration of this frantic female, for the act of murder and suicide which we have described; but we must confess our total inability to appreciate the heroism of a piece of cruelty and cowardice, involving a large amount of brutal daring, but wholly destitute of moral fortitude.

Carthage was now utterly destroyed, and Scipio, who had been the main instrument of its having been set on fire, is said to have shed tears over its smouldering ashes; but we should be inclined to attribute the fact to the smoke having got into his eyes, rather than to any feeling of humanity. Even those who give him credit for sensibility, accuse him of selfishness, for they say that he alluded to the possibility that the same fate would befal his own country; and they add that, while thinking of his home, he quoted Homer, who had foretold the doom of Troy through the mouth of Hector.* The Romans having possession of the place, razed to the ground every part that had escaped the flames; but they lowered themselves even still more completely than they levelled the city. Thus fell a place which had maintained a noble rivalry with Rome, and which, in many respects, surpassed her proud competitor.

The greatness of Carthage had been, undoubtedly, the cause of that littleness of feeling which had been manifested towards it by Cato, who could not bear the idea that there should exist a city rivalling in

---

* " The day shall come when Ilium's self shall fall,
With Priam and his strong-spear'd people all."—*Iliad*, vi. 446.

grandeur the place he inhabited. The walls, which were triple, were divided into two stories, the upper for men, and the lower for brutes ; the former comprising barracks for soldiers, and the latter being fitted up as stables for elephants.

The chief glory of the place was, however, to be found in its aqueducts, which ran in a long line of seventy miles, and of which the people had more reason to be proud than of even a still longer line of ancestors. That a place surrounded almost by aqueducts should have been destroyed by fire, is an extraordinary fact, though it is possible that turncocks may have been neglectful, and if called upon to turn the water on, they may have turned it off in favour of some more agreeable engagement.

There were not so many spoils as had been expected, for everything was spoilt by the mischief that had been done, and though there had been plenty of gold, the fearful amount of violent change had so scattered the gold, that there was not so much remaining as there otherwise would have been. With a touch of that honour which the proverb says is to be found among thieves, Scipio called upon the places formerly plundered by Carthage to reclaim their goods ; and the people of Agrigentum demanded a brazen Bull they had once used as an instrument of torture, though the invention was so discreditable to humanity, that its inventors ought to have been ashamed to ask for it back again. Among the prizes secured by the Romans, was a very small parcel of books, including a little work on agriculture, by Mago, which had taught the Carthaginians to till the earth, though not how to keep their ground, for they had lost every foot of it.

Carthage became a province of Rome, under the name of Africa, and Scipio, who subsequently styled himself Africanus, enjoyed one of those triumphs, which were in fact disgraces to the object they were designed to honour. Part of the " triumph " consisted in the barbarity of throwing as food to lions the fugitives that had fallen into his hands, and games were celebrated, in which death to the conquered was the chief sport to the conqueror.

Macedonia, which was groaning under the freedom forced upon it by Rome, was glad to become the slave of everybody who offered to ease it of the obnoxious burden. The Macedonians, therefore, became the dupes of three impostors in succession, who, with all their imposition, were less objectionable than the hardships imposed by Rome in her character of liberator to the world in general. The impostors—one of whom was a runaway gladiator—were in turn subdued, and Macedonia was swallowed up by Rome's insatiable appetite for conquest.

Of the three pretenders just alluded to, the only one who had been able to maintain his ground—though, by the way, the ground was never his to maintain—was a young man, who declared himself to be Philip, the son of Perseus. The youth was certainly very like his alleged father ; and, upon the strength of the resemblance in features, he put upon his claim such a bold face, that the Macedonians favoured it. They put their crown upon his head, and the kingly name seemed to have invested the young adventurer with a tower of strength; for he was successful in an attack upon the Romans, under the consul Juventius. The impostor, however, soon lost control over himself, and there was at once an end to his influence over his new subjects. They threw him off, and he was compelled to take refuge in a Court inhabited by one Bysas, a petty Thracian prince, who gave up, or, more probably, sold, the fugitive, who had sought his hospitality. The pretender, who had led away so many others, was eventually led away himself, and made to march as a "frightful example" in the triumph of Metellus.

About this time the Achaians, who had entered into a league, began to quarrel among themselves; for Sparta, like a spoiled child, wanted to have its own way, and sulked, as it were, alone in a corner, apart from the rest of the confederacy. Rome was appealed to for advice, and Roman ambassadors came to Corinth; but they were so unpopular, that on a visit to the theatre, where they had gone, expecting fair play, they were insulted and pelted by the audience. This irritated the Romans, and an army was sent, under Mummius, to encounter the Greek general Diæus, who made so certain of victory, that he had seats erected for the women and children to see him win a battle. He had prepared everything in the neighbourhood of Corinth, and appropriating the privilege of the brave who are said to deserve the fair, he clustered a large bevy of female beauty round the spot of his intended achievement. The ladies were all expectation, and Diæus was all confidence, until Mummius made his appearance, and in a very few minutes sent Diæus flying towards Megalopolis. Here he entered his own abode, and setting fire to the premises, celebrated, with the most dismal of house-warmings, the defeat that took the place of his intended victory.

Mummius, thinking it idle to pursue the fugitive, preferred following up his advantage, and arrived at the gates of Corinth, which had been left wide open by the citizens. The place was deserted; and Mummius not only sacked its palaces, but ransacked its private houses, and, looking into its magazines, extracted from them some very valuable articles. So little, however, did he understand or appreciate art, that when sending valuable pictures or pieces of sculpture to Rome, he told the sailors, that if any damage was done on the voyage, he would make them execute objects precisely similar to those with which he entrusted them. Among the pictures was the celebrated "Bacchus" of Aristides, —which was so perfect as to be looked upon as one of the wonders of the world—and, when consigning it as part of a cargo of curiosities, he declared that, if any injury was done to it, the ship's painter should immediately paint another. Such was the barbarism of the destroyers of Corinth, that this picture was only rescued by Polybius from the hands of the soldiers, who were gambling on its face, and who, with every throw of the die, took off a portion of its colour.

The scenes enacted during the pillage of Corinth were barbarous in

the extreme, and involved the total destruction of what may have been
termed one of the chief pillars of civilisation—or, at all events, its
Corinthian capital. Many of the Roman soldiers, intoxicated with
success and something more, perished in the flames, to which the city
was doomed by the barbarous order of Mummius. When the conflagration

Bacchanalian Group, from a very old Vase.

first commenced, it is said that a liquid metal was seen to flow through
the streets, which induced the invaders to rush forward in the hope
of profiting by such a strange metallic currency. Those, however,
who laid their hands upon the tempting issue, as it ran from the banks
on either side of the thoroughfare, found it a mass of floating fire, with
which they terribly burned their fingers. On cooler examination the
material proved to be a fusion of beautiful ores, to which the name of
Corinthian brass has since been given.

Greece was now at the feet of Rome, which trampled not only on her
fallen foe, but upon all the obligations of honour and morality. The
population and wealth of Corinth were disposed of—the former by
murder, and the latter by robbery. Greece was formed into a Roman
province under the title of Achaia, and Mummius, glorying in, rather

than being ashamed of, his share of the work, took the surname of
Achaicus. We may instance as a redeeming feature of the period, the
erection at Rome of a clock, which was in some degree at variance with
the time ; for the useful arts were neglected amid the pursuits of war
and rapine. The clock consisted of a bottle with a narrow neck, filled
with water, divided into twelve measures, to mark the hours ; but it
was only a minute observer that could ascertain the minutes. The only
mode of telling the time at Rome, had been previously by means of
the sun-dial, which was, of course, useless in the absence of sun, and
those who were particular to a shade, could derive from it no assistance
in their evening arrangements.

We dwell with some satisfaction on the introduction of the apparatus
we have described ; for the mere manifestation of a desire to note the
progress of time is indicative of a wish to make an improved use of it.
The application of the bottle to a wholesome purpose must also be a
cheering symptom, when it is met with among those who had previously
looked at the bottle as the means of killing time, rather than as an
instrument for making its flight perceptible.

CHAPTER THE TWENTY-SECOND.

WARS IN SPAIN.　　VIRIATHUS.　　DESTRUCTION OF NUMANTIA.　　THE SERVILE
WAR IN SICILY　　APPROPRIATION OF PERGAMUS.

WAR had become so familiar to the Romans, that they never felt at
home unless they were fighting abroad, and the sword was the only
thing they took in hand with real earnestness. The intoxication of
success, like other habits of intoxication, cannot be easily got rid of, and
the Romans sought to indulge their thirst for conquest in a manner
wholly at variance with sober judgment. Their design was to conquer
Spain, and in the execution of this design they cruelly executed large
numbers of the Lusitanians, who had laid down their arms, in consequence of a promise that if they quitted the field of battle, they
should be allowed quiet possession of the fields of peaceful industry.
On this assurance, they divided themselves into three parts, and were
then—as we are gravely assured by the chroniclers—treacherously cut
into several thousand pieces. One of the few that escaped was
Viriathus, who combined the qualities of the wolf and the lamb, for
he had turned a desperate robber, after having been employed as a
gentle shepherd. Abandoning the honest hook of a pastoral life, he had
adopted the more crooked ways of the common thief; and he seems
to have gradually stolen upon the confidence of his countrymen, until
they made him a general. He had passed his early days among the
mountains, and was prepared for the ups and downs of life, which he
afterwards experienced. His predatory properties had taught him how
to attack, and his practice as a robber—which rendered it necessary for
him frequently to keep out of the way—had familiarised him with the
art of avoiding an enemy. He would appear suddenly from the thick of
a thicket, and after doing considerable mischief, he would find concealment in the hollow of some rock which his companions would never
split upon. Though he had commenced his career as a poor country
clown, he had trained himself to perform feats of activity worthy of the
most experienced Harlequin. Life, which is a drama in the case of
most men, was, in his case, a series of scenes in a pantomime. He was
here, there, and everywhere, when he was not expected, and he was
immediately nowhere when his opponents were in pursuit of him. His
policy was first to scatter, and then to destroy; to divide an enemy *en gros*,
and cut it to pieces *en detail*. He had encountered Vitellius, the Roman
Prætor, near a place called Tribula, where the latter got into the utmost
tribulation by being led through briers and bushes into an ambush,
where he lost half his army. The other half lost him, for he was
killed by the sword of some one who did not know him, though, had he

been known, the acquaintance would, most probably, have been cut in the same barbarous manner.

Viriathus for some time baffled the enemy by cunning and address, or rather by having no address at all, for he had no fixed residence ; and there was, consequently, much difficulty in finding him. At length he fought a battle, in which he was so far successful that a peace was concluded, in which he was acknowledged as the friend and ally of Rome; but having no one to save him from his friends, he was basely murdered in his sleep by some Lusitanian assassins that the Roman

Assassination of Viriathus.

general had hired. The instigators of this barbarous act refused to pay when the sanguinary work was done; and the murderers, in making a demand on account of their crime, may be said to have, figuratively, cut their own throats, for they were threatened with punishment for the iniquity they confessed themselves guilty of. After the death of Viriathus, the Lusitanians having lost their head, were without the brains necessary to defend themselves, and fell an easy prey into the hands of Q. Pompeius. This individual was the son of a musician ; but instead of following his father's profession, he had become the leader of a warlike band, and he found the soldiers willing instruments to play into his hands, or act in concert with him, for the gratification of his personal ambition. He attacked Numantia, though with so little success, that he was compelled to conclude a peace ; but treacherously declaring that the conclusion of a peace meant the beginning of a war, he renewed hostilities at the first convenient opportunity. Subsequently, C. Hostilius Mancinus commenced an attack, but 10,000 of his men having been killed, and 20,000 more being blocked up in a ravine, he could not exactly see his way out of it without a surrender. The Numantines refused to treat with him, until young Tib. Sempronius Gracchus, whom they trusted, came forward to pledge his honour that Numantia should be fairly treated. The Senate, however, repudiated the arrange- ment, and the honour of young Tib. remains among the enormous stock of unredeemed pledges which history has handed down to us.

The Romans began to feel that none but the best man was likely to win, and they accordingly looked out for the best man, whom they found in Scipio Africanus, the destroyer of Carthage. He was sent against Numantia, which he surrounded by fortifications, in order that he might starve out the inhabitants by keeping them in, and he did his utmost to restore the discipline of the Roman army. He hardened the soldiers by making them carry loads of wood, a novel plan of providing them with a billet; he forced them to sleep on the ground, which they complained of as hard ; and he allowed them no other cooking utensils than a saucepan, which caused the indignation of many to boil over.

Numantia stood upon a lofty rock, and its inhabitants displayed a courage worthy of its high position. The river Durius (now the Douro) washed its feet; there were forests on either hand ; while the mounds and ditches abounding in the vale before it, rendered any attempt to approach it in the front almost unavailable. Scipio Africanus soon perceived the hopelessness of succeeding by a direct attack, and he pro- ceeded, therefore, to raise round the place a double stockade, to prevent any aid in the form of a stock of provisions being carried into it. He impeded the navigation of the river by throwing across it large beams, perforated with swords, which, revolving with the tide, cut off all com- munication by means of water.

Notwithstanding all the precautions that had been taken, a party of about half-a-dozen young men, having slipped through the lines—and very hard lines they were—succeeded in reaching the town of Lutia. The head of the party, holding an olive-branch, begged for assistance with such effect, that the Lutians offered to lend him a hand in his terrible emergency. Scipio, who had been in pursuit, no sooner heard of the Lutians having offered to lend a hand, than he savagely declared that they should have no hands to spare, and he barbarously ordered the cutting off of the hands of four hundred citizens.

The Numantines being completely hemmed in, were unable to obtain provisions ; but though reduced at last to eat cats, they became only the more dogged in their resistance to the enemy. Eventually, they begged for a truce of three days, which they employed in destroying their wives and children—a species of heroism not easily understood; for to kill those who are dear, by way of protecting them, is a mode of insurance of which we must dispute the policy. The men were so sadly dispirited, and so fearfully cut up by their own or each other's swords, that the conquerors had only a remnant to take, in the shape of population, when they entered the city.

In conformity with the custom of the period, Scipio Africanus Minor, whose atrocities, in connexion with the siege of Numantia, have branded his name for ever with disgrace, proceeded to make arrangements for a triumph. Instead of feeling a decent shame, he manifested a most unbecoming pride in what he had done ; and to identify himself more completely with the horrors of the siege, he took the name of Numantinus. So thoroughly had starvation done its work, that of the few citizens who were found alive, only fifty were in sufficiently good condition to appear in the show got up in celebration of his dishonourable victory.

While Rome was thus extending her arms, she may be said to have been painfully on the stretch ; and Scipio, during his consulship, seeing the republic was likely to outgrow its strength, caused prayers to be said for its safety. Rome was certainly in danger, though from a different cause than that which had been apprehended; for the free population had been greatly reduced by war, and the captives, or slaves to circumstances, had been vastly multiplied. The office of the latter was to tend flocks ; and they were so thoroughly regarded as a portion of the stock, that they were treated like brutes by their masters.

The system of slavery which existed at Rome, had so much influence upon her fate, and is calculated to afford such an insight into her morals, that the fetters she placed upon others may be regarded as so many links in her history. We will, therefore, break for a moment the chain of narrative, and proceed to a brief consideration of the Roman system of slavery and chains, to which we cannot hope that the attention of the reader can remain long riveted.

According to the strict letter of the Roman law, a master could treat, or maltreat, his slave in any way he pleased, either by death, sale, or punishment. Though the slave could hold no property, he had the power of taking anything he could get, but simply as a medium for conveying it to his master. So thoroughly were the slaves looked upon as articles of traffic, that they were liable to be pledged or put into pawn— a position in which they were the subjects of a melancholy sort of interest.

The demand for slave labour in Rome was caused by the annual consumption of the free population in war, at whose bidding many who should have remained to cultivate the land, were sent forth to plough the ocean. The result was a redundancy of slave population, accustomed to agricultural labour of every kind, and which, having been already brought under the yoke, had become sufficiently brutalised to do the work of oxen. The chief supply of slaves was drawn from the prisoners taken in war, and an army was generally attended by dealers, who, in case of a glut, could frequently buy a lot cheap ; and at the camp of Lucullus they were being picked up for about three shillings and three-pence of our money—or four drachmas. In Rome it was usual to sell slaves by auction, and, as if the poor wretches were not already low enough, they were knocked down by the hammer. The dealers were in the habit of practising the same sort of tricks to conceal the defects of a slave, as are, in these days, employed to hide the faults of a horse, and it was customary therefore, in purchasing, to require a warranty. The character was often suspended on a scroll round the neck, and their chief recommendation consisted in a guarantee that they would neither commit suicide, nor steal—having no tendency to make away with either themselves or their master's property. There was a con-siderable variation in the value of slaves, and fancy prices have been known to be given for some curious specimens of captive humanity. A fool has been known to fetch 20,000 sesterces—about one hundred and seventy pounds—a sum that would seem to show that folly was scarce ; but when we remember how wise a man is required to make a fool, we may take it for granted that the wisdom comprised in the subject of the bargain was the rare and costly part of it. Literary men were often exposed for sale like cattle when they happened to be slaves, and the useful hack, or occasionally the literary lion, might be seen chained to a pen in the public market-place. Slaves had no distinctive dress ; and when it was once proposed to give them one, the measure was rejected, on the ground that it might show them their numerical strength, and that if they once saw their power by obtaining their livery, they might attempt to take up their freedom. It was deemed better to keep them in the dark, by clothing them in sombre colours, and their numbers not being manifested to them by any peculiar dress, it was not likely they would unite in order to redress their grievances.

There is, however, something elastic in human nature, which causes it to rise after being trodden on. Such was the case with the slaves, who began to swell with indignation, which was rendered particularly tumid by the inflated and inflating eloquence of one Eunus, a Syrian, who was a member of their own body. This individual possessed the art of oratory in a high degree, and there is nothing more stimulating to the breeze of discontent than the breath of an enthusiastic demagogue. He persuaded the slaves to revolt, and while preaching to them the doctrine of equality, he claimed to be not only their leader, but their prince and ruler—a species of practice which is not uncommon with the propounders of the most levelling theories. Pretending to possess the gift of prophecy, he predicted that he would be a king one day; and the rich, putting a mimic crown on his head for a few hours, jeeringly told him that he had been a king one day—or at least half a day, and that his prediction had been therefore verified. The slaves, however, put faith in him, and shouldering their spades, axes, poles, and hatchets, made themselves, as well as their implements, the tools of Eunus. No less than 70,000 slaves acknowledged as their head the man who taught them that they ought to have no head at all, and he urged them to a merciless massacre of their vanquished foes, while inculcating the doctrines of humanity. Rage without restraint, and revenge without reason, were, however, of no permanent avail, and the slaves under Eunus were soon routed by the disciplined forces of the Consul, Rupilius. He besieged Tauromenium; and the slaves, by being completely shut in, were altogether shut out from the chance of obtaining provisions. Their condition from day to day was so desperate and monotonous, that, with nothing to eat, they furnish but sorry food to the historian. Having swallowed their last morsel, the inhabitants could not satisfy their hunger by bolting the gates, and Rupilius was admitted within the city. Eunus escaped into a cutting in the rocks; but when he relied on the friendly shelter of the cave, he found it a hollow mockery. His retreat was discovered, and he was taken into custody with his cook, his confectioner, his butler, and his buffoon, who, with the exception of the last, must have held sinecures in their master's limited establishment. The buffoon must have been worked the hardest of the party, for the pursuit of mirth under difficulties is one of the most melancholy tasks that can be imposed on the professed humorist. Eunus himself was transferred from his subterranean cellar to an underground cell, where it is said he was devoured by rats; but happily this horrid tale receives no authentic ratification at the hands of history.

The Servile War had not yet ceased, when Attalus, the King of Pergamus, died, and left no sign; for there was no succeeding king's head for the crown of Pergamus to rest upon. It was fortunate, perhaps, that Attalus left no heir; for had there been any inheritor of his qualities as well as his title, the perpetuation of a nuisance would have been the deplorable consequence. The man was so thoroughly wicked that it is charity to pronounce him mad, and we accordingly set him down as a lunatic, though we feel scarcely justified in acquitting him of his many crimes on the single ground of insanity He is said to have been so much addicted to the practice of poisoning his relations, that he found it cheaper to grow his own plants; and he cultivated the hemlock, or the night-shade, as others grew their own faba or cicer, their beans and chickweed. Death lurked at the root of everything his garden contained, and it is probable that he sent many a present of putative mushrooms to his unsuspecting kindred. So odious had he become, that it is said he would have been murdered, if he had not died a little too soon for the arrangements of the assassins to be completed.

Having been in the habit of expressing his will very briefly in his
lifetime, it is not surprising that he should have left at his death a

Arrest of Eunus.

will, so short, that it· purported to say in four letters all he desired
His last testament was comprised in the characters P. R. H. E.;
and all his property was supposed to be represented in this small
collection of capitals. The Romans affecting to be initiated in the
meaning of these initials, declared them to signify, *Populus Romanus
hæres est*, Let the Roman people be the heirs of my property. Regarding these letters as letters of administration, the Romans possessed
themselves of all the effects of Attalus ; but the will was disputed by
the next of kin, one Aristonicus, a natural brother, whose claim to
succeed, as a member of the testator's line, was stifled by a rope, with
which the unfortunate claimant was cruelly strangled.

Pergamus became a Roman province under the name of Asia Proper—a species of appropriation which there was nothing to justify.

Rome was now in the position of a man who had outgrown his strength, or rather of an adult still wearing the clothes of its infancy. Its measures had been adapted to a social body which had since spread itself in all directions, while the constitution, with which it was clothed, had not been extended to the new growth; and the extreme points of the Republic were therefore reduced to all sorts of extremities. The people at large had become so miserably poor, that they were easily bribed to become the tools of their own further abasement; and they were not only ready to sell themselves for a mere nothing, but to lend themselves to almost anything.

The tribuneship, which had been originally a purely popular institution, had changed, or rather lost, its character. Instead of being stationed outside the entrance of the Senate House, to prevent the door from being opened to abuse, the Tribunes were, by a law of C. Atinius, constituted *ex-officio* members of that aristocratic body. The design of the tribuneship was to insure to the people a certain number of friends invested with high authority; but the people were eventually anxious to be saved from their friends—a result that is by no means rare in ancient or modern history. As the bitterest vinegar can be made from the most generous wine, the sharpest of despots is often created out of the blandest of demagogues.

So great had the power of the Tribunes become, and so much had it been abused, that even the Senate grew jealous of it; and a law was enacted to bring the tribuneship under the operation of signs and omens. These were interpreted by the Augurs, who of course had the power of reading in the lightning, and hearing in the reports of the thunder, whatever it suited their purpose to circulate.

Aristocracy had lost its exclusive privileges; but these had only become more objectionable by being spread over a larger surface; for they were now extended to a certain portion of the plebeians, who went by the name of *novi homines*, or upstarts. These were distinguished from the Nobiles, or, to speak shortly, the nobs, who enjoyed the right of having the images of their ancestors in wax; but this *jus imaginum*, as it was termed, conferred only an imaginary dignity. There was no legal privilege attached to the sort of nobility above described; but those persons who were qualified by the possession of the waxen forms of their fathers, were looked upon as men making in society a highly respectable figure.

Notwithstanding the liberty which is declared by republicans to be inseparable from the Republican form of Government, laws were passed to restrain the liberty of private action in the days of the Roman Commonwealth. By the Orchian law, made in the year of the city 572 (B.C. 181), the number of guests that might sit down to dinner was limited; and as a further illustration of republican freedom, it may be mentioned that the entertainer was obliged to keep open his doors.

so that all who were freely-and-easily inclined might enter his house to see that the law was complied with. Twenty years later, it was decreed by the law of Fannius, that no entertainment should cost more than one hundred asses, or six shillings and five-pence farthing, on high days and holidays ; on ten other days in the month, the meal was not to exceed thirty asses, or one and eleven-pence farthing ; but on ordinary occasions seven-pence farthing was the figure to which even the richest man was to limit the cost of his dinner. The law not only interfered with the bill of expenses, but with the bill of fare ; and, under the Consulship of M. Scaurus, the dormouse was excluded from the dinner-table as an enervating luxury. Vegetables were allowed to any extent, and bread might be eaten at—or even beyond—discretion.

To such a ridiculous extent did the Romans carry their interference with the private expenditure of each other, that when Crassus and Cn. Demetrius were Censors, they endeavoured in the most absurd manner to damage each other's popularity. Demetrius publicly charged Crassus with having been guilty of extravagance for going into mourning on the death of a favourite fish ; and Crassus retorted by declaring that Demetrius had lost three wives without exhibiting signs of mourning for any one of them.*

* Macrobius, Saturnal., lib. ii., c. 1.

CHAPTER THE TWENTY-THIRD

**THE GRACCHI AND THEIR MOTHER. RISE AND FALL OF TIBERIUS
AND CAIUS GRACCHUS.**

A PEOPLE trained to live chiefly on spoils taken from others must be
continually spoiling itself for any peaceful occupation; and those whose
chief support is the sword, must be always destroying the food they live
upon. When foreign means are exhausted, it becomes necessary to
look at home, and those who have existed by robbing strangers, are no
sooner deprived of their external sources of support, than they begin to
rob each other. Such was the order—or rather the disorder—of things
in Rome, where wealth had got into the hands of the few, and the social
fabric, like a building too heavy at the top, was in immediate danger of
a downfall. There were large classes of persons who were assured that
they were perfectly free; but, though enjoying the freedom of air itself,
they found in it no element of comfort, when they had nothing more
substantial than the air to live upon. Deprived of every inch of land, there
was but a flatulent sort of satisfaction in the enjoyment of the atmosphere, nor could the most long-winded of orators impress the people with
the idea that life could be maintained by simply imbibing the breath of
liberty. They were informed that they were the lords of the earth; *
but this mockery of respect was simply insulting the emptiness of their
mouths by a scarcely less empty title. The plebeians were like a
number of ciphers without a preliminary figure, and, though possessing
all the materials of strength in their vast body, were powerless until a
head could be found for them. This at length appeared in the person
of Tib. Sempronius Gracchus, the grandson of the elder Scipio, and as
two heads are said to be better than one, Tib. united his brother Caius
with him in the office of leader to the great plebeian movement.

The elder Gracchus had been tutored by his mother Cornelia—one
of the earliest members of the ancient and honourable order of blue-
stockings. She had superintended the education of her children, and
had personally tutored them in eloquence; an art of which the female
tongue is peculiarly capable. Her own house was the resort of some of
the first philosophers of the day, who, like many modern philosophers,
were thoroughly impressed with the idea that the way to penetrate the
youthful mind, is to continue for ever boring it. In this manner the
understandings of the young Gracchi had been thoroughly drilled, and
the treasures of science had been admitted at so many apertures, that
the only fear was lest the treasures, through some of the numerous

* Plut., Tib. Gracch.

The Mother of the Gracchi.

openings by which they had got into the mind, might find their way out again.

Tib. had already won some reputation in Spain, and was returning home, when he saw the Etrurian estates of the wealthy being cultivated by foreign slaves in chains, whose bonds not only bore the seal of degradation for themselves, but were the means of fettering native industry. These slaves were housed and huddled together in places called Ergastula, which were literally workhouses, but practically, prisons. They are said to have been built under-ground in the shape of vaults; but, in giving this account of their construction, there has perhaps been some misconstruction on the part of Columella, who is the chief authority for the statement.

We must now return to Tib. Gracchus, who had, by this time, returned to Rome, and had formed the noble resolution of remedying abuses, though he knew that loud abuse of himself would be the inevitable consequence. He had seen that the aristocracy had got possession of nearly all the land, allowing the plebeians to have no share in it, except the ploughshare, and even this was often denied them by the employment of slaves instead of the free agricultural labourer. Tib. was learned in the law, and recollected the existence in the books of the old statute of Licinius, which had fallen into disuse, and the renewal of which he thought might put new life into the plebeian body. By this law, no one was allowed to occupy more than 500 jugera—about 330 English acres—of the land of the state; but the state of the land exhibited a very different distribution of the public property.

The poorer occupants of the soil had been compelled by their necessities to sell to the richer, and Tiberius made the popular but scarcely honest proposal, that those who had bought should give back to those who had sold—a suggestion which was hailed by the masses as the happy inspiration of a patriot. The idea was simple enough, and if simplicity is an element of grandeur, the notion was so far a great one; though, as it is based on the principle, that when a man has sold everything he possesses, the purchaser or the possessor should hand the property back to the original vendor, the project is not well adapted to business purposes. The suggestion was, however, one which enabled a patriot to go to the country with a " cry," and though the end proposed was laudable enough, the means, which involved an interference with the means of the wealthy, could not command the general approval. It is true that much of the property had been unfairly obtained, and that much more was held in illegal quantities; but some had been the subject of regular sale, and the general confiscation proposed was but a Procrustean measure of justice.

The plan was of course opposed, and the term of " selfish aristocrat " was liberally, or illiberally—for they are unfortunately too much alike, sometimes, in their political sense—bestowed on every one who did his utmost to protect what the law had allowed him to regard for years as his own property. Common sense, however, began so far to prevail over

clamour, that the proposal of Tib. Gracchus was modified to some
extent, and the distribution of the surplus land was confided to a
permanent commission of three men, who were called the Triumviri.   In
order to give something like consistency to the measure, it provided,
that the land which had been taken away from its old possessors should
not be sold by the new; and thus a sort of uniformity was observed
by robbing the former, and restricting the latter; so that the principle
of not being able to do what one likes with one's own, was affirmed in
each instance.   The injustice of the whole proceeding was so palpable,
notwithstanding the "popularity" of the scheme, that a compensation
clause was introduced to indemnify those who had built houses at their
own expense upon the ground; but nothing was awarded to those who
had only built upon it their hopes of being allowed to continue in quiet
possession of the property.

Party feeling ran, of course, exceedingly high, or, in other words, its
proceedings were extremely low on both sides. Tib. Gracchus was
lauded by the people as the essence of everything noble, and denounced
by the patricians as the incarnation of everything contemptible.   On
one side he was hailed as a patriot, and on the other side he was hooted
as a fraudulent demagogue ; so that if everything that went in at one ear
went out at the other, his head must have been a thoroughfare for every
kind of vehicle of abuse and flattery.   The Senate took the meanest
means of revenge, and reduced his official salary to one denarius and a
half, or about a shilling a day in English money. Tiberius, thus
curtailed of the means on which he lived, declared there was a conspiracy against his life, and rather prematurely went into mourning for
himself, to excite the public sympathy   Putting his children into
black, he took them with him from house to house, requesting that they
might be taken in as orphans ; but the public refused to be taken in by
a trick so obvious.   False accusations were, however, brought against
him ; and a next-door neighbour stood up in the Senate, declaring that
he had that morning observed a diadem and a scarlet robe delivered at
the back door, which proved that Tiberius intended to usurp the regal
authority.   In order to obtain the weight of an official position for his
reforms, Tiberius got himself elected tribune of the people, and the apparently inevitable effects of taking office were at once shown in his introduction of a modified edtion of the measure he had previously clamoured for.

The aristocratic party set every engine and every old pump at work
to throw cold water on his project, and they at length persuaded one of
his colleagues, named Octavius, who was played upon as easily as an
octave flute, to take part against him.   The mode of opposition resorted
to by Gracchus was rather more effective than constitutional, for he
called upon the people to dismiss his colleague—an arrangement almost
as equitable as it would be for one judge to insist upon the dismissal of
another, who might refuse to announce himself submissively as "of the
same opinion" with his learned brother. When, however, the people
are once fairly off, in a certain or uncertain course, they seldom think

how unfairly their precipitancy may operate. They had set their hearts on a particular measure, and they refused to be guided by their heads; but without deliberation, drove away every obstacle that impeded the accomplishment of their wishes. As Octavius still held his position, Gracchus gave notice that he had a resolution to propose; and, on the following day, he moved the removal of his colleague. Octavius, however, met the proposed resolution by a remarkable display of resolution on his own part, and he declared that he should stick to his office, notwithstanding the other's unfriendly offices. These means having failed, Tiberius made a personal appeal to his colleague, and pointed out to him the gracefulness of a voluntary resignation; but Octavius, who rated himself very highly, objected altogether to the voluntary principle. Tiberius next attempted to starve his colleague out by sealing up the treasury; but the sealing made no impression on Octavius, who retained his official seat until it was drawn from under him by the mob, and he fell to the ground, between the two stools of himself and his unscrupulous colleague. A client or creature of the Gracchi was elected in the place of the deposed Tribune, who had been got rid of by upsetting one of the most important forms of the constitution—that form being no other than the bench occupied by one of the highest officers of the government. Octavius was hurried out among the mob, who thrust him about in every direction; but, when it came to the push, Tiberius Gracchus endeavoured to pull him through his difficulties. The effort was almost vain; and Octavius owed his life to a faithful slave, who lost an eye in seeing his master through the dangers that surrounded him. After this manifestation of the popular opinion, no Tribune ventured to have an opinion of his own—or, if he had, he kept it to himself, with a prudent regard to his personal safety.

The new bill for distributing the soil became at once the law of the land, and the two Gracchi—Tib. and Caius—with Appius Claudius, the father-in-law of the former, became a permanent triumvirate. This desire of the temporary holders of power to change their tenancy at will to a life estate, has been in all ages conspicuous. The stability of authority is so desirable, that a fixed executive seems to be everywhere a natural want; but the mushroom might as well seek to substitute itself for the oak, whose roots have struck deep into the soil, as the mere chief of a revolution might hope, without any hold on the affections of a nation, to become the founder of a dynasty.

Tib. Gracchus, in the true spirit of a patriot by profession, proposed limiting every power but his own, which he sought to render as extensive as possible. When his term of office had legally expired, he declared that the safety of the republic required his re-election, and he accordingly forced himself on the attention of the electors as the only desirable candidate. On the day previous to the election, he spent all the afternoon in the mourning he had already bought, and leading his children by the hand, he exhibited himself and them as the " un-happy family," in the public thoroughfares. The election had already commenced, on the

following day, when the Conservative party objected to it on the ground
of illegality.   The proceedings were already opened, when Tib. Gracchus
set out on a canvass, expecting that his canvass would enable him to
reach the desired point with a wet sail and flying colours.   Not content

Tib. Gracchus canvassing.

with going alone to solicit the electors, he took one of his own boys in
his hand, and he got all the mothers on his side, by introducing what
may be termed child's play into his electioneering movements.   In the
afternoon, the candidate doubted whether he would go personally to the
poll, when his friends—some of them from whom he would have been
glad to have been saved—assured him that he had better go, for there
was no danger.   Taking their advice, he had got as far as the area in

front of the Capitol, when he was seized with the irresolution of an area-sneak, and hanging about the spot, he refused to go further. A debate was in progress among the senators, when one of them, P. Scipio Nasica, called upon the house to come to the door, and save the republic by sacrificing Tiberius. The whole assembly rushed upon its legs and its crutches; some of the members seized hold of sticks, others snatched up their clubs, and declared that the vengeance of the clubs should fall on Tiberius. In this spirit they sallied forth, and looking for Gracchus, they soon knocked dissension on the head, by one of those blows which

Melancholy End of Tib. Gracchus.

disposed of any pretensions he might have had to a crown when they first encountered him. His brother, Caius Gracchus, fell politically with his relative; but without resigning his office, he abandoned his post, and he withdrew to a little place he had in the country, though neglecting to give up his place in the triumvirate.

Scipio Æmilianus was on his return from Spain to Rome when he heard of the death of his brother-in-law; and, quoting a line from Homer, to the effect that

" All thus perish who such deeds perform,"

..e declared that his relative Tib. had met with such a fate as his antecedents warranted. Scipio at once assumed the leadership of the Conservatives, or rather of the destructives; for their Conservatism consisted merely in a desire to keep all they had unfairly got, while their policy tended to break all the bonds of mutual interest and goodwill, which can alone permanently bind society.

The plebeian party became quite as unreasonable on one side of the question, as the patricians had been on the other; and C. Papirius Carbo, a demagogue, who had got the place of tribune, proposed that the people should have the right of re-electing the same person to the tribuneship over and over again,—a suggestion designed to render his own position permanent. Scipio Æmilianus opposed the measure to the utmost; and after going home one night, he had no sooner finished his supper, than he began to cram himself for a speech, with which he contemplated coming out on the day following. He was, however,

Scipio Æmilianus cramming himself for a Speech after a hearty Supper.

found dead in his bed ; and, though probability points to apoplexy as the cause, the historians have—without much, indeed, of evidence— returned a verdict of Wilful Murder against C. P. Carbo. We have no hesitation in acquitting him of this dreadful crime ; but we cannot say that we shall be able to allow him to quit these pages without a stain on his character. It is to be regretted that the Senate had not the courage to institute an inquiry at the time when the occurrence took place, and when only the real facts could have been ascertained ; for such a course would have saved considerable trouble to those chroniclers who are always ready to frame an entirely new set of circumstances of their own, to replace those which contemporaneous investigation has omitted to supply us with.

Caius Sempronius Gracchus was getting daily more tired of his thoroughly retired life ; and, being an excellent spokesman, he began to flatter himself that the commonweal might profit by his services. He is said to have been urged on by his brother's ghost; but there is reason to believe that he was impelled by a more commendable spirit. This fraternal shade is stated to have appeared to him in his dreams ; but the matters he now began to take in hand were not those which he could afford to go to sleep over.

In republics, where he who is the humble servant of the people to-day, may be, to-morrow, the people's master, talent is looked upon with jealousy by the governing power, which, while ostensibly employing an able instrument, may be, in fact, promoting a dangerous rival. Thus, when the head of a nation is removable, it is reluctant to employ the best men, lest they prove better than the head itself, and aspire to the very highest position.

Where the form of government is monarchical, it is to the interest of the ruler to avail himself of the ablest assistance he can obtain ; for, being himself irremovable, he becomes the fixed centre towards which the glories and successes of his ministers and servants continually gravitate.

It was on the principle of getting rid of a dangerous rival, that the republican government had sent away Caius Gracchus from Rome,— where he might have been everything—to Sardinia, where he would almost inevitably sink to nothing. He was himself apprehensive of this result, and he consequently returned to Rome, leaving Sardinia without the leave of any one. His duty should have kept him abroad, but ambition urged him home ; and, in a republic, there is little to insure the fidelity of one who, though the servant of the Government to-day, may be its master to-morrow. Leaving the interests of his country in Sardinia to take care of themselves, this professed patriot came to look after his own interests in Rome, and took his talents into the political market. He immediately stood for the tribune-ship ; and though he had abandoned one post—that of Quæstor in Sardinia—he was elected to the more important post, which might, indeed, be termed the chief pillar of popular liberty.

R

Though he had, of course, solicited and obtained his high office on purely public grounds, he at once endeavoured to use it for the gratification of personal animosities. His first two measures were proposed with a view to avenging his brother's death; and he sought to give the intended new laws a retrospective effèct, for the purpose of gratifying his private enmity. He introduced a law to prevent a person deprived by the people of any office, from being appointed to the public service again; but this exalted patriot withdrew the bill to please his mother. He carried various measures of more or less value, and among them was a law for the establishment of granaries for supplying the poor with corn at a very low price; but though this might have been very attractive to buyers, and insured a brisk demand, it does not seem calculated to encourage growers and sellers to such an extent that a supply could always be relied upon. Of course, the deficiency had to be made good from the pockets of the public; and therefore the process amounted to little more than receiving with one hand what had been paid by the other.

The privilege of purchasing cheap corn was not limited, as some * have supposed, to the poor; but every citizen could claim his share; and even Piso, a Consul—though perhaps he was one of the greatly reduced Consuls—had been shabby enough to demand the privilege. Piso had been an opponent of the law; and Gracchus, seeing him among the crowd receiving a bushel of the cheap grain, taunted him with his inconsistency in taking advantage of a corn measure which he had set his face against. The answer of Piso was sensible and just; for, said he, "though I had a strong objection to your giving away my property, I think I have a right to try to get my share of it." Another of his enactments vested the right of putting a Roman citizen to death, in the people themselves, a measure that was no doubt theoretically attractive, though practically inconvenient. To vest in the public at large the privilege of applying the sentences to the highest offences, would really be giving a nation so much rope, that business would be suspended very often, instead of the criminals.

Caius Gracchus next applied himself to Law Reform with considerable zeal; but it was not so much the law itself, as those who administered it, that required amendment. Those who held the scales of justice, used to weigh only the gold of the suitors; and the judges were so far impartial, that they had no bias towards any particular side, but favoured that which was the most liberal in bribing them. Many of the defendants had been guilty of extortion, which was a common practice with the judges themselves; and therefore a rude sort of honour, commonly known as honour among thieves, was not altogether banished from the judgment-seat. Caius Gracchus, however, caused a law to be passed, in which we trace the origin of that glorious institution, familiarly known as " twelve men in a box," so dear to the

---

* Plutarch implies that it was so ; but Cicero relates anecdotes showing the fact to have been otherwise.

hearts, and sometimes, also, to the pockets of Englishmen. The law alluded to, provided for the trial of causes by a middle class of equites or knights, who were, literally speaking, men who could keep a horse, and who, on the same principle adopted in modern times as to the keepers of gigs,* were considered to be respectable.

The Senators had made a practice of acquitting all criminals of their own class, and, by acquitting themselves thus shamefully, they had become guilty of the grossest corruption ; but the equites were frequently regardless of equity, and were found leaning with undue leniency towards offenders of their own order. Gracchus had now become the popular idol, but he never had an idle hour, and was always busy in building up a reputation for himself by the construction of works of permanent utility. He knew that general occupation is necessary to public content, and he felt that as long as he could keep the hands of the multitude employed on bricks and mortar, he was, in reality, cementing his own power. This policy placed considerable patronage at his command, and he rallied round him a crowd of contractors and artificers, who, but for his power of giving them something better to do, would, perhaps, have been contracting the bad habit of political agitation, or resorting to every kind of revolutionary artifice.

The greatest political work of Caius was that in which he did the least ; and his legislative successes sink into insignificance by the side of the real grandeur of his extensive failure. This was his attempt to extend the franchise to all the Italians, and the other allies ; but Rome refused to aid him in the grand design, and determined to rivet upon Italy those Italian irons with which Rome at a future period was destined to burn her fingers. So popular was Caius Gracchus, that, upon his re-election to office, the people, who could not get near enough to the Campus Martius on account of the crowd, voted for him from the tops of houses or unfinished buildings ; and many came up to the poll by climbing an adjacent scaffold.

He who would keep himself constantly sailing before the wind raised by the breath of public applause, must be for ever on some new tack ; for no airs are more variable than those which the people are apt to give themselves. Caius Gracchus was soon destined to discover the fact that, amid the storms of political life, the highest point can be safely occupied by none but the political weathercock. He had too much rigid inflexibility to turn with every breeze ; and instead of being moved by each passing gust, he was simply dis-gusted by the vacillation exhibited.

The aristocratic party, perceiving this, resolved to beat him with his own weapons ; and they prevailed upon M. Livius Drusus, his colleague in the tribuneship, to outbid him by all sorts of extravagances for the prize

---

* The following question and answer, uttered in a Court of Law on a modern trial, are well known :—

Counsel. " What do you mean by respectable ? "
Witness. " He keeps a gig."

of popularity.   When Gracchus proposed to distribute land among the poor at a small fixed rental, Drusus moved, by way of amendment, that they should have it for nothing at all; and as to the corn in the public granaries, if Gracchus said the people ought to have it at half price, Drusus would insist upon their right to be paid for the trouble of walking away with it.   The people, as a matter of course, followed the man who was most profuse in his promises, rather than him who had been the most liberal in his performances.   Caius Gracchus was, in the mean time, induced to go to Africa to mark out the ground for a new city

Rash Act of Caius Gracchus.

The reporters of the period—who were, no doubt, in the pay of his opponents—circulated all kinds of ill-natured stories, in which it was alleged that the omens had been unfavourable; that the flags had been blown down, or the pavement blown up; and that the wolves had eaten up every flag-staff—a thing not very easy to swallow. On his return to Rome, from which he had been absent only seventy days, he found Drusus amazingly popular, and every nose turned up at himself, which induced him to recognise a general snub in the faces of many of his old followers. He offered himself a third time for the tribuneship, but he was at the bottom of the poll, and an election row commenced, when an officious lictor lost, first, his fasces ; secondly, his securis—which he had done his utmost to secure ; and ultimately his life, in the scuffle. Caius Gracchus, who had mainly endeavoured to keep the peace, knew he would be accused of breaking it, and he accordingly ran as fast as he could ; but in scaling a wall to get into another street, he unfortunately sprained his ankle. His friends continued to carry him until, moved by a sudden instinct of self-preservation, they dropped an acquaintance it would have been no longer safe to keep up, and poor Caius was left alone with a single manservant. His pursuers being at his heels, the ex-tribune desired the faithful attendant to stab him, and the man was too much in the habit of obeying his master's orders to hesitate. Having respectfully run his employer through, he found himself so terribly out of place in the world, that, apologising for the liberty, he finished himself off with the same dagger.

A reward of its weight in gold had already been offered for the head of Caius Gracchus, when one Septimuleius, having picked it up, carried it home, and plumbed it with lead before he took it to the authorities. Opimius, the Consul, weighed it, and exclaiming, " Bless me ! seven pounds and a half ! " threw down in exchange for the head, the same quantity of the precious metal. His customer having gone away, Opimius proceeded at his leisure to examine his bargain. " Well ! " said he, " I don't know that it 's worth its weight in gold, but the offer was my own, and I must make the best of it." On a minuter inspection, he detected the trick that had been played, and though he had looked upon Caius as somewhat leaden-headed, he at once perceived that nature had not been the only plumber employed in this disgraceful transaction.

All the friends of Gracchus were cast into prison and slain ; but it was astonishing to observe how contracted his circle became when it was known that ruin awaited every member of it. They who had been his intimates made the sudden discovery that they had never known him at all, and others, who had been too frequently in his company to repudiate the acquaintance, declared that they had been grievously mistaken in his character. Several of his radical associates joined the aristocratic party, and his friend Carbo was so severely bantered on his having gone over to the other side, that after trying both sides, he took refuge in suicide as the only side left for him.

Rome owed much to the Gracchi ; but it paid them both off in a most unsatisfactory manner. Tiberius was an orator of such power, that, to prevent his voice from being too loud, he took with him a piper—paying the piper out of his own pocket—to prevent him from pitching it too strong when he was addressing the multitude.   Tiberius Gracchus was the first orator who introduced the graces of action into the art of public speaking ; and he was in the habit of rolling, as it were, from side to side, which gave him great sway with his audience.

Caius Gracchus was a man of action, rather than of words, and was the first to divide distance into portions of one thousand paces, each of which he called a mile, and which was one of his really useful measures. He was also the inventor of milestones, and of those stations for awkward equestrians, which enabled many to ride the high horse, who would otherwise have been placed on their own humble footing.

The two Gracchi owed, no doubt, to the teaching of their mother, much of their success—if, at least, that can be called success which ended in the violent death of both of them.   Cornelia was, however, a little too much addicted to making prodigies of her sons ; and it is said of her, that, on one occasion, when receiving a visit from a Campanian lady, who came to display her jewels, the mother of the Gracchi, having privately sent for the children, exclaimed, as they stole gently in with their nurse, " These are my jewels : what do you think of them ? "   So maudlin was her maternal sensibility, that she never spoke of her sons without tears, which were always responded to by the infants them- selves, with sympathetic, but uncomfortable, moisture.   Nothing, how- ever, can damp parental love; and, to a fond mother's feelings, childhood has no unpleasant features ; though it is different to him who, if approaching them at all, prefers looking at them in a drier aspect.

CHAPTER THE TWENTY-FOURTH.

THE JUGURTHINE WAR. WAR AGAINST THE CIMBRI AND TEUTONI.

WHILE Rome had been making the numerous conquests already described, self-conquest—the most important conquest of all—had been altogether lost sight of, and she had failed in obtaining the victory over her own vices. Though she possessed, nominally, a constituted body of rulers, money was actually the governing power; and so debasing is its influence, that it is more fatal to the liberty of a people to be ruled with a rod of gold, than with a rod of iron. No consideration but pecuniary consideration had any weight, corruption presided in the courts of law, the people were bought by the Senate, and the Senate sold the people. In the army there was a system of shameless plunder on the part of the commanders, and the soldiers followed their leaders with avidity.

Numidia had, since the death of Masinissa, been ruled over by his son Micipsa, who, by his will, put his kingdom, as it were, into commission, by giving it to his two sons, Hiempsal and Adherbal, conjointly with a lad whom he had adopted, and whose name was Jugurtha. Jugurtha was a person of excellent manners and genteel address, an excellent horseman, the first to strike the lion* in the field, and himself a lion much run after in society.

On the death of Micipsa, when the three rulers came to the throne of Numidia, they found the accommodation rather insufficient, and Jugurtha insolently threw himself down in the middle of it. By this act the two sons of Micipsa were practically set aside, and Jugurtha assumed that in himself alone the monarchy was centered. His next act was to propose the abolition of the acts of the last five years of Micipsa's reign, declaring that they ought all to be dotted out, on the ground of the old man's dotage. Hiempsal, with a touch of sarcasm, assented to the proposal, observing—" We shall then get rid of you, as your adoption was an act performed within the prescribed period." This attempt to be funny was a serious matter to Hiempsal, for Jugurtha caused the would-be wag to be murdered in the palace.

After this instance of sharp practice, on the part of Jugurtha, Adherbal began to tremble in his shoes lest he might be made to walk in his brother's footsteps. This fear was so nearly on the point of being realised, that Adherbal took to flight, and ran all the way to Rome, to ask for aid; upon which a commission of inquiry, consisting of ten members, was despatched to Numidia.

To refer any matter to a commission, has always been considered

* Sallust, Jugurthine War, c. vi.

equivalent to laying it per nanently on the shelf; and such might have been the result of the quarrel of the Numidian princes, had it not been for the fact that Jugurtha had settled the dispute in his own way, before the commissioners had even opened their inquiry. By the time they had arrived on the spot to which they had been sent, they found one of the parties dead, and the other in possession of all that he desired. Jugurtha was, of course, the survivor in this affair; and when the ambassadors, on their arrival, expressed their astonishment at their services having been dispensed with, he, by offering them something for their trouble, sent them home fully and shame-fully satisfied.

Every spark of honour was not, however, extinct in Rome; for the tribune, C. Memmius, who had not received, or, indeed, had not been offered, any of Jugurtha's gold, became virtuously indignant at the disgraceful harvest made by the ten commissioners. His agitation was so far successful, that war was declared, and the Consul, L. Calpurnius Bestia, with his legate, M. Æmilius Scaurus, were sent to invade Africa. Bestia immediately made the best bargain he could for himself, by concluding a peace with Jugurtha, on certain terms, for which the Roman Consul's own terms were most exorbitant. He and his legate, Scaurus, accepted a nominal surrender of all Jugurtha's tents, horses, and elephants; but he was allowed to reserve nearly the whole of his canvas booths and his menagerie.

When the tribune Memmius heard of the venality of the ambassadors, and of the money they had corruptly made by their services abroad, he, whose duties kept him at home, became more indignant than ever. He denounced, in abusive language, the abuse of which they had been guilty, and succeeded at last in carrying a motion that Jugurtha should appear to answer for his offences of bribery and corruption before the Senate. The summons was carried to Africa, by the stern and incorruptible Cassius, who refused every offer of cash, and insisted on the personal appearance of Jugurtha at the time and place appointed. The artful Numidian came with a very small retinue and a very long purse; for he knew that in meeting such an antagonist as Rome, he should not have to draw the steel from the scabbard, but the gold from the treasury. He threw purses in all directions; and so extensive was his bribery, that the criminals who had accepted his money were a strong majority over the few who were qualified, by not having participated in the offence, to sit in judgment over it. Memmius, who had seen none of Jugurtha's gold, insisted on his giving up the names of those who had received it; but there was such a vehement and general shout of " No," that any further inquiry as to who were the culprits, would have been quite superfluous.

The only punishment the Senate ventured to inflict upon Jugurtha, was a sentence of banishment; and it was indeed quite natural that the dishonourable members should have been glad to send speedily out of the way the principal witness to their own turpitude. As Jugurtha quitted Rome, he expressed his disgust at her venality, in a sentiment

which came with but an ill grace from an accomplice in her infamy.
"Oh!" he exclaimed, with an air of affected horror, "Oh! thou
venal city; thou wouldst sell thyself to perdition, if thou couldst only
find a purchaser!" The exact point at which this claptrap was uttered,
who was at hand to hear it, and supposing the reporters to have been
present, whether they proceeded to take it down, are points which the
historians have not shown any disposition to look into.

After the retirement of the only witness, the inquiry into the
bribery cases was prosecuted with considerable vigour. Scaurus, who
had been one of the chief delinquents, attempted to expiate his own
faults by getting himself appointed a member of the committee, and
passing as severe sentences as he could upon his fellow criminals.

War with Jugurtha was again declared; for it was one of the
most prolific sources of a profitable job to those in power. The Consul,
Spurius Posthumius Albinus, was despatched with an army to Africa;
but he soon came home, like his predecessors, with a large fortune,
which seemed to be the kind of fortune of war that attended all who
went to fight against Numidia. He left the army under the guidance
of his brother Aulus, who, with his officers, were easily bribed into
accepting any terms, provided they were of a pecuniary nature, that
Jugurtha proposed to them. The Senate, however, refused to ratify
the dishonourable peace concluded by Aulus; and thus, by the somewhat dishonest process of repudiating the acts of an authorised agent,
Rome was again free to make a further property of the Numidian
sovereign. At last, however, the affair was placed in honourable hands,
by the appointment of Metellus (Q. C.) to the command of the army.
His probity placed him far above any bribe that Jugurtha could offer;
and though it is a maxim with many, that every man has his price, it
may be said of Metellus that his moral standard was too high for any
pecuniary standard to be applied to it.

With the generosity of true genius, Metellus selected as his legate
a man capable of sharing with himself any of the honours that might
be gained in the wars about to be undertaken. This man was Caius
Marius, who had been, in early life, a labourer; but, while working
with the spade, he felt sure that something would eventually turn up
in his favour. He had served as a common soldier, but proved himself
no common man; and he rose, step by step, to a highly respectable
position. Vanity, however, was one of his weak points, and he fell into
the hands of an old Syrian fortune-teller, who resorted to all sorts of
tricks to persuade him that he was destined for the highest honours.
He mentioned his aspirations to Metellus, and hinted at the possibility
of his obtaining the Consulship; but his superior officer burst into a
loud laugh, which, instead of putting Marius out of conceit, put him
further into it. He proceeded to Rome, and, by a series of popular
speeches, in which he promised everything to the people, he, of course,
gained their suffrages. Having obtained the Consulship, he was despatched to finish the war against Jugurtha; but Metellus, having first

pretended that there was nothing more to be done, for that he had settled the whole business himself, resigned his post to Marius.

Peace had indeed been already concluded with Jugurtha ; but Rome, with its habitual want of faith, re-opened the war, which terminated at last in Jugurtha's being taken prisoner. He was drawn behind the chariot of Marius—a situation little less exalted than being tied to a cart's tail, and in that position received the pelting of a pitiless storm of mud from the congenial hands of a cowardly populace. Being thrown into a damp dungeon, he—as we are told by the grave historians—still preserved his wit ; for he exclaimed, as he entered his prison, " By Hercules, what a cold bath ! "—a touch of humour which seems to us remarkable for neither breadth, point, nor neatness. When, however, we consider the moisture of the circumstances under which he was placed, we cannot be surprised that he should have failed in an attempt at dry humour.

The war with Jugurtha was no sooner at an end, than Rome found herself threatened by the swords of half-a-dozen different foes ; and, in default of being able to cut herself into six, for the purpose of dividing her strength, she seemed in danger of such a cutting-up at the hands of her enemies. It would be a tedious task to unravel the excessive tangle into which the threads of history are thrown by the windings of those numerous lines of barbarians who kept themselves suspended over Rome at about this period. The Cimbri, a Celtic race, entered into an alliance with the Teutoni—a German band—and threw themselves upon Gaul ; which was unable to throw them off again. They encountered the Consul, M. Junius Silanus, to whom they applied for a country to be assigned to them ; but, as this modest request could not be attended to, they set upon Silanus, and gave him a sound beating. At length the Consul, Q. Servilius Cœpio, offered to meet the difficulty, and approached the Rhone, but the Cimbri cut to pieces 80,000 soldiers and 40,000 camp followers ; at least, if we are to believe the authorities, who are always ready to mince men, though never mincing matters. Cœpio—according to the same authentic accounts—was glad to make his escape across the Rhone with a handful of men, and the term, "handful" is in this instance not misapplied ; for as the number is said to have been exactly ten, he might have easily told them off on his fingers. As if to show that they had not been actuated by mercenary motives, the Cimbri threw into the river the whole of their booty ; and, not satisfied with spoiling the foe, they proceeded to spoil the property taken in battle.

It says little to the credit of Rome that her dangers seemed to damp the ambition of her citizens, and no one evinced an anxiety for the perilous honours of the Consulship. Those among the aristocracy who claimed a sort of prescriptive right to the government in times when there was everything to be got, now that there was a prospect of everything being lost, shrunk from the responsibility of a high position. The plebeian, Marius, was declared to be the only man for the situation ; and, instead of being obliged to solicit the Consulship, it was thrust upon him even before he had returned from Africa.

His first care was to get together an army capable of bearing the fatigues of a military life, in preference to those who were only fit to support its gaudy trappings. He enlisted large numbers of working men, and tested their strength by putting into their hands a spade before he entrusted them with a sword, subjecting them to all sorts of privations, and putting them even upon reduced rations—an experiment that was by no means rational. Many of the soldiers, who, under a generous diet, would have become strong healthy men, dwindled to mere skeletons, and many of the recruits were reduced so low that their strength was past recruiting. Those who were able to stand against the fatigue, were hardy enough to stand against anything; and, in order to give them the benefit of a lengthy training, he refused to accept battle until a convenient opportunity. He allowed the Teutoni to pass his camp, and, as they did so, they inquired tauntingly if there were any messages or parcels for Rome, as they—the Teutoni—were on their journey thither. Marius pursued them to Aquæ Sextiæ—now Aix—and purposely pitched his camp in such a place, that water could not be obtained without a fight for it. Every soldier who went down to the river was obliged to draw his sword as he drew the water he required, and, while he fought with one hand, defended himself as well as he could with a bucket in the other. The Teutoni were completely defeated, and rushed, for safety, to their wagons ; but all who remained in the rear, together with many who had got into the van, were cut to pieces.

Marius had no sooner disposed of the Teutoni, than he heard that the Cimbri were pouring themselves all over the plains of Lombardy ; and, proceeding to meet them, he threatened to " turn their bones into whitening for the fields," a menace that proves the practice of bone manuring to be an agricultural process of great antiquity. He drew up his army near Verona, at a place called the Campi Raudii, and found the front ranks of the Cimbri linked together by chains,—an arrangement adopted, probably, to prevent their running away, and making them feel bound to stand against the enemy. Marius, with considerable tact, got into such a position that the sun got into their eyes, and the wind blew their noses. Unable to look their danger in the face, they were sent winking and sneezing to destruction.

Marius celebrated the success of the day in a magnificent triumph, and paraded, among his trophies, a Cimbric king of such a gigantic height, that, notwithstanding his humiliating position, everybody looked up to him.

For the sixth time the consulship was bestowed on Marius, though not without a vast amount of bribery on the part of the successful candidate, who, while he corrupted the electors with one hand, raised a temple to Virtue and Honour with the other. He had now become so inflated with vanity, that he came swelling into the Senate in his triumphal robes ; but he was so coldly received, that he pretended he had forgotten to change his dress, though his astonishment was as clearly put on as his objectionable attire. He caused to be engraved upon his buckler the image of a Gaul pulling out his tongue ; an allegory rather difficult to comprehend, except by adopting the somewhat vulgar reading, that the design was emblematical of the fact that, after the victory of Marius, the Gaul might as well pull out his tongue at once, as there could be no chance of his giving a licking to the Romans.

Marius was so popular, that he was acknowledged as the third founder of Rome ; Romulus, Camillus, and himself being figuratively regarded as so many bricks that the city had been built upon.

Success had rendered Marius so arrogant, that he committed many illegal acts, declaring that, amid the clashing of the swords of war, the silent motion of the sword of justice could neither be heard nor attended to. His morbid appetite for mob popularity caused him to enter into a disgraceful alliance with an unprincipled demagogue, named L. Appuleius Saturninus, whose performances equalled his promises ; but he always promised one thing, and performed another. He adopted the extremely liberal side in politics, and proposed, among other liberal measures, that every member of the Senate should bind himself by an oath to support some very liberal law for dealing with property, by taking it from those who had it, and giving it to those who were ready to take it. This friend of freedom suggested, further, that every senator attempting to exercise a free will, should pay a heavy penalty. One of the aristocratic party having ventured on proposing an amendment, was driven from the Senate by a shower of missiles. Another having suggested that he heard thunder—a sign at which the Assembly should have broken up—was told that there would probably be some hail, with hail-stones of real stone, if he opposed the project of Saturninus. Marius had the courage to declare that he would never take the degrading oath ; Metellus seconded his resolution ; and the whole Senate, with one voice—which turned out, ultimately, to be *vox et præterea nihil*—swore that they would never swear to what the people had dared to demand of them. Notwithstanding this spirited proposition, Marius had not sufficient bravery to brave the popular clamour, and his courage had died away before five days had expired. Having called a special meeting of the Senate, he intimated that second thoughts were sometimes best, and that, after his first thought, there had occurred to him a second, which he proposed that they should place upon their minutes. He concluded by intimating that he had been pelted in public for the part he had taken, and, as the people were determined, apparently, on having their fling, there was little use in opposing them. He declared his attachment to his native soil ; and, though he had always kept it in his eye, he objected to its being thrown in his face by his own countrymen. He finished by proposing that the oath should be taken, with a mental reservation that it should not be kept—a disgraceful compromise between cowardice and conscience, which the Senate without hesitation assented to. There was, after this, so little disposition to freedom among the members, that Metellus Numidicus was the only one who held out; and he, instead of remaining to battle with the abuse, preferred sneaking away from it into voluntary exile.

Saturninus not only put himself up for the tribuneship a third time, but endeavoured to get the Consulship for one Servilius Glaucia; and these noisy demagogues—by way of guiding the people in their choice —coolly murdered C. Memmius, who had started as an opposition candidate.

Marius now began to perceive that he had connected himself with a disreputable set, and finding his popularity on the wane, he repudiated his new political allies as suddenly as he had joined with them. He drove Saturninus to the Capitol, where, being without provisions, the demagogue found himself at last driven to an unprovisional surrender. Saturninus, Glaucia, and others were put to death by the command of Marius, who thus regained the good opinion of the people, though he had, in fact, simply trampled under foot, when down, those whom he had taken by the hand when they were uppermost. Having so far reinstated himself in the favour of the public, Marius retired into private life; and it was time that he should do so, while he had yet a certain amount of popularity left to fall back upon.

Law Reform, and the extension of the franchise, had now become the two great questions of the day; for the tribunals were courts of in-justice, and the Italians thought that as much weight ought to be allowed to the Italic as to the Roman character. It was the policy of the Senate to purchase popularity at almost any price, and the members were ready to outbid each other by the most extravagant offers, for the object of their ignoble competition. Among the boldest of the bidders was M. Livius Drusus, the son of old Drusus—the colleague of Gracchus —who seems to have inherited his father's propensity for sacrificing all his principle, in order to convert it into political capital. Young Drusus is said to have been a remarkable man, because, when Quæstor in Asia, he dispensed with the insignia of office, preferring to depend upon his own personal bearing, and, perhaps, wishing to save the cost of those externals which, sometimes, take from the public functionary quite as much in the way of emolument, as they bring him in the way of dignity. He had been elected to the Tribuneship, and in that capacity he did everything he could to catch the breath of popular applause, which often sullies the brightness of the object that seeks to reflect the evanescent vapour

One of the principal propositions of M. Livius Drusus was, that the judges should be liable to be brought to trial themselves, for their mode of conducting the trials of others. This attempt to undermine the independence of the judicial order, was shown to be so fatal to the administration of justice, that the people, who, after all, require only to be convinced of what is right in order to take the right direction, repudiated the proposal which Drusus had intended to be the means of misleading them, and obtaining for himself—under false pretences—a little additional popularity. It was pointed out to them, that a judge who felt every trial at which he was presiding to be his own, and who would be always divided between the calm demands of justice on one hand, and the unreasoning voice of public clamour on the other, would feel himself exposed to a pressure that would prevent him from maintaining an upright position. Notwithstanding his failure in this instance, M. Livius Drusus made himself the champion of the movement, and opened his house every evening, to give political advice gratis to all who were desirous of consulting him. He was engaged in this manner during one of his evenings at home, when he was suddenly stabbed by a shoemaker's knife ; and though the assassin was never discovered, the blow was supposed to have been connived at by some persons who had persuaded the cobbler to risk his awl in the dangerous effort. As a Roman could never die without a claptrap in his mouth, Drusus was of course prepared with a neat speech on the melancholy occasion. Having ejaculated, " Oh ! thou ungrateful Republic, thou hast never

Drusus is stabbed, and expires gracefully.

lost a more devoted son ! " he arranged his toga in becoming folds, and bowing to circumstances—bowing, perhaps, to the audience as well—he gracefully expired.

The Italians, being deprived of the support of Drusus, were more than ever oppressed, and the multitude, whom it is customary to regard as synonymous with the liberal party, became vehement in denouncing the idea of allowing an equality of rights to all classes of Roman subjects. The Italians, therefore, came to the resolution, that if Rome was not to exist for them, it should not exist at all ; but that they would either bring the city to the ground, or raise themselves from the dust to which injustice had lowered them. Several of the Italian nations formed themselves into a league, but never did a league go to such lengths as the one in question ; for some of its members murdered the prætor, Servilius Cœpio, and his legate, who attended a meeting in the hope of conciliation at the Theatre of Asculum.

The next step of the Italians was to start a republic of their own, under the name of Italica; and by way of giving it an imposing appearance, it was to have a senate five hundred strong—though in a deliberative assembly numbers are not so much an element of strength as of weakness. It was to have two annual consuls, and no less than twelve prætors ; it being perhaps the policy of the framers of the constitution to have plenty of patronage to tempt adherents to the new government. The two consuls first appointed were Silo Popædius, a Marsian, and C. Papius Mutilus, a Samnite, who took the field with great vigour, but took little else in the first instance ; for Silo fell in the fight, though Mutilus, whose army was terribly mutilated, obtained some success in Campania.

Though the Italians had commenced their operations as fast friends, they loosened considerably in their friendship as the war advanced, and made separate treaties of peace, by which Rome was enabled to deal with them piecemeal, instead of being compelled to stand against their united efforts. The Samnites evinced their old obstinacy, and waited, as usual, to be cut to pieces, before they abandoned the hope of holding together. When the sword had been busy among them for three years, there remained still a mass of sufficient importance to induce the Romans to offer the franchise to all who would lay down their arms ; and of this proposal the Samnites at last reluctantly availed themselves.

Rome having acquired a large accession of new citizens, was puzzled to determine what to do with them. Had they been distributed amongst the thirty-five country tribes, the old members would have been swamped by the new, and the latter were, therefore, formed into—some say six, some say eight, and some say fifteen separate bodies. Such is the disagreement of the learned doctors on this head, that we cannot put confidence in one without discrediting two ; and we consequently take the more impartial course of believing none of them So great is the discrepancy of the authorities on nearly every point, that, for the sake of history, we can only hope they do not go for their facts to the same sources which have supplied their figures. It is true that they usually profess to deal with round numbers alone ; and perhaps if

every number employed were literally round, it would represent the
sum of what is known with certainty on the subjects that are spoken of.

The fact, however, is indisputable, that, in the times to which our
history relates, the weaker states were the prey of the stronger,—might
overcame right ; and the only mode by which a small society could save
itself from destruction by one power, was by the sale of its independence
to another.   Those places which were incompetent to practise the noble
art of self-defence, could only obtain protection against violence on the
right hand, by submitting to robbery on the left ; and the Romans,
who were usually appealed to for aid, always plentifully helped themselves at the cost of those by whom their help was required.

By the foreign policy of Rome, ambassadors were always planted in
all places of importance, to interfere in the quarrels between nations
and their kings ; and the ambassadors took care, by fomenting quarrels,
that there should be no lack of material for their diplomacy.   The cost
of intervention fell heavily on those upon whom it was bestowed, but it
eventually helped to ruin Rome itself; for neglect of one's own affairs
is the inevitable consequence of interfering with the affairs of one's
neighbours.   The professed object of this meddling on the part of the
great republic, was to give to other states the benefit of freedom.
There is, however, no slavery more abject than that which induces a
nation to accept a foreign, instead of a domestic, tyranny.   Those who
are willing to import their independence from abroad, will never find it
flourish at home ; and there is not a more melancholy object—as
recent events have proved—than a transplanted tree of liberty.

CHAPTER THE TWENTY-FIFTH.

MITHRIDATES, SULLA, MARIUS, CINNA, ET CÆTERA.

OLLOWING the order of dates, we come to Mithridates, the son of old Mithridates the Fifth, surnamed Eupator, who had been a fast ally of Rome; but his son, who was much faster in another sense, soon came to hostilities.

The birth of young Mithridates had been, according to Justin,* signalised by the appearance of a wondrous comet, which was, probably, an idle tale; but those whose eyes are always strained towards a rising sun, are liable to be dazzled by all sorts of illusory visions.

If the comet was to have brought prosperity to Mithridates, the consignment must have been dropped on the way, inasmuch as none of it reached the young prince, whose early years were passed in hot water; for he was in one continual perspiration, caused by the constant discovery that his life was in danger. His grandmother, Laodice, had killed five of her children, when young Mithridates, fearing that infanticide might run in the family, resorted to matricide, as an alternative for checking the fearful disease, and, according to Appian,† murdered his mother. It is said that his guardians did their utmost to get rid of him, by encouraging him in all sorts of dangerous games;—that they

* Some say that Just-in was just-out, on this occasion, for that no comet appeared at the time stated. See Justin, xxxvii. 2, *et seq.*

† " De rebus Mithridaticis."

S

gave him weapons for playthings, and that one of his toys was a real sword, with which the child might have accidentally cut the slender thread of his own existence.

They mounted him, also, upon the highest horses that could be found, which was the height of cruelty ; but though the animals often kicked and hurled the youngster from his seat, fortune always decided the throw in his favour. He soon acquired such skill, that he was deep enough to meet the most fearful amount of plunging; and when placed upon a determined jibber, he could always back out of his danger. Though the horses given him to ride were quite unbroken, his neck remained entire ; and he at length became such an excellent horseman, that he could travel on horseback—according to Polybius—125 miles a day, a length to which we are not prepared to go with the ancient historian. Young Mithridates, going at full gallop, for several successive hours, presents a spirited picture to the mind's eye, but duty compels us to pull him up at the turnpike of truth ; for we can allow no evasion of the important trust of history.

Among his other accomplishments, it is said that he could hurl the javelin to such a distance, that the enthusiasm of the spectators would be roused to the utmost pitch ; but we are obliged to add, that his power in throwing the spear was not equal to that of the chroniclers in throwing the hatchet.

His guardians having failed to kill him by physical force, attempted to do so by the force of physic, and were continually giving him poisonous drugs, which, though exceedingly unpleasant, he was not nice enough to reject, for he had the bad taste to swallow them. They put him through a course of hen-bane, but he was now no chicken, and had learnt to neutralise the effects of the bane by a powerful antidote. So admirably did the latter answer its object, that he could swallow arsenic by the drachm without a scruple, and his inside was rendered thoroughly poison-proof, though there is an utter absence of historical proof to support the statement.

In order to harden himself externally, as well as internally, we are informed that he would lie at night in the open air ; but we do not believe he was any more hardened by lying than those who make the statement. He would trust to the chase for a dinner, and he was often very hard run for a meal, which he sometimes sought by a contest with a wild beast; and the question then was, whether the latter was to be cooked, or Mithridates himself done for.

The excitement of an encounter with some ferocious animal furnished the continual source of a *sauce piquante* to what he took to eat, which formed food for his courage as well as for his appetite. He was well versed in physics, which he was continually imbibing at the hands of his enemies, and, in accordance with the saying *fas est ab hoste doceri*, he turned the dosing to good account by studying the power of antidotes. He became a master of languages, and taught himself ; so that he was, in fact, his own master and his own pupil. His object appears to have been to save the trouble and expense of diplomatic agents, by qualifying himself to talk with all foreign ambassadors, and to prevent the chance of matters being misinterpreted through the mouth of an interpreter.

Those historians who have built up a considerable fabric on inconsiderable grounds, do not hesitate to add to their fabrications another story, by describing Mithridates as a giant in growth, and as a lad so tall that he might have overlooked an ordinary ladder.

Such had been the education and pursuits of the young man whom we find occupying the throne of Pontus, and interfering in the affairs of Cappadocia, to which he undertook to supply a king, from his own family, whenever a vacancy happened. Rome, also, began to take an interest in Cappadocia, and the only party without a voice in the affair, consisted of the Cappadocians. They were assailed with the offer of freedom and a republic at the point of the sword, on one side,—while, on the other, they were asked to pin their faith to a monarchy which would otherwise be pinned to them by the blades of a foreign army. The Cappadocians had a wholesome horror of republican freedom, especially when imported from abroad ; and Rome, therefore, sent them a king, who was accepted until his throne was overthrown by Mithridates— the Cappadocians having to pay a heavy fine on each change of government.

The king, who was thoroughly put out by Mithridates, applied to Rome, which raised an army in three divisions ; but the Romans were so hated in Asia Minor, that they encountered every opposition from the inhabitants. Appius and Aquilinus, who were leaders of two of the divisions, soon fell into the hands of Mithridates, and it is said that he punished their avarice by pouring melted gold down their throats ; but this is more than any one could swallow.

The Roman Senate, irritated by defeat, called upon L. Cornelius Sulla —or Sylla, as, by an alteration of the first syllable, he is sometimes called—to take the command of the army. The family boasted of its antiquity, though one family must be quite as old as another, if everybody's pedigree could be traced ; and the real wonder would be to find a man whose ancestors had a beginning, instead of the ordinary case of one with an apparently endless line of progenitors. The family of Cornelius Sulla claimed connection with that of Cornelius Rufinus, who, in the year of Rome 540, instituted the Ludi Apollinares, in honour of Apollo, and in conformity with the directions of the Sibylline books, from which he had taken the name of Sibylla. This had, according to the interpretation put upon it by family pride, been corrupted into Sulla ; and such is the empty boast of ancestry, that even corruption is eagerly acknowledged as a proof of ancient lineage. The father of L. Cornelius Sulla had left little—not even an unsullied name—to his son, but had been equally wasteful of fortune and character. The boy was clever and quick, but his speediness speedily degenerated into fastness. Having neither morality nor means, he took a cheap apartment, where he entertained a low set, and there was nothing to be envied either in his room or his company.

In early life he had distinguished himself as a soldier in the Jugurthine War; and he subsequently obtained the office of Prætor, in which he won the affections of the people, by introducing into the entertainments of the amphitheatre the extraordinary attraction of 100 real lions.

These noble animals had been the gift of a Mauritanian king, and as Sulla might have wished the present absent, if he had been saddled with the cost of the keep of no less than one hundred monarchs of the forest, the donor forwarded a band of Moors, who were to serve as food for the lions, by being turned into the arena with them when occasion required.

Sulla had excited the jealousy of Marius during the Jugurthine War, and the latter, though now a man of seventy, still cherished his old animosity with all the obstinacy of a most inveterate veteran. He was still ambitious of the laurel, though he should have been thinking only of the cypress; and with one foot in the grave, he was anxious to march with the other at the head of an army. Limping into the Campus Martius, where the soldiers were being drilled, he placed himself by the side of the youngest, and hobbled through the exercise with an air of ill-assumed juvenility. His feeble evolutions excited a mixed feeling of ridicule and disgust among the lookers-on, instead of obtaining for him the command to which he aspired. Having been disappointed of producing the effect he had anticipated, he had recourse to his friend, the tribune P. Sulpicius, who exercised a sort of reign of terror by means of 3000 gladiators, whom he always had about him. This formidable band of armed ruffians went by the name of the Anti-Senate of Sulpicius, who employed them to carry any measure he proposed, by showing the point of the sword to those who did not see the point of his argument. In order to gain time, the Senate appointed a series of holidays, or Feriæ, during which all business was suspended for the celebration of public sports, which often enabled the authorities to play a game of their own, by delaying any measure that was opposed to their interests. After a brief interval, the Senate appointed Sulla to the chief command, whereupon the Anti-Senate appointed Marius; and the former had no sooner heard the news, than he marched upon Rome with the whole of his army. The utmost consternation ensued; for no army having been expected at Rome, there had been no preparations for defence; and though the gates were closed, they were almost as crazy and unhinged as the terrified inhabitants.

A feeble attempt was made to bolt the doors against Sulla and his soldiers, but it was impossible to bar their entrance. As they marched through the streets, they were assailed from the houses with showers of

Marius discovered in the Marshes at Minturnæ.

brick, which, though very destructive, could not have been so damaging as the modern mortar. Some of the inhabitants were armed with slings, and now and then an arrow was discharged from a bow window. Orders were immediately given to set fire to the quarters whence the annoyance proceeded, and the directions were acted upon with that indiscriminate ferocity which is too often displayed by an incensed soldiery against an unarmed populace. The anger excited by the few was vented on the unoffending many, and the troops performed, with savage alacrity, the most humiliating service on which they could have been employed—the butchery of their defenceless fellow-citizens.

The leaders, or, rather, the mis-leaders of the people in this miserable conspiracy, were the first to seek their own safety in flight, and the tribune P. Sulpicius, who had set the example of employing brute force, evinced the most cowardly haste in running away from it, when he seemed likely to become one of its victims. Marius made for the marshes near Minturnæ, where he stuck in the mud, and covered his reputation with a number of stains that are quite indelible. On being discovered in his ignoble retreat, by those who had pursued him through thick and thin, he was dragged to the town and lodged in the nearest station. A price had been put upon his head, but the article does not seem to have been worth much, for he had shown very little sense in the part he had been playing. His gray hairs, or, perhaps, rather, his

" Who dares kill Marius ?"

total baldness, still commanded so much of sympathy, that nobody
evinced a disposition to become his executioner, until a Cimbric soldier
undertook the discreditable office. He approached the veteran with a
drawn sword, but Marius had got into a dark corner, and succeeded in
frightening the man-at-arms by putting on a voice of the most dismal
character. The soldier fancying himself in the presence of a ghost,
failed in plucking up a sufficient spirit; and when a moan was heard—
inquiring, "Who dares kill Caius Marius?" the would-be assassin,
having flung down his sword, ran away, exclaiming—"Not I, for
one, at any rate!" The soldier, of course, exaggerated the cause of
his fears, and declared that the eyes of Marius had appeared to him
like two candles burning in their sockets. The inhabitants of Minturnæ
became as nervous as the panic-stricken soldier, and put Marius on
board a ship, which, after being tossed about for several days, came to
an anchor, or ran aground, high and dry, on the fine old crusted port of
Carthage. Here he rambled about the ruins, and rested his aching
head upon its broken temples. The Roman Governor, Sextilius, not
knowing what to do with such an embarrassing visitor, sent a messenger
to request him to "move on;" but the exile, with a dignified air,
claimed his right to repose upon the dry rubbish. "Tell thy master,"
he observed to the officer on duty, who had respectfully told him he
must "come out of that," in compliance with the orders of the authorities,—"Tell thy master that thou hast seen Marius, sitting on the
ruins of Carthage." The intelligence was not new, but it seems to have
been rather startling, for it had the effect of causing Marius to be
allowed to remain; and we will, therefore, leave him there, while we
proceed with the march of our history.

Sulla having reduced the city to the most complete subjection, made
a merit of not pursuing his vengeance farther against the defenceless
inhabitants; and so great was his confidence in the efficacy of his
work, that he acquiesced in the appointment of L. Cornelius Cinna, a
partisan of Marius, to the consulship. Sulla proceeded to Greece,
where he blockaded Athens, whose inhabitants he plundered, as a practical acknowledgment of their worth; and he spared their lives, to show
how he valued their ancestors. He manifested his respect for their arts
by robbing their city of its chief ornaments; and he paid their learning
the compliment of stealing their principal libraries.

In the meantime Cinna had entered on the duties of the consulship
at Rome, but there the truth of the maxim, that two heads are better
than one, was rendered extremely doubtful by the constant dissensions
between himself and his colleague. The latter was Cn. Octavius, who
opposed whatever the former recommended; and while one tried to
carry his measures by brute force, the other endeavoured to defeat them
by armed violence. Cinna appealed to the mob, and Octavius trusted
to the army, both forces being the principal movers under a republican
rule or misrule, and both being equally repugnant to the spirit of

constitutional government.   The arms of such a republic might have for
its supporters the bludgeon and the sword, with the figure of Liberty

Marius in the Ruins of Carthage.

battered and bleeding, slashed and sabred, gagged and fettered, in the
middle.   Octavius and the sword had, on this occasion, got the upper
hand ; and Cinna, the clubbist, was glad to break his bludgeon or cut
his stick, in flying from the city.

The Senate decreed that he had forfeited the consulship, and Cinna,
having been well received in the Italian towns, decreed that the Senate

had forfeited their authority. The Government was thus reduced to two negatives, which could not make an affirmative; and in the midst of a theoretical perfection of republican forms, there existed only the substance of practical anarchy. The inhabitants of the Capitol, with the sword at their throats, elected a Consul, who was, of course, declared by the executive to be their free choice; while the people in the provinces protested, as loudly as they dared, against the violence that had been done to all the principles of law and liberty. Cinna, who had possessed himself of large sums of public money, employed bribes and promises to get himself acknowledged as the lawful Consul, for it is customary with despotism, acting under the name of freedom, to rob the people with one hand, in order to corrupt them with the other.

The veteran Marius, who, after making his bed on the ruins of Carthage, was not too anxious to lie there, had been wanted to join the party of Cinna, and the great captain of the age was received with enthusiasm, in consideration of the great age of the captain. Papirius Carbo and Q. Sertorius also gave in their adhesion; but Cn. Pompeius, who was stationed with an army at Umbria, waited to see which side would pay him best, and of those who would bid the highest, he was prepared to do the bidding. Marius, in the meanwhile, landed in Tuscany with a few friends; but to excite commiseration, he dressed himself in rags, which was, indeed, putting on the garb of poverty. He spoke so repeatedly of his reverses, and touched so frequently on his old clothes, that the subject was completely threadbare. Rags are seldom attractive, but in this instance, they were successful in obtaining for the wearer a large crowd of followers.

Cn. Pompeius had at length consented to espouse the cause of the Senate, but the alliance was one of interest on his side, for he would not espouse anything without a very large pecuniary settlement having been made in his favour. He met the army of Cinna under the walls of Rome, but both forces were enfeebled by sickness. Each party proceeded to do its best, but the soldiers on both sides were so wretchedly ill, that none of them could, for one moment, stand at ease; and all were much fitter to be in bed than in battle. A storm did sad havoc among the defenders of Rome, and a flash of lightning falling naturally upon the conductor of the army, caused the death of Cn. Pompeius. The gates of the city were thrown open, Cinna was restored to the Consulship, and though there had been an understanding that no blood should be shed, Marius set a band of slaves and mercenaries upon the defenceless people.

Under the pretence that he would only act according to law, this sanguinary impostor, declaring himself an exile, pretended that he would not enter the city until the sentence should be repealed; and with a sword at every throat, he demanded an expression of the voice of the people. The decision need scarcely be told, and Marius entered the city, where, standing behind Cinna's consular chair, he made a series of savage grimaces at his intended victims. Among these was the Consul, Octavius, who, soothed by the soothsayers into the belief that he had nothing to fear, boldly refused to fly, until some hired assassins exe-cuted their task, by executing the unhappy officer. He met his death while still maintaining his seat, and expired in the arms of his arm-chair of office.

Marius being now master of the situation, did all he could to make the situation vacant by a system of indiscriminate murder. The heads of the nation were not only imprisoned, but struck off. The two Cæsars were savagely seized and killed, while Marc Antony—an orator of con-siderable mark—had concealed himself in a place that was made known to Marius. The tyrant was at supper when he heard the news, and as if determined to sup full of horrors, he started up with a determination to witness the murder, which he desired should immediately take place ; but his friends pacified him with the assurance that the head should be brought in to him.

If the chroniclers are to be credited, Marc Antony owed his detection to his fastidiousness as to the sort of wine that was placed before him. While in concealment, his daily supply was procured from a neighbour-ing tavern, by a messenger who was in the habit of tasting several bottles before he was satisfied. This excited the curiosity of the land-lord, who became anxious to know the name of his very particular customer. The messenger, on one occasion, had taken so much of the wine in, that he let the truth out, when the wine-merchant treacherously proceeded to betray the hiding-place of Marc Antony. Soldiers were sent to his lodgings ; but he grew so eloquent over his generous wine, that he excited among the guards a generous spirit. His life would probably have been spared, had not the tribune Annius rushed up-stairs, and himself struck off the head of the unhappy Antony.

Several men of consideration, in the most inconsiderate manner, killed themselves, to avoid the fate which was intended for them by Cinna, and that still greater sinner, Marius.   Q. Lutatius Catulus proceeded to the temple, and getting into a corner among the statues of the gods, placing himself opposite Pan, perished by the fumes of charcoal. Merula, the Flamen of Jupiter, may be said to have snuffed himself out, or extinguished his own vital spark ; for, seating himself in the portico of the Capitoline, he calmly made preparations for suicide, and took off his flame-coloured cap, in which it was not lawful for him to expire.   Producing some surgical instruments from his pocket, he sat ruminating over his case, and taking out a lancet, he showed that he was no longer in the vein to live, but quite in the vein to die, for he opened an artery.   The tyrant himself took to drinking in his old age, and frequently rolled about in a state of frenzy, under the impression that he was commanding an army against Mithridates. He ultimately drove himself to *delirium tremens*, and he contracted a

constant shake of the hands by his frequent use of cordials.   He died
after a short illness, on the 15th of January, B.C. 86, without having
devoted himself to that sober reflection, which would have induced him
to repent of his numerous enormities.   Such was the end of a man,
whose faults have been sometimes glossed over with the varnish of
flattery, though at the hands of truth they can only receive an appropriate coat of blacking.

Marius in his Old Age.

CHAPTER THE TWENTY-SIXTH.

DEATH OF CINNA. RETURN OF SULLA TO ROME. C. PAPIRIUS CARBO.
DICTATORSHIP OF SULLA.

LIBERTY being now established on a republican basis, by the massacre of all who had a word to say against the military usurper Cinna, that individual began the task of consolidating his power. He nominated L. Valerius Flaccus to the consulship; and those of the aristocracy who wished for freedom, were free to leave Rome if they did not like living under a tyrannical government. To speak openly in the forum or the courts of justice, was prohibited ; and the scantiness of the reports that have come down to us of the events of the times, can be no matter of surprise, when we consider that the reporters were not permitted to give an account of actual occurrences.

It was necessary to amuse the masses by what are termed liberal measures, and as an excess of liberality, it was proposed that every debtor, paying one fourth of his debt, should be released from all further liability to his creditor. This was sure to be a popular act in a country already ruined by political agitation, and the despotism to which it frequently leads ; and, as the debtors were by far the most numerous class, a sort of general Insolvent Act was hailed with acclamations by a bankrupt community.

Sulla, who was still in Greece, refused his allegiance to the despot at home, and L. Valerius Flaccus was sent to supersede him in the command of the army. Flaccus was not popular with his soldiers, and as the head of the Government had set the example of setting aside all law by a *coup d'état*, an imitator was soon found in the person of one Flavius Fimbria, a lieutenant, who, by a *coup de tête*, got rid of his obnoxious general. Flaccus being thus disposed of, Fimbria promoted himself to the chief command ; but, cowardice and cruelty going hand in hand, he took his own life on hearing that Sulla was setting out against him. The soldiers of Fimbria, with the most revolting faithlessness, revolted to Sulla, who was now master of Asia. He called upon the conquered nation for 20,000 talents, and as the subdued people had not so large a sum by them, they were obliged to borrow it with one hand at enormous interest, in order to pay it with the other. The Roman capitalists lent the cash, and the Roman soldiers assisted them with their swords to draw a ruinous per-centage from the unfortunate borrowers. Sulla now prepared to march upon Rome, where Cinna had re-elected himself as Consul, in conjunction with one Papirius Carbo, a political incendiary, who acted like so much touch-paper and coal upon the flame of discord. Intending to meet their rival, they proceeded with an army into Italy; but the soldiers no sooner found themselves on the Italian soil, than they declared their determination to remain there. Cinna called them together, and endeavoured to persuade them to go forward, but even when he gave the word of command there was no advance on his bidding. From passive resistance they proceeded to active insubordination, and, denouncing him as a tyrant whom it was high time to see through, they perforated him with their swords in several places.

On the death of Cinna, legal authority began to raise its humbled head, and Carbo was summoned to hold a Comitia at Rome; but on the day appointed, the attendance of voters not promising a satisfactory result, the augurs declared the auspices unfavourable, and dissolved the meeting.

A deputation had been sent to Sulla to endeavour to make terms, but the members of the deputation were forced to return without any terms having been agreed upon. Sulla did not march immediately upon Italy, but went to Ædepsus, in Eubœa, for the benefit of the hot baths, though he did not limit himself to the waters, for he addicted himself to the spirits abounding in the neighbourhood. He amused himself in the society of those who are sometimes said to live upon their wits, though their existence is really derived from the want of wit in others. Sulla, however, had a counterpoise to any demerits of his own, in the still greater demerits of those who were opposed to him.

The new Consuls were L. Cornelius Scipio, a highly respectable man, and C. Julius Norbanus, a mere creature of Carbo. Against these leaders Sulla marched from Greece in the rudest health and the most exuberant spirits. His pockets, however, were as light as his heart; but this signified little, for the troops were so devoted to him that there was not an officer unattached; and so far from making any difficulty about their pay, they undertook to raise money among themselves, if necessary, for the use of their leader.

The expedition landed at Brundusium, where the inhabitants received Sulla with open arms, or rather without any arms at all, for they permitted him to occupy the place without opposition. Passing through Calabria and Apulia, he approached the encampment of Norbanus, in the neighbourhood of Capua, and sent ambassadors to treat; but their treatment was anything but courteous. They were insulted by all kinds of abuse, and it is said that they had a great deal more thrown in their face than mere reproaches. When Sulla heard of their reception, or rather their rejection at the enemy's camp, he fell upon it with such force that everything fell under him.

He next turned his attention to L. Scipio, whose army went over in a body to the side of Sulla, while Scipio and his son were sitting together, talking over general matters in the tent of the general. L. Scipio had despatched his son with directions for the right division, when the youth returned to say, that of the right division, there was not one man left; and when Scipio himself went to look after his men, he found there was not one remaining, even for the look of the thing, to mount guard at the tent of their commander. He, of course, proposed a series of strong resolutions, seconded by his son, that all those who had joined Sulla were enemies to the state; but the state in which he then was, rendered his denunciations idle, if not. ridiculous. The position of Sulla was becoming rather alarming to the party of Carbo, who caused himself to be appointed Consul, for the year B. C. 82, in conjunction with young C. Marius, who, as the heir of his father, had inherited a large stock of wickedness. Cn. Pompeius had already sent in his adhesion to Sulla, who had received him as a very promising young man, for he had a fair share of popularity, and a good amount of property. Young Pompey was opposed to old Carbo, and the former so harassed the latter, that his temper, always sour, became equal to carbonic acid in its inflammable tendency.

Sulla took young Marius in hand, and followed him up to a place called Sacriportus, where, in consequence of a dream—for the ancients were addicted to taking advice with their eyes shut—an attack by the former on the latter was resolved upon. Sulla ordered his soldiers to advance, but they were so fatigued that they fell asleep on the road, and caused their leader to wonder what they could possibly be dreaming of. Instead of their being equipped in the arms of the warrior, they were stretched in the arms of Somnus, and Sulla, though reluctant to go counter to his dream, perceived the folly of marching to battle with a somnambulist army. He gave orders, therefore, to halt, and the men had commenced digging the foundations for a camp, when the cavalry of Marius rode up for the purpose of annoying them. Irritated by the conduct of the enemy's horse, the soldiers of Sulla kicked against it, and even while engaged in their work, picked out, with their pickaxes, a few of the foremost of the Marian army. This led to a general engagement, in which Sulla's forces forgot their fatigue, and pursued the enemy to the neighbouring town of Præneste, the gates of which were shut in such haste, that all the fugitives had not time to get in, and Marius himself was pulled up by a rope over the wall, together with a few immediate hangers-on, who had tied themselves to his fortunes. Sulla is said to have slain 20,000 men, and to have taken 8000 prisoners, while he lost only twenty-three; but as he is his own authority for the statement,* we must take in a purely figurative sense many of his figures.

The Marian party, fearing that the successes of Sulla might encourage resistance to the despotism still prevailing at Rome, determined on getting rid of the principal politicians of the day, the heads of the National Assembly of the period. The modern practice might have been to have shut up the place of meeting, and prevent the members, by armed force, from going in—slaughtering them, of course, in case of their perseverance; but the Marian policy was to summon them to the Curia Hostilia, and having got them in, to butcher those who attempted to go out again.

* As quoted by Plutarch, in Sulla, c. 28.

The prætor, L. Damasippus, was entrusted with this sanguinary business; and every eminent politician, who was suspected of having an independent opinion of his own, was at once massacred. This step was declared to be necessary to give strength to the Government, and to insure the unanimity of the nation, by cutting the throats of all who ventured to be of a way of thinking contrary to that of the ruling power. Unfortunately, some of the best and wisest men of the day were blind to the virtues of the chief of the republic; and the whole of these, including Q. Mucius Scævola, the eminent jurist, were unceremoniously sacrificed.

The news of the success of Sulla at Sacriportus, caused a panic among those who had been combining the butcher's business with that of government at Rome, and the perpetrators tried to fly when they heard the enemy was approaching the city. Sulla, leaving Lucretius Ofella to keep watch at the gates of Præneste, lest Marius should attempt to creep out, marched in person on the capital. Directing his steps towards the Colline gate, he found there an army of those same Samnites, who had been previously cut into so many pieces, and who were ready to be cut into so many more, should occasion require the alarming sacrifice. Their general, Pontius Telesinus, rode in front of them, entreating them to come and be killed for positively the last time; and the dux had sufficient influence to induce them to rush like a flock of geese on their own destruction. The victory of Sulla was complete; and Pontius Telesinus having been overlooked by the foe in the heat of battle, supplied the omission in the business of the day by making away with himself—after the usual cowardly fashion of the heroes of antiquity.

Sulla's success seemed only to have effected a change of tyrants; and his conduct proved that the monster grievance of Rome was the series of inhuman monsters who had got hold of the government. The atrocities attributed to Sulla are, however, so enormous, as almost to border on the burlesque; and it is comfortable to feel in the exaggeration a ground for hope that in the account furnished by the historians, much may fall under the head of " Errors excepted."

It is said that 3000 of the enemy at Antennæ implored his mercy, which he granted, on the understanding that they were to assassinate their associates—a service that was performed with brutal eagerness. When the 3000 claimed their own pardon as a reward, they were, according to Plutarch, conveyed to Rome, and butchered with a few thousand others, who had the misfortune to differ in opinion with the chief of a republican government.

It was found so extremely embarrassing to heads of families and others who were liable every day or hour to be cut off, that it was at length proposed, as a matter of convenience, that Sulla should save time by publishing a short list, containing the few names of those whom he did not intend to sacrifice. He replied, by bringing out a very long list of those he did, which he stated to be merely the first number of a serial work, which he did not pledge himself to complete within any particular period. As every copyright is liable to be infringed, the work of Sulla was the subject of numerous imitations; and there were many who made lists of their own, containing names disagreeable to themselves; so that no man could walk the streets without the chance of reading his own death-warrant on the walls of the capital. Sulla, in many instances, offered rewards for the heads of his victims, and his doors were beset from morning till night with the cry of, "Butcher!" by those who called for the sums they had earned as slaughtermen. Assassinations proceeded to such a fearful degree, that Q. Catulus asked Sulla, in confidence, whether it was the intention of the latter to spare any human being at all? for there seemed a chance of his having no one left to rule over but himself; and such a man was likely to find self-government exceedingly difficult.

While these things were going on at Rome, Marius was besieged in Præneste, from which he tried to make his escape through the common sewer; a mode of insuring his life that was far from dignified. He, however, was espied through an iron aperture, which was so grating to his feelings, that he called upon his slave to run him through; when the faithful fellow immediately bored him to death with a trusty and rusty weapon.

Sulla, the perpetrator of all the acts of despotism and cruelty which are above described, was without any legal authority, and had no more right than the meanest subject of the republic to the power which he exercised. His reign was a reign of terror, supported by the swords of a sordid soldiery. Of the two Consuls, Marius was already dead; and Carbo, being taken prisoner, was condemned to death; so that Carbo— the blackness of whose conduct justified his title of the coal—was soon reduced to ashes.

The senate, which had been cut down by assassination to suit the views of Sulla, elected L. Valerius Flaccus as interrex, who immediately caused Sulla to be invested with the power of doing whatever he liked, as long as he liked; or, to use the official phraseology, made him dictator for an unlimited period.

On receiving his appointment, the first measure of Sulla was to reward the tools who had assisted him, and L. Valerius Flaccus was immediately made master of the horse, while the military murderers, who had acted as executioners in the execution of his plans, received grants of land in the places which had been unfavourable to the tyrant. He courted a certain sort of popularity by extending the suffrage to some 10,000 emancipated slaves, who retained enough of their slavishness to cause them to vote as their master desired. He affected to reconstitute the legislative body which he had illegally destroyed, and he sent into it a quantity of that noxious scum which, in the troubled waters of revolution, is frequently cast up to the surface of society.

Having established his position through the brutality of one part of the people, and the cowardice of the other, he set about the business of a reformer; and, though he did much harm, the little good that he accomplished must not be denied to him. Being a despot by nature, he limited, as far as he could, the popular element in the constitution, by curtailing the power of the tribunes ; and he increased the government patronage by adding to the number of pontiffs and augurs, so that he might have the privilege of appointment to lucrative, but useless, offices. His changes in the criminal code were, however, really beneficial, for he made murder, whether committed by poison or violence, a crime by law ; and, indeed, it was necessary that the point should be clearly defined, for military murders at the hands of the executive had been so numerous that it was reasonably doubted whether human life was henceforth to be protected at all by the government. Many old laws were re-enacted, though they had never been repealed ; but the usurpers of power had so thoroughly trampled on every legal form, that it was impossible to know which of the laws were to be regarded as imperative on the people.

Sulla, and his friends, boasted that his firmness had given tranquillity to Rome ; but tranquillity can scarcely be a desirable condition to one whose quietude is the result of a gag in the mouth, a sword suspended over the head, and chains on every part of the body. The repose, or rather, the stillness thus obtained, was no less costly than inconvenient, for there was a wholesale confiscation of the property of all who were supposed to entertain views different from those of the government. The iniquities of the master will often be followed by the man, and, in conformity with this rule, a fellow, named Chrysogonus, one of Sulla's creatures, caused the murder of Roscius of Armenia, in order to get the opportunity of robbing him. The property of Roscius was knocked down at a mock auction to a bad lot of ruffians, who were there to intimidate the auctioneer into doing their smallest bidding. Everything went for positively nothing, and Chrysogonus was understood to have got nearly the whole of it at a ludicrously low figure.

The laws made by Sulla, though perhaps plain enough in their purport, had an ambiguity in their application which was extremely inconvenient. Though binding at some times, in some places, upon some persons, they were not so at other times, in other places, upon others. He had laid it down as a rule that no one could be elected consul until he had been prætor ; though, in the case of his own adherents, Sulla was not at all particular. When, however, L. Ofella, the commander at Præneste, who had never been prætor, put up for the consulship, Sulla declared such conduct was not to be put up with at all, and had him killed in the middle of a morning's canvass. The people were rather angry at the outrage, when Sulla, walking among a group with a sword in his hand, " demanded silence for an anecdote." * A circle drew round him, tremblingly alive to what he was about to say, when the despot proceeded as follows : " A labourer," said he, " was at work at the plough, when he was annoyed by insects, which caused him to stop and beat them off by dusting his own jacket. Finding himself

* Vide the account given by Appian, c. 102.

annoyed a second time he took off his jacket and threw it into the fire. Now, I advise those whom I have twice conquered not to oblige me to try the fire." The people, who knew something of Sulla's threatened fire, dreaded it with all the horror of a burned child, and he was left to pursue his career of unchecked atrocity.

A man who has the cruelty of a brute has, generally, the other debasing appetites of the lower order of animals; and Sulla had as much of the sensualist as of the tyrant in his character. To a thirst for blood he added the appetite of a glutton; and, having amassed enormous wealth by murder and rapine, he longed for the opportunity to expend his ill-gotten means in idleness and debauchery. He accordingly called the people together in the forum, and, having walked up and down for some time asking if anybody dared to make a charge against him, he resigned the dictatorship. This abdication has been lauded by some as a proof of magnanimity and disinterestedness; but, to sum up the truth in a few words, he had practised human butchery as a trade, and, having realised an enormous fortune, he retired from business. Having secured all the profits that were likely to accrue from his unprincipled career, he left to others the difficult work of sustaining the results of his policy. He retired to Puteoli, where he passed much of his time in the company of actors, and became the intimate associate of one or two popular low comedians. In his sober moments—which were very few during the latter part of his life—he wrote his own memoirs, and was employed upon the work until within a few days of his death, which happened B. c. 78, when he had reached the age of sixty. Seldom had a man, who had reached but three-score, left so many scores unsatisfied. Such was his cruelty, that he delighted in loading prisoners with fetters, and then shedding their blood, which caused it to be said of him that he was no less fond of mangling than of ironing. He had so little regard for old associations, that when one of his acquaintances reminded him of the days when they lived in the same house—Sulla paying 2000 sesterces for the basement, and his former friend 3000 for the first floor—the Dictator refused to spare his fellow-lodger's life, but brutally remarked, that the story, whether upper or lower, was an old one, and had long ago lost its interest. It is said that dungeons or cellars were attached to Sulla's house for the purpose of keeping a supply of human beings always on hand for occasional sacrifice. The manner of his death rendered him an object as repulsive as he had become by his mode of life; for, his licentiousness led to a disease which developed itself in the generation of vermin in his skin; and he may be said to have been almost eaten up with corruption before he expired. By his own desire his body was burned; as if he had thought that fire might act in some sort as a purifier of his memory. The ladies of the nobility threw perfume on the funeral pile,* but it was too late to bring him

---

* Plutarch in Sulla, c. 38.

into good odour. Numerous attendants carried spices of every kind; and, in addition to the ordinary mace-bearers, there were several officers laden with cinnamon. The fact of incense having been offered at the funeral pile of such a monster, is enough to incense any one who reads a statement so humiliating to humanity.

Funeral Pile of Sulla.

In personal appearance Sulla was by no means attractive; for he had a quantity of green in his eye, an abundance of red in his hair, and a profusion of purple in his countenance. His face was, like his character, full of spots; and those who accused him of aspiring to the purple, said the fact might be read in his look, for his cheeks were of blue, and caused himself, as well as his acts, to wear a very dark complexion. He was coarse in his manners, and had no appreciation of any kind of delicacy but the delicacies of the table. Notwithstanding the unpleasant features of Sulla's person and character, he was married five times; for divorce had become so easy, that a man could always put his old wife away when he wished for a new one.

CHAPTER THE TWENTY-SEVENTH.

REACTION AGAINST THE POLICY OF SULLA.   SERVICES OF Q. SERTORIUS.
METELLUS.   CN. POMPEY.   SPIRITED STEPS OF SPARTACUS.   THE
IRATE PIRATE.

Cæsar and Pompey very much alike,
especially Pompey.

HE tyrannical acts of Sulla had smothered, but not extinguished, the flame of liberty, and every piece of injustice had been so much fuel heaped upon a smouldering fire. At the death of Sulla, the population consisted of little else than those who had been beggared by a rapacious soldiery, and the military desperadoes who had done the tyrant's work; a melancholy combination of the victimisers and the victimised. The Consuls were M. Æmilius Lepidus and Q. Lutatius Catulus; the former having enriched himself by connexion with the dictator's party, but the tide having turned, he turned with it, in the hope that it might again lead on to fortune. Catulus, on the other hand, adhered to the policy of Sulla; and there being reason to fear that the two Consuls would get up a quarrel—in the course of which the lookers-on would be robbed—the Senate made the Consuls swear that they would not take up arms against each other. The oath was readily taken, and no less readily broken by those republican chiefs, who came into violent collision near the very gates of Rome; and Lepidus, having got the worst of it, fled to Sardinia, where, having laid down his plans for the future, he laid down himself, and died rather unexpectedly.

Several of the laws of Sulla were so manifestly unjust as to be indefensible even by his own partisans; and many of them were repealed under various consulships. Cn. Pompey, who had been a warm adherent of the dictator, had a much warmer feeling for himself, and he courted popular favour by the promise of many reforms which involved a compromise of his former principles. The republic was, in fact, the sport of a set of unprincipled men, who were trying, by every artifice and crime, to get to the head of it. They cared nothing for the public interests, but thought only of their own; which will be too often the case when the chief power in the state is open to any who will make the highest bid for it. Pompey had gone into the market with his abilities when tyranny required tools; but perceiving that demagogues were now in demand, he endeavoured to make a profit of popular principles. Others had embarked on the same voyage, shifting their course with the breath of public opinion, and having no rudder but self-interest. One of these was L. Licinius Lucullus, a man of excessive wealth, which he used, or rather abused, in excessive luxury. He employed art for the purpose of opposing nature; and, among other pieces of prodigality, he endeavoured to convert a portion of the sea into a private fish-pond. This he attempted at his winter residence near Naples; where, by a cutting through the rocks he formed an opening into the bay, and kept upon his own premises a continual supply of fresh fish in a reservoir of salt water. His tastes were not, however, limited to the pleasures of the dinner-table; for he had not only studied the law, and had the Twelve Tables at his fingers' ends, but he had collected a library of such vast extent, that it comprehended a store of information far beyond the comprehension of its owner.

M. Licinius Crassus was another candidate for power, which he sought rather by means of his wealth, than his talents; for he had far more money than wit; and Crassus often evinced signs of crass ignorance.

Almost the only illustrious man of the period was C. Julius Cæsar, who could turn his hand, no matter what was in it, to anything. He was as ready with the pen as with the sword; but the latter was not sharper than his tongue; while his mind was so capacious and elastic, that it could adapt itself to small or great things with equal facility. A very little subject is often lost in the vast expanse of a very great intellect; and a diminutive understanding cannot afford space for the admission of a grand idea; but there was suitable accommodation for either one or the other, or both at once, in the self-adapting mind of Cæsar. He was an author without jealousy, a scholar without pedantry, and a politician without quackery.

These, and other illustrious men, flourished in Rome about this time; but Pompey, who had a natural love of pomp, possessed the art of concentrating upon himself the rays reflected from the brilliant personages who surrounded him; so that it was difficult to distinguish at all times between him and the other men of distinction of the period.

During the lifetime of Sulla, Q. Sertorius had been serving, or rather commanding, in Spain, where he held the post of prætor, and was engaged in keeping the interests of his party—that of Marius—alive, by killing all who were opposed to them. His professed object was to unite Spaniards and Romans as one people; but his mode of reconciling any differences was to put to the sword those who, after he had put their opinions to the test, were found to disagree with him. Sulla had sent an army, under C. Annius, to attack Sertorius in Spain, when Sertorius, looking upon C. Annius as a mere deputy, with whom a deputy on his side might deal, despatched Julius Salinator to meet the envoy. The result proved that the prætor had done wisely in acting on his discretion, rather than giving way to any sudden impulse of valour; for Salinator, whom he had sent as a substitute for himself, was killed, when, in his capacity of proxy, he approximated too closely to the enemy.

Sertorius, who had sent out Salinator as a sort of feeler—not exactly expecting that the latter would have to feel his death-blow—perceived there was little prospect of his own success ; and he made his escape to Africa. While in Mauritania, having no quarrel of his own, he interfered in the quarrels of other people; and there being two claimants to the Mauritanian crown, he supported one, and—by way of keeping his hand in—picked the pocket of the other. His meddling having paid him extremely well, he made up his mind and his luggage to retire into private life, and an account he had heard of the Canary Islands tempted him to deposit his well-feathered nest in that congenial locality.

The Lusitanians, however, who had been robbed by the Romans belonging to Sulla's party, having a vague idea of the propriety of setting a thief to catch a thief, entreated Sertorius to defend them against their enemies. The engagement was entered into after some little delay as to the terms; when Sertorius set to work with so much ardour, that he was soon fighting four Roman generals at once; and, what was still more remarkable, he was getting decidedly the best of it. His mode of warfare was to pour down from one fastness to another with such speed, that his foes never knew where to have him, until he had them in the most unexpected manner. If they began to march, says Plutarch, he was upon their heels,—if they sat still, he was upon their back,—and if they invested a town, he turned the investment to his own profit by intercepting all their convoys. The enemy had no resource against his arms but their own legs, for flight was their sole safeguard.

Not satisfied with fighting the battles of the Spaniards, he began regulating their civil domestic affairs, and endeavoured to translate the Spanish into the Roman character. His object was to establish a Roman republic in Spain; but it is difficult to manufacture a foreign article of native materials. He appointed 300 persons as a senate ; and, though the greater part were Spaniards, he took as many proscribed Romans as he could find, in the hope that they would serve as a sort of Roman cement, to make it hold together. He established a school—a classical academy—where Latin and Greek were taught, and where the pupils wore boys' tunics, after the Roman fashion.

Sertorius was a general favourite with all classes, besides the classes of the school; and happening to have a favourite fawn, which followed him wherever he went, flattery declared the fawn was sent him by the gods, as a mark of favour.

Fortune appeared to favour him in all he undertook ; and even Q. Metellus, with a large army, could produce no effect,—a failure that was attributed to the age and imbecility of that illustrious veteran. Sertorious was joined by Perperna, who, on the strength of the forces he brought, expected to share in the command ; but such is the influence of success, that Perperna's men repudiated their own leader, and insisted on having Sertorius as their general.

Sertorius and his young Friends.

The constant arrival of unfavourable news at Rome, at length induced Pompey to exclaim—"This will never do; I must go and settle the matter myself;" for Pompey's conceit induced him to conceive that he should easily conquer Sertorius. The latter was besieging Lauro, the modern Liria, to which the former advanced for the purpose of relieving it. There was, near the walls, a hill that it was important to possess, and both parties tried for it; but Sertorius, setting his eye on the top, was the first to get up to it. Pompey, with consummate vanity, expressed his determination to dislodge the fellow forthwith, and sent a message to the town, desiring the inhabitants to sit upon the walls, that they might see how cleverly he would dispose of their enemy. Sertorius, on hearing the boast, observed, smilingly, that "a general should watch behind as well as before,"—an observation that Pompey, who did not see behind him at the time, would often afterwards look back upon. Sertorius had, in fact, a very considerable reserve, with which he hemmed the besiegers in while he burned the inhabitants out, to the utter astonishment of Pompey, who, though near enough to the flames to warm his hands, could not interfere without burning his fingers.

Pompey was, nevertheless, impatient to measure swords with Sertorius; an operation which, though it seems indicative of coming to close quarters, must always keep a soldier at arm's length, at least, from his antagonist. Desirous of all the glory that might be obtained, Pompey, hearing that Metellus was coming up with assistance, resolved on precipitating a battle, and he accordingly commenced one rather late in the afternoon, though he knew he might be quite in the dark as to the issue. Sertorius and Pompey each advanced at the head of a division, but by some accident they did not happen to meet; and each of them came back to the main body of his army with the conviction that he had been victorious. On the renewal of the conflict the generals met, the armies knocked their two heads together, when Pompey, being stunned by the blow, and having no one to advise him what to do, took to flight for the purpose of consulting his own safety.

Though apparently invincible by his enemies, Sertorius was not safe from his friends, for he was murdered at a dinner-party given to him by Perperna. The cloth had not been removed, when Sertorius was startled by a singular *entrée*, in the shape of a band of assassins, who set upon him and slew him. So much was he respected by the Spaniards, that it is said his death brought dying suddenly into fashion, and many killed themselves at his funeral, for the purpose of taking Sertorius as their pattern. Perperna immediately declared himself commander-in-chief, but he was quite unfit for the place, and in his very first engagement he was cut to pieces, with the whole of his army. Whether they were literally cut to pieces, is a matter of doubt to us, though the account is placidly adopted by the graver historians; but when we consider the quantity of cutting and coming again of the same parties—as exemplified particularly in the case of the Samnites—which we are continually called upon to place faith in, we find belief rather difficult.

While these things were proceeding in Spain, the slaves were going on in the most perplexing manner in Italy and its neighbourhood. Some of the ablest of them had been trained in gladiatorial schools to afford amusement in the Circus; but this outrage to humanity brought much misery in its train to those who were the cause of it. The slaves were exercised in the use of all sorts of weapons, and humanity was lowered by hiring them out for shows on public occasions. Being skilled in the employment of the sword, they began to think of wielding it against their oppressors, instead of trying it upon each other, and about seventy of them escaped under the leadership of a Thracian of their body, named Spartacus. Being unprovided with arms, they plundered the cook-shops, where they seized spits for spears, skewers for daggers, carving knives for swords, dripping-pans for shields, and basting-spoons for general purposes. They next entered the shops of the carpenters, and seized the tools of the workmen, many of whom concealed the implements of their industry; but, if a saw happened to show its teeth, it was immediately captured. Their party, though at first small, was increased by all the runaway debtors of the district; for it is a remarkable fact, that those who owe

privately more than they can pay, are often foremost among those
who talk the loudest about what they owe to the public interests.
They took up their position on Mount
Vesuvius—an appropriate place for
a breaking out—and their numbers
having swelled to 10,000, they poured
themselves down, like a devastating
stream of lava, on many neighbouring
towns, which were speedily laid in
ashes. Spartacus pushed forward as
far as the foot of the Alps; but his
followers were intent on returning to
Rome, in order to sack it, and add
its contents to their baggage. M.
Licinius Crassus was sent after him;
and having undertaken to overtake
him, came up with him in Lucania.
The slaves fought like lions, or,
rather, with the ferocity of the brutes
with whom they had been taught

Armed Slave.

to contend, and were, in some instances, victorious.

Crassus had sent Mummius to keep the army in check, but the latter
had received particular directions not to fight; for the object of the
republican general was to take all the glory for himself, irrespective of
his country's interests. Mummius, however, had the same feeling, and
was desirous of winning a reputation, regardless of the orders of his
superior; for he knew that a military success, in the unstable condition of the executive, would, however irregular, be passed over by the
people, and perhaps made a stepping-stone for himself to supreme
power. His men, who were not actuated by the same personal motives
as himself, saw the insufficiency of their force, and, being seized with a
panic, ran away, without stopping to draw their swords from their
scabbards. Spartacus formed the idea of passing into Sicily, and proceeded to Rhegium, where he bargained with some pirates to supply
him with vessels; but after pretending much friend-ship, they never
furnished him with any ship at all, though he had paid the knaves the
price of a small navy.

Spartacus found himself blockaded in Rhegium; and Crassus, cutting
a trench all round, thought to prevent all egress from the place; but
neither Crassus nor his trench proved deep enough to answer the
purpose proposed, for Spartacus filled up a portion of the ditch, and
walked over it. Crassus, now fearing that his cause was lost, sent to
Rome for the assistance of Pompey, who, priding himself on his previous
victories, and mentally ejaculating, " I 'm the only man; they 're always
obliged to send for me," proceeded to meet Spartacus. No sooner had
Crassus sent for help, than he recovered from his panic, and sent to say
he should require no aid; but he had calculated in the absence of the

host, for when the host of Spartacus appeared, Crassus found it no easy
matter to contend with them.   The latter, however, grown too confident
of success, determined on running the chance of striking or receiving a
decisive blow, notwithstanding the misgivings of their leader.

Spartacus commenced the day by sending for his horse, and killing
it, to the utter astonishment of the spectators, and the intense bewilderment of the unfortunate animal.   " If I win the day," said he, " I shall
have many better horses ; but if I lose it, the poor creature would be
useless to me in my very humble walk of life, or my more probable
walk out of it."   Such was his only mode of accounting for an act,
which none who pitied the suffering of an equine animal could regard
with equanimity.   On the day of the battle, Spartacus was soon
wounded, but falling on his knees, he continued to fight in that uneasy
position.   Being at last overpowered, he fell, with 40,000 of his
men, who, according to the authorities, were sent to destruction ; but

Spartacus.

though there is no hesitation in saying where they went, the question where they came from, is one which the grave historians have paid no attention to. Of the whole 40,000 who are said to have been found dead upon the field, it is asserted that two only had their backs to the foe ; but we suspect that if there had been time for the defeated to have turned themselves round, there would have been many more in the same position.

Crassus marched towards Rome, expecting to be received with enthusiasm ; but Pompey who had met and exterminated 3000 Thracians, sent a letter home, declaring that " what Crassus had done was all very well, but that he (Pompey) had really put an end to the war by his act of determined butchery." Knowing the value attached by a military republic to a sanguinary act, he was sanguine enough to expect the office of Consul. This he obtained in conjunction with his rival Crassus, who laid himself out, and laid out a considerable sum of money as well, for the purchase of mob popularity. He gave the people corn for nothing, and invited them to dinner-parties of 10,000 at a time; but his prodigality only proves the extent of his plunder, for nothing could have gone into the public mouth, but that which had in some shape or other come out of the public pocket. Pompey, on the other hand, practised the profession of humility, which perhaps answered better in a double sense ; for it was certainly cheaper, and possibly somewhat more effective, than ostentatious prodigality. He used to lead his own horse in a procession, to show that he was a simple *eques*, on a footing of equality with other citizens. When his consulship was at an end, he retired into a private station, where he lived like a prince—a style that seems to be much in favour with those who preach the doctrine of perfect equality.

It was impossible for such an active participator in public affairs to remain wholly idle ; and the alarming spread of piracy soon gave him an opportunity for really honourable distinction. The pirates were becoming a scourge to Rome, but Rome had richly deserved it, for it had been her own injustice that had called into existence these dangerous enemies to humanity. They consisted, in the first instance, of men ruined by Roman extortion, who took to the mountains and the sea, where the true excitement of the ups and downs of life may be most vividly experienced. These men had in time been joined by the once rich and noble, some of whom, having sold the wives and families they could no longer keep, began to plough the ocean as the only field of enterprise. Piracy thus became a regular business of man, just as in more civilised times it has become a regular part of the business of bookselling. Towns were plundered, the cattle were carried off, and the inhabitants walked off to captivity. The rich were frequently kidnapped on the roads, and nothing but a handsome ransom would obtain their liberty.

The pirates had been often reduced, but had never been rooted out ; and the tribune, A. Gabinius, proposed, therefore, that Pompey should be called upon to do extraordinary things with extraordinary powers. He was to have supreme command for three years, during which period he was to have whatever was asked, and to order everybody or everything that he required. He took his own measures extremely well, and took the measure of the pirates also with such effect, that he soon drove them from all their fastnesses, with a speed quite marvellous. Though his extraordinary powers had been conferred upon him for three years, he had such still more extraordinary power over himself, that he made a voluntary surrender of the former, when the object for which they had been entrusted to him was accomplished. Everything was achieved in three months, during which period he had taken several towns, none of which he had kept to himself, though one of them, in Cilicia, called Soli, he made a solitary exception of, by giving it the name of Pompeiopolis. The people of Soli talked a mixed dialect of Asiatic and Greek, which caused such a confusion of speech, that a great deal of confounded nonsense was the result; and it is said that the word solecism, as applied to an inaccuracy of speech, is derived from the name of the place alluded to.

That the Romans should have been hostile to piracy is somewhat inconsistent with the principle, or rather the want of principle, on which they acted themselves, for they pirated almost everything. Their literature was mere piracy from the Greeks; and according to some authorities, the Romans pirated even from the pirates themselves; for the former are said to have pirated from the latter the idea of the system of the Zodiac.

The pirates carried on their lawless trade with such success, that they had a fleet of more than 1000 galleys, many of them being handsomely gilded—a fact that glossed over in the eyes of many the iniquity of the means by which such wealth had been acquired. A dash of gaiety is said to have pervaded the enormities of these lawless depredators; and when among their prisoners they captured a Roman of high rank, they would politely request him to walk into the sea; for " to enslave one of the lords of the earth was an act they could not think of being guilty of." Young Julius Cæsar, who fell into their hands when a mere boy, on his voyage to Rhodes, appears to have met them more than half way in their sallies of humour. They asked twenty talents for his ransom, when he offered them fifty; and even then was so little anxious to leave them, that he remained thirty-eight days after having paid his money and become entitled to his quittance. During his stay among them he wrote satirical verses on their barbarous mode of life, and parried off their swords by the still keener weapons of ridicule. The pirates were amused by the sallies of their prisoner, who conveyed to them all the bluntness of truth in all the sharpness of epigram. They were sorry enough to part with him, when the money for his ransom arrived; but they had reason to be still more sorry when they met him again; for when he did so, it was only to capture them and carry them to Pergamus.

CHAPTER THE TWENTY-EIGHTH.

WHILE Pompey had been busy in punishing the pirates, Rome had something to fear from another quarter; for Mithridates had been everywhere beating up for recruits to beat down the Commonwealth. He was extremely rich, and had an army of 150,000 men; for the trade of war is unhappily one of those in which there is never any lack of hands ready to wage war, when their wages can be relied upon.

Bithynia was one of the first objects of the attack of Mithridates, who was opposed by the Consul, M. Cotta; but the place was burned to the ground, and the ashes of poor Cotta were found in the condition of terra cotta among the ruins. Lucullus, the colleague of Cotta, was sent into Asia with a great army, which attacked Mithridates with such effect, that the king only saved his own life by emptying his pockets of all the money he had about him, and making a scramble of it among the hostile soldiers. The mercenaries, in fighting with each other for the loose silver, forgot to make sure of the sovereign. Mithridates fled to his son-in-law Tigranes, who, having named the metropolis Tigranocerta, after himself, had established himself as King of Armenia. Lucullus proceeded across the Tigris, and required that Mithridates should be given up; but Tigranes, looking at his venerable though determined father-in-law, referred the legate for an answer to the old gentleman. The King of Pontus answered by requesting that the enemy would come and take him, which the Romans were actually about to do, when Mithridates and Tigranes thought it safer to run for their lives; Tigranes ingloriously taking his crown from his head, and putting it in his pocket, to avoid being recognised.

The treasury of Tigranocerta, with a surplus of two millions sterling, fell into the hands of the Romans, who seized on the spoil, and who had become so independent by their temporary wealth, that they criticised, approved, and abused or disobeyed, when and why they pleased, the orders of their general.

Mithridates, taking advantage of this state of things, collected a numerous army, and fell wherever he could upon the Roman garrisons. On one occasion he approached so near the enemy as to be within a stone's throw, and as they happened to be throwing stones, he received one on the knee; while an arrow, fixing itself under the eye, at once opened it to the full extent of his danger. He soon recovered from the effect of his wounds, and was ready by the ensuing spring to attack C. Triarius, when a Roman soldier, disguised as a native, pretended to whisper something in the ear of Mithridates, at the same time giving him a most unfriendly poke in the ribs with a concealed weapon. The King was so unprepared for the wound that he fainted right away, and his troops were so taken up in catching him, that they forgot to catch the foe, who were suffered to escape, though they might otherwise have been easily seized upon. Mithridates, having come to, expressed his anger at the carelessness of his officers, and, notwithstanding his wound and his age, he would have attempted the pursuit—under difficulties— of the enemy. The next morning he renewed the attack on Triarius, and cut to pieces 7000 men ; an operation, however, which seems almost too extensive for even the scissors of Fate, and we cannot help regarding it, therefore, as a sheer invention of the graver historians.

Pompey was now sent to supersede Lucullus in the command ; a measure that had become doubly necessary, for Lucullus had not only failed as a leader, but his soldiers were daily refusing to follow him. When his troops approached within a short distance of Mithridates, they seemed more inclined to engage with him in a friendly than in a hostile sense, for many of them joined his forces. Soon after the arrival of Pompey, a battle was fought by night on the banks of the Euphrates. The moon, being near its setting, had lengthened the reflection cast by the Roman troops, and the soldiers of Mithridates, mistaking the reflection for the substance, began fighting most energetically with mere shadows. Every missile, thrown apparently into the midst of the Romans, was as ineffective as a miss, and the soldiers of Mithridates believing the foe to be invulnerable, fled in a state of panic. The King himself fought valiantly at the head of his body-guard ; a corps which counted among its members his own wife, who, in the arms of a man, committed fearful havoc upon the Roman soldiery. Notwithstanding the powerful assistance of this strong-minded and able-bodied woman, Mithridates was compelled to fly, though he made extensive arrangements for renewing the war on the first favourable opportunity. This opportunity seems never to have arrived, or, if it came, it was lost by the treachery and cowardice of his son Pharnaces, who persuaded the soldiers that his father was an old fool to think of fighting with the Romans. Several of the principal officers took the same view of the subject, and joined in a conspiracy to depose the King, for the purpose of setting up Pharnaces as his substitute.

Mithridates was in bed one morning, when, woke by a considerable shouting under his window, he heard the words, " Pharnaces is king ! " and sent to know the meaning of such an outcry. The answer was unsatisfactory, when the veteran, mounting his charger, made a speech on horseback, which nobody listened to. His son gave orders that he should be seized, when the old man, putting spurs to his horse, galloped up a hill, which for a man in the decline of life, who had been going down hill rather rapidly, was a bold and hazardous experiment. From the eminence he had gained, he saw the depth to which he had fallen ; for he witnessed the coronation of his son Pharnaces, amidst the acclamations of the army. The poor old man was so affected at the sight, that he took from a fold in his dress a deadly drug, which, in anticipation of an alarming self-sacrifice, he always carried about with him. He was about to take off the mixture, when his two daughters, who were standing at his side, entreated the privilege of a drink at the deadly decoction. For some time he hesitated; but he was at length touched by their looks of mute entreaty at the fatal liquid. Dividing the contents of the bottle into three parts, he gave a dose to each of his daughters, reserving a dose for himself; and on a signal from the old

Mithridates, his rash act.

gentleman, the two young ladies swallowed the nauseous stuff they had so earnestly solicited.

The poison took effect at once upon the females; but their father experienced only a disagreeable taste, without the deadly result he had looked for. Though too much for two, it was not enough for three, and the poor old man tottered about in a state of nausea, unattended with danger. Having been previously tired of existence, he was now thoroughly sick of it, and turning to a loyal servant at his side, he requested that he might immediately be put out of his misery. The faithful fellow, making a compromise between his morality and his duty, turned away his eyes, and held out the point of his sword, when Mithridates, coming speedily to the point, fell on the outstretched weapon.

Thus ended the Mithridatic War, as well as Mithridates himself;

and his cowardly son Pharnaces sent in his adhesion to Pompey, acknowledging, in a spirit of humility and subservience to Rome, that he only held his kingdom at the pleasure of the Senate.

The character of Mithridates has been drawn by so many different delineators, that his portrait, as taken by the historians, presents a daub in which it is difficult to recognise the true features.   So many skilful artists have been employed upon the task, that we hesitate in submitting Mithridates to a fresh canvassing at our hands ; nor are we desirous of using the pencil, as some have done, for the purpose of imparting additional blackness.   Some of those who have taken the sketch in hand, have thrown in the shadows with a ten-pound brush, while others have clothed him in several coats and overcoats of varnish,

Mithridates.

for the purpose of glossing over the defects of his character. All are ready to admit that he was an able ruler ; but he had not that perfect uprightness and straightness which give to a ruler the qualities most to be desired. He could speak twenty-five different languages; and thus he was often able to talk over those with whom he might not have been able to come to an understanding, had his conversation been less versatile. He was of gigantic stature, which caused him to be looked up to by those who were placed under his authority. Notwithstanding his excessive height, he was not at all ungainly in his appearance, but his well-moulded frame was a perfect picture.

His fondness for the fine arts was exhibited in the rapacity with which he seized upon the choicest efforts of human genius, which were in turn stolen from him by other amateurs, whose patronage of talent was evinced in the ardour with which they appropriated the result of its labours. In Sinope, one of his cities, was found an astronomical sphere, which seems to show that the science of the stars was within the circle of his knowledge. In one of his fortresses was discovered a statue of himself no less than twelve feet high, in pure gold, which proved not only the value he set upon himself, but showed how completely he was wrapped up in the precious metal.

Credit has been given him for the possession of many domestic virtues ; because, though he was cruel to one half of his numerous wives, he treated the other half with considerate tenderness. He excited the terror of his foes, but enjoyed the affection of his servants ; and though hated in the field, he was beloved in the kitchen. According to Paterculus, Mithridates was a man of whom it is difficult to speak, and still more difficult to say nothing.* The same authority confers upon him a character for greatness of mind during the whole of his life ; but when, having a great mind to kill himself, he prevailed on a slave to put him to death, he evinced—to use a contradictory expression—a vast amount of mental littleness.

* Mithridates, Ponticus Rex, vir neque silendus, neque dicendus sine curâ. Vell. Paterc., lib. ii., c. 18.

CHAPTER THE TWENTY-NINTH.

CONSPIRACY OF CATILINE. INTRODUCTION OF CICERO. CÆSAR,
POMPEY, CRASSUS, AND CO.

REPUBLIC without republicans may be an exceptional state of things; but ancient as well as modern history furnishes proof that the existence of a republic is not incompatible with the absence of anything for which such a form of government is usually desired. It is now an ascertained fact, that the people have no greater enemies to liberty than themselves; and that universal suffrage is the surest instrument to effect the objects of a despot. Equality, in a republican sense, seems to imply a condition in which all are equally debased; and a nation appears to be never so thoroughly slavish as when it is free to choose its own ruler.

The Romans had for some time been in the habit of placing themselves in the hands of a succession of tyrants and knaves, who obtained popularity by the display of the worst attributes. One would win the public voice by his boldness as a thief; another would render himself the elect of the people by his sanguinary successes as a wholesale murderer. It is unfortunate for what is termed the liberal cause, that the vulgarest qualities often attract the largest share of applause; and that those who are entrusted most freely with the confidence of the people are almost always the most unscrupulous in betraying it.

Rome had now sunk to the lowest condition; and society, under the republic, had become so dissolute, that its dissolution might be looked for as a natural consequence. Among the nobles of the period was a certain mass of cruelty and corruption, under the name of Sergius Catiline. He boasted of a long line in connection with his family tree; but a much shorter line, in connection with any ordinary tree, would have been more appropriate to his merits. Having spent all his own money, he spent as much as he could of other people's, by running into debt as deeply as possible. In order to meet some of his old engagements sufficiently to enable him to contract new, he murdered his brother, with a few more of his family connections, and, in fact, justified the opinion formed of him on account of his antecedents, by killing his

U

relatives. Having obtained a Prætorship in Africa, he followed up his career of private swindling, by the wholesale practice of public robbery. He used his office for the purposes of extortion; and the only proof he gave of exactness was in the exactions to which he submitted all who were under his authority.

On his return to Rome he hoped to have a wider scope for his dishonesty in the office of Consul, to which he aspired; and he formed a party of ruined spendthrifts, whose only chance of supporting themselves was by supporting him as a candidate for power. These desperadoes had nothing to lose, and everything to gain,—all that they had to lose being their own, and all that they had to gain being the property of others. Catiline had attracted the sympathies of these adventurers by promising to divide among them all the official salaries; and he had rallied round him a considerable number of adherents by offering to the " million " an opportunity of helping themselves to that which did not belong to them. He professed to be able to relieve all classes at once, by relieving the poor of their burdens, and the rich of their property. The dregs of the populace were easily stirred up, and even some of the nominal nobles were base enough to join in a conspiracy against their own order. The object of the conspiracy was to murder the whole of the senate by a massacre *en masse;* but the scheme was frustrated by that treachery which is almost sure to be found among a set of men who are banded together for a bad purpose. One Curius was induced to gratify the curiosity of a woman, named Fulvia, with whom he was in love; and the secret having reached female ears, flew to the tip of a female tongue, when the secret oozed out as naturally as water finding its level.

Cicero, who had been the competitor of Catiline for the Consulship, soon became aware of the facts; and the former resolved to try and talk the conspiracy down, by making it the subject of several bursts of indignant eloquence.

On the entrance of so illustrious a person as Cicero on the historical scene, it is fit that we should act the part of cicerone, for the purpose of introducing him. This celebrated character was born on the 3rd of January, in the year of the City 647, at Arpinum, where his father had a seat before the future orator was capable of standing. His grandfather was a man of some consideration, pecuniary as well as moral; for he was possessed of some property, and looked up to as an authority in questions of local politics. He had two sons, the eldest of whom, Marcus, was the father of the celebrated Marcus Tullius, from whom the family has derived that indelible mark which time is not likely to obliterate. After receiving the rudiments of his education at his native place, he was sent to Rome, where he studied Greek; and the flame of oratory was first kindled in his mind by contact with the Greek poetic fire. As soon as he had assumed the toga, he became wrapped up in manly pursuits, and was placed under the care of Mucius Scævola, the augur, who augured extremely well of his pupil. The young Cicero

soon evinced a turn for poetry, which caused his head to be constantly
running upon poetical feet; and he came out rather strong in numbers

Fulvia.

at a very early period. At the appointed age he joined the army; for
the laws of his country required that on his entrance into life he should
incur the risk of being sent out of it. He was present in the Marsic
War, at the taking of the Samnite camp; but being in-tent on another
part of the field, he saw little of the battle. At the end of the war he
devoted himself to literary pursuits, and wrote his work *De Inventione*,
which, in accordance with the maxim that necessity is the mother of
invention, no doubt derived its existence from the author's necessities.

He next studied the art of reasoning, under Diodorus, who came to
live under Cicero's roof, so that the latter probably found, or rather
provided, lodging, while the Stoic " stood " the logic, which was
undoubtedly a reasonable consideration for the accommodation afforded

him. In his twenty-sixth year Cicero came out regularly as a professed
orator; and the public voice soon accorded to his own a reputation of
the highest character.

After talking incessantly for nearly two years, he found it necessary
to take breath in retirement; and proceeded to Athens and to Rhodes,
where he cultivated a more subdued style of oratory, getting rid of a
disagreeable redundancy of action, and avoiding that motion, of course,
of the arms, which is the common defect of the youthful advocate.

On his return to Rome, after an absence of two years, he appeared
in the courts of law with distinguished success, and had the next best
business to those popular leaders, Cotta and Hortensius. The three
learned brethren were all of them successful candidates for the offices of
Consul and Quæstor, in the last of which capacity Cicero was sent to
Sicily. There his chief employment was to keep up a good supply of
wheat for the capital, and, by the production of large crops of corn, he
cultivated his growing popularity. During his Quæstorship he visited
Syracuse, and discovered the tomb of Archimedes, which was thoroughly
overgrown with briers, presenting an apt monument to one who had
trodden, during life, the thorny paths of science. Cicero left the
island with the pleasing idea that all Rome had been resounding with
the praises of his administration; but, on landing at Puteoli, he was
not a little disgusted at meeting a friend who asked him "where he had
been, and what was the latest news in the city?" Cicero, at once perceiving that out of sight and out of mind were the same thing, determined to keep himself henceforth in the public eye to prevent its being
shut to his merits.

It was not long after this period of his history that he came into
collision with the conspirator, Catiline, whom he denounced before the
assembled Senate, in an oration which has been preserved to this day,
by the pungency of its sarcastic reasoning. Every sentence smacked of
Attic salt, and every word was so much pepper to the guilty Catiline.
The latter attempted a reply; but the senators were seized simultane-
ously with one of those coughs which spread like an influenza over an
unwilling audience. The mask was now fairly torn off; and Catiline
stood revealed in all his naturally atrocious features. He fled from
Rome; but Cicero continued to show that though his hostility was all
talk, it was of the most effective kind; for he sent forth speech after
speech, and every sentence involved a sentence of "guilty" against Catiline. All those conspirators who had remained in Rome were seized, and
strangled by the executioner, who, when they cried for pity, abruptly
choked their utterance.

The conspiracy, though in great part stifled, was not wholly extinguished; for Catiline did his utmost to keep it alive, by assembling an
army in Etruria. There he was to have been opposed by the Consul,
C. Antonius; but that individual pleaded illness, and declared that a
severe headache would preclude him from encountering the din of war,
while a hoarseness, which he said had seized him by the throat, incapa-

Cicéro dénonçant Catilina

citated him, as he alleged, for giving the word of command on the field of battle. His troops were, however, so determined on action, that they no sooner heard of their general being an invalid, than they insisted that his appointment was invalidated, and they proceeded to business under the command of his legate, M. Petreius. A fierce battle ensued, at Pistoria, and both sides fought like lions; though, to say he fought like a tiger would have been more appropriate to one of the race of Cati-line. Nobody fled, if the accounts are to be believed; but 3000 conspirators fell with their swords in their hands, causing a perfect mountain of slain; and, to crown the whole, their leader is alleged to have formed the summit of this cadaverous pyramid. Those of the conspirators who were not killed by the sword were suffocated under the heaps of their companions; and the conspiracy itself was effectually smothered.

Cicero having saved his country, went out of office,—a course exactly opposite to that followed by modern statesmen, who sometimes quit the service of their country when they have placed it in danger. He received the thanks of the Senate; was hailed as Pater Patriæ, the father of his country, and was invested with a civic crown,—a headdress of oak-leaves; the material being a fitting type of that popularity which falls away and is scattered to the winds with such fatal facility.

The fickleness of public favour was speedily shown in the case of Cicero; for it was proposed that Pompey should be recalled from Asia, to restore the Constitution; it being one of the inconveniences of a republic, that though the constitution is said to be always the best in the world, it is always in need of a succession of restoratives. Pompey landed at Brundusium, where he disbanded all his army, in order to show his attachment to republican simplicity,—a term which is often misapplied; for the simplicity of republicans consists chiefly m their aptitude for being imposed upon.

Though Pompey arrived at Rome without his soldiers, he took care to show his grateful sense of services to come, by causing every man of them to receive a sum equal to about forty-five pounds sterling from the public treasury. He devoted a portion of his gains to building a temple, ostensibly to Minerva, but, in reality, dedicated to himself; for it was inscribed with an account of his victories.

Having sought in vain the support of the Senate, he abandoned the aristocratic party, and threw himself upon the people, who received him with open arms; but the arms that are open to admit a candidate for popularity are often equally open to let him fall from his position.

As Pompey is destined to lose his life before the end of the chapter, it may be as well to give some account of his birth, that the reader may be able to estimate the loss at its true value.

Pompeius Cneius was born on the 30th of September, B.C. 106, a few months later than Cicero, and breathed his first at about the time when Jugurtha breathed his last, in a Roman prison. The family of Pompey belonged to the plebs; and one of his ancestors may be said to have lived upon air, for he was by profession a flute-player. His father, Pompeius Strabo, had imbibed aristocratic ideas, and fought in the Marsic War; but he seems to have despised the laurel of fame for the more profitable branch of plunder. His wealth had been considerable; and after his death his son was accused of having participated in the ill-gotten gains, when young Pompey, knowing the corruption of the tribunals, married the daughter of the judge, as a sure mode of getting a decision in his favour.

His acquittal followed as a matter of course; for when public officials were immersed in every kind of selfishness and degradation, the sinking of the judge in the father-in-law was comparatively venial. By dishonest means the elder Pompey had come to a great estate, from a low condition; and the son sought to hide, in the abundance of his means, the meanness of his origin. He became proud and upstart, evincing a predilection for aristocracy, which often animates those of lofty talent and low birth; who frequently affect the littlenesses of the nominally great, instead of showing that true greatness can exist among the so-called little. Self-aggrandisement was his grand, or rather his petty, object; and he owes to his ignoble attempts to elevate himself, the low place he occupies in the opinion of the impartial historian.

Soon after his return from Asia to Rome, he celebrated a triumph, which had all the attributes of a vulgar puff; for there were carried before him long lists of his achievements, followed by several wagon-loads of goods, the produce of much pillage. Finding his political designs opposed by Cato and others, he was anxious to form a party of his own; and C. J. Cæsar, who saw the necessities of Pompey, determined on turning them to his own advantage. He made overtures, to which the other listened, and effected a reconciliation between Pompey and Crassus, who having both met, were capable of contributing in more senses than one to the success of the plans of Cæsar. These three men entered into a sort of political union, which is usually distinguished by the name of The First Triumvirate.

Cæsar had become Consul in the year of the City 694, (B.C. 59) when the party of the Senate, wishing to have a check upon him, practised every sort of bribery to obtain the election of one Bibulus as his colleague. This individual was a mere nobody, with a remarkable deficiency of head; and the small wits of the day were accustomed to date their notes " in the Consulship of Julius and Cæsar," instead of in the Consulship of Cæsar and Bibulus.

It is a remarkable fact that despotism always looks for its tools among those whom it designs for its victims; and there are no instruments so ready as the people themselves to put an end to popular liberty. It is the policy of a tyrant to destroy all power but his own; and the destruction of legal authority is always favourable to those who are playing the game of unprincipled ambition. Cæsar began by flattering the people at the expense of the Senate; and he enacted that records of the proceedings of the latter should be published under the title of

Acta Diurna, which may be regarded as the origin of our journals of the House of Commons, and our daily newspapers. A second measure was a sort of Insolvent Act, for the benefit of the farmers of the public revenue, who, in their anxiety to obtain the contract, had offered more than they could pay for the privilege of collecting the taxes. His third great project was an agrarian law, in conformity with which any pauper citizen who could show at least three children—whether genuine, or borrowed for the occasion, it might have been difficult to ascertain—were entitled to a grant of land in Campania. This premium on improvident marriages called forth such an overwhelming demonstration of paternity, that the ground in Campania fell far short of the quantity of fatherland that was required; and it was necessary to purchase several thousands of acres, in order to widen the field for the operations of Cæsar. Bibulus opposed the measure; but his opposition, though for the moment busy, proved idle in the end; when, disgusted with failure, he shut himself up in his house for the rest of the year; and every one said that he had been completely shut up by his more powerful colleague.

Cæsar was now more desirous than ever of a near alliance with Pompey; and, in order to draw the bands closer, the former gave his daughter in marriage to the latter, though the gentleman was obliged to put away his old wife, Mucia, to make room for the new; and the lady, Julia, was under the necessity of breaking off an engagement with an intended husband. In order to constitute a strong family party for carrying on the government, Cæsar himself married Calpurnia, the daughter of L. Calpurnius Piso, who, by means of private influence, was made Consul for the ensuing year with A. Gabinus.

It was customary for a retiring Consul to have a province assigned to him for a single year; but Cæsar having worked all the principal public departments with tools of his own, obtained, by a flagrant violation of the Constitution, a prolonged lease of his own power. The rich provinces of Cisalpine Gaul and Illyrium were assigned to him for five years; and Transalpine Gaul was afterwards added by the Senate, because they saw the people were so completely under his influence, that they would either have given him all he asked, or he would have taken all he wanted without asking it.

Among the members of the aristocracy of this degenerate age of the Roman republic was one Clodius, whose name, like himself, was a corruption of Claudius, for he belonged to the family of the Claudii. This disreputable profligate had obtained an infamous notoriety during the festival of the *Bona Dea,* whose rites were celebrated on the first of May; and being conducted exclusively by women, the ceremony was no doubt one of a most confused and tedious character. Clodius having disguised himself in a female dress, passed unnoticed amid the din of many tongues, till female curiosity detected him in a flirtation with the wife of Cæsar, whose house was the scene of the festival. Clodius was brought to trial for the offence, and sent a retainer to Cicero, with instructions to the orator to prove an *alibi*. Instead of following the modern professional course of adopting any falsehood, however gross, for the sake of a client, Cicero hurried into the opposite extreme, and, indignantly throwing up his brief, not only rushed into the witness-box

Cicero throws up his Brief, like a Gentleman.

to give evidence against the accused, but blew up his cause in an explosive burst of eloquence. Notwithstanding this remarkable instance of honesty at the bar, there was so much corruption on the bench, that Clodius bribed the judge by throwing into the scales of justice a sum of gold which turned the balance in his favour. Clodius threatened revenge, and promised to stick to Cicero through life, for having cast him off, and refused to stick to him at such a momentous crisis.

Cæsar, who was the person most interested in the subject of the law-suit, allowed it to give him very little uneasiness; for having divorced his wife, he continued on terms of friendship with Clodius. The latter became a candidate for the tribuneship; but being disqualified by his high birth, he got himself adopted into that for which nature had best adapted him—a very low family. By a bargain with the Consuls he obtained their support; for he promised that if they helped him to the tribuneship, he would assist them in helping themselves to a rich province at the close of their year of office. The disgraceful arrangement was completed,—the plunderers paying each other at the cost of the public welfare.

Clodius immediately began to exercise his public authority for the gratification of his private feelings; and got a law passed for the sole purpose of destroying Cicero. The orator looked to the triumvirate for protection; but Pompey went out of town; Crassus remembered an old grudge; and Cæsar sided with his friend Clodius. Cicero, without waiting to take his trial, left the city, amid the lamentations of all the good, who formed a mourning party, far more select than numerous. After his departure, sentence of outlawry was passed upon him; his house on the Palatine, and his two villas, were by the hand of demolition brought to the ground, while the rest of his property was brought to the hammer at a public auction.

Clodius having been successful in the gratification of one of his personal animosities, began to look about for other victims against whom he could put in force the power with which "the people" had entrusted him. Recollecting that he had once been in the hands of pirates, and that Ptolemy, King of Cyprus, had declined to rescue him, he passed a law that Ptolemy should be at once deposed; and he, in order to kill two unfortunate birds with one stone, got rid of Cato, by sending him to take possession of Cyprus as a Roman province. Ptolemy, instead of meeting the matter with spirit, met it with a dose of laudanum, and so far forgot himself as to seek in suicide forgetfulness of his sorrows.

Cicero employed his exile in lamenting his fate; and though by profession a dealer in philosophy, he had no stock on hand for his own use, when its consolation was required. He sent whining letters to his wife; and his signature was so bedewed with tears, that he left a blot upon his name, through his unmanly weakness.

Clodius being no longer Consul, a portion of the incubus which stifled the breath of freedom was removed, and the public voice ventured to make itself heard in demanding the recall of Cicero. The orator returned in triumph; and he showed his gratitude by supporting any measure that was proposed by any of those who had been influential in bringing him home again. His advocacy was demanded, and freely given, in favour of many a disgraceful proceeding on the part of his friends; and he undertook the defence of Gabinius, who had carried on a system of extortion in Syria.

Rome was now completely in the hands of an ambitious party, which, by means of armed mercenaries, disposed of the lives, the liberties, and even the opinions of the citizens. Pompey and Crassus, at the instigation of Cæsar, put up for the Consulship a second time, when an opposition candidate, L. Domitius, having come forward, his servant was cut down by the soldiers before his face, as a hint to those who should presume to hold an opinion adverse to the existing authority. The candidate having seen the skull of his domestic split, feared an equally decisive plumper for his own poll, and retired into private life, leaving the executive to be re-elected without any attempt at opposition. The temporary powers of each member of the triumvirate were, by treachery and violence, prolonged for five years; and Cato, who ventured on an opinion that the step was not quite in accordance with the constitution or the law, was unceremoniously thrown into prison. Right was in all cases made completely subservient to might; and the competitors for power kept armed ruffians in their pay, whose collisions with each other were often of the most desperate character. In one of these encounters between the creatures of Clodius and the mercenaries of Milo, the former was killed, which caused the latter to be put upon his trial. Cicero was engaged to defend the accused; but Pompey, who hated Milo, had taken care to surround the former with an armed force, which so intimidated Cicero, that his tongue stuck to his mouth, when he himself ought to have stuck to his client. The orator had not a word to say for himself, or rather for Milo; and as not a sentence was said in his favour, a sentence was pronounced against him. He went into exile at Marseilles; and Cicero, with tardy zeal, wrote a defence when the trial was over. He sent a copy of it to Milo, who pronounced it excellent in its way, but a little too late; and he added, in writing to Cicero, "If you had only delivered it in time, you would have delivered me from the dilemma I was placed in."

CHAPTER THE THIRTIETH.

OVERTHROW OF CRASSUS.　DEFEAT OF POMPEY.　DICTATORSHIP AND DEATH
OF CÆSAR.　END OF THE ROMAN REPUBLIC.

ÆSAR'S proceedings in Gaul are sufficiently familiar to enable us to treat them with a sort of contempt, by omitting even the heads of the oft-repeated tale from our history. Though his arms were abroad, his eye was at home, and he watched the affairs of Rome with a jealous interest. His confederates, Pompey and Crassus, had quarrelled; and the former fell out with Cæsar; so that there was a difference between the triumvirate, though they were all three alike in their unscrupulous designs upon the commonwealth.

Crassus was busy in his province of Syria, laying his hands on every thing of any value, until somebody laid hands upon him, notwithstanding his worthlessness. His engagement with the Parthians was a short passage in his life, which led to his death; for he had been induced by treachery to plunge into the mess of the Mesopotamian deserts. There he encountered an army which endeavoured to strike terror into the Romans, by brayings, bellowings, the beating of drums, and every kind of hollow artifice. The Parthians, who were skilful in the use of the bow, sent forth such a shower of arrows, that fury darted into many an eye, and on many a lip there was a quiver. Crassus began to faint, and went into a sort of hysterics, highly incompatible with historic dignity. The enemy, however, tried a feint of a different kind, and pretended to run away; but when pursued, turned suddenly round, galloped upon the Romans through a sand-hill, thus raising so much dust, that the latter were obliged to lick it, as their mouths were full of it. In this position they were assailed with arrows, which having been shot at their feet, pinned many of them to the ground; and their hands being skewered in the same manner to their breasts, they could neither fly nor defend themselves.* The horses might still have charged; but when the poor creatures arrived at the Parthian pikes, they were obliged to pull up rather suddenly. The cavalry being cut

---

* Those who doubt the accuracy of this description, may consult Plutarch's " Life of Crassus."

to pieces, Crassus and some of his footmen retired to a sand-hill for safety; but they soon found the error of building their hopes on such a foundation. Crassus himself hid his head in the sand, and would see nobody; but ultimately he was induced to enter into a negotiation with the Parthian general. In the course of the parley a little misunderstanding arose, when some of the parties present began to push each other about, first with their hands, then with their clenched fists, and ultimately with their weapons. At length Octavius, who had accompanied Crassus, drew his sword, and killed a groom, when somebody else killed Octavius; and the assassination having once fairly—or unfairly—set in, Crassus himself was soon disposed of. The King of the Parthians caused the head of Crassus to be filled with gold, as in his lifetime he had devoted all his faculties to the accumulation of the metal.

By the death of Crassus, the triumvirate was reduced to a duumvirate, and jealousies arose between Pompey and Cæsar; but as the people seemed to think that two heads at loggerheads were better than one having everything its own way, the opposing tyrants were left by the public to fight their own battles. The great prize for which they were now contending was the army, which is too often exposed to the degradation of being reckoned upon as the sure means of crushing everything in the shape of law and liberty.

Cæsar had certainly obtained the attachment of his soldiers; for he had shared their dangers; but the vain upstart, Pompey, had no more claim upon the army than he could establish by corrupting them. Cæsar held them by their affections, but Pompey hoped to unite them to him by those golden links which never fix themselves to the heart, though effecting a sort of temporary hanging-on to the pocket. Cæsar stood on the bank of the Rubicon, which divided his province of Gaul from Italy, and, looking at the surface of the river, he was soon absorbed in his own reflections. He knew it was against the law to cross the stream with an army; but after looking at both sides, and feeling his position to be that of sink or swim, he made a bold plunge, with one of his legions after him. The Rubicon was now passed; and Pompey, hearing of Cæsar's approach, was struck with such a panic before he had received any real blow, that he had at once quitted the city. So great was his haste, that he omitted even to follow his natural bent, and went away without robbing the treasury. The tyrant is so frequently associated in the same person with the coward, that the ignoble retreat of Pompey was the natural sequel to his previous despotism; for that which passes for boldness of action may be prompted by the fears of the knave, instead of by the courage of the hero.

Cæsar arrived at Rome, which had become freed from the presence of one tyrant, to receive another; and the people certainly deserved all they got, or rather all they lost; for they conferred upon the despot many marks of popularity. When he wanted money, he burst open the treasury-door like a thief; and when opposed in the name of the law, he cut down everything in the shape of objection, like a butcher.

Cæsar next proceeded to Spain, but only to be recalled as Dictator, to which office he had been illegally nominated by one of his creatures, the Prætor, M. Lepidus. Having laid down the dictatorship in eleven days, during which period he laid down the law on some very important questions, including that of debtor and creditor, Cæsar abandoned his legislative pursuits, and started in pursuit of Pompey. The latter had proceeded to Greece, where the former suffered much inconvenience in trying to manage the movements of his army. Only a portion of his troops having got across the water, he became so impatient at the non-arrival of the rest, that he went to see after them by going to sea himself in disguise, on board a small fishing-boat. The winds were extremely contrary, and were blowing the vessel back, with a force threatening to dismast her, and to the utmost dismay of the master, when Cæsar, who was sitting at the stern, put on a stern look, exclaiming, " *Quid times? Cæsarem vehis.*" " What are you afraid of? You carry Cæsar as a passenger." At this moment the vessel gave a lurch, and the heels of Cæsar were suddenly brought to

" Quid times? Cæsarem vehis."

the level at which his head had the moment before been visible. The mariner was about to ask for further explanation, and had got " *Quid ?* " in his mouth, when a wave completely washed him up, and he remained in soak for the rest of the voyage. The vessel was driven back, and Cæsar, who was wet through, as well as in despair, sat wringing alternately his hands and his toga.

At length, soon after his return to his camp, his army was brought to him by Antony; but provisions were so scarce, that the soldiers had to live upon bark, which proves that the unlucky " dogs of war " were exposed to the most biting necessities. There, however, they continued, without being subdued; and, indeed, the bark seems to have made them more than usually snappish; for they threw some of it into the hostile camp, and declared they would live upon grass; nor would they lay down their swords while there was a single blade remaining.

Cæsar encountered some slight reverses, and took up his quarters at Pharsalia, where he might have been blocked in and starved out, had not Pompey been taunted into attacking him. Cæsar was delighted at that imprudence, the fruits of which were speedily shown; for Pompey's army was utterly routed; and Pompey himself, retreating to his tent, was literally sick at the disgusting result of his enterprise. " The way in which my soldiers turned their backs," exclaimed Pompey to an intimate friend, " has positively turned my stomach;" and he was only sufficiently recovered on the following day to start *viâ* Lesbos for Egypt. There ill-fortune still awaited him; for Ptolemy, the young king, instead of receiving the outcast with hospitality, was advised to put him to death, as a little compliment to Cæsar. Septimius, a Roman, who had served under Pompey, was sent to meet him, with instructions to stab him in the back; and the victim had no sooner felt the blow, than, according to the custom of the period, he arranged the folds of his robe across his face, so that although very disgracefully killed, he might very gracefully expire. His wife, Cornelia, who witnessed the scene, sailed away as fast as she could from the melancholy sight, leaving no one but an old servant, named Philip, to perform not only the funeral, but all the characters that the performance required. He was, in fact, the undertaker of the whole of the sad ceremony, and attended as sole mourner at the melancholy undertaking.

On the arrival of Cæsar in Egypt, he was welcomed by having the head of Pompey put into his hand; but the former turned away in disgust, and at once dropped his old animosity.

Being detained by contrary winds at Alexandria, Cæsar entered into the disputes between Cleopatra and her elder brother Ptolemy; when the young lady, relying on her powers of fascination, caused herself to be brought, concealed in a mattress,* into the presence of the Roman general. Having emerged from under the bed, she pleaded her cause so earnestly, that he went to war on her account with her brother, who

---

* This story of the mattress, though gravely told, is somewhat doubtful, and is hardly worth the straw involved in it.

ultimately fell into the water; thus causing the drowning of himself and all his enmity. Cleopatra reigned in Egypt; and Cæsar was so enslaved by her charms, that he remained nine months on a visit; nor would he have torn himself away, but for the intelligence that Pharnaces, the son of Mithridates, was endeavouring to recover his father's lost possessions. Hurrying to Pontus, he looked out for the enemy, drew his sword, struck one decisive blow, and in the memorable words, " *Veni, vidi, vici,*" he set an example of the laconic style, which no writer of military despatches has since followed.

Disturbances had by this time broken out at Rome ; and in order to repair the evil, Cæsar was obliged to repair himself to the capital. So much enthusiasm had been excited by the battle of Pharsalia—for the people are always too ready to lick the hand which seems capable of striking them—that Cæsar had been elected Dictator for one year, Consul for five, and Tribune for his whole lifetime.

The fact is, that Rome had become so thoroughly tired of the continual contests for the chief power, which a republican form of government necessarily invites, that the nation yearned for a permanent head, and eagerly adopted the very first that offered. It was thought better to be the slaves of one despotic adventurer, than the victims of half-a-dozen; and even absolutism was preferred to the republican system, which had kept the country so long exposed to laceration at the hands of those who were trying to snatch it from each other, without being able to govern it.

After a short stay in Rome, during which he exhibited his power by making various arbitrary changes in the Law and Constitution—for it is the tendency of a republic to place a whole nation at the will of one man —Cæsar proceeded to Africa, with the view of quelling there the party opposed to him. He marched against Utica, which was governed by Cato, who, when he ought to have been preparing to fight, was standing upon ceremony, and politely insisting that Scipio ought to take the command, as being the man of the highest rank present. Scipio, who was not ambitious of the foremost place in the field, declared that the pretended deference to his rank was rank nonsense, and that Cato must assume his proper position. The Governor, however, persisted ; and Scipio went forth to fight; but he seems to have killed nobody except himself, while Juba and the legate Petreius, two other brave fellows on the same side, slew each other.

Cato, trembling for the fate of Utica, called a meeting of the Senate, which resolved unanimously to run away; and the Governor went home to supper. On retiring to his chamber he called for his sword, which was nowhere to be found ; and he became so irritated, that he savagely struck the domestic who returned without the missing weapon. At length it turned out that " one of the young gentlemen had got it ;" for the sword was brought to Cato by his eldest son, and it was quietly put away for the night under the old gentleman's pillow. Cato went to bed, and fell asleep while reading one of Plato's dialogues. Waking again at dawn, he rose, and having methodically finished the perusal of the dialogue he had commenced over-night, he ran himself through the body. His attendants rushed in, and sewed up the wound ; but they had no sooner turned their backs, than—if we are to believe the authorities, which we confess we cannot at all times — he either undid the numerous stitches in his side, or ran himself through the body again ; and, with a compliment in his mouth to the excellence of the reasoning of Plato, expired.

Cato was only eight-and-forty at the time of his death ; and therefore, though in the course of nature too young to die, he was quite old enough to have known better than to kill himself. The graver historians inform us, that " he died the death of a hero and a philosopher;" but being unable to appreciate the heroism of running away from misfortune, instead of meeting it, or the philosophy of refusing to endure what one cannot cure, we must beg to be allowed to differ from the serious writers, who generally hold up suicide as a subject for respect and admiration. Cæsar was, of course, deeply affected on hearing of Cato's decease ; but such affectation was common in those days ; and there was nothing extraordinary in Cæsar's having gone into mourning for the man whose death he had long been compassing.

The victorious general now returned to Rome, where he might have obtained as long a lease as he pleased of almost unlimited power. He was named Dictator for ten years ; and, instead of pursuing the ordinary practice of tyranny, which abuses the greatest power to gratify the pettiest spite, Cæsar not only made no proscriptions, but declared a general amnesty. He celebrated four triumphs, and gave a succession of banquets ; for he knew that there is no more portentous grumbling than that which proceeds from an empty stomach.

Being entrusted with supreme power, he turned it, in many instances, to good account ; and introduced, among other wholesome regulations, the very valuable reform of the Roman Calendar. This was an improvement, not merely for the day, but for all time, and has handed down the name of its author to every age, and every civilised country, in every almanack.

In these and similar salutary occupations he was disturbed by an insurrection in Spain, headed by the two sons of Pompey, Cneius and Sextus, whom he encountered, on Saturday, the 17th of March, B. C. 45, on the field of Munda. The battle, though ultimately decisive, was at first doubtful ; for Cæsar's troops had commenced retreating, when their want of spirit so dispirited him, that, as they ran away, he was near making away with himself, by the mere force of sympathy. By a last effort, however, he succeeded in stopping the fugitives, and asked them if they were mad, to display such flightiness. His appeal was successful ; and, having first come to themselves, they fell upon the enemy. Cneius made for the shore, and was getting into a ship, when a rope caught his foot, and he remained tied by the leg in a most perilous position. Having endeavoured for some time to effect his own extrication from the cable, which proved utterly impracti-cable, he called to one of his companions, who endeavoured to cut the rope, and in doing so, wounded Cneius. The unhappy sufferer attempted to. fly, but being pursued to within an inch of his life, he naturally had not a foot to spare; and finding himself deprived of the use of one of his legs; he was, of course, in a sad hobble. He had got on shore, and had just placed his foot in a doctor's hands, when he was overtaken and killed by the enemy. His brother Sextus made his escape; and his hopes of rulership being at an end, he commenced the trade of a robber, which is not a very different kind of business from that of government in the days of military despotism.

On Cæsar's return to Rome he was received with increased adulation, though his victory had been over the Romans themselves ; who, by acquiescing in their own degradation, became fully deserving of all the acts of tyranny they were made the victims of. Success, however, is the idol to which the multitude will bow, let the object of adoration be either good or evil ; and it is only when the latter encounters the fall, which, sooner or later, must be its inevitable fate, that the *Vox Dei* is really echoed by the *Vox Populi*.

We must, however, accept with caution the accounts of the rejoicings that are described as attending the dictatorship of one who had so completely subjugated his country, that murder or banishment, without trial, had become the certain fate of every one who should venture to express the smallest disapprobation of any of his measures. Nothing is easier than for one who has a drawn sword ready for every hostile throat, to style himself the " father of his country," and to exercise the ancient privilege of paternity by taking the lives of such of his children as might rebel against his parental authority. It was easy to decree a thanksgiving of fifty days, and to obtain its outward observance, when instant death at the hands of a mercenary might be the fate of any one expressing a doubt as to having much to be grateful for. The statues of the usurper were placed in all the temples ; but this was no test of true popularity; for if an armed band should break into our house, take forcible possession of all its contents, rob us of all we possess, and spend a portion of the proceeds in placing a bust of the head of the banditti in our principal apartments, it would be no proof of his being a favourite of ours. He decreed himself imperator, or Emperor, for life,—a proceeding no less impudent than that of a burglar, who, having broken into our premises, calls himself the landlord of the property. He declared his own person sacred—a poor consolation for a tyrant who knows that there is a curse which must eventually be brought terribly down upon all injustice and iniquity. He seized upon half the magistracies, as his own private property, to be given away by himself; and he virtually seized upon the other half, by claiming the nomination of the candidates. He was, in fact, supreme and sole master of the Republic ; and without any one of the conditions which are absolutely essential to the permanency of power. His usurpation had neither law, morality, justice, nor reason—nor even that hollowest of all mockeries, expediency—to rest upon. The first utterance of the public voice, when free to speak, must have overwhelmed him with one shout of indignant execration; and the first movement of the popular arm, when freed from its ignoble paralysis, must have hurled him from power.

Some supporters of the miserable and unprincipled fallacy, that the end justifies the means, have pointed to some of Cæsar's salutary acts, as an excuse for his usurpation; but that right can never result from wrong, is shown in the fate which the Dictator soon met with. His aim was evidently the monarchy; and his adherent, Antony, caused a statue of Cæsar to be crowned; when two Tribunes seeing the diadem, and perceiving that there was an intention of trying it on, ordered it to be taken off again. The Dictator of the republic was so offended at this outrage on the symbols of monarchy, that he was on the point of putting the Tribunes to death, when it was suggested to him that exile might do as well, and he accordingly sent them into banishment.

It is one of the numerous penalties of iniquity, that its own example may be followed in opposition to itself; and that he who uses lawlessness and violence to attain his ends, may find them conducing to his own, in a sense he had not expected. The sentiments which, in contact with the open air of freedom, form the wholesome breath of public opinion, can never be stifled and pent up, without generating the foul and dangerous vapours of conspiracy. This noxious poison speedily forms itself among an enslaved people, and an explosion eventually takes place, which removes a load of oppression, and clears the political atmosphere.

A conspiracy had been for some time forming against Cæsar's life; and a band of about sixty, headed by M. Brutus and C. Cassius, had resolved on his downfall. The Dictator kept continually aiming at the crown, which he might perhaps have worn in dignity and safety, had he sought to gain it by honest means; for the nation had become so heartily sick of the alternate farce and tragedy of a Republic, that the necessity for some permanent authority based on law was on all hands admitted. He had, however, tried to effect his object by the cunning of a knave, the audacity of a thief, and the inhumanity of a butcher.

When a sovereign is really wanted, much may be done for a candidate who has circumstances, seconded by prudence, honour, and ability, on his side; but that crown is not worth an hour's purchase which is seized by force, fraud, and cruelty. The last trick of Cæsar, in trying to turn his usurpation into a right, was a pretence that the Sibylline books, having declared the Parthians could be conquered by none but a king, it was necessary to make him one. The Senate was to meet to consider the matter, on the 15th of March, in Pompey's Curia, where now stands the Palazzo Massimi. The professional augurs had already begun to prophesy, on the strength of those shadows which precede coming events; and Cæsar was so puffed up with self-conceit, and the people had been so long his abject slaves, that he had almost learned to believe the world would never throw off the atom that had got to the top of it. His wife had, it is said, an unfavourable dream, on the day previous to the meeting; but Cæsar smiled at her warnings, and told her that her night-mare proceeded from some ridiculous mare's nest. Cæsar walked down to the house of assembly, chatting arm-in-arm with the Consul, Decimus Brutus. Seeing in the crowd an augur, who had told him to beware of the Ides of March, Cæsar observed, smiling, "Well, here they are; and here am I;" to which, "Wait till they are gone, and then where are you?" was the only reply of the soothsayer.

The secret of the conspiracy, which had been hitherto well kept, now began to ooze out in all directions; and nearly everybody that Cæsar met thrust a paper into his hand, or dropped a whisper into his ear; but he would read and listen to nothing.

The Senators rose on his entrance; and when he took his seat the conspirators got round about him, until one of them, Metellus Cimber, came rather intrusively to close quarters, with a petition. Cæsar gave him a slight push, as a hint to him to keep his distance; and Cimber, as if to catch himself, took hold of the Dictator's toga, which was the signal agreed upon. Casca instantly stabbed him in the neck, when Cassius followed up the blow with a poke in the ribs; and Brutus had raised his hand with a dagger in it, when Cæsar exclaiming, "Et tu, Brute!"—And you!—you, Brute!—staggered to the foot of Pompey's statue, that he might form a *tableau* as he expired.

The republic was now virtually, if not nominally, at an end, though a faint struggle was still made by the murderers of Cæsar, who ran through the streets, proclaiming that they had killed a king, but obtained no praise for the achievement. Antony, on the other hand, created an immense sensation, by exhibiting the identical toga in which Cæsar had fallen, and thrusting his ten fingers through twice as many large holes, which he declared had been made by the assassins' daggers. Not satisfied with making the most of Cæsar's wardrobe, Antony appropriated the money of the deceased; and while the widow was wrapped in grief, with her face buried in her hands, her late husband's friend was carrying off all he could lay his hands upon. Antony had been at once grasping and prodigal, giving away with one hand what he had snatched with the other; and buying at a liberal price what he had no means of paying for.

His rival in the contest for the supreme power was Octavius, the son of a daughter of Cæsar's sister, and who, with no other qualification than that of nephew to his uncle, had the impudence to claim absolute dominion over a great but broken-spirited nation. This individual was without character or courage; and though afraid to be left in the dark, he was still more afraid of the light; for he felt that his own actions would not bear looking at. His cowardice had the usual effect upon him, for it made him cruel; and though there was nothing but his name to make him a favourite with the army, he had betrayed the soldiers into the disgrace of turning their arms on their fellow-citizens. By a constant use of the name of his uncle, he succeeded in cozening a people who sought only permanence in their institutions; and Antony being ultimately subdued, more by his own feebleness as a voluptuary,

than by the strength of his opponent, an empire fell into the hands of
Octavius.   He was invested with the title of Imperator for life ; and
he retained his position till his death—a circumstance to be attributed
to the conviction that had been brought home to the popular mind, that
the constant changing of the head of a State is a source of constant
danger to the peace and happiness of the whole community.

The End of Julius Cæsar.

LONDON: BRADBURY AND EVANS, PRINTERS, WHITEFRIARS.

Now available in its first English edition

A HISTORY OF
ROME

From Town to Empire and
From Empire to Town

Erik Christiansen

First published in 1989 in Danish, this new English
version of Eric Christiansen's "History of Rome"
offers a broad outline of Roman
history based on recent research
and current scholarly debate. It
follows the political, social, and
economic events from Rome's
foundation in 753 BC to the
decline nearly 1,400 years later.

Eric Christiansen, who has been
an internationally renowned
scholar of Roman history for 25
years, wrote for students of
Roman history who "want an accessible, comprehensive view of the development and disintegration
of the whole Roman civilisation" (from the author's
Foreword), but his book is also well suited for
teachers and students of other fields who need a
concise and reliable introduction into this fascinating field.

13 maps, 221 p. (1995),
Casebound
ISBN: 0-86516-269-7

ROME
AND HER KINGS:
EXTRACTS FROM LIVY

Edited by
W. D. Lowe
and
C. E. Freeman

This graded reader with connected excerpts
from Livy's first book of the history of Rome
is recommended to students who have had
the basic introductory sequence of Latin. The
book features notes, vocabulary of proper
names, Latin-English/English-Latin vocabulary, exercises and maps.

The text was designed to stimulate students;
reinforce their knowledge of grammar and
syntax; offer an opportunity to engage in
creative Latin composition; and provide
background for appreciation of Livy.

maps, 110 p. (1988), Paperback,
ISBN: 0-86516-000-7

A Handbook of Latin Literature
H.J. Rose

THIS TEXT IS A MUST

for anyone who:
teaches or reads
Latin and Modern
Literature

600 p., (1936, rpt. 1996),
Paperback, ISBN 0-86515-317-0

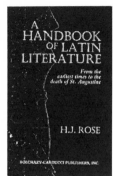

[Rose's] book in fact has its value as a dictionary of Latin literature besides that of a history.
—Times (London) Literary Supplement

This edition provides complete analyses of the most prominent works of Latin literature, setting them in their historical context and alongside their contemporaries, rating their relative importance in their own time and in later periods, and exploring their influence on subsequent literatures and Western civilization.

Each known work is discussed and analyzed in terms of content, chronology, genre, significance, meaning, genetic relationship to other works, ancient and modern scholarship and influence.

- indispensable reference tool for teachers and students
- affordable, comprehensive edition
- astute and sensitive analysis
- unsurpassed in scholarship and usefulness
- extensive bibliography by Professor E. Courtney
- all authors of pagan and Christian Latin literature including:
  Augustine, Boethius, Caesar, Catullus,
  Cicero , Horace, Livy, Lucretius, Martial,
  Ovid, Plautus, Servius, Terence, Vergil

Guide to the Aqueducts of Ancient Rome

Peter J. Aicher

GUIDE TO THE
AQUEDUCTS OF
ANCIENT ROME

PETER J. AICHER

illu., maps, xiii,
183 p. (1995),
Casebound
ISBN: 0-86516 -271-9

illu., maps, xiii,
183 p. (1995),
Paperback
ISBN: 0-86516-282-4

Aicher has crafted an ideal introduction and a valuable field companion for navigating the Roman aqueducts. Features new maps, schematic drawings, photographs and reprints of Ashby's line drawings.

From the armchair tourist to the field explorer, travellers of all ages and stages will enjoy this fascinating depiction of ancient Rome's immortal achievement in engineering and architecture.

"Enlivening and fascinating ... this guide can serve both the appreciative tourist and the serious student ..."

—**Robert Rodgers**,
University of Vermont

"Extremely well written, with valuable maps and detailed directions to the remains. There is no comparable book for anyone interested in the Roman Aqueduct system."

—**Harry Evans**,
Fordham University

Responsible Popularization

see

The other half

of Classical Scholarship

THE CLASSICAL
BULLETIN
A Journal of Scholarship since 1925

VOLUME 72   1996

1000 Brown Street
Wauconda, IL 60084
847/526-4344; Fax: 847/526-2867